I0024192

PRAISE FOR DEI EXPOSED

"Ridgley rips away the façade of Diversity, Equity, and Inclusion, exposing both its unscientific foundations and its objectives, which run precisely counter to its attractive packaging. Drawing from extensive research and firsthand observations, the author reveals the striking contradictions between DEI's stated aims and its practical effects. In this penetrating investigation, Ridgley methodically dismantles the modern Diversity, Equity, and Inclusion movement, challenging its core premises and examining its real-world impact on institutions and communities. Drawing from extensive research and firsthand observations, the author reveals the striking contradictions between DEI's stated aims and its practical effects. Through rigorous analysis, Ridgley demonstrates how certain DEI practices and theories fail to withstand scientific scrutiny while often producing outcomes that oppose their purported goals. This unflinching examination cuts through rhetoric to expose the movement's internal contradictions and consequences. Provocative yet meticulously researched, this book offers readers a compelling reexamination of one of today's most influential social movements. Whether you're a policy maker, business leader, educator, or concerned citizen, Ridgley's insights will fundamentally transform how you view contemporary conversations about diversity and equity in America.

– Ram Mudambi, Frank M. Speakman Professor of Strategy, Fox School of Business, Temple University

"Dr. Stanley Ridgley's *DEI Exposed: How the Biggest Con of the Century Almost Toppled Higher Education* is a powerful indictment of the multi-billion-dollar DEI industrial complex and the cowardice of the "intellectual" class. With razor-sharp analysis, Dr. Ridgley dissects how higher education compromised itself, abandoning merit and intellectual vigor in favor of pseudoscience and ideological conformity. Our colleges and universities have surrendered to the DEI racket for far too long and squandered billions in tax dollars. As Dr. Ridgley puts it, the DEI agenda is nothing more than an "anti-Enlightenment and ideological program to fundamentally change higher education." On the frontlines of the fight to reclaim academia, he delivers a bold call to action – a blueprint to restore higher education to its original purpose: the pursuit of truth through critical inquiry, the free flow of information, and robust standards that uphold meritocracy. This is a must read for anyone who values intellectual honesty and the future of higher education."

– Nicholas Giordano, Professor of Political Science and Host of The P.A.S. Report Podcast

"The DEI monster has continually sprouted new tentacles, and Stanley Ridgley has given us a long-term account of how it came to be its lurid self. His documentation of its expanding set of fake words and fake claims – from 'racial battle fatigue' to 'microaggressions' – will serve as the standard account of how this noxious ideology got a hold on our society before anyone had noticed, to quote a phrase, that we couldn't breathe."

– Bruce Gilley, Presidential Scholar-in-Residence, New College of Florida, and author of *The Case for Colonialism*

"Ridgley explains how the modern-day academic bureaucracy's obsession with so-called "diversity, equity, and inclusion" has forged a path for radicals to become judge, jury, and executioner across academia."

– Zack K. De Piero, Ph.D., litigant in the landmark case *De Piero v Penn State*, over reckless implementation of DEI programs

DEI
EXPOSED

DEI EXPOSED

Copyright © 2025 by Stanley K. Ridgley, PhD

All rights reserved under the Pan-American and International Copyright Conventions. This book may not be reproduced in whole or in part, except for brief quotations embodied in critical articles or reviews, in any form or by any means, electronic or mechanical, including photocopying, recording, or by any information storage and retrieval system now known or hereinafter invented, without written permission of the publisher, Armin Lear Press.

ISBN (paperback): 978-1-963271-73-7
ISBN (hardback): 978-1-963271-74-4
ISBN (eBook): 978-1-963271-75-1

ARMINLEAR

Armin Lear Press, Inc.
215 W Riverside Drive, #4362
Estes Park, CO 80517

DEI
EXPOSED

HOW THE BIGGEST CON OF THE CENTURY
ALMOST TOPPLED HIGHER EDUCATION

Stanley K. Ridgley, PhD

ARMINLEAR

I dedicate this work to several irreplaceable souls. My wife, partner, inspiration, and love of my life, Lory, whose support for me has always been unwavering. And to our children— Andrea, Caitlyn, Nathan, Lauren, and Michaela—who will enjoy the fruits of an America whose founding principles are being restored, even as you read this.

CONTENTS

INTRODUCTION

"I think DEI is a fraud and what we're seeing now on campuses is proof of that."[1]
— **Congressman Burgess Owens, Utah**

"This growing multibillion-dollar industry was embedded into so many powerful public and private institutions so quickly that due diligence was skipped and costly failures guaranteed."[2]
— **Conor Friedersdorf, *The Atlantic***

What, exactly, is wrong with Diversity, Equity, and Inclusion?

Isn't it noble, moral, right and proper? Isn't DEI just teaching about slavery, teaching about race, ensuring that everyone gets a fair shot? You know, "level playing field" and all. It's just plain common sense, isn't it?

---

1   Fabiola Cineas, "How Republicans are weaponizing antisemitism to take down DEI," VOX, December 21, 2023: https://www.vox.com/24010858/republicans-antisemitism-dei-diversity-equity-inclusion-jewish-students

2   Conor Friedersdorf, "The DEI Industry Needs to Check its Privilege," *The Atlantic*, May 31, 2023: https://www.theatlantic.com/ideas/archive/2023/05/dei-training-initiatives-consultants-companies-skepticism/674237/

Isn't it the "right thing to do"?

These are just some of the platitudes of the con-artists working the diversity hustle for profit, and no—it's actually none of those things.

These common misrepresentations are just a few among many that are key to making the Big Con of DEI work. The Foundation for Individual Rights and Expression (FIRE) observes that

> [B]eyond being a mere abbreviation for those three terms, "DEI" is also the blanket label for a body of thought that includes a much larger collection of ideas, research, scholarship, practices, and proposals—including "anti-racism," "intersectionality," "critical race theory" and more. In our institutions of higher education, that larger constellation of concepts can grow into an ideological orthodoxy that affects everything from faculty hiring and tenure to campus programs and policies.[3]

If anything, FIRE's assessment is understated. DEI is a strange and alien world of paranoia, pretense and make-believe. It's a world of funhouse mirrors in old carnival shows that distort reality rather than mirror it.

DEI appears as a chameleon, adapting itself to the situation and as the situation demands. It can be whatever is needed at a particular moment in time, with the only criteria the survival of DEI and its lavishly compensated bureaucracy and the maintenance of its monumental Con Story.

---

3   "DEI in higher ed: When it's constitutional and when it's not: If it chills, curtails, or compels expression, it's a free speech problem," FIRE website, 2024: https://www.thefire.org/research-learn/dei-higher-ed-when-its-constitutional-and-when-its-not

If we are permitted for a moment to admire elaborate confidence games, and the con artists who implement them, then let's reserve superior acclaim for the Big Con of DEI, the most elaborate, sensational con game of the 21st century. The DEI Con has enriched thousands of hustlers nationwide. It has embedded many hundreds of apparatchiks and supernumeraries in college bureaucracies, and it will require herculean efforts to root them all out. And it continues to attack the average person for the most dubious of ideologically motivated reasons in "training" sessions, both on the campuses and in corporate America.

I first heard the actual acronym *DEI* expressed while I was in a 7-11 on the campus during the early days of the Covid pandemic, and it was two masked graduate students discussing the wonderful employment possibilities of this new initiative, which sounded like someone trying to monetize *kumbaya*. Already steeped in Leftist ideology and its tactic of renaming and relabeling its hooey for new generations of suckers, I was only vaguely aware that this was just the latest brand for the newest social justice foray in higher education.

"Diversity" had already been around for many years, its hustlers scratching at the university door. Not actual diversity, mind you, but the skin-deep diversity of noxious racialism tarted-up with fake Enlightenment discourse. This concept of "diversity, equity, inclusion" quickly metastasized until it was everywhere, and this was no accident. It was a bureaucratic initiative designed to anchor a new raft of social justice programs as an inescapable presence on the campus. With especial privileges conferred on DEI because of the unfortunate death of George Floyd, this "diversity" would bypass the faculty. It would, in fact, bypass vetting of any sort.

Organized and coordinated with the support of off-campus activist groups like NADOHE, NASPA, ACPA, and NACADA,[4] it would be imported wholesale from the many hundreds of diversity hustlers around the country and given a pass as it goose-stepped through the gates of academia.

It was no accident that it was violence and the threat of violence that opened the door for this effervescence of DEI. It sounded absurd. *I* knew it was absurd; I knew it was a con. *Most* people likely knew it was a con but then, most people on the campuses also knew to keep their mouths shut in a time of hair-trigger tempers and performative chaos unleashed by well-funded activist groups. No college administration wanted the summer violence of 2020 overflowing onto the campuses. And so they opened the university to barbarian ideas rather than the barbarians themselves.

This was the madness of crowds brought *en masse* onto the campuses, and it was wildly successful. It achieved this success with a superb combination of psychological factors—relentless hustling, a primitive ideology suffused with mysticism and "indigenous knowledges" and the barely concealed violent urges of quasi-communist and terroristic revolutionaries. All of this protected from criticism and even the mildest of questioning.

You knew something was terribly wrong with it.

Anyone on a college campus subjected to the mediocrity of a DEI hustler knew there was something wrong with it. It was not noble. It was not idealistic. It was not the many wonderful things its proponents said. It was one thing to the public, and it was

---

4   NADOHE—National Association of Diversity Officers in Higher Education, NASPA—National Association of Student Personnel Administrators, ACPA—American College Personnel Association, and NACADA—National Academic Advising Association.

another altogether when enacted on the campuses. It was weird and alien and hateful at its core, but the public is rarely exposed to any of this. It was the classic Potemkin village offering, with a façade masking a racialist substance.

DEI has a front stage, and it has a backstage. In other words, it was a con. In fact, it was the Biggest Con of the 21st century, with America's universities the biggest suckers imaginable. And the crowning achievement of Western civilization—the modern university—tottered under the debilitating assault of mediocrity, racialism, and pseudoscience.

I suppose that folks duped by the big con will eventually retreat in their embarrassment at having been fooled by one of the shadiest Con Stories ever deployed. Even now, DEI is in retreat. As it plays out in its final act, I assure you that it will dissipate in a flurry of new acronyms and new labels designed to hide its failure. Its proponents will roll out new slogans to replace the vapid "Diversity is our strength." Already, "inclusive excellence" is supplanting DEI as this trusty acronym becomes freighted with failure.[5]

The Con Story will morph and adapt. Reluctantly. Buzzwords will change, new slogans will be coined, but the underlying ideology will remain the same as it always has. It must serve yeoman's duty for the Big Con.

Elaborate and elegant Con Stories have played major political roles for centuries, baiting and hooking marks with promises of utopia. The most convincing Con Story of them all is that of Karl Marx, whose fabulous pseudoscience has duped millions of the credulous to support murderous regimes in the name of "social

---

5   "NADOHE ... offers insights ... to guide institutions in their quest for inclusive excellence." NADOHE website: nadohe.org

justice." It still does. Con Stories are essential to convincing gullible people to act in ways that simply make no sense to a normal person, who is tethered to reality. We saw an example of the Con Story's power in December of 2024.

A Con Story duped a privileged 26-year-old by the name of Luigi Mangione to commit murder on the streets of New York.

Equity and the Assassin

On December 4, 2024 in the early morning hours on a New York City street, Luigi Mangione shot in the back a man he'd never met, who had done him no harm, whose business paid for the health care of 29 million Americans.

So what does DEI have to do with the assassin Luigi Mangione?

Mangione exemplifies what can happen when persons become infected with ideology to the point that they act on that ideology—no matter how unharnessed it is from reality.

This was the case with the shooter, who killed a man for what a theory told him, not for what he, Mangione, knew to be the case. Mangione killed for the same reason that extremist ideologues and world-changers always kill. His ideology told him the villain to target, and he acted.[6] And as a result, "Mangione was indicted on a charge of murder in the first degree in furtherance of terrorism, Manhattan prosecutors announced December 17."[7]

---

6   Theo Burman, "Luigi Mangione Manifesto: Read Reported Document in Full," *Newsweek*, December 11, 2024: https://www.newsweek.com/luigi-mangione-manifesto-full-document-1998945 https://www.newsweek.com/luigi-mangione-manifesto-full-document-1998945

7   Alex Sundby, John Doyle, Layla Ferris, Laura Doan, Emma Li, Kerry Breen, "What we know about Luigi Mangione, suspect charged in UnitedHealthcare CEO's killing," CBSNews.com, December 20, 2024: https://www.cbsnews.com/news/luigi-mangione-healthcare-ceo-shooting-what-we-know/

In a bizarre outpouring of sympathy, across the nation, people cheered and made him a sex symbol.[8] Even university professors responded approvingly, oddly enough at Mangione's *alma mater*, the University of Pennsylvania. At Penn, Professor Julia Alekseyeva called Mangione the "icon we all need and deserve."[9]

The approving public reaction to the assassin's deed may be difficult for the average person to fathom. The celebration of the ideologically motivated murder certainly surprised many persons grounded in the realities of daily life, classically educated in personal morality with a keen sense of right and wrong and personal responsibility. One murder-celebrant, the ex-*Washington Post* reporter Taylor Lorenz expressed "joy" at the assassination of Brian Thompson and, on national television, nervously doubled-down on her support of the killer. "It feels like justice," she said.[10]

All this support for murder, as awful as it is, should really surprise no one. It has been a feature of hard-left political thought for centuries. Leftists of various stripes have always embraced "revolution" and violence for a more "just" society (as long as it requires nothing dangerous from armchair revolutionaries who serve as comfortably compensated faculty or as reporters safely removed from consequences). After all, "By any means necessary" *is* a leftist trope. Leftists have always been divorced from notions of

---

8   Sonam Sheth, "Luigi Mangione: In Familiar Trend, Alleged Killer Becomes Online Sex Symbol," *Newsweek*, December 10, 2024: https://www.newsweek.com/luigi-mangione-online-sex-symbol-1998794

9   Zachary Schermele, "University of Pennsylvania professor apologizes for posts lauding Luigi Mangione," *USA Today*, December 11, 2024: https://www.usatoday.com/story/news/education/2024/12/11/luigi-mangione-julia-alekseyeva/76925248007/ https://www.usatoday.com/story/news/education/2024/12/11/luigi-mangione-julia-alekseyeva/76925248007/

10   Isabel Keane, "Ex-WaPo reporter Taylor Lorenz tells Piers Morgan she felt 'joy' over assassination of UnitedHealthcare CEO Brian Thompson: 'Feels like justice,'" *New York Post*, December 10, 2024: https://nypost.com/2024/12/10/us-news/ex-wapo-reporter-taylor-lorenz-says-she-felt-joy-over-assassination-of-unitedhealthcare-ceo-brian-thompson-feels-like-justice/

personal responsibility and tend to evaluate individual people and their actions based on a hazy notion of world history, making tenuous connections between individual actions and the grandiosity of historical movements. In such a scheme, people are judged guilty or innocent based on which "side" of history they embrace, with the trope of "social justice" woven seamlessly into the narrative.

Their notions of "justice" are not personal and derived from actual events. Rather, they are rooted in "cosmic justice."[11] It's a Manichean world these people inhabit, in which good and evil are clearly distinguished and people on each side of the binary divide are deserving of their fate. Killers are lionized, their victims dismissed as collateral damage in the quest for the common good. Leftists believe that nobility attaches itself to those who act for "social justice," whether it's assaulting Jewish students on campus in the name of "decolonization," or shooting an innocent man in the back in the name of anti-capitalism.[12]

Let's be clear. People who think this way are dangerous. They are not temperate, they do not compromise (except for the moment's expediency), and they are certainly not swayed by the better "argument." These are the kinds of people who hide inside a crowd, usually masked. Many of them are disturbed mentally.

It's easy to identify the people who are moving in the Mangione direction, inspired by corrupt ideas and urged to do something rather than sit idle. This is a social pathology, and examples of it are too numerous for any polity to be comfortable. Look to the

---

11   Thomas Sowell, "The Quest for Cosmic Justice," *The Hoover Digest*, January 30, 2000: https://www.hoover.org/research/quest-cosmic-justice

12   Graeme Wood, "Luigi Mangione's Commonplace, Deplorable Politics," *The Atlantic*, December 11, 2024: https://www.theatlantic.com/ideas/archive/2024/12/luigi-mangione-manifesto-healthcare/680962/

universities for examples, scourged as they were with violent anti-Semitic demonstrations for much of 2024.

Columbia students and college students on campuses nationwide believed themselves instructed to act out a murderous ideology that they call "decolonization," which is the justifying label they affix to their violent activities. They did so throughout 2024, playing the roles scripted for them. They hearken to the call in the seminal article "Decolonization is not a metaphor," the gauntlet for action thrown down in one of the dozens of ersatz academic journals created for the purpose.[13] They issue a challenge and a charge for the many potential Mangiones-in-training right now.

DEI is no different in its call for action grounded in social fantasy, cosmic justice, and "theory."

DEI: a Feverish Fantasy of Cosmic Justice

DEI doctrine declares that somewhere, someone of the same ethnic caste as you has been wronged. Maybe. You don't know for certain.

You *do* know that your job, your responsibility, is to take umbrage. You should be offended. It's *your obligation* to recognize fabricated social injustice and to ignore the vast reality of millions of non-incidents of so-called injustice. Moreover, if you are of the same ethnic caste as the villain, you should feel guilt—*collective* guilt. When something happens that conflicts with the notion of "cosmic justice," it's time to move into action. When a ne'er-do-well called George Floyd, who had fentanyl and methamphetamine in him according to the autopsy, is murdered by a rogue cop, it's time

---

13   Eve Tuck and K. Wayne Yang, "Decolonization is not a Metaphor,"
     Decolonization: Indigeneity, Education & Society, Vol. 2, No. 1, 2012.

to *defund the police* and fix the "system."[14] When a drugged-up, 6-4, 300-pound thief is killed while attacking a police officer, it's time to shake-down corporate America to the tune of millions of dollars, because police killed an unarmed Black teen.[15]

This is the core of successful social movements and social hustles—to contrive a winning narrative out of confusing facts and isolated incidents to portray a fictional pattern, a nationwide epidemic of, well, *something* that can be used to make a buck. When the social movement is also a social hustle, the combination is too powerful to resist, for Con-artists *and* their suckers.

If you believe that there is no link between the kind of social fantasy that motivates a Luigi Mangione to backshoot a man he doesn't know on a New York street and the kind of DEI fantasy that dictates a racialist split on the college campus that slots persons into good and evil, then try this test yourself. I give you a guarantee that persons who cheer the killer Luigi Mangione for his assassination of Brian Thompson *also* fully support DEI's personnel, programs, policies, and enforcement mechanisms on the college campuses. Go ahead, ask a person who cheers the assassin if he also supports DEI.

You already know the answer, don't you? And why is that?

It's because this type of person is animated by a vision of the world crafted by some dead scribbler and is a prisoner of ideology, forfeiting the reliable information provided by his own senses and experience. Former communist and public intellectual Arthur

---

14   "Defund the Police": https://defundpolice.org/
15   Department Of Justice Report Regarding The Criminal Investigation Into The Shooting Death Of Michael Brown By Ferguson, Missouri Police Officer Darren WilsoN, Department of Justice Memorandum, March 4, 2015: https://www.justice.gov/sites/default/files/opa/press-releases/attachments/2015/03/04/doj_report_on_shooting_of_michael_brown_1.pdf

Koestler provides a sense of the laser-like intensity of the true believer, who is overwhelmed by righteousness. Koestler relates his own moment in his description of the recruit's universal experience of epiphany, what happens when a narcotic narrative meets the mind groomed with ideology and leads to an emotional embrace. It's what happens when a sucker falls hard for a Con Story:

> [S]omething had clicked in my brain like a mental explosion. To say that one had "seen the light" is a poor description of the mental rapture . . . . The new light seems to pour from all directions across the skull; the whole universe falls into pattern like the stray pieces of a jigsaw puzzle assembled by magic at one stroke. There is now an answer to every question, doubts and conflicts are a matter of the tortured past—a past already remote, when one had lived in dismal ignorance in the tasteless, colorless world of those who *don't know*. Nothing henceforth can disturb the convert's inner peace and serenity—except the occasional fear of losing faith again, losing thereby what alone makes life worth living, and falling back into the outer darkness, where there is wailing and gnashing of teeth.[16]

The powerful epiphany that Koestler describes is the relief that the prepared mind feels when his delusions coalesce into a simple belief system that slots or rejects facts accordingly, and complex reality becomes a mere latticework of categories.

---

16   Arthur Koestler, in Richard Crossman (ed.), *The God that Failed* (New York: Bantam Books, 1959, 1949), p. 19.

* * *

The DEI Con begins simply enough. One of the faces of DEI is that of a kind of exaggerated affirmative action. Supporters say that it simply ensures justice and equal treatment, basically following civil rights law.

This is the first and perhaps the most important deceit in the entire DEI Enterprise. DEI proponents commit fraud at the very beginning. They either misrepresent DEI as a sensible, commonplace, and benign pursuit of merit and excellence, or they simply allow persons to provide their own reasonable definitions of diversity. But of course these common-sense *ad hoc* definitions have nothing to do with the actual DEI agenda. And that's the idea. But if that's the case, what's the need of a multi-billion dollar DEI industry that is nothing but an elaborate affirmative action program with illegal appendages? That kind of doubt is simply swept away in the urgency of the moment.

DEI recruits its supporters into a gaslit world of fake results and Newspeak transformations of reality. It's an Orwellian place where material success is branded failure, where failure is valorized, and where cheating is rewarded with million-dollar salaries, and the cheaters feted and celebrated.[17]

Even by the standards of the university, where so-called "difference" is robustly cheered, this seems a bit much. It's all orchestrated and kept on life support by the con-artists who set the entire project in motion and who benefit from the bureaucracies constructed to mask for as long as possible the relentless drain on the budget with no commensurate value added.

But we sense that change is afoot.

As universities that prop up the DEI racket march toward insolvency, the minds of those who control the purse strings are becoming focused. It's a given that hundreds of years of business wisdom has been ignored for as long as possible by the moguls of higher education. They have subsidized DEI, castigated their own institutions, and doubled-down on their witless pursuit of "social justice" until, now, when it's almost too late. The treasury is nearly empty, and this is usually the point when business wisdom is suddenly rediscovered in higher education.

On that business wisdom point, we can look to the master entrepreneur and phenomenal businessman Steve Jobs for insight on what is, after all, a business conundrum.

Wisdom from a Master Entrepreneur

Jobs coined many business aphorisms during his 35-year career. One of his most merciless tropes was his concept of A players and B players. This was his relentless assessment of his own business talent at Apple.

You were either an A player, or you were a B player. Steve wanted teams of top-notch performers, and he abhorred what he called B players. Aside from being called a "bozo," Steve had no greater insult than to identify you as a "B Player."

Unless he considered you a "C Player."

He morphed this into one of his sage management principles many years ago. Jobs identified a negative cascade effect when business standards of performance are lowered. The A players hire B players and then B players hire C players.

"It's too easy, as a team grows, to put up with a few B players, and they then attract a few more B players, and soon you will even have some C players," he recalled. " . . . A players like to work only with other A players, which means you can't indulge B players."[18]

The indulgence of B players may have been a bridge too far for the demanding Jobs, but it serves as the identifying marker for *Diversity, Equity, and Inclusion.*

It is a program that appears explicitly designed to search out and solicit B-Players. In fact, a familiar pejorative emerged in the years since DEI became a buzzword in business, in academia, and in government—the notion of a "DEI hire."

To some, the term DEI hire was just another denigration of the just efforts to fully include oppressed and "marginalized" minorities in American society. But the term appeared to have legs, especially as negative anecdotal evidence mounted.

The rapid installation of DEI regimes in business and in academia and in virtually every other aspect of society led inevitably to the pejorative notion of the DEI hire. However unjust the appellation in any individual case, the specter of thousands of unqualified persons entering the workforce and professions rang true.

Anecdotes abound.

The evidence has *necessarily* been anecdotal since few have dared to study systematically the impact of mass hiring of protected classes of people and elevating them over persons more objectively qualified. The negative results have been disastrous, while the positive results have been vaporous feelings-based satisfaction over the achievement of artificial and arbitrary "social goals" of representation.

---

18   Walter Isaacson, *Steve Jobs* (New York: Simon & Schuster, 2011), p. 181.

The Tale of the Tourist Submarine

Oceangate was an American company that operated private undersea tours, and the company's infamous "tourist submarine" is one particularly tragic example of what a commitment to DEI can yield.

The tourist submarine is what happens when social goals supersede proven standards carefully developed over hundreds of years.

The deep-sea submarine, called Titan, was a vanity project of a billionaire. In this case, the submarine was constructed by a company that apparently ignored mundane requirements, such as expertise, experience, even common sense. The Oceangate CEO Stockton Rush blatantly stated that "50-year-old white men" who were ex-military submariners were not welcome as sub pilots in his company.

In effect, Rush reversed the Jobs dictum to employ A players. These ex-military submariners were the A Players in this slice of private maritime business. Not only were these A Players not selected, but they were also actively shunned in favor of a development team with B-Player qualifications.

Rush himself exerted B-Player mentality boasting of the navigation tools aboard the Titan, as he steered the Titan submersible with a "cheap Amazon video game joystick."

The Titan imploded while submerged two miles down in the Atlantic in summer of 2023.

On a dive to view the wreck of the Titanic, located more than 12,500 feet below the surface, the Titan's hull caved in a millisecond, immediately killing the sub's four passengers and CEO Rush, the sub pilot.[19]

Stockton Rush could not have been clearer in sacrificing safety and standards on the altar of political posturing and "inspiration." He sacrificed his life, in fact, for DEI.

It's a horrific tale of the consequences of DEI—the elevation of superficial, non-essential characteristics as employment criteria, in this case a high-stakes life-and-death situation. The Titan project was designed and executed by B Players, because the most qualified A Players were excluded from consideration. Why?

Because they weren't "inspirational," said Rush.[20]

DEI is a B and C player Program

The unfortunate tale of the tourist submarine is more than a lesson in billionaire hubris and eccentricity. It's an instructive dynamic of what happens when you ignore competent A Players in favor of B Players, based on criteria that have nothing to do with the mission of the firm.

Tourist Submarine has become short hand for the kind of programs that celebrate vaporous social goals while simultaneously ignoring hard-won knowledge about reality, particularly the clear relationships between cause and effect.

The unspoken assumption is *always* that there is enough slack in the rope so that these superficial social goals can be fulfilled while we simply prestidigitate competent results into existence.

19 Sam Cabral, "'All good here': Titan sub's last messages before implosion," BBC News, September 16, 2024: https://www.bbc.com/news/articles/cx2kk1g66n7o
20 Jesse O'Neill, "Titanic tour CEO didn't hire '50-year-old white guys' because they weren't 'inspirational,'" *New York Post*, June 21, 2023: https://nypost.com/2023/06/21/why-stockton-rush-didnt-hire-50-year-old-white-guys-for-titanic-sub-tours/

If we pursue these diversity goals—if we hire contingents of B Players—good things are bound to happen. If they don't, well, we'll just pretend.

We don't know how or why, but "diversity is our strength."

This pretense of top-notch results gives rise to what has been called "gaslighting." Where stakes are low, and where bullshitting and jargon reign supreme, this gaslight tap-dance can survive for a long time. In high-stakes situations, however—in the case of the tourist submarine where lives are at stake—the pretense of results is predictably disastrous.

Other examples present themselves, where the pretense of results is shrouded in a toxic cloud of verbiage. The infamous Bud Light advertising campaign serves as a cautionary business case, in which radical and unsound marketing decisions were based on nebulous social goals rather than on sound business principles.

In 2023, a strange beer advertising campaign was constructed around the transition of a young male into a would-be female, a small-time actor who decided to turn a possible self-obsession into a public spectacle. Thus did Dylan Mulvaney become a national figure. No discernible reason could be found for this association with a popular beer brand, nor was there any indication how this might benefit the brand financially or appeal to the brand's customer base.[21]

The market responded, predictably in fact, and the disaster of the campaign could not be covered up. The responsible marketing

---

21   Jay Hodgkins, "New UVA Darden Case Examines How Bud Light Cracked Open a Can of Controversy," *The Darden Report*, University of Virginia, December 12, 2023: https://news.darden.virginia.edu/2023/12/12/how-bud-light-cracked-open-a-can-of-controversy/

executive (a Harvard and Wharton School graduate) and her boss were both suddenly gone from Anheuser-Busch.[22]

In high-stakes life-and-death situations or in business, where outcomes can be measured, the social engineering of wishful thinking quickly collides with reality. It may be quick and disastrous, as in the cases of the tourist submarine and Bud Light's rapid collapse in market share, or it may be cloaked and drawn-out and quietly shelved.

This is a clarity denied to the non-profit world. This is the world of feelings and causes, where storytelling and, yes, con games play a large role in fooling people to commit to absurd ideas.

The Absurd Finds its Way to the Colleges

In the non-profit world, results are not easily measured, and America's sprawling higher education system of colleges and universities are part of that world. This renders them the perfect petri dish for con games of various types. It's one reason why hokum finds its way in, and why it remains ensconced even as profound absurdities pass as results.

The colleges are an eccentric place where eccentric personalities find a home. Eccentricity, in fact, is commonplace and expected, which renders it no longer eccentric. The absurdities on the campuses are not simply tolerated; they are nurtured and promoted.

DEI is one such profound absurdity.

The basis for so-called DEI is vague and constantly shifting and depends on the needs of the moment. DEI is slippery and the

22 Henry Rodgers, "EXCLUSIVE: SOURCE: Top Anheuser-Busch Marketing Executives Responsible for Boycott Are No Longer Employed," The Daily Caller, June 27, 2023: https://dailycaller.com/2023/06/27/anheuser-busch-marketing-execs-bud-light-not-employed/

people who serve as its primary avatars—chief diversity officers and various other executors—are slippery as well.

DEI is grounded in nothingness, such that anyone who claims to be a "practitioner" is, by definition, second-rate. Just as a chemist who practices alchemy is, by definition, second-rate. Or a B player.

But in the heat of political warfare and cultural battle, none of that matters. All of it is washed away with the cringiest slogan of the century.

"Diversity is our strength!"

DEI's mantra is the clear winner. And it's not even close.

"Diversity is our strength!" must be one of the most vapid, laughable slogans ever contrived by man. This is true in business, in government, and it is certainly true in academia. It captures the disaster of DEI in a microcosm.

That disaster began long ago, percolating in odd corners of academia and out in the hinterlands in small firms running consulting hustles, solitary peanut grifters selling "antiracism" to credulous school boards, and extremist academics peddling myth as history. Prescient authors warned that this peripheral pseudo-academic enterprise could present higher education with real problems if given license on the campuses. One voice who recognized the threat was public intellectual Dinesh D'Souza, whose 1991 book *Illiberal Education* sounded an early tocsin.[23] Another volume that called out fake scholarship was Mary Lefkowitz's *Not out of Africa*.[24] These were welcome voices, but without institutional resistance, the early diversity grifters and their short cons continued to grow in numbers and influence on the campus.

---

23 Dinesh D'Souza, *Illiberal Education: The Politics of Race and Sex on Campus* (New York: The Free Press, 1999).
24 Mary Lefkowitz, *Not out of Africa: How "Afrocentrism" Became An Excuse To Teach Myth As History* (New York: Basic Books, 1997).

It emerged in full-bloom when, in 2020, the death of an intoxicated crook in the streets of Minneapolis led to a summer of riots, arson, and violence in America's streets, fueled by the militants of Black Lives Matter and amplified by hysteria engendered by a COVID pandemic that originated in Communist China—it was a perfect storm of events. It was conveniently labeled a "Racial Reckoning."

The deceitful DEI narrative was founded in myth, but it had just the kernel of truth to give it traction. And every good con artist knows that's all that is needed for a sucker to take the bait: "One of the most powerful aspects of a great con game is how it often uses the truth to support a lie."[25]

The orgy of violence in 2020 hit America's campuses hard, as skittish university presidents succumbed to fears of the unrest spreading to their institutions. The Racial Reckoning con propelled mediocre scholars to academic stardom—Ibram Kendi and Robin DiAngelo—and elevated others to regular stints on cable news shows—Eddie Glaude and Elie Mystal. Meanwhile, progressive activists leveraged numerous policy and structural changes into the universities under the all-purpose rubric of social justice.

The juggernaut gained momentum steadily, and all the con needed was a brand name, a catchy acronym, but nothing to warn the rubes that Marxism was storming back with a vengeance. It had to be non-threatening and lofty and aspirational, perhaps even vaguely deceptive with echoes of an Enlightenment trope.

This movement would be called *Diversity, Equity, and Inclusion*.

This DEI would be administered on campuses by a new

---

25   R. Paul Wilson, *The Art of the Con* (Guilford, CT: Lyons Press, 2014), p. 78.

bureaucratic hierarchy, a Frankenstein mash-up that mimicked the real-life Commissar system of the 1940s Soviet Union, the enforcement teams of Ray Bradbury's *Fahrenheit 451*, and the Ministry of Truth in George Orwell's *1984*.

This bureaucratic carbuncle would be embedded into all aspects of the university. DEI functionaries would play a politicized role in all university activities, irrespective of bureaucrat expertise. The project has been successful, at least in terms of personnel hired and budgets provided.

Since DEI elbowed its way onto the campuses, it has metastasized into a multi-billion dollar a year business. The Big Con has never before seen this magnitude of lucre. Today, DEI is a multi-faceted business, overfunded and overstaffed, and with no discernible mission save to provide cover for administrations to say, "We're doing the work of antiracism."

This is a slick and processed DEI in 2025. It has its pseudoscientific creed, it boasts a pantheon of saints, it has its true believers, it has its well-heeled mandarin class, it has its obedient footsoldiers and credulous allies, it has its generous share of suckers, and it has generated a growing list of genuine victims who have run afoul of DEI's inquisitional enforcement agencies.

It also has its critics.

These voices have grown more vocal with each passing year and with every absurd indignity inflicted upon the great majority who increasingly see DEI for what it is—a bloated and racialist discriminatory bureaucracy that adds no value to the university community.

The new presidential administration of Donald J. Trump surely recognizes this and has stated clearly that a new sheriff is in town. DEI is on the hot seat from the very top, and we discuss this welcome development in the final chapter.

* * *

How the American university came to this sorry situation is a tale worth the telling, an adventure of carnival barkers and small-time hustlers aiming for the big-time, an unbelievable story of racialist gurus cashing in on the scam before time ran out and America wised up.

DEI Exposed dissects and examines the fraud of DEI, which is indeed the *Biggest Con of the Century*. Each chapter focuses on a key aspect of DEI that demonstrates its pervasiveness in the university, its authoritarian structure, its coercive character, its origin in fantasy, its con-artists, swindlers, and fakes, and its victims. To communicate this fascinating story, the book follows loosely a structure crafted around the stages of any successful generic confidence game:

1. finding a suitable victim
2. gaining the victim's trust
3. persuading the victim to commit to a scheme that will benefit him or her
4. getting money from the victim
5. finally, placating the victim in order to quell any uneasy feelings about the situation."[26]

---

26 C. R. D. Prus and Robert C. Sharper, *Road Hustler* (Lanham, MD: Lexington Books, 1977), cited in Terry Williams and Trevor B. Milton, *The Con Men: Hustling in New York City* (New York: Columbia University Press, 2015), p. 7.

The nation has always been afflicted with small-time diversity hustlers. These are "consultants" who hang out their shingles to mark them as experts who can workshop-away your sins. Just like fortune tellers, tarot readers, and astrologers, "diversity consultants" typically earn their keep from the short con. This is a quick-hit engagement and doesn't depend upon or even count on repeat business.

In the confidence lingo, it's called "peanut grifting."

The summer of 2020 changed all of that. In the ensuing year, DEI was launched as an institutional long con at almost every American university.

At places like Princeton, Harvard, Duke, Michigan, Berkeley, UCLA, Penn, and many others, the lofty values that created the modern Enlightenment university were quickly abandoned by the persons entrusted to safeguard them—university faculty and frightened college administrators. Instead of policy, research, and teaching guided by logic, reason, progress, scientific method, humane values, the peripheral concern of DEI moved to center-stage.

This was the chance to establish lavishly compensated DEI positions in an entirely new bureaucracy for extremists who would "do the work" of *antiracism*. It was administrative bloat on steroids as an entire cadre of hustlers streamed into the university to staff a new authoritarian DEI hierarchy tasked to impose these phony values. They would police the university's students and faculty, and they would enforce the new racialist creed of DEI. These hustlers were funded lavishly and given power to "boldly transform higher education." This new DEI bureaucracy would serve as a modern Commissariat to enforce the new anti-Enlightenment orthodoxy on campuses nationwide and collude with off-campus professional associations.

The only surprise was how meekly the intellectual class capitulated to bald pseudoscience and allowed the imposition of a nationwide program of systematic, codified bigotry. DEI grifters had targeted them because they were easy "marks." DEI zeroed in on their key weakness and exploited it. It was *j'accuse*, and DEI bureaucrats would administer the indictment.

The fraud was obvious to anyone who paused and considered. It could not continue indefinitely. Something would give. Money and patience are in short supply, and it was only a question of which would deplete first, especially when so much was being squandered on outright intellectual chicanery.

The time has come for DEI's own reckoning, a corrective backlash that could not arrive soon enough. *DEI Exposed* is part of that reckoning.

A Time for DEI Reckoning

It is time to tell the sordid and deceitful story of DEI. This is *not* the standard yarn of DEI as a noble cause that would root out the "systemic racism" and the "culture of white supremacy" of our universities.

Rather, the entire narrative of deceit, coercion, swollen salaries, phony scholarship, codified bigotry, paranoia, and a sophisticated protection racket all occurred unmolested—aided and abetted in most cases by simpering college administrations. Stripped of its soaring rhetoric and coarse hyperbole, DEI is an uncomplicated con game. Grifters contrived a story to attack campus moralizers at their weakest point, and they simultaneously offered expensive absolution to those saddled with guilt.

It's time for a book on DEI that exposes it as a racialist confidence game run by clever grifters, assorted charlatans, and oblivious foot-soldiers. Breathtakingly ambitious, sprawling, and lucrative—DEI is the Biggest Con of the 21st Century.

1
BLUEPRINT FOR THE BIG CON
THE POWER OF VIRTUOUS VICTIMHOOD

"The true con artist doesn't force us to do anything; he makes us complicit in our own undoing. He doesn't steal. We give. He doesn't have to threaten us. We supply the story ourselves. We believe because we want to, not because anyone made us. And so we offer up whatever they want—money, reputation, trust, fame, legitimacy, support—and we don't realize what is happening until it is too late."[27]

— Maria Konnikova, bestselling author and worldclass poker player

---

27 Maria Konnikova, *The Confidence Game: Why We Fall for It . . . Every Time* (New York: Viking, 2016), p. 6.

One of the most well-known of con games is the swindle involving a "Nigerian Prince." It works like this:

The term "Nigerian Prince" has become nearly synonymous with the first email scams of the nineties. Mostly targeting individuals, these emails often came from allegedly wronged and robbed Nigerian nobility, who asked for financial assistance and promised millions in repayment as soon as they regained access to their wealth. Despite their absurdity and the huge sums of promised money, people fell for these scams by the thousands.[28]

This con has already passed into legend and become the punchline for the ubiquitous online cons that clutter the internet.[29] A "con" is a swindle designed to separate a person, persons, or entire institutions from sums of money, great and small. Cons are predatory and take advantage of the vulnerable, the dishonest, the stupid, the greedy, and the weak.

Diversity, Equity, Inclusion is a Con.

While DEI for decades was the province of the short con practiced by small-time grifters, it recently exploded into prominence as the biggest, most ambitious, and most expensive Con-Game of the 21ˢᵗ Century. It belongs in the pantheon of the great swindles and scams of history—Charles Ponzi's "Swampland in

---

28   Mike Britton, "The Nigerian Prince is Alive and Well: Cybercriminals Use Generative AI and New Themes to Run Their Scams," AbnormalSecurity. com, September 14, 2023: https://abnormalsecurity.com/blog/generative-ai-nigerian-prince-scams

29   The Nigerian Prince is a retooling of the classic con called the "Spanish Prisoner," a mail scam that offers the chance to receive a portion of great wealth, if the mark puts up "good faith" money to assist the prisoner. Megan Leonhardt, "Nigerian prince' email scams still rake in over $700,000 a year—here's how to protect yourself," CNBC, April 18, 2019: https://www.cnbc.com/2019/04/18/nigerian-prince-scams-still-rake-in-over-700000-dollars-a-year.html

Florida,"[30] the South Sea Bubble,[31] Dutch "Tulipmania,"[32] and the dot-com bust of 2000.[33]

This chapter 1) reveals the basics of the confidence game and the hustle, 2) explains what motivates people who practice the grift, 3) explains the essential elements of the con game—the role of stories, lies and deception, 4) shows how the grifters follow a standard progression to identify and dupe their marks with a convincing story, 5) explains how the DEI story is crafted with a convincing attractive façade and actual backstage elements of the DEI scam.

The Hustle and the Big Con of the "Racial Reckoning"

I use the term "hustle" here and quite often in this book. It's a verb and it's also a noun. What does it mean to "hustle" someone? What is the *DEI* hustle?

We have several versions of the concept of "hustle," all of which capture the unsavory sense of the word. A hustle is a scheme, elaborate or simple, to convince a person to part with his-or-her money by virtue of deceit. Synonyms for hustle are con, flim-flam, swindle, fleece, or grift. There is always an element of dishonesty and deceit in the hustle.

---

30 https://www.amazon.com/Bubble-Sun-Florida-Brought-Depression/dp/1982128372

31 Terry Stewart, "The South Sea Bubble: The 18th century version of the Dot Com Boom - and Bust!" Historic UK: https://www.historic-uk.com/HistoryUK/HistoryofEngland/South-Sea-Bubble/

32 Dave Roos, "The Real Story Behind the 17thCentury 'Tulip Mania' Financial Crash," History.com, August 4, 2023: https://www.history.com/news/tulip-mania-financial-crash-holland

33 "The Late 1990s Dot-Com Bubble Implodes in 2000," Goldman Sachs: https://www.goldmansachs.com/our-firm/history/moments/2000-dot-com-bubble

Merriam Webster provides this:

> to sell something to or obtain something from (someone) by
> energetic and especially underhanded activity : **swindle** *hus-*
> *tling* the suckers, an elaborate scam to *hustle* the elderly[34]

This from the Cambridge dictionary:

> to forcefully encourage someone to buy something, or to
> cheat someone; to try to persuade someone, especially to buy
> something, often illegally: The Hustle is a dishonest way of
> making money:[35]

From the Collins Dictionary:

> If someone **hustles**, they try to earn money or gain an advan-
> tage from a situation, often by using dishonest or illegal means.[36]

You get the idea.

A synonym for the Hustle is the Con, which is "to make someone believe something false, usually so that that person will give you their money or possessions."[37] A hustle usually denotes a short-con, sometimes called a "peanut hustle." For much of the existence of the diversity scam, it remained the province of the small-time operator, the "consultant" willing to give debunked

---

34 https://www.merriam-webster.com/dictionary/hustle
35 https://dictionary.cambridge.org/dictionary/english/hustle
36 https://www.collinsdictionary.com/dictionary/english/hustle
37 https://dictionary.cambridge.org/dictionary/english/con

"implicit bias training,"[38] or to tell you the bluff of how "diverse" teams out-perform others,[39] or to call your employees "racist" for a hefty fee.

All Cons—short or long—follow a sophisticated progression that relies upon understanding the psychology of motivation. This is true whether of the Nigerian Prince variety or of the more complex and financially rewarding Big Cons.

All con artists follow some variation, even people who ordinarily do not spring to mind as "conmen." These are the various cults—both religious and secular—whose repertoire of recruitment strategies are some of the most highly developed. Cults offer what Maria Konnikova calls "the scam of all scams." This is the "scam of belief, the most profound yet simple belief we have about the way the world works, why life is the way the way it is."[40]

The unusual characteristic of the DEI hustle is that perhaps a majority of Americans know that it's a con *and yet play along with it.* They do this, because to *not* play along can mean trouble, lots of it. Sometimes serious trouble of the sort to threaten one's livelihood.

The best conmen are fabulous students of behavior, and capable of recognizing and sizing up a "mark." This is as true of DEI grifters as it is of the basest street hustlers who fleece victims in games of Three-card monte.

Although the details may vary, all flimflam games rely on

38 David Randall, "The Implicit Bias House of Cards," *City Journal*, October 3, 2023: https://www.city-journal.org/article/the-implicit-bias-house-of-cards#:~:text=The%20implicit%2Dbias%20theory%20(also,but%20the%20Open%20Science%20Foundation's

39 Jeremiah Green and John R. M. Hand, "McKinsey's Diversity Matters/Delivers/Wins Results Revisited," *Econ Journal Watch*, 21(1), March 2024: https://econjwatch.org/articles/mckinsey-s-diversity-matters-delivers-wins-results-revisited

40 Maria Konnikova, *The Confidence Game*, p.307.

their basic ability to make a lie look like the truth. Even today, confidence artists continue to work their scams with great success. Time and again, people from every walk of life demonstrate their ability to abandon common sense and believe in something that is simply too good to be true by succumbing to the con man's call.[41]

Con-artistry has developed a colorful original lingo to capture the rambunctious knavery of the enterprise.[42] It is a world of con-artists, marks, ropers, chumps, shills, inside men, and peanut grifters.[43]

The Psychology of the Hustler

As you likely surmise, con artists are persons psychologically different from you and me. Grifters are motivated by gain, of course, and their personalities often show signs of the Dark Triad of psychopathy, narcissism, and Machiavellianism.

Psychopaths exhibit tendencies to "lie, manipulate, and break the rules." They "lack empathy, guilt, remorse, and fear and ... [are] unconcerned with their behavioral transgressions." Says Konnikova, "Psychopathy is a sort of biological predisposition that leads to many of the behaviors we expect from the confidence artist."[44] Narcissism, too, includes the grifter markers of a sense of grandiosity, entitlement, self-enhancement, inflated sense of worth, and a propensity to manipulate others. Finally, Machiavellianism is characterized by the ability to convincingly lie and skillfully manipulate others to get what is desired.

41 Mary Darby, "In Ponzi we Trust," *The Smithsonian*, December 1998: https://www.smithsonianmag.com/history/in-ponzi-we-trust-64016168/
42 David W. Maurer, *The Big Con: The Story of the Confidence Man* (New York: MJG Books, 1940, 1968, 1999), p. 278-310.
43 "The SPYSCAPE Glossary of Con Artist Slang": https://spyscape.com/article/spyscapes-glossary-of-con-artist-slang
44 Maria Konnikova, *The Confidence Game*, p. 23.

Not all persons who display Dark Triad personality traits become grifters. But all grifters display these traits: "[A]ll three entail a socially malevolent character with behavior tendencies toward self-promotion, emotional coldness, duplicity, and aggressiveness."[45] The authors of an important study on Dark Triad personalities spare no pejoratives in describing these persons as "social parasites who intentionally attempt to extract resources from their environments without providing any benefits."

> [P]redatory social parasites can use a variety of mimicry and deception strategies to integrate themselves into different communities so that they can extract resources either all at once or over time. An example of the former would be when a con artist convinces someone to entrust them with their life savings in a fraudulent Ponzi scheme [internal references removed].[46]

Whether social parasites or practitioners of con-artistry, the persons drawn to the grifting life have developed a keen skillset that merges practical deception techniques with the type of personality capable of pulling them off.

---

45 Delroy L. Paulhus and Kevin M. Williams, "The Dark Triad of personality: Narcissism, Machiavellianism, and psychopathy," *Journal of Research in Personality* 36 (2002), p. 557.

46 Ekin Ok, Yi Qian, Brendan Strejcek, and Karl Aquino, "Signaling Virtuous Victimhood as Indicators of Dark Triad Personalities," *Journal of Personality and Social Psychology: Personality Processes and Individual Differences*, Vol. 120, No. 6, (2021), p. 1636.

Elements of a Successful Con

Every con plays its own scenario, but its essential elements are the same for every con. To run a Con, professional scammers follow a formula, and it relies upon a keen understanding of human nature.

> 1) finding a suitable victim, 2) gaining the victim's trust, 3) persuading the victim to commit to a scheme that will benefit him or her, 4) getting money from the victim, 5) finally, placating the victim in order to quell any uneasy feelings about the situation."[47]

The progression of the Con begins with the Grifter and the Mark—the swindler and the sucker.[48]

The Grifter has a tale to sell that appeals to the base desire of a potential mark, and the mark is eager to part with a sizable chunk of personal wealth (or an organization's budget) for anything that can satisfy that desire. For those attracted to get-rich-quick schemes, easy lucre is certainly the goal. But in the political realm, greed for money is not necessarily all that is in play.

Finding a Suitable Victim—The Mark

Who is the mark for the DEI grifter who plies his trade on the college campus? Why does the mark find this DEI so appealing?

The credulous marks for the DEI Con on the university campuses are special—they certainly believe themselves to be,

---

47 C. R. D. Prus and Robert C. Sharper, *Road Hustler* (Lanham, MD: Lexington Books, 1977), cited in Terry Williams and Trevor B. Milton, *The Con Men: Hustling in New York City* (New York: Columbia University Press, 2015), p. 7.
48 A detailed slang description of this progression—The Put-up, The Play, The Rope, The Tale, The Convincer, The Send and the Touch. along with examples, is provided in Maria Konnikova, *The Confidence Game: Why we fall for it . . . Every Time* (New York: Viking, 2016).

and it is this specialness that renders them vulnerable to the DEI hustle. We can identify two "special" groups, distinguished by the psychological vices that render them vulnerable.

First, there are academics who are generally smarter than average people—and they *believe* themselves much smarter than, say, the pipefitters and electricians, the policemen and carpenters, the factory workers and grocers who make our society function. Sociologist Edward Shils distinguishes between the highfalutin intellectuals and this laity of common workers.[49] Most of these academics are on the political left and fervently want a better world. They also consider themselves nobly motivated and more virtuous than the norm, deeply concerned as they are with the ever-ubiquitous social justice.

> The vision of the anointed is not simply a vision of the world in a functional causal sense, it is a vision of themselves and of their moral role in that world. *It is a vision of differential rectitude.* It is not a vision of the tragedy of the human condition: Problems exist because others are not as wise or as virtuous as the anointed.[50]

These are *smart, good people,* who also happen to demonstrate a proclivity toward vanity and narcissism, and "pompous or eccentric personality traits."[51] The source of their vanity and narcissism is their belief that they have developed what they call "critical consciousness," a Marxist notion that gives them special access to

---

49 Edward Shils, *The Intellectuals and the Powers and Other Essays* (Chicago: University of Chicago Press, 1972), p. 17.
50 Thomas Sowell, *The Vision of the Anointed* (New York: Basic Books, 1995), p. 5.
51 Deborah L. Rhode, *In Pursuit of Knowledge: Scholars, Status, and Academic Culture* (Stanford: Stanford University Press, 2006), p. 2.

discern the contradictions of power and privilege in any society, and this sets them apart from the vast majority of persons who are afflicted with "false consciousness."[52] They position themselves on the moral high ground, and as one scholar notes: "People are never more sincere than when they assume their own moral superiority."[53] This posture of moral superiority *vis-à-vis* less enlightened colleagues and the hordes of laity concerned with the mundanity of living, is a major component of what is called "cultural capital," which is the chief currency of academics employed in higher education and who are consumed with studying "vital facts."

> With this striving for contact with the ultimately important comes self-esteem which always accompanies the performance of important activities. One ... must bear in mind the crucial significance of the self-regard which comes from preoccupation and contact with the most vital facts of human and cosmic existence, and the implied attitude of derogation toward those who act in more mundane or more routine capacities.[54]

These largely white, liberal, racially aware intellectuals possess a keen superiority of their own cognitive and moral rectitude, and they constitute the first group of marks.

The **second** group of marks is a much larger coterie of college employees also targeted by DEI grifters. They want to be considered "university people" and "college educators." They, too, fancy

---

52 "False Consciousness" simply means disagreement with the premises and arguments of Critical Consciousness, a concept that is most closely associated with the Brazilian Maoist educator Paulo Freire. See Paulo Freire, "Conscientisation," *Cross Currents*, 24 (1), 1974.
53 Thomas Sowell, *The Vision of the Anointed*, p. 3.
54 Edward Shils, *The Intellectuals and the Powers*, p. 17.

themselves smarter-than-average folks, equally vain and narcissistic, but their limitations saddle them with intellectual timidity and fatalism, even as they adopt the same superior posture as their more august models within the faculty.

> Vain individuals desire to be admired by the social group to which they wish to belong and thus are motivated by a desire to be esteemed. Because they strive to be admired, they are unable to accept their limitations. Narcissists also want to be admired [and] are also unable to accept that they have any limitations.[55]

If anything, these ancillary support staff are even more vulnerable to the Big-Con than academics, because the basis of their "specialness" is even more fragile. Many of them are employed by student affairs, and they take their cues from social justice ideologues. They actually run their own fake college-within-a-college, pretending to be professors and teaching fake courses in what they call the "co-curriculum."[56] These are also *good people* in their own minds.

What do all of these people want for themselves? For the intellectually vain and narcissistic progressive and the battalions of less-talented campus minions, the goal is to amass the valuable currency of higher education—*prestige of the virtuous*. Sociologist Pierre Bourdieu called this currency "cultural capital."[57] This means opining about vague and aspirational goals that contribute

---

55   Alessandra Tanesini, *The Mismeasure of the Self: A Study in Vice Epistemology* (New York: Oxford University Press, 2021), p. 127.

56   I have written extensively about this sprawling fake "co-curriculum" in a previous work. See Stanley K. Ridgley, *BRUTAL MINDS: The Dark World of Left-wing Brainwashing in our Universities* (New York: Humanix, 2023), p. 89-105.

57   Pierre Bourdieu, *Homo Academicus* (Stanford: Stanford University Press, 1984).

to an amorphous common good, but not necessarily demanding anything of substance. It must be the *right kind of virtue*, not the virtues of the laity.

The Achilles Heel of Campus Marks

This is a particular type of virtue that is unconnected with doing good works for others. Rather, it's vanity harnessed tightly to the trope of social justice. Thus, it relies upon a particular grand narrative that is focused on this vanity. This is the Achilles heel of campus intellectuals—their vanity and self-image of themselves as *good* people committed to eliminating oppression in all its forms and working hard for what they believe to be a common good. Economist and public intellectual Thomas Sowell has called this type of person a member of the campus "anointed."[58]

It is precisely this psychology of superiority that renders university bureaucrats and faculty prime *marks*, with the entry point their intellectual and moral vanity.

> The confidence artist will do everything in his power to bring our better-than-averageness front and center. Grifters appeal to our vanity, not about just anything, but about the things that are most central for us—after all, they've spent the entire put-up casing our psychology . . . . The more exceptional we see ourselves, the easier we may be to con.[59]

Such would-be campus sophisticates are akin to the New Yorker, who has been described as "The best sucker that ever was

58   Thomas Sowell, *The Vision of the Anointed.*
59   Maria Konnikova, *The Confidence Game,* p. 179.

born. He is made to order for anything. You can't knock him. He loves to be taken because he is wise."[60]

The DEI Story—*Gaining the Victim's Trust*

The key to the successful confidence game is to obtain the trust or the "confidence" of the mark, and grifters do this by telling a story that is tailored to the weaknesses and wants of the mark.

It's amazingly easy to gain the trust of someone with a targeted campaign that may seem random or spontaneous, but which is carefully planned and utilizes techniques of psychological manipulation. No con can succeed without this trust-building phase.

Just how did DEI grifters use all of the foregoing to craft an effective story?

With a keen knowledge of the psychological weaknesses of white liberal intellectuals and their hangers-on, here's what they did . . .

The Tale

A convincing tale is told, with a bit of truth at its core. It is this core truth that attracts the mark, who readily believes the tissue of lies spun out of the kernel of truth. The best con-artists know this, and they are spectacular story-tellers.

It's remarkably easy to tell a lie when it is accompanied by something real that appears to support that lie. Con artists have a talent for spotting facts that can be distorted in their favor. The believability of a good scam depends on roping the

---

60 David W. Maurer, *The Big Con: The Story of the Confidence Man* (New York: MJG Books, 1940, 1968, 1999), p. 255.

right mark and telling him something he is either inclined to believe or can be convinced of using proven techniques that have a powerful influence over anyone under the right circumstances.[61]

The DEI Big Con began in 2020 with a kernel of truth in Minnesota, with the death of George Floyd. He was, indeed, killed by a policeman. It was from this singular incident and its months-long violent aftermath that a grandiose epic of nationwide systemic oppression was spun—the myth of "white racist America."

Riots rocked cities in 50 states, sponsored and egged on by the multi-million dollar activist group called Black Lives Matter The scale of damage was staggering. It comprised more than 8,700 protests in 68 cities from May 25 to July 31 of 2020.[62] The total cost of ravaged neighborhoods and businesses destroyed likely exceeded $2 billion.[63] A compliant media dutifully reported all of this as righteous punishment of "white racist America." It was this broad indictment that pounded home the fraud that America was irredeemably racist and a veritable hellhole of oppression and discrimination. This was the Con Story, and no one could escape the indictment. *Everyone* was guilty, universities too.

Universities were *especially* guilty, in fact.

The Con Story targeted college campuses, and with no exemptions for the good white folks. Well-heeled white liberals were culpable, too. Faculty, staff, students—*all* were complicit

---

61 R. Paul Wilson, *The Art of the Con*, p. 81-82.
62 Major Cities Chiefs Association, "REPORT ON THE 2020 PROTESTS AND CIVIL UNREST," October 2020: https://majorcitieschiefs.com/wp-content/uploads/2021/01/MCCA-Report-on-the-2020-Protest-and-Civil-Unrest.pdf
63 Brad Polumbo, "George Floyd Riots Caused Record-Setting $2 Billion in Damage, New Report Says. Here's Why the True Cost Is Even Higher," Foundation for Economic Education, September 16, 2020: https://fee.org/articles/george-floyd-riots-caused-record-setting-2-billion-in-damage-new-report-says-here-s-why-the-true-cost-is-even-higher/

in maintaining the invisible structures of "systemic racism" just like the *hoi polloi* in the streets of Indianapolis, in Jacksonville, in Shreveport, in Bozeman, and in hundreds of other places.

This was the universal guilt-trip of "White Racist America" that roped-in the campus contingent of suckers—many thousands of them. It was the classic "resource extraction strategy" practiced by con-artists, which combined *victim-signaling* with *virtue-signaling* to create a dual message and construct called *virtuous victimhood.*

Bitter Medicine

> "For the first time in my life, I feel guilty about being white," my student admitted in shame. His voice barely rose above a whisper. He hunched over in embarrassment, his cheeks flushing."[64]

This virtuous victimhood Con Story was a hard pill for white liberal intellectuals to swallow.

More than that, it posed an insurmountable challenge to everything that gave their lives meaning—their conception of themselves as good and noble persons battling oppression in all its forms in their striving for a better world. DEI indicted them *all* as complicit in the ubiquitous white supremacy culture. Said Barbara Applebaum:

> All whites, by virtue of systemic white privilege that is inseparable from white ways of being, are implicated in the production and reproduction of systemic racial injustice. ...

---

64 Michael Eric Dyson, *Tears we Cannot Stop: A Sermon to White America* (New York: St. Martin's Press, 2017), p. 96.

How do white people reproduce and maintain racist practices even when, and especially when, they believe themselves to be morally good? How do these practices function to protect their white moral innocence? What allows whites to see themselves as part of the solution and to deny that they are part of the problem?[65]

For good measure, Applebaum cited two other accusers, Sherry Marx and Julie Pennington: "[T]o the good whites the racism they perpetuate is invisible to them, hidden by their helpful, knowledgeable and well-intentioned practices."[66]

Applebaum was just one of the dozens of Gurus of the DEI indictment Con Story, who had been preparing the ground for the intrusion of DEI folderol into the universities. Chapter 2 looks more closely at their core message. That core is the same for all of them—Emory University's George Yancy is one of the meanest of the DEI gurus, awash in his own righteousness, as is Georgetown University sociologist Michael Eric Dyson. These two race-baiters have labored long in the vineyard of the white indictment and have constructed the scaffolding of the DEI Con Story.[67] Dyson, especially, brings an evangelical spirit of the preacher to the indictment as he literally calls on America to "repent of whiteness":

---

65 Barbara Applebaum, *Being White, Being Good: White Complicity, White Moral Responsibility, and Social Justice Pedagogy* (Plymouth, UK: Lexington Books, 2011), p. 179-180.
66 Barbara Applebaum, *Being White, Being Good*, p. 180.
67 George Yancy, *Backlash: What happens when we talk honestly about racism in America* (Lanham, MD: Rowman & Littlefield, 2018); Michael Eric Dyson, *Tears we Cannot Stop: A Sermon to White America* (New York: St. Martin's Press, 2017).

It is my faith that helps me see how whiteness has become a religion. The idolatry of whiteness and the cloak of innocence that shields it can only be quenched by love, but not merely, or even primarily, a private, personal notion of love, but a public expression of love that holds us all accountable. Justice is what love sounds like when it speaks in public.[68]

Dyson is skilled with the lingo and litany of accusation: White fragility, White innocence, White grief, White supremacy, White racism, White silence, White complicity.

Even as the white intellectual considers himself the paragon of moral propriety and racial rectitude, Dyson and the other DEI gurus indict the campus white intellectual as guilty. In his *Sermon to White America*, Dyson thundered:

> [In] my insistence on holding you accountable for privilege, for tiny but terrifying aggressions, for condescension, for any of the everyday racial slights that reinforce white supremacy, I have invoked again your sense of your guilt. I am not just a person, but a pointing finger, a scold, a challenge to the authority you were given as a birthright and that you cannot bear to relinquish.[69]

This attack on the self-conception—the very identity—of the liberal intellectual is a recurrent DEI theme. It creates the

---

68 Michael Eric Dyson, *Tears we Cannot Stop*, p. 100.
69 Michael Eric Dyson, *Tears we Cannot Stop*, p. 103.

frantic distress linked to "cognitive dissonance."[70] DEI racialists attack white intellectuals in a way that intentionally creates this dissonance.

> Inclusion programs that deconstruct systemic oppression and the role of dominant ideology generally involve confronting privilege and the complexities of intersecting identities in ways that bring about "intellectual vertigo" and "ontological dizziness." This sense of disequilibrium comes from having to *reconceive the self in relation to others in ways that are counter to one's understanding of one's social and political position in society.*[71] [italics added]

Thus, the liberal white intellectual is no longer special, and his "critical consciousness" has not saved him from complicity in the base sins of the masses. He is just as guilty of these racial sins and no better than any rural Alabama bumpkin or Oklahoma hayseed or knuckle-dragging Donald J. Trump supporter in this racial reckoning. This attack on his self-image is catastrophic—he is *desperate* to atone, and he will pay any price, bear any burden to scrub out the stain of "racism" that has lumped him in with the rabble.

This was how a magnificent, grandiose Con Story of "fall and redemption" came together. It was a major cultural narrative of *virtuous victimhood* to set up the campus marks for fleecing.

---

70 "If two elements are dissonant with one another, the magnitude of the dissonance will be a function of the magnitude of the elements." Leon Festinger, *A Theory of Cognitive Dissonance* (Stanford: Stanford University Press, 1957, 1985), p. 16.

71 Sherry K. Watt, "Privileged Identity Exploration (PIE) Model Revisited," in Sherry K. Watt (ed.), *Designing Transformative Multicultural Initiatives* (Sterling, VA: Stylus, 2015), p. 41-42.

The Con Story—*Fall and Redemption*

The story accuses campus intellectuals of the most devastating sins, transgressions that contradict their very sense of self. The tale said that you, too, are guilty. You are not special, noble, or good. DEI condemned them but would also provide a way out. At a price. DEI doctrine would create the problem and then provide the means to solve it. With their fall-and-redemption offer to white liberal intellectuals, DEI proponents set up a scam of *virtuous victimhood* designed to extract resources from the *faux* guilty.

Under this devastating challenge that stripped away the prestige and moral sanctimony at their core, vain intellectuals and their fellow-travelers of the campus would pay *anything* to shed their guilt and restore their elevated self-conception, and this included payment of fabulous sums of scarce financial resources. They could again become *good people*.

Thus, DEI provided an easy path to absolution for imagined sins and a tonic for those eager to repair their damaged egos for the public perception of the virtuous.

DEI grifters, who are motivated by cash—and lots of it— were pleased to provide the easy good feelings that the intellectuals demanded and *still* demand. DEI offers a creed to assuage the guiltiest liberal and to coerce the most intransigent of conservatives.

That the push for DEI in the universities was all about relieving the guilt of white liberal intellectuals and nothing else was brutally articulated by *The Atlantic's* Conor Friedersdorf, who pointed out the skewed morality of DEI's Big Con:

> So how strange—how obscene, in fact—that America's professional class largely reacted to Floyd's murder not by lavishing so much of the resources spent in his name on helping poor

45

people, or the formerly (or currently) incarcerated, or people with addictions, or the descendants of slaves and sharecroppers, or children of single mothers, or graduates of underfunded high schools, but rather by hiring DEI consultants to gather employees together for trainings.[72]

* * *

The scaffolding of DEI's Big Con is brilliantly simple: We are victims, we are virtuous, you are guilty, you must pay reparations to gain absolution, and here's how you can do it.

DEI grifters create the problem in the university, and then they offer to solve the problem. They artificially manufacture the guilt for the mark, and they then provide the absolution for the guilt.[73] This is a sophisticated version of the protection racket that is familiar to anyone who has watched gangster films of the 1930s that features versions of the well-known veiled threat: "That's a nice (university) you have there. It'd be a shame if something were to happen to it."[74] But was the story of the Con Story good enough?

Would the colleges buy into the con?

The story was key, and this was the story's pivot point.

---

72   Conor Friedersdorf, "The DEI Industry Needs to Check its Privilege," *The Atlantic*, May 31, 2024: https://www.theatlantic.com/ideas/archive/2023/05/dei-training-initiatives-consultants-companies-skepticism/674237/

73   Lisa Spanierman, "White Guilt in the Summer of Black Lives Matter," in Katharina Von Kellenbach and Matthias Buschmeier (eds), *Guilt: A Force of Cultural Transformation* (New York: Oxford University Press, 2022), p. 41-58. Professor Spanierman of Arizona State University contributed a major element of the DEI big con by advocating the use of psychological techniques to generate fake guilt, which would then translate into the mark's readiness to "do the work" for social justice.

74   *The Public Pays: Startling Expose of Modern Racketeering* (October 10, 1936), "In this MGM Crime Does Not Pay series short, a protection racket preying on milk distribution is broken through the persistence of law enforcement and the courage of a local businessman." https://www.themoviedb.org/movie/130386-the-public-pays

* * *

"Persuading the victim to commit to a scheme that will benefit him or her"

> Storytelling is the oldest form of entertainment there is. From campfires and pictograms—the Lascaux cave paintings may date as far back as 1700 BCE—to tribal song and epic ballads passed down from generation to generation and city to city, it is one of the most fundamental ways humans have of making sense of the world . . . . That's precisely why they are such a powerful tool of deception, and so vital when it comes to the play. When we're immersed in a story, we let down our guard.[75]

Everything would hinge on whether the universities took the bait. The urgent reason given for the embrace of DEI was that racism was *rampant* on the campuses. Thus, the bait was "rampant racism."

This was a lie of immense scale at the core of the Con Story. This lie was so big and egregious, in fact, that only an intellectual could engage in the mental gymnastics to believe it.

This was the moment that colleges and universities would either call bullshit on the entire DEI enterprise . . . or capitulate. How would the colleges respond to this blatantly obvious fraud?

They caved.

The story was too good, the accusation was crafted too on-the-mark, like a surgeon wielding a scalpel. The smart, *good*

---

75 Maria Konnikova, *The Confidence Game*, p. 100-101.

people on the campuses took the bait and the hook was firmly in place. Once the "guilt" and sin of the university had been simply assumed into existence, the backdrop of the con was established and conmen could begin the *Play*.[76] Says Konnikova:

> After the mark is chosen, it is time to set the actual con in motion: the play, the moment when you first hook a victim and begin to gain her trust. And that is accomplished, first and foremost, through emotion. Once our emotions have been captured, once the con artist has cased us closely enough to identify what it is we want, feeling, at least in the moment, takes over from thinking.[77]

The Play was brilliant:

1. Universities would be accused of "rampant racism," "White supremacy," "institutional racism," "complicity in systemic racism" according to the grand narrative contrived by critical racialists and neo-Marxists.

2. Antiracist Task Forces would be handpicked by simpering presidents and would quickly confirm that, yes, the universities were guilty of the sin of racism— lots of different "racisms," in fact. An amorphous "racial climate" was interminably negative.

---

76 Maria Konnikova, *The Confidence Game*, p. 89-127.
77 Maria Konnikova, *The Confidence Game*, p. 92.

3. Shady con artists would be imported into the universities and paid lavishly to castigate suckers eager to don the hairshirt of penance. In exchange for extravagant salaries and increasing power and personnel, DEI cadres and their colluding consultants would provide indulgences, much as did the medieval Catholic Church.[78]

4. The newly minted DEI bureaucracy would provide racial absolution through the instrument of "training," narratives of "oppression," and the imposition of a new orthodoxy on the campus.

5. For those unresponsive skeptics who resist the absolution phase, their fates would be decided in other ways—perhaps with the anonymous snitch lines set up to report them, perhaps with a "bias response team," or vague and anonymous complaints on student evaluations, or outright coercion, discipline, and dismissal in the case of faculty.

In this way, universities acted in a contrived moral panic to address a range of problems that existed only in the minds of those who saw opportunity in the death of a crook in Minneapolis. It was the perfect con, a con that is literally hundreds of years old—the scam of the fortune teller who creates an imaginary dilemma and then offers a solution. The scam of the gangster's protection racket.

---

78 Robert Ekelund, et al, *Sacred Trust: The Medieval Church as an Economic Firm* (New York: Oxford University Press, 1996), p. 70.

Hundreds of colleges and universities with no connection to the events in far-off Minnesota agreed to don sackcloth and ashes and to solicit absolution that carried an exorbitant price tag.

Victims and Villains identified

College presidents tested the political winds and saw fit to abandon their principles. **They embraced the contrived guilt, and they sought the absolution that only DEI could provide.** They rushed almost unanimously to pronounce on the crime in Minneapolis in confessions of complicity. They issued sycophantic public statements, each more anguished than the last. They begged for absolution for vaguely articulated sins, and they promised to do better.[79] Public handwringing was now obligatory and accorded new cachet, and confessional racialist workshops multiplied faster than coronavirus in the colleges, all based on the fabulous fraud of rampant racism.

This was the "Put-Up" of the Big Con—*virtuous victimhood*—and once it was established, the "Play" commenced, and the money began to flow. By summer of 2021, the ideological locomotive was chugging along at top speed and the money, power, and people poured onto the campuses in such quantities that nothing could stop it. Opportunists saw a chance for their own big score, and no one receiving a share of the loot wanted it to stop.

---

79 A compendium of these statements can be found here: Lindsay McKenzie, "Calls for Change," Insidehighered, June 1, 2020: https://www.insidehighered.com/news/2020/06/02/higher-ed-leaders-address-protests-racial-tensions-and-killing-george-floyd. See also Amy Guttman, "Statement on the Death of George Floyd," *Penn Today*, May 20, 2020: https://penntoday.upenn.edu/announcements/statement-death-george-floyd

Conclusion

In this chapter, I defined what it means to run a scam or "confidence game." We learned that the diversity grift has a decades-long history loitering on the periphery of higher education as a "short-con," the province of peanut grifting consultants. By way of the events in this chapter, we see how DEI has acquired Big Con status.

The media created the sensational histrionic brand of the "racial reckoning" that launched DEI as an official social movement and made the Big Con possible, with White Racist America the dark mega-canvas of the narrative.

For a con to work, the tale told must have important accurate details to make the lies easier to swallow. Equally important, the bait for the con must consist of something the mark wants badly. This bait is not always money. In this case, the virtuous victimhood Con Story convinced vain white intellectuals and their hangers-on in the staff that they were guilty *en masse* and that expensive DEI programs could return them to the moral high ground.

The backdrop for the DEI con is the "racial reckoning," which manufactured and amplified a problem of "white racist America" that was exemplified on the college campuses by "rampant" and "systemic racism."

This "racism" would be rubber-stamped by a university "task force" that would verify that, yes, racism was rampant and a serious problem. The findings of the task force are essential to the success of the con. It offers a self-indictment of the school and offers recommendations by the very people who stand to profit from the recommendations.

As for the marks, all are guilty of this racism, which goes strangely unspecified, but which can be remedied with large budgets and larger bureaucracy. The DEI Con Story executes the resource extraction strategy employed by DEI con-artists as *virtuous victimhood*. The dual signaling of virtue + victim is a powerful tonic, especially employed against the white liberal university establishment, which is more than ready to lavish riches on these self-proclaimed victims. This is the payout of the Big Con.

In return, DEI offers to its marks absolution for imagined sins of faculty, staff, and students. Even institutional absolution. To receive this absolution, the *good people* of the campuses must accept a raft of radical and permanent changes to their schools. DEI demanded that they inject systemic bigotry into the university, institutionalize it, give it respectability. They would "boldly transform higher education" according to a clearly expressed racialist ideology.[80] The newly ensconced bureaucracy of well-funded commissars makes this absolution not only possible, but compulsory. While some have welcomed the absolution, others who offer "diversity resistance" must be trained.

Such is the barely believable background of the Big Con of DEI.

The following chapters detail the pathology of DEI—the who, the what, the where, and the results of this debilitating DEI creed that has invaded and continues to erode the nation's universities.

---

80 The seeds of this critical racialism were planted decades earlier. Its proponents trace their lineage back to the original neo-Marxist theorists, and these contemporary advocates are clear on their Marxist roots. Critical Race Theory is nothing more than the transmogrification of Marxist theory into a racialist iteration. This was clearly stated in the foundational weekend conference in Madison, Wisconsin in 1989, which included all the key personnel—Kimberly Crenshaw, Richard Delgado, Derrick Bell, Mara Matsuda. See Richard Delgado and Jean Stefancic, *Critical Race Theory: An Introduction* (New York: New York University Press, 2001), p. xvii.

2
THE DEI CON STORY

YOU CAN'T SPELL DECEIT WITHOUT DEI

"A well-executed play doesn't just capture your emotion in the moment; it makes you more susceptible to the precise version of reality a confidence artist wants to create to further his scheme. ... Visceral cues, like the basic emotion brought forth by a powerful story can override even motivation. Instead of processing a message logically, we act like the unmotivated person and take in all the wrong things. That's the power of the play. Even if we're trying hard not to get conned, if the play unrolls in the right way, it eventually won't matter; the narrative sweep will take over."[81]

— Maria Konnikova

---

81 Maria Konnikova, *The Confidence Game*, p. 110-111.

The so-called racial reckoning of 2020 was a brilliant weave of minimal facts and a trainload of fiction. The George Floyd affair opened the floodgates for opportunists, peanut hustlers, and big-time grifters. It was like the Wild West, and the Gold Rush was on.

This was a market flush with marks, eager for guilt, influential self-flagellants ready to take and spread the myth, and campus social climbers ready to mouth what is likely the most idiotic slogan of the 21st Century: "Diversity is our strength."

For a Big Con to work, even one with a spectacular set-up like the "racial reckoning," it must be legitimized in ways that make sense to the mark. Thus, it's important to offer evidence and substantiation in the language the mark uses and in forums that the mark trusts. The clincher should carry heft for the mark.

The biggest cons are categorized as *Big Store* games, which require elaborate planning, even props and stages. The most prominent are **The Wire, The Rag**, and **The Payoff**, and for these an elaborate stage setup is manufactured to play the mark. In The Wire, for example, the mark believes that they are in an actual betting establishment and privy to early inside information on the winners of races—and wins a fortune betting on that privileged information.[82] The con depends upon the mark buying into the lie entirely. Hence, the need for accuracy in the performance down to the finest detail.

> The store [became] a pretentious institution where men high in
> the social and financial world could be played for scores which

---

82 If this Big Con seems familiar, it's likely because this was the swindle portrayed in the 1973 film *The Sting*, which starred Paul Newman and Robert Redford. The film was based on the 1940 book by David Maurer, *The Big Con*: https://www.imdb.com/title/tt0070735/

ran into the hundreds of thousands of dollars, a prosperous establishment which was well calculated to arouse the larceny in the soul of the mark once he saw it in action.[83]

If universities and their shrewd faculty, administrations, and staff were to be hoodwinked, the same commitment to detailed accuracy was necessary.

As we've seen, the perfect Big Store to tackle the university is the con called *Virtuous Victimhood*. This is the elaborate resource extraction charade to convince innocent people that they are guilty villains, who have harmed innocent victims, and that they must pay those victims in the interests of "restorative justice."[84] What renders *Virtuous Victimhood* especially powerful is that universities are persuaded that they must actually *train* students, faculty and staff into villainhood or victimhood. Most of them are guilty and a minority of them are victims.

But how to convince the smartest people in America to accept this absurdity?

In this con, the best evidence to convince university academics and academic audiences appears in scholarly books and in scholarly journal articles. These have typically been the venue for reliable knowledge generated from rigorous research. Some call this evidence-based research. The high quality of these sources

---

83 David W. Maurer, *The Big Con: The Story of the Confidence Man* (New York: MJG Books, 1940, 1968, 1999), p. 18-19.
84 Lydialyle Gibson, "Restoring Justice: Exploring an alternative to crime and punishment," *Harvard Magazine*, July-August, 2021. "The person who has committed the crime takes responsibility, expresses remorse, and offers a detailed public apology; victims give voice to their pain, their feelings, and their needs. Then the group comes to consensus on a set of actions that the offender can take to meet those needs, repair the harm, and prevent further offenses." https://www.harvardmagazine.com/2021/06/features-restorative-justice

elicits the trust of university audiences, which unfortunately also renders these sources as targets for cooptation by grifters of all sorts. The point, of course, is to influence belief, and the closer the lie is presented in terms trusted by the mark, the more likely the Big Con will succeed.

And thus, an entire industry has emerged to launder the main ideas of the DEI Con Story. This "industry" includes the founding of what can be called "cargo cult" journals, radical book publishers, and the establishment of fake "co-curricula" of seminars and workshops in the universities. The method is to repeat, repeat, repeat. This *idea laundering* is a way to generate "symbolic capital" through repetition in as many places as possible, to give the false impression that problematic assumptions have achieved the status of accepted fact. This repetition is a characteristic of all totalitarian entities, as Polish academic Leszek Kolakowski reminds us:

> In the functionaries' minds, the borderline between what is "correct" and what is "true," as we normally understand this, seems really to have become blurred; by repeating the same absurdities time and again, they began to believe or half-believe in them themselves.[85]

This body of faux scholarship constitutes a *hoax literature* from which campus con-artists draw freely.

Worse, ideas laundered in this way can be smuggled into the mainstream of academia through the side door and posture as genuine, accepted knowledge. This is how some of the most ridiculous

---

85   Leszek Kolakowski, "Totalitarianism and the Lie," *Commentary*, May 1983: https://www.commentary.org/articles/leszek-kolakowski/totalitarianism-the-lie/

of assertions make their way onto the campus, unexamined and unchallenged. Public intellectual Dinesh D'Souza recognized this technique of the charlatan scholar at the beginning of the century:

> Through professionalized jargon, however meaningless, critics assert their claims to special expertise and consequently to special recognition and privilege. And these intellectual gymnastics have now become very profitable in the academy.[86]

DEI cadres are quick to provide expensive absolution to a cowed populace of willing suckers or "marks." Their story is convincing to their marks, because it offers these marks something they desperately need. It taps into the emotions to elicit an emotional response, and it counts on the dismissal of rationality.

But in the final analysis, DEI is nothing but an elaborate Con Story constructed from the raw material of exaggerations, half-truths, and lies.

Let's dismantle this edifice of lies.

The Kernel of Truth and the Biggest of Lies

The biggest lie of DEI began with an unfortunate truth—the death of George Floyd on May 25, 2020 in Minneapolis. Even today, it is rare to attend a diversity training session that does *not* mention the death of Floyd.

Floyd's demise formed the basis of the myth, and here marks the beginning of the DEI Big Con. While every death is tragic, there was nothing exceptional in the singular death of an

---

86   Dinesh D'Souza, *Illiberal Education*, p. 181.

intoxicated suspect at the hands of a multiethnic team of Minneapolis police to suggest that the nation's police were engaged in some sort of systematic targeting of black Americans. The facts did not substantiate it, as scholar Heather MacDonald has carefully documented.[87]

Nevertheless, the gears of what would become the Big Con of *virtuous victimhood* were set in motion with a series of simple and simple-minded tales. The theme of these yarns was tailor-made for the future marks in business and, especially, in the universities.

Abortive attempts at exploiting death had been made earlier. The self-defense shooting of Trayvon Martin in 2012 by George Zimmerman was one such event. It launched the trope of the "unarmed teen," and it triggered the launch of the Black Lives Matter movement, which gouged millions of dollars in donations from businesses and eventually morphed into a major scam as the founders—self-professed Marxists—exited the organization as rich women. BLM would become a major player in the violence to come in 2020.

The Trayvon Martin case was followed by another abortive attempt to sensationalize a shooting. This was the death of Michael Brown in Ferguson, Missouri in 2014. Brown was a 6-4, 300-pound giant who had just come off a strong-arm robbery of a grocery store, was high on drugs, and was walking down the middle of a busy street when he was confronted by police officer Darren Wilson, who ordered him off the thoroughfare. Brown moved immediately to assault Wilson and was fatally shot. Wilson was found innocent, but the incident was quickly torqued into

---

87   Heather MacDonald, *The War on Cops* (New York: Encounter Books, 2016).

another tale of an "unarmed teen" shot by the police, as if Brown were a 13-year-old innocent on his way to violin practice.

It was the death of George Floyd, however, that gave the opportunists the perfect hook for the Con Story they needed to trigger a transformation of society. While most persons are familiar with the basic story of the Floyd death, I relate the tale here with the particular details highlighted that gave the story such power.

The Accidental Martyr of Minneapolis

The summer of 2020 propelled George Floyd into the role of unlikeliest of saints. The reaction of violence and vandalism to this accidental martyr revealed a shocking impotence of state governments in their abdication of their responsibilities to protect their citizens.[88]

The violence was not random. In fact, it was systematically organized and orchestrated, much of it by the multi-million-dollar activist group BLM and by a shadowy crypto-terrorist group of white radicals called "antifa." Sympathetic pundits quickly labeled this organized chaos a "Racial Reckoning." But to most of America it looked like a celebration of urban violence, arson, assault, looting, vandalism, statue-toppling, and riots. Little of this seemed to have anything to do with the death of the hapless Floyd, killed by a rogue policeman in Minneapolis. But hectoring voices in the media and public intellectuals of every stripe chastised the country.

The race-driven mania sucked in many who should have known better, but who saw a chance to earn moral credentials on the cheap with no immediate downside. This led to an explosion in

88 Nicole Chavez, "2020: The Year America Confronted Racism," CNN: https://www.cnn.com/interactive/2020/12/us/america-racism-2020/

major media of fakery called "gaslighting"—this was the transformation of what people could see for themselves into a fraudulent pseudo-reality, and it was exemplified by the "mostly peaceful protests" trope that was widely ridiculed on social media.[89] This trope appeared in a CNN media segment from Kenosha, Wisconsin, by Omar Jimenez. While viewers watched the reporter, a building behind him engulfed in flames, and the chyron on the screen read: "FIERY BUT MOSTLY PEACEFUL PROTESTS AFTER POLICE SHOOTING."[90] The phrase "mostly peaceful protests" became a punchline for the social fantasy joke enjoyed by those more closely attuned to reality than to a fake alternative. Social critic Christopher Rufo espied this change in media coverage that sought to reframe positively what people saw with their own eyes, with rampant criminality passed through the filter of ideology and euphemism.[91]

This gaslighting became almost routine, and it eroded public trust in national media as, simultaneously, problematic coverage of the COVID pandemic was doing the same.[92] Even the medical profession began to delegitimize itself with its public embrace of street violence as a "public health" crisis more urgent than containing what was hysterically portrayed as a killer virus. Thus, medical

89 Isaac Schorr, "A Misleading Attempt to Bolster the 'Mostly Peaceful' Riots Narrative," *National Review*, September 8, 2020: https://www.nationalreview.com/2020/09/a-misleading-attempt-to-bolster-the-mostly-peaceful-riots-narrative/
90 Joe Concha, "CNN ridiculed for 'Fiery But Mostly Peaceful' caption with video of burning building in Kenosha," The Hill, August 27, 2020: https://thehill.com/homenews/media/513902-cnn-ridiculed-for-fiery-but-mostly-peaceful-caption-with-video-of-burning/.
91 Christopher F. Rufo, *America's Cultural Revolution: How the Radical Left Conquered Everything* (New York: Broadside Books, 2023), p. 126.
92 Merriam-Webster named "gaslighting" its word of the year for 2022, as online searches for the term increased by a staggering 1,740 percent. Ella Feldman, 'Gaslighting' Is Merriam-Webster's Word of the Year,' *Smithsonian Magazine*, November 29, 2022: https://www.smithsonianmag.com/smart-news/gaslighting-merriam-webster-word-of-the-year-180981203/

THE DEI CON STORY

doctors seemed to lose their minds as they approved and excused tightly packed urban protests in the midst of a pandemic.[93]

This gave the green light to big-city street dancing as a public health contribution, while at the same time, government cracked down on religious services and funerals.[94] Fifteen persons were arrested in New Jersey for attending the funeral of a rabbi, and similar absurdities played out nationwide.[95] Public intellectuals hailed the time as a "Summer of Racial Reckoning" for America, which was the moralizing label used to justify nationwide violence and the burning and looting of neighborhoods.[96] This appeared almost as orchestrated collective insanity. Even as the chaos seemed just that—chaotic—it seemed too contrived to pass the smell test, and it promised disaster for the immediate future.

Built by Guilt—*DEI's White Supremacy Scam*

[B]efore a single element of the actual con is laid out, before a single persuasive appeal is made, before a mark knows that someone will want something, anything at all, from him, the emotional channels are opened. And as in that first rush

---

93 Kim Bellware, "Calls to declare racism a public health crisis grow louder amid pandemic, police brutality," *The Washington Post*, September 15, 2020: https://www.washingtonpost.com/nation/2020/09/15/racism-public-health-crisis/
94 Samirah Majumdar, "Key findings about COVID-19 restrictions that affected religious groups around the world in 2020," *Pew Research Center*, November 29, 2022: https://www.pewresearch.org/short-reads/2022/11/29/key-findings-about-covid-19-restrictions-that-affected-religious-groups-around-the-world-in-2020/
95 "Coronavirus Latest: Lakewood Officers Break Up Large Funeral Gathering Violating New Jersey's Stay-At-Home Order," *CBS News*, April 2, 2020: https://www.cbsnews.com/philadelphia/news/lakewood-township-police-15-charged-funeral-violating-nj-stay-at-home-order-coronavirus/
96 Ailsa Chang, Rachel Martin, Eric Marrapodi, "Summer of Racial Reckoning," *NPR*, August 16, 2020: https://www.npr.org/2020/08/16/902179773/summer-of-racial-reckoning-the-match-lit

of romantic infatuation, we abandon our reason to follow our feeling.[97]

The Floyd story gained overnight mythic status and elicited emotional power of the type most likely to trigger a tsunami of fake guilt in America, especially on the college campuses. Coupled with the psychological manipulation advocated by Professor Lisa Spanierman at Arizona State University and others similarly motivated, fake guilt could be generated to motivate persons to "do the work" of social justice. Campus classrooms were a superb venue for this type of manipulation, where a gigantic scam could be proffered almost unchallenged.[98]

This scam was "white racist America" awash in "white supremacy."

This theme had variations—"white supremacy," "white privilege," "white racism," "white innocence."[99] It was the perfect malevolent Dark Triad construction—fake victimhood coupled with virtue.[100] It was a politically contrived Con Story designed to inflame the emotions in blatant defiance of a reality most everyone saw and experienced for themselves. But the extremist story performed exactly as expected. Konnikova contends that: "The more absorbing the story, the stronger the effect. And that's

---

97 Maria Konnikova, *The Confidence Game*, p. 92.

98 Katharina Von Kellenbach and Matthias Buschmeier (eds), *Guilt: A Force of Cultural Transformation* (New York: Oxford University Press, 2022).

99 OiYan A. Poon, "Ending White Innocence in Student Affairs and Higher Education," *Journal of Student Affairs*, Vol. XXVII, 2017-2018.

100 The "Dark Triad" is a cluster of psychological traits often found together having malevolent qualities—Machiavellianism, narcissism, and psychopathy. Delroy L. Paulhus and Kevin M. Williams, "The Dark Triad of personality: Narcissism, Machiavellianism, and psychopathy," *Journal of Research in Personality* 36 (2002): https://www2.psych.ubc.ca/~dpaulhus/research/OCT/ARTICLES%20&%20CHAPTERS/JRP%202002%20Paulhus-Williams.pdf

what the play is all about-finding the best approach to get the strongest effect."[101]

This narrative rapidly penetrated the nation's college campuses, spurred on by clenched-fist activists, diversity peanut grifters, and their fellow-travelers, who quickly fell into line. This was a window of opportunity to "boldly transform higher education."[102]

It didn't matter that universities had nothing to do with the death of Floyd.

It didn't matter that the larger "killer police" narrative was false.

It didn't matter that inequities in higher education were being addressed briskly since the passage of the Civil Rights Act more than half a century earlier.

It didn't matter that the nation's campuses are arguably some of the least racist places in America, according to Harvard law professor Randall Kennedy.[103]

But as is the case so much of the time where extremist political causes are involved, the truth is the first casualty. The truth doesn't matter. It's simply another obstacle to be overcome in the transformation of higher education into an instrument for the anti-intellectual indoctrination of students and for the reshaping of society into a crucible of emasculated and race-obsessed would-be intellectuals squabbling over spoils in what has been called *competitive victimhood*.[104]

---

101 Maria Konnikova, *The Confidence Game*, p. 103.
102 https://myacpa.org/
103 Randall Kennedy, "How racist are universities, really?" *The Chronicle of Higher Education*, August 12, 2020: https://www.chronicle.com/article/how-racist-are-universities-really
104 Timothy C. Bates, Clara Grant, Leila Hobbs, Claire Johnston, Shahrzad Moghaddam, Kate Sinclair, "Virtuous Victimhood as a Dark Triad resource transfer strategy," *Personality and Individual Differences*, 234 (2025), p. 1.

The Con Story of DEI did everything it was supposed to do. It created a resource extraction narrative driven by the con of *virtuous victimhood*. The core of the narrative was "killer cops." With this Con Story repeated and amplified nationwide, it became incredibly easy to extract resources from those portrayed as guilty, and in this *all* of society was guilty. This is why universities were targeted and the fakery employed in the way it was, targeting higher education at its weakest point. The university, this least likely of villains, had to be portrayed as victimizer, a *systemic* victimizer. People in charge of the purse-strings *had to be convinced* that they were villains. The con of virtuous victimhood was tailor-made for the universities' white liberal intellectuals and their fellow-traveling staff. It tapped into what psychologists know about victimhood culture.

Here we examine the cascade of dishonesty, deception and lies of DEI that have bedeviled the universities and have proven so difficult to dislodge. Dismantling the DEI con won't be easy. Says Konnikova: "An expertly planted belief is a nearly impossible thing to shake."[105]

DEI's Potemkin Façade

The imaginative Con Story is like a magnificent deceptive façade on a building that obscures the decay behind the front. Let's call this narrative façade the *frontstage*. Behind it is the truth of the matter, the *backstage*. These are the guts of the Con that the con-artist would prefer that you never see.

The lies of DEI form a useful public face of the doctrine. A term for this is the *Potemkin village*, a Russian term that refers to

---

105 Maria Konnikova, *The Confidence Game*, p. 309.

adding a freshly painted façade to the exterior of buildings to mask the interior rot.[106]

Behind the front is the DEI "backstage." This is where the actual noxious victim/villain doctrine is spun out on campuses. Many folks go all-in on the diversity, equity, and inclusion project, not recognizing that DEI has this two-faced characteristic.

This *frontstage/backstage* tactic is a reliable tool, especially in universities, which have uncritically embraced DEI and have installed a phalanx of racialist bureaucrats to maintain the virtuous victimhood fiction. Yale research psychologist Irving Janis called these true believers "mindguards," those who administer the political orthodoxy. This is a classic example of what Janis identified as "groupthink," in which skepticism and doubt about the orthodoxy are prohibited.[107] The frontstage fraud is maintained, and anyone who questions this fraud is attacked. Simple requests for evidence are treated with hostility, which is a key marker for conspiracy theory.[108]

Let's look at both faces of DEI's Con Story.

The Front

The public face of DEI consists of sloganeering for an agenda of positive abstractions, seemingly admirable and even utopian. It offers a lyrical tale steeped in moralizing yet short on specifics.

106 Ishaan Tharoor, "Top Ten Weird Government Secrets," Time, August 6, 2010: https://content.time.com/time/specials/packages/article/0,28804,2008962_2008964_2009010,00.html
107 Groupthink is "a mode of thinking that people in a group engage in where striving for unanimity overrides the motivation to realistically appraise alternative courses of action." Message from the Chief, Safety and Mission Assurance, "Watch out for Groupthink," SMA News, July 2024: https://sma.nasa.gov/news/sma-news-archive/watch-out-for-groupthink
108 Stanley K. Ridgley, "The Conspiracist Fantasy of University Bureaucracies," *Minding the Campus*, November 28, 2022: https://www.mindingthecampus.org/2022/11/28/the-conspiracist-fantasy-of-university-bureaucracies/

Indeed, DEI messaging is so aspirational that few persons could find anything objectionable.

DEI pronouncements are suffused with the minimal expected program activity to provide a patina of legitimacy to the entire enterprise. Enough generic rhetoric of Enlightenment values is woven throughout the DEI lingo to establish familiarity and to resonate with reasonable people.

DEI afficionados use familiar words and phrases, but they define them differently so that programmatic radicalism is masked with a patina of reasonableness. Authoritarians—and totalitarians—from the middle of the 20th century have utilized this technique with skill to gain popular support for pernicious programs. Novelist George Orwell was not a linguist, but as a practicing wordsmith, he understood this better than most. His dystopian novel *1984* contains an elaboration of what he called *Newspeak*. He warned of the linguistic gymnastics that authoritarians use to dupe and cajole those who are ruled, and he created Newspeak to capture the notion that language can control reality. This has become the best-known example of language manipulation in the quest for political power.

DEI has developed its own variation of Newspeak.

Much of the DEI discourse sounds like a program grounded in traditional liberalism, with fingers crossed that folks believe that "equity" and "equality" are one and the same. This crude resemblance to liberalism gets DEI's nose in the tent, with references to "educating for freedom," "emancipation," "love," "community," "dialogue," "belonging," "engaging with difference," and even the occasional reference to "science." This is akin to the deceptive lingo used by cults to attract recruits—the Unification Church, for example, relies on "peace and unity" as the attractive slogan and the technique of love bombing to bait the cult's hook.[109]

I speculate that many persons enamored of DEI's façade initially have no idea that the *backstage* even exists, let alone the toxic ideology that animates it. This is why so many otherwise intelligent persons are eager to "do the work" of the virtuous victimhood Big Con.[110]

These people have switched off their critical faculties to favor a feelings-based posture. They embrace the idea of viewing the world through an "equity lens," which is otherwise known in mainstream academia as *confirmation bias*, the cherry-picking of data to confirm an already-held dubious belief.

They buy into the façade of their own mental devising, and they simply remain unaware of the actual agenda and noxious ideology—whether through averted gaze, simple disinterest, inability to grasp what goes on, the psychological need to be a foot-soldier follower, or the artificially induced need to pay penance.

This is an intentional deception, of course, that is essential to the Big Con. Behind this benign *frontstage* façade, we find *backstage* DEI.

---

109 Nancy Jubb, "The Unification Church": Who We Are," Family Federation for World Peace and Unification, PR Newswire, September 14, 2021: https://www.prnewswire.com/news-releases/the-unification-church-who-we-are-301377078.html According to Margaret Singer, Love Bombing "involves long-term members' flooding recruits and newer members with flattery, verbal seduction, affectionate but usually nonsexual touching, and lots of attention to their every remark. Love bombing—or the offer of instant companionship—is a deceptive ploy accounting for many successful recruitment drives." Margaret Singer, *Cults in our Midst* (New York: Wiley, 1996), p. 114.
110 Stanley K. Ridgley, "Doing the Work" of the Antiracism Cult: *Cultists always attack a recruit's belief system and "sense of self,"* BrutalMinds.com, September 6, 2023: https://brutalminds.com/?p=1511

Backstage DEI—*Behind the Façade*

Backstage DEI is as far from Enlightenment thinking as one can get. In fact, it's grounded in a pre-Enlightenment Manichean ideology of paranoia and conspiracy.

This is the anti-scientific world of the "medicine wheel" and the "talking stick" and the "spirit animal," a world of hyper-suspicion, delusions, and ethnic discipline, where minority professionals are cautioned that "skinfolk are not always kinfolk."[111]

Contrary to the optimism of the Enlightenment—logic, reason, progress, scientific method, self-critique, humane values—the DEI backstage is a construct of virtuous victimhood. It is a binary world of arbitrarily defined *villains* and *victims*, of "agents and targets."[112] It's a fantasy world of "storytelling" and "autoethnographies" and "lived experiences" and "counternarratives" and "*testimonios*" and "indigenous" enchantment.

This ideology is commonly called *antiracism*, and it undergirds DEI and its raft of "training" activities.[113] This construct of Antiracism-as-Business was fingered more than three decades ago as a burgeoning grift. Said hate hoax expert Laird Wilcox in 1994:

> In recent years "anti-racists" have proclaimed that virtually every behavior and institution in our society is covertly racist. Anti-racism has become a small industry in the United States.

111 A quote attributed to author Zora Neale Hurston and repeated often to attack minority scholars who do not engage in the groupthink of DEI orthodoxy, as here: https://upcolorado.com/utah-state-university-press/item/3794-presumed-incompetent-ii
112 Maurianne Adams, Lee Anne Bell, Pat Griffin, *Teaching for Diversity and Social Justice* (New York: Routledge, 1997).
113 Stanley K. Ridgley, "Campus 'Anti-Racism' Is a Degenerating Research Program: A theory that cannot accommodate reality is fatally flawed," James G. Martin Center for Academic Renewal, September 8, 2023: https://www.jamesgmartin.center/2023/09/campus-anti-racism-is-a-degenerating-research-program/

Entire career fields are built around defining and combatting "racism" in one form or another. As individual problems are solved and offensive behaviors disappear, the definition of racism is broadened again and again to include more and more behaviors, hence we have the problem of "increasing" bigotry and intolerance. I suspect the last thing many professional anti-racists want is a truly race-neutral society. They have developed a vested interest in the continuation of the problem, a kind of "co-dependency" relationship, if you will.[114]

Wilcox was nothing else if not prescient. The Orwellian contrivance of antiracism has metastasized into big business, but has little to do with battling actual campus racism. It has everything to do with codifying a paranoid conspiracy theory into university policy and contriving an elegant victim-signaling Con Story to extract the maximum of resources from higher education: "Resource transfer from non-victims would include money, transportation, offers of accommodation, as well as forgiveness for transgressions."[115]

The conspiracy theory identifies its racial scapegoat in the form of a pseudocommunity of persecutors, a key marker of paranoia.[116] Paranoia informs DEI and its vision of the world and is the source of much of its deceit. We will examine this paranoid basis of DEI in detail in Chapter 3. Here we preview this paranoid

114 Laird Wilcox, *Crying Wolf: Hate Crime Hoaxes in America* (Olathe KS: Laird Wilcox, 1994).
115 Timothy C. Bates, Clara Grant, Leila Hobbs, Claire Johnston, Shahrzad Moghaddam, Kate Sinclair, "Virtuous Victimhood as a Dark Triad resource transfer strategy," *Personality and Individual Differences*, 234 (2025), p. 2.
116 Norman Cameron, "The Paranoid Pseudo-Community," *American Journal of Sociology*: Vol 49, No 1 (1943) and Norman Cameron, "The Paranoid Pseudo-Community Revisited," *American Journal of Sociology*: Vol 65, No 1 (1959).

vision as it contributes a major component to DEI's Con Story. It elicits feelings rather than appeals to rationality, and it sets up the virtuous victimhood framework.

DEI's Paranoid Vision of the World

The paranoid conception of the world as populated with enemies has endured throughout history in various forms literary, academic, even scientific. Paranoia appears in literature and is the animating plot-mover of Cervantes' great novel *Don Quixote*.[117] It is ubiquitous in philosophy.[118] In its most consequential form, it has appeared in political systems, codified, organized, and instrumental.[119]

Closely tied to this paranoid vision that inspires so much of the human condition is the language that is used to build it. A particular sort of language serves as a marker for paranoid belief systems, and the critic and literary scholar Michal Glowinski tells

---

117 "[Don Quixote] is beginning to recognize the limitations upon his heroic powers; but his paranoid sense of the meaningfulness of every element of his experience has not left him. He is still a prey to the 'omnipotence of thoughts', even when no longer the bearer of omnipotence." John Farrell, *Freud's Paranoid Quest: Psychoanalysis and Modern Suspicion* (New York: New York University Press, 1996), p. 106.

118 John Farrell, *Paranoia and Modernity: Cervantes to Rousseau* (Ithaca: Cornell University Press, 2006). Farrell identifies a "generation of postwar French intellectuals who, under the broad banners of Nietzsche, Marx, and Freud, carried the suspicion of society to new depths: Jean-Paul Sartre, for whom the "gaze" of others imposes a fundamental experience of the alien; Louis Althusser; for whom the discourse of responsibility is a primary instance of ideology; Jacques Lacan, for whom language itself is the source of our unnatural submission to the Father; and Michel Foucault, who speaks in terms of an unlocatable and alien *power* that infiltrates every particle of social being. When these notions become dominant, we have passed the point at which it is possible to make a distinction between paranoia and anything else to which the term could be meaningfully opposed." [p. 4] As well, Jean-Jacque Rousseau is credited with crystallizing the elements of modern paranoia: "In Rousseau's confessional works, we see him struggling mightily to cope with what he himself takes for an astonishing fact—the existence of an all-powerful conspiracy focused in hostility against him in order to remove him from the sight of posterity. Rousseau believes in this conspiracy—the evidence is all around him—but he is unable truly to make sense of it." [p. 290]

119 Michal Glowinski, *Totalitarian Speech*. Stanley Bill (trans.) (Frankfurt am Main: Peter Lang, 2014).

us how this works. Glowinski studied paranoid belief systems for decades, he lived inside a conspiracist regime for many years, and his focus on language control as a vital component of such systems demonstrates how they give rise to ideology.

> The words we use not only convey a certain vision of the world; they also influence its construction. They make—or at least they can make—their own contributions, and thus they easily fall victim to various kinds of manipulation. From the very outset, I wish to make the following assertion: it is possible to examine the conspiracist vision of the world from a linguistic point of view, since it represents a certain way of speaking and a certain way of constructing discourse. Therefore, we may also choose to view it as a set of metaphors, idioms or well-worn phrases, which are often essentially neutral in themselves, but which lose this neutrality when harnessed within a specific type of argument. Then they become vehicles and agents of a specific way of understanding the world. ... How does the conspiracist vision of the world—understood as a peculiar form of discourse or a certain way of using linguistic resources—develop? ... A more or less latent notion of conspiracy remains the discourse's main defining feature.[120]

This suspicious "way of understanding the world" is simple and simple-minded, a binary world of good and evil, of those who conspire and those who are conspired against. This, Glowinski calls the "conspiracist vision of the world."

---

120 Michal Glowinski, *Totalitarian Speech*. Stanley Bill (trans.) (Frankfurt am Main: Peter Lang, 2014), p. 233-234.

This paranoid and conspiracist worldview permeates DEI. It informs DEI's language lies, and it animates "training" sessions in the universities nationwide. I deal with these extensively in Chapter 5 on DEI trainings.

Small wonder that *backstage* **DEI is kept obscured behind the** façade, and it's unsurprising that many persons are duped into embracing the agenda under such sketchy pretenses.

The Rampant Racism that Wasn't—*The Central Lie of DEI on the Campus*

Was this strange notion of rampant racism fake? Of course it was. *Rampant racism* was uttered repeatedly, but no one would say exactly what, where, or who constituted this racism. Moreover, it was dangerous to even ask the question lest the query itself trigger an avalanche of invective accusing the inquirer of racism.

For instance, more than 350 faculty and staff at Princeton University signed a public letter alluding to how "rampant" racism, "systemic racism," and "antiblack racism" "continue to thrive" at Princeton:

> Anti-Black racism has hamstrung our political process. It is rampant in even our most "progressive" communities. And it plays a powerful role at institutions like Princeton, despite declared values of diversity and inclusion .... At this moment of massive global uprising in the name of racial justice, we the faculty—Black, Latinx, Asian, and members of all communities of color along with our white colleagues—call upon the University to take immediate concrete and material steps to openly and publicly acknowledge the way that anti-Black racism, and

THE DEI CON STORY

racism of any stripe, continue to thrive on its campus. We call upon the administration to block the mechanisms that have allowed systemic racism to work, visibly and invisibly, in Princeton's operations.[121]

But *Atlantic* writer Conor Friedersdorf asked the most obvious question of the letter's signatories: "Can you give any examples of 'racist behaviors, incidents, research, and publication' at Princeton in, say, the last 15 years, that exemplify what you want to see disciplined?"[122]

No one answered, of course.

In a pattern that has been repeated pathologically nationwide for years, the avatars of "antiracism" refuse to provide the evidence that could clinch their claims and convince people to take them seriously. Harvard's Randall Kennedy mocked the lack of anything remotely resembling the racist hellhole that was alleged of Princeton in the breathless letter.

> If Princeton's racism was as conspicuous as alleged, one would expect the ultimatum's authors to be able to dash off some vivid, revealing examples. Instead, they refer with unsatisfying generality to "micro-aggression" and "outright racist incidents," leaving readers uncertain about what, precisely, they have in mind.[123]

---

121 Faculty Letter, July 4, 2020: https://docs.google.com/forms/d/e/1FAlpQLSfPm feDKBi25_7rUTKkhZ3cyMICQicp05ReVaeBpEdYUCkyIA/viewform

122 Conor Friedersdorf, "The Princeton Faculty's Anti-Free Speech Demands," *The Atlantic*, August 4, 2020. https://www.theatlantic.com/ideas/archive/2020/08/what-princeton-professors-really-think-about-defining-racism/614911/

123 Randall Kennedy, "How racist are universities, really?"

So why do they not answer the most basic queries about their frantic charges? Why, in fact, do they bristle angrily at the routine questions asked of anyone who levels such preposterous charges?

The answer is part of the weakness of DEI and a key marker for one of the major contentions of this book. The hostility toward routine questions asked of the truth claims of any doctrine is a tell for conspiracy theory. The Diversity, Equity, Inclusion doctrine is grounded in conspiracy, and *this* strange omission of substance in the accusations is a feature of such charges of racism.[124] Repeatedly, the architects of the new campus racialist regimes refused to provide even the barest of examples of the malady that was supposedly out-of-control on their campuses. When questioned, even gently, they would bristle and exhibit the behavior of conspiracy theorists—they cite the very act of requesting proof or examples as all the evidence necessary to substantiate such racism.[125]

This mendacious Princeton model was the template employed nationwide with weary regularity and with no pushback by people who ought to know better. Indeed, people who are *paid* to know better. They seemed helpless in the face of the con, even eager. This is the result of one of the most powerful psychological ploys ever foisted on the university—*virtuous victimhood*.

This dynamic is the classic logic of virtuous victimhood—a story claims victimhood status for a group and simultaneously

---

124 Jovan Byford, *Conspiracy Theories: A Critical Introduction* (New York: Palgrave Macmillan, 2011, 2015). See also, Jovan Byford, "How to spot a conspiracy theory," The Conversation, March 16, 2020: https://theconversation.com/how-to-spot-a-conspiracy-theory-when-you-see-one-133574
125 I've personally dealt with this conspiracist mindset on the campus.

acquires *moral immunity*[126] against criticism: "[V]ictims are enabled to claim not only compensation from nonvictims, but also immunization from claims on their own moral transgressions—whether by deceit, intimidation, or even violence—in transferring resources to themselves or to their social group."[127] Said Wilcox again with keen prescience:

> Powerful racial and ethnic interest groups have compelling reasons to manipulate the rules and to keep up an appearance of perpetual victimhood. Not only is it extremely useful in promoting a political agenda, but it can have considerable financial benefits to the "victims" as well.[128]

Conclusion

DEI's racialist project on the campuses is profoundly unoriginal. Stripped of the lies of its fake Enlightenment rhetoric, DEI offers little more than a resource extraction strategy called *virtuous victimhood*. The Con Story itself is a persuasive confabulation of the coercive, crypto-Maoism of prior generations. It's been refurbished to accommodate a new conceptual scapegoat to replace the *bourgeoisie*, the kulaks, and the capitalist roaders. The new villains of

126 "In other words, victim status can morally justify the use of deceit, intimidation, or even violence by alleged victims to achieve their goals. Relatedly, claiming victim status can lead observers to hold a person less blameworthy, excusing transgressions, such as the appropriation of private property or the infliction of pain upon others." Ekin Ok, Yi Qian, Brendan Strejcek, and Karl Aquino, "Signaling Virtuous Victimhood as Indicators of Dark Triad Personalities," *Journal of Personality and Social Psychology: Personality Processes and Individual Differences*, Vol. 120, No. 6 (2021), p. 1635.
127 Timothy C. Bates, Clara Grant, Leila Hobbs, Claire Johnston, Shahrzad Moghaddam, Kate Sinclair, "Virtuous Victimhood as a Dark Triad resource transfer strategy," *Personality and Individual Differences*, 234 (2025), p. 1.
128 Laird Wilcox, *Crying Wolf: Hate Crime Hoaxes in America* (Olathe KS: Laird Wilcox, 1994). See also Noah Rothman's essay "Identitarianism" in his book *Unjust: Social Justice and the unmaking of America* (Washington, DC: Regnery, 2019), p. 1-32.

convenience are "whites," "whiteness," "white supremacy," and "white privilege." This is the social fantasy of the folks who "do the work."

Every aspect of DEI is connected to some untruth, either great or small. Beginning with the lie of university complicity in the death of a doped-up crook, it spun out in a predictable deceptive logic with the fraud of "rampant racism" on the campuses. Convincing persons that "racism" is rampant in the least racist places in America was a *tour de force*, and it worked, with a story crafted for a special type of person, intellectually primed to receive the story.

Whether it's the fake credentials of the DEI Gurus, or the fakery of their "scholarship," or the false front of DEI to lure people to sign on, or the coercive accusations of "racism" and "complicity," or the litany of manufactured "evidence" of rampant racism, the hallmark of DEI is fraud. The notion of DEI as a con constructed with lies naturally leads to the unraveling of the scaffold of lies that maintains the façade of the doctrine.

The rest of this book focuses on the various personalities, doctrine, budgets, and programs that maintain the edifice of DEI on the college campuses.

3
PARANOIA AND *VIRTUOUS VICTIMHOOD*

"IT HAS ALL BECOME CLEAR TO ME"

*"How much happier you would be if you only knew
that these people cared nothing about you! . . . You
would break out of this tiny and tawdry theatre in
which your own little plot is always being played, and
you would find yourself under a freer sky, in a street
full of splendid strangers."*[129]

— G. K. Chesterton, author and philosopher

---

129 G. K. Chesterton, "The Maniac," *Chesterton Collected Works, Volume 1:
Heretics, Orthodoxy, The Blatchford Controversies* (San Francisco: Ignatius
Press, 1986), p. 223. Published originally in 1908.

If you've followed our universities, you already know that much of higher education seems committed to normalizing the abnormal.

Students matriculating for the first time discover this quickly, during orientation. A constant message new students hear is that they must suspend judgment on virtually every oddity they encounter, great or small. They are urged to "become comfortable with difference" instead of encouraged to exercise their critical faculties to render important value judgments.

In fact, value judgments are to be suspended until "values clarification" programs can go to work on the students' psyches. So-called values clarification training was originally conceived as a neutral heuristic whereby students would come to understand their own values and, hence, adjust their expectations and behaviors accordingly. In this way, they might live a life aligned with these discovered values.[130]

But then, as with so many useful psychological techniques, the "neutral" aspect of values clarification was undermined by the reformers. The bad guys got hold of it and turned it to their own nefarious ends. It became a "values replacement" exercise.

Harnessed to a political purpose, values clarification was a way to change the belief systems of students and, perhaps, even faculty. Change them to what? Why, to the orthodoxy embraced by the university's social justice claque. Some have recognized the morphing of values clarification into "morally dangerous indoctrination."[131] The objections to "values clarification" instruction are

---

130 Richard A. Baer, Jr., "Teaching Values in the Schools: Clarification or Indoctrination?" *Principal*, v61 n3, January 1982: https://blogs.cornell.edu/envirobaer/publications/teaching-values-in-the-schools-clarification-or-indoctrination/

131 Lisa Marie Contini, "Values Clarification Destroys Conscience," *The Homiletic & Pastoral Review*, November 2020: https://www.catholicculture.org/culture/library/view.cfm?recnum=3512

many, and yet values clarification is an essential part of the DEI training project.[132]

The obvious question offers itself: What values? Whose values?

The values agenda of DEI is clear, and it informs all activities on the campus with which it is involved. The *virtuous victimhood* Con requires that persons be slotted into one of two roles—villains or victims, oppressors or oppressed. DEI offices actually train persons to perform according to their assigned roles in this binary scheme. DEI cadres work hard to turn normal people into either arrogant and demanding paranoid victims, or into obsequious and repentant persecutors who constitute a "pseudocommunity" of racist villains.

In fact, DEI attempts to normalize the abnormal. It does so in this way.

The DEI "profession" attracts persons who display the characteristics of those who suffer from a particular type of malady that can be found in the DSM-5—*paranoid personality disorder*.[133] This isn't to say that all or even most DEI personnel are paranoiacs, just that virtually all of them display the victim behavior associated with paranoia. Moreover, the individual problem of paranoia becomes the *group* problem of conspiracy theory as the campus DEI project attracts persons of like-mind into campus DEI cadres. A circle of reinforcement forms, as a critical mass of these personalities coalesces.

---

132 The objections include: Violation of a person's right to privacy; Values clarification becomes psychotherapy; It threatens pluralism and liberal democracy; It displays bias against authority, traditional morality, and duty; It serves as a "religious position; It coerces "response to the mean". Richard A. Baer, Jr., "Teaching Values in the Schools: Clarification or Indoctrination?" *Principal*, v61 n3, January 1982, p. 20-21, 36.

133 The *Diagnostic and Statistical Manual of Mental Disorders*, 5th edition, is used by medical professionals to diagnose mental illnesses. https://www.psychiatry.org/psychiatrists/practice/dsm

This chapter illustrates how DEI's Con Story incorporates racialism into its training regimen. It is convincing chiefly because of its simplicity. A major problem with this entire project is that it not only is a con game that enriches thousands of diversity staffers at the expense of students and parents, but it's a con game with negative impact on the psyches of students. This impact is more than simply noticeable. Values clarification has resulted in the increasingly wholesale corruption of a student generation into an attitude of what has been called "safetyism."

In their 2018 book *Coddling of the American Mind*, Greg Lukianoff and Jonathan Haidt identified this trend in America's colleges and universities.

> "Safetyism" refers to a culture or belief system in which safety has become a sacred value, which means that people become unwilling to make trade-offs demanded by other practical and moral concerns. "Safety" trumps everything else, no matter how unlikely or trivial the potential danger.[134]

Students are recruited into the con game to become carping victims who demand payment or to become simpering guilty penitents eager to pay restitution for imagined sin. DEI's con also impacts the funding of research, the quality of education, the cost of education, and the future survival of the university as a respected institution that produces trustworthy scientific knowledge.

Let's see how all of this works to create a paranoid construct of reality in the university consisting of the paranoid and their persecutors, which is proselytized to students and faculty.

---

134 Greg Lukianoff and Jonathan Haidt, *The Coddling of the American Mind* (New York: Penguin Press, 2018), p. 30.

Contrived Allies, Imagined Enemies, and Virtuous Victimhood

Universities nationwide employ thousands of diversity bureaucrats to preach an either-or doctrine. These cadres are controlled in a hierarchy, usually topped by a well-paid assistant provost, whose salary can approach a half-million dollars. The basic doctrine encourages its targets to behave like paranoiacs—hyper-suspicious, hyper-sensitive, hostile, grandiose and bombastic victims, neither accountable for personal failure nor responsible for their actions. Bureaucrats learn to do this in train-the-trainer "institutes," conferences, webinars, and various confabs sponsored by a network of supportive off-campus non-profits—NADOHE, NASPA, ACPA, NACADA. The doctrine encourages what has been identified in psychology as *virtuous victimhood* and the dual behavior of *victim signaling* combined with *virtue signaling*. This virtuous victimhood is aberrant behavior motivated by the Dark Triad traits of Machiavellianism, Narcissism, and Psychopathy.[135]

Big Con artists and many hundreds of peanut grifters alike use *victim/virtue-signaling* to bring in the cash. These are characteristics of what has become known as "Victimhood Culture."[136] Such a culture renders it financially and psychologically advantageous to announce victim status publicly.

The entire logic of DEI's Big Con is built on this idea of virtuous victimhood. 1) Claiming victim status for profit and payouts (a version of the "protection racket") and 2) Asserting

135 Ekin Ok, Yi Qian, Brendan Strejcek, and Karl Aquino, "Signaling Virtuous Victimhood as Indicators of Dark Triad Personalities," *Journal of Personality and Social Psychology: Personality Processes and Individual Differences*, Vol. 120, No. 6, 2021. "Individuals with Dark Triad traits—Machiavellianism, Narcissism, Psychopathy—more frequently signal virtuous victimhood," p. 1634.
136 Bradley Campbell and Jason Manning, *The Rise of Victimhood Culture* (New York: Palgrave Macmillan, 2018).

moral immunity to justify use of "deceit, intimidation, or violence" to receive that payout. In psychology's academese, it looks like this.

> *Victim signaling* allows victims to pursue an environmental resource extraction strategy that helps them survive, flourish, and achieve their goals in situations that are responsive to their claims. By resource extraction we mean that resources are transferred from either individuals or larger institutions to the person who signals victimhood .... Claiming victim status can also facilitate resource transfer by conferring *moral immunity* upon the claimant. Moral immunity shields the alleged victim from criticism about the means they might use to satisfy their demands. In other words, victim status can morally justify the use of deceit, intimidation, or even violence by alleged victims to achieve their goals. Relatedly, claiming victim status can lead observers to hold a person less blameworthy, excusing transgressions, such as the appropriation of private property or the infliction of pain upon others, that might otherwise bring condemnation or rebuke. Finally, claiming victim status elevates the claimant's *psychological standing*, defined as a subjective sense of legitimacy or entitlement to speak up.[137]

It's a brilliant ploy, and it's been successfully refined and rolled out by campus diversity staff. Entire university bureaucracies have been constructed on this logic, which ensures the propagation of a paranoid world view imposed as reality on students, faculty, and

---

137 Ekin Ok, Yi Qian, Brendan Strejcek, and Karl Aquino, "Signaling Virtuous Victimhood as Indicators of Dark Triad Personalities," *Journal of Personality and Social Psychology: Personality Processes and Individual Differences*, Vol. 120, No. 6, 2021, p. 1634,1635.

staff. These are symptoms of *paranoid personality disorder*, the psychopathology that figures prominently in this book. This disorder is even more severe when it is so advanced that the patient suffers delusions of persecution.

What sort of behavior emerges from members of a group grounded in such a shared delusional belief system? How might the delusionary system be codified into an ideology? These are not idle questions. The answers to these questions reveal the origins of DEI victimhood culture in the psychopathology of paranoia and its growth into a systemized conspiracist belief in a shared, but false, reality.[138]

In the relaxed university venue, great leeway is granted to what is called neurodiversity. This means that persons with cognitive or personality challenges find their way to campus in numbers greater than the norm. While "counseling" services are offered as a hat-tip to the burgeoning mental health crisis on campuses, borderline personalities typically do not receive treatment for their delusions. Instead, in the case of the race-based brand of paranoia discussed here, the malady and its associated delusions become the basis for training. They are theorized and elaborated into a comprehensive racialist belief system with its core tenets shielded from challenge. The persecutory delusions themselves are affirmed, amplified, and subsidized. They inform a bureaucratic system of training, of monitoring, of judging, and of punishing. Extending the scenario, the delusionary belief system is cushioned from

---

138 John T. Jost, Alison Ledgerwood, and Curtis D. Hardin, "Shared Reality, System Justification, and the Relational Basis of Ideological Beliefs," *Social and Personality Psychology Compass* 1, 2007; Glenn Roberts, "The Origins of Delusions," *British Journal of Psychiatry* (1992), 161; Gerald Echterhoff, E. Tory Higgins, and John M. Levine, "Shared Reality: Experiencing Commonality With Others' Inner States About the World," *Perspectives On Psychological Science*, Vol. 4, No. 5 (2009).

criticism by an administrative *moral immunity* and simultaneously subsidized and proselytized to a larger captive audience—students, faculty, and staff.[139]

With time, the system grows increasingly divorced from the actual world. It is this conspiracist belief system that informs and animates DEI.

This is the elaborate basis for the Con Story of DEI—a conspiracist racialist belief system informed by the pathology of paranoia that extracts resources from people and institutions convinced that they are victimizers. This is what happens when persons who share a common victimhood pathology are recruited and clustered in a unit that is funded and given support to train others in the shared doctrine that informs the pathology.

The ideology incorporates this binary of "allies" and "enemies," and it requires the acceptance of this primitive binary model as its fuel for expansion. The model replaces all other conceptions of the world that are not thoroughly dominated by racialist assumptions—in a world of only allies and enemies, the struggle is constant.

At the Racialist Core of DEI, we find the Villain

This is a world created by the paranoid and their fellow-travelers, and they serve as actors performing a standard DEI plot in every show, before every audience. That plot revolves around a single, crystal-clear idea. That idea is . . . well, let a racialist thought leader tell you herself.

---

139 "[B]elief systems may achieve *invulnerability* against empirical evidence . . . [P]seudoscience and other belief systems are immunized against disconfirming evidence and rational criticism." Maarten Boudry and Johan Braeckman, "Immunizing Strategies and Epistemic Defense Mechanisms," *Philosophia* 39 (2011), p. 145, 159.

If you are white in a white supremacist society, you are racist. If you are male in a patriarchy, you are sexist. If you are able-bodied, you are ableist. If you are anything above poverty in a capitalist society, you are classist. You can sometimes be all of these things at once.[140]

That, in 52 words, is the core of the DEI project.

The key to understanding this is that the author of this quote, racialist Ijeoma Oluo, believes that she lives in a "white supremacist" society. It takes her 216 pages of her *New York Times* bestselling book to get to this upshot. But at least she's honest about it. It may be embellished, it may be cushioned with rhetoric to disguise it, and it is likely denied when a racialist is cornered in front of an unsympathetic audience. But this is the core belief that animates *all* of the racialists. Without exception.

And if you believe that Ijeoma Oluo is an outlier or extremist of some sort, understand that she served as the opening keynote speaker at the 2023 Conference of the National Association of Diversity Officers in Higher Education (NADOHE). Oluo's racialist views are considered normal and routine by diversity grifters.[141]

This is how "white people" became the enemy of DEI on the campuses. White people constitute a manufactured pseudocommunity—the easily identifiable villains—to blame for every shortcoming. Psychologist Norman Cameron identified this behavior of the paranoid:

---

140 Ijeoma Oluo, *So you want to talk about race* (New York: Seal Press, 2018, 2019), p. 216-217.
141 NADOHE: Delivering on the Promise, Annual Conference, April 2023: https://nadohe.memberclicks.net/2023-conference-speakers

The final delusional reconstruction of reality may fall into an integrated conceptual pattern that brings an experience of closure: "I suddenly realized what it was all about!" the patient may exclaim with obvious relief at sudden clarification. The intolerable suspense has ended; the strangeness of what has been "going on" seems to disappear, and confusion is replaced by "understanding," and wavering doubt by certainty.... In short, the pseudo-community reduces the hopeless complexity and confusion to a clear formula. The formula—"the plot"—the patient can now apply to future events as he experiences them and fit them into the general framework of his reconstruction.[142]

We can see that a single premise resides at the heart of DEI: *All whites are racist and this racism is permanent.* This is the DEI premise that identifies the enemy and populates the paranoid *pseudocommunity*. The useful corollary of "all whites are racist" is that *only* white persons can be racist. A web of stories and anecdotes are spun around this pseudocommunity of white racist persecutors.

[P]sychotic delusions of persecution represent a desperate attempt to justify suspicions, to account for failure, and to explain the spying and persecution of others. All the pieces fall neatly into place with the invention of a *pseudocommunity*.[143]

---

142 Norman Cameron, "The Paranoid Pseudocommunity Revisited," *American Journal of Sociology*, Vol. 65, No. 1 (July 1959), p. 56. See also Norman Cameron, "The Paranoid Pseudocommunity," *American Journal of Sociology*, Vol. 49, No. 1 (July 1943).

143 James, D. Page, *Psychopathology: the Science of Understanding Deviance* (2e), (Chicago: Aldine Publishing, 1975), p. 296.

DEI emerges from this core in a relentless, destructive logic that is unconnected to reality and which is characteristic of *all* totalist ideologies.[144]

The message may be muted, cushioned, or offered in an oblique manner, but it is there in classrooms, in workshops, in journal articles, in books, in conferences, in lectures, on the streets. It informs every policy prescription and every *New York Times* bestseller by hustlers like Ibram Kendi, Robin DiAngelo, Ta-Nehisi Coates, Ijeoma Oluo, Layla Saad, and many others. It informs the bombast of media con-artists, such as Al Sharpton, Elie Mystal, Joy Reid, Melissa Harris-Perry and any of an assortment of those striving for a slice of the media spotlight. And it is repeated as a form of racialist Newspeak identified by Francoise Thom: "Newspeak is nothing but a series of magical incantations, disguised as a chain of self-evident axioms."[145]

All whites are racist.

It is a phrase with endless utility, and it constitutes the creation of a paranoid pseudocommunity on which to blame the ills of the world and from whom to extract resources. It's a magical incantation that originates in paranoia. As Hannah Arendt tells us, it is this core lie of a totalist ideology that informs every other aspect of the ideology regardless of actual experience in what we call the "real world."

All whites are racist.

Everything in the "real world" is interpreted by this conspiratorial core myth, no matter what occurs. "As soon as logic as a

---

144 Hannah Arendt, *Totalitarianism: Part Three of The Origins of Totalitarianism* (New York: Harcourt, 1951, 1976), p. 165-172.
145 Françoise Thom, *Newspeak: The Language of Soviet Communism* (London: Claridge Press, 1989), p. 14.

movement of thought . . . is applied to an idea, this idea is transformed into a premise."[146]Once a person, even a quite intelligent person, submits to this core myth, the rest of the doctrine follows easily, and they become consumed. Take, for instance, this example from a faculty member at the University of New Mexico, brought into the racialist fold:

> [T]he white person needs to accept and admit that he is the oppressor, that is, he is necessarily racist as a consequence of his structural and epistemological standing as a member of the white race . . . . The best a white person can be is a white anti-racist racist. As white anti-racist racists, reborn whites work against white supremacy by working with race-radical people of color and remembering that we will always have blindspots to our own whiteness.[147]

In venues great and small, critical racialists are recruited and paid to attack unsuspecting white folks and to perhaps cajole and convince more innocents that they, too, are guilty and must become members of the pseudocommunity of persecutors. Here is another example that is, unfortunately, typical of the genre of diversity race hustlers:

> All white people are racist, so I put this up because I really want any white person in the room to know, up front, that this is what we're dealing with. That it's not going to be this coddling of white tears and what that looks like. . . . No you're always

---

146 Hannah Arendt, *Totalitarianism,* p. 167.
147 Ricky Lee Allen, "Whiteness and Critical Pedagogy," *Educational Philosophy and Theory,* Vol. 35, No. 2, 2004, 129-130.

going to be racist actually. So even when you're on your path to trying to figure out how to be a better human being—because I believe that white people are born into *not* being human. Like that actually instead of people of color and black folks being dehumanized that actually everyone is dehumanized within white supremacy. That y'all are born into a life to not be human, and that's what y'all are taught to do, to be demons. So in this particular way white people are all racist.[148]

This is the litany of Antiracism and DEI, and I suggest you read it again so there is no mistaking the meaning.

Whites, according to this view, must recognize their positions as whites, as whites in a racist system, and ultimately as racist whites. That is they must embrace the oppressor label at the same time that they challenge oppressor identity and behavior.[149]

On and on the litany goes, and it is these racialist hustlers who have dominated campus DEI since 2020. They have embedded themselves in lucrative positions of power, they have constructed

---

148 https://www.youtube.com/watch?v=5keqoXClrq0 (accessed September 15, 2020). The Video has since been removed for violating Youtube "hate speech" policy. This particular workshop was conducted for a group of approximately 20 white persons by someone called Ashleigh Shackelford, who is representative of the cadre of independent racialist contractors. She advertises herself as "a queer, agender Black fat femme writer, artist, and cultural producer. Ashleigh is a contributing writer at For Harriet, a community organizer at Black Future, and the creator of a body positivity organization Free Figure Revolution. She is a run-on sentence repeat offender and a Ratchet Black Feminist dedicated to dismantling anti-Blackness." See http://ashleighshackelford.com/
149 Jennifer L. Eichstedt, "Problematic White Identities and a Search for Racial Justice," *Sociological Forum*, Vol. 16, No. 3 (September 2001), p. 460.

and expanded their bureaucracy, and they continue to do so today despite signs of an initial rollback that is building momentum.

This chapter describes the construction of this paranoid world on the campuses, explains how belief in this paranoid construct is reproduced and disseminated, and identifies it as the central plot of *virtuous victimhood*.

What is Paranoia?

G. K. Chesterton was an English Catholic poet, philosopher, essayist, and literary critic whose most productive period spanned the first three decades of the early 20th Century. His wit, his prose style, and the depth of his learning and thought were respected by both friend and foe. He earned the honorific Prince of Paradox. One of his most powerful essays—"The Maniac"—appeared in his work *Orthodoxy*, published in 1908.

The essay captures a spirit of mind that a lay person recognizes as paranoia. It's a pathological paradigm that guides thinking. But it is something much more than this, and Chesterton captures the claustrophobia, the peerless logic, the sinister suspicions that taint reasoning and that channel thought along the well-worn grooves of mind that circle endlessly round and round, like an old phonograph record. For the paranoiac, the song is always the same, and it's a lament in minor key.

Chesterton provides a philosopher's insight that methodically disassembles the pathology of the self-absorbed man. This is an ill man who constructs social reality according to his internal rhythms and whims, according to personal philosophy that is always developing *ad hoc*, from moment to moment and enlarging his sense of self. It is this paradigm of paranoia that drives a person to create a fantasy world driven by a single, swollen idea. Chesterton seemed comfortably familiar with today's paranoiacs entrapped in the web of race-obsessed DEI:

> Are there no other stories in the world except yours; and are all men busy with your business? ... How much happier you would be if you only knew that these people cared nothing about you! How much larger your life would be if yourself could become smaller in it; if you could see them walking as they are in their sunny selfishness and their virile indifference! You would begin to be interested in them, because they were not interested in you. You would break out of this tiny and tawdry theatre in which your own little plot is always being played, and you would find yourself under a freer sky, in a street full of splendid strangers.[150]

We see this person today running DEI offices in the universities. He pays fealty to a single idea, a single motivating conception, a single engine that motors the world that is embodied in ... himself. Such a person yields no surprises.

> He is in the clean and well-lit prison of one idea: he is sharpened to one painful point. He is without healthy hesitation and healthy complexity. ... His cosmos may be complete in every rivet and cog-wheel, but still his cosmos is smaller than our world. ... It has just the quality of the madman's argument; we have at once the sense of it covering everything and the sense of it leaving everything out.[151]

---

150 G. K. Chesterton, "The Maniac," *Chesterton Collected Works*, p. 223.
151 G. K. Chesterton, "The Maniac," *Chesterton Collected Works*, p. 225.

This century-old colorful narrative characterizes the modern paranoiac of our time as diagnosed in the various editions of the *Diagnostic and Statistical Manual of Mental Disorders* (DSM) published by the American Psychiatric Association.[152] We sometimes encounter this type of person in our own lives.

When we encounter such a person, at this point in the story we ordinarily recognize that paranoia *is* a problem. We conclude that the person suffering from an apparent psychopathology ought to be evaluated and suitably treated.

Psychologists have learned a lot about paranoia in the 100-plus years since Emil Kraepelin first argued that paranoia is a specific type of mental affliction: "The different forms of delusion—the delusion of greatness and insignificance, the delusion of sin, the physical delusion of persecution, and so on—have often been considered as characteristics of distinct forms of disease."[153]

Symptoms of Paranoia?

Here is what we know about paranoia and how the policies, programs, procedures, and personnel of DEI are permeated with this fearful malady and exhibit the symptoms. Let's be clear on this—for many of these persons, the behavior is chosen and not part of a mental illness. The paranoid story appeals to them, to their vanity, to their sense of not measuring up, and it provides an external reason for personal failure—these are the perpetual victims of DEI. These personnel display paranoid characteristics through their writings and their speeches, and their training programs aim to instill paranoid behavior in others.

---

152 https://www.psychiatry.org/psychiatrists/practice/dsm
153 Emil Kraepelin, *Lectures on Clinical Psychiatry* (New York: William Wood & Son, 1904), p. 140.

Let's begin with several descriptions of paranoid personality behavior. This lays the groundwork to demonstrate how paranoia lies at the core of DEI doctrine.

> *Paranoia* is a constitutional mental disorder that is limited in symptomatology to well-systematized and stable delusions of persecution and grandeur. The delusional system is skillfully and logically elaborated, so that if the fundamental hypothesis (which is often inaccessible to examination) is granted, the ideas expressed appear reasonable and probable. Apart from their unshakable delusions, paranoiacs are sensible and coherent in their thinking and behavior.[154]

This initial characterization of paranoia has been substantiated in subsequent years.

Theodore Millon provides this description of symptoms in 1969, and his description captures the spirit of DEI a half-century before its ascendance:

> Paranoids are constantly on guard, mobilized and ready for any emergency or threat. Whether faced with real dangers or not, they maintain a fixed level of preparedness, an alert vigilance against the possibility of attack and derogation. There is an edgy tension, an abrasive irritability and an ever-present defensive stance from which they can spring to action at the slightest hint of threat. This state of rigid control never seems to abate; rarely do they relax, ease up or let down their guard.

---

154 James Page, *Abnormal Psychology* (New York: McGraw-Hill Book Company, Inc., 1947), p. 284.

Beneath the surface mistrust and defensive vigilance in the paranoid lies a current of deep resentment toward others who "have made it." To the paranoid, most people have attained their status unjustly; thus, he is bitter for having been overlooked, treated unfairly and slighted by the "high and mighty," "the cheats and the crooks," who duped the world. Only a thin veil hides these bristling animosities.

Unable to accept their own faults and weaknesses, paranoids maintain their self-esteem by attributing their shortcomings to others. They repudiate their own failures and project or ascribe them to someone else.[155]

Paranoiacs live in a hostile world, with enemies threatening them constantly. This puts immense stress on the paranoiac, who yearns for answers to the complexities of life. He seeks a framework of understanding to make sense of his environment: "In paranoid reactions, the individual becomes completely dominated by a preoccupation with enemies, real and imagined; every aspect of life comes to be intimately related to the struggle, until finally the paranoid person gives the impression that he or she literally has no other reason to live."[156]

Further research on the effects of paranoia show that the person afflicted needs answers for the inexplicable events around them, which all seem to happen *to* them. The paranoiac seeks *the*

---

155 Theodore Millon, *Modern Psychopathology* (Philadelphia: W. B. Saunders Company, 1969), p. 328-329.
156 Robert W. Rieber, *Manufacturing Social Distress: Psychopathy in Everyday Life* (New York: Plenum Press, 1997), p. 80.

answer. They need an identifiable enemy, someone or some group that threatens them and which they can blame for the happenings in their life.

How might people behave in such a binary system of belief? How might they train others to behave in such a system? The behavior of the people trapped in the race-based DEI conspiracy of villains-and-victims, oppressors-and-oppressed, evil-and-good is predictable. This conspiracist belief system is captured in the personal narrative of Kurt Snyder in one of the most famous cases of acute paranoia:

> My concept of THEM grew and began to color every experience I had. After a few months, everything that happened to me was somehow related to THEM, or was caused by THEM. When I started experiencing problems with my home computer, I blamed THEM. When I got a parking ticket, it was THEIR influence with the police that got me in trouble. Every thought I had was somehow associated with THEM .... THEY were a concept in my mind that expanded beyond my own control. The concept of THEM was taking over all my thought processes, in every way possible. I could not think about anything or anyone without making some type of association with THEM. THEY were everywhere, involved with everything.[157]

---

157 Kurt Snyder, "Kurt Snyder's Personal Experience with Schizophrenia," *Schizophrenia Bulletin*, vol. 32 no. 2, (2006), p. 210.

In layman's terms, the paranoiac protects himself and his self-esteem by blaming others when he is shown to be incompetent, and he always defaults to such explanatory behavior, blaming members of the pseudocommunity for his travails.

This core myth of paranoid racialist DEI is powerful, seductive, and simple. It is grounded in prejudice and is manifested in bombast. It's justified by outright pseudoscience based on the evidence-free assumption of a "racism" that is all but absent in any meaningful form on campuses. Indeed, the absence of evidence and the hostility toward requests for such evidence of "racism" is the hallmark of conspiracy theory[158] and pseudoscience.[159] Conspiracy theory expert Jovan Byford observes that this is the most important feature of conspiracy theories: they are, as with pseudoscience, self-sealing and irrefutable.

> Logical contradictions, disconfirming evidence, even the complete absence of proof have no bearing on the conspiratorial explanation because they can always be accounted for in terms of the conspiracy: the lack of proof about a plot, or any positive proof against its existence, is turned around and taken as evidence of the craftiness of the secret cabal behind the conspiracy and as confirmation of its ability to conceal its machinations.[160]

Brian Keeley adds to this the quixotic notion:

---

158 Jovan Byford, "How to spot a conspiracy theory when you see one," *The Conversation*, March 16, 2020: https://theconversation.com/how-to-spot-a-conspiracy-theory-when-you-see-one-133574

159 Massimo Pigliucci and Maarten Boudry (eds.), *Philosophy of Pseudoscience: Reconsidering the Demarcation Problem* (Chicago: Chicago University Press, 2013).

160 Jovan Byford, *Conspiracy Theories: A Critical Introduction* (New York: Palgrave Macmillan, 2015), p. 36.

[C]onspiracy theories are the only theories for which evidence against them is actually construed as evidence in favor of them. The more evidence piled up by the authorities in favor of a given theory, the more the conspiracy theorist points to how badly "They" must want us to believe the official story.[161]

The Modern Paranoid Style—*Basis of DEI Conspiracy*

The profile of the paranoid personality has been developed and sharpened over time. Those with the disorder display all of the following characteristics, often in exaggerated form:

1. Displacement of Responsibility
2. Suspiciousness
3. Grandiosity
4. Delusional Fixity
5. Creation of a Paranoid Pseudocommunity
6. Creation of an Interpretive System.

In the next section, I explain each of these characteristics.

1. Displacement of Responsibility

The paranoiac absolves himself of blame by externalizing the source of his troubles in "forces and influences that surround him."[162] This reflexive externalization of blame displays elements

---

161 Brian L. Keeley, "Of Conspiracy Theories," *The Journal of Philosophy*, Vol. 96, No. 3, March, 1999, p. 120.
162 William Meissner, *The Paranoid Process* (New York: Jason Aronson, Inc., 1978), p. 36.

of denial and projection and helps to protect self-esteem. Rather than accept personal responsibility, the paranoiac rejects the notion that he can affect his environment and that therefore he is absolved of blame for his troubles. Others are responsible, and these others mean him harm.

Campus DEI people and programs are grounded in this externalization of blame, rarely holding individual persons responsible for their actions or inactions in the achievement of goals. In fact, in the case of the "microaggression" myth, the externalization of blame is automatic and the "victim" is believed *automatically*.

2. Suspiciousness

The hyper-suspicion of paranoia means that the paranoiac constantly tests his own view of reality. He maintains a hyper-vigilance that is "almost scientific in its interest in assimilating the available data of reality to the paranoid construction."[163] Suspiciousness is manifested in the constant evaluation of new data and its slotting within the delusional belief system of enemies and allies.

> The primary defence mechanism [was a] retreat to the paranoid position. This came out as a rigid clinging to attitudes of suspicion and hostility even in circumstances where they consciously felt that some of this suspicion was not justified by the situation they were actually experiencing.[164]

163 William Meissner, *The Paranoid Process*, p. 36.
164 Elliott Jaques, "Social Systems as Defence Against Persecutory and Depressive Anxiety," in Melanie Klein, Paula Heimann, R. E. Money-Kyrle, *New Directions In Psycho-Analysis* (London: Maresfield Library, 1977), p. 492.

3. Grandiosity

Delusions of grandeur perform a safety function that preserves the paranoiac's self-esteem. Grandiosity is a persistent characteristic of the paranoid style.[165] This sense of grandeur preserves the delusional belief system in its insistence upon "the rightness of the construction and the goodness of its formulation."[166] It springs from a sense of being underappreciated and overlooked. The current term for this is "marginalized." It can be manifested in melodrama and the attribution of great significance to mundane gestures and pedestrian events.

DEI writers evince a tendency toward self-valorization. Ta-Nehisi Coates and Ibram Kendi exhibit this in their writings, particularly in Coates's various memoirs. In a later chapter, I describe the DEI "navel-gazing" technique, whereby the gurus of DEI posture on an imaginary high ground, where every man and woman is literary royalty with nary a discouraging word to point out the emperor's nakedness.

4. Delusional Fixity

Paranoiacs desperately avoid admission of error, inadequacy, or of the recognition of a personal defect. This requires all-out devotion to the delusions of the DEI belief system. Deviation from DEI orthodoxy is simply not permitted. DEI personnel maintain their delusional belief system at all costs: "The paranoid conviction of rightness, therefore, can be seen in terms of its function

---

165 Rebecca Knowles, Simon McCarthy-Jones, Georgina Rowse, "Grandiose delusions: A review and theoretical integration of cognitive and affective perspectives," *Clinical Psychology Review*, 31 (2011), pp: 684-696.
166 William Meissner, *The Paranoid Process*, p. 37.

in maintaining self-esteem at one level, or in the maintaining of psychic integrity at another."[167]

The people and programs of DEI demonstrate a perdurable fixity of its core myth by ritualization of belief and preservation of its founding tenets.

5. Creation of a Pseudocommunity of Persecutors

Paranoiacs construct an imagined pseudocommunity of persecutors. This is one of the key markers for DEI, and its foundational element. DEI programs are constructed around this core fabrication that "all whites are racists." Campus DEI offices maintain this essential fraud, and it informs all of their activities. DEI's persecutory belief system points the finger at "a unified group which has a definite plot aimed at the patient as the intended victim."[168]

This element of the paranoid style consists in defining one's enemies.

> One of the clearest manifestations of paranoia is the discovery of enemies, both real and (more typically) imagined. The term "enemy" is in itself a paranoid definition of an other: "enemy" designates "an unfriendly or hostile person; one that cherishes hatred, that wishes or seeks to do ill to another," according to the Oxford English *Dictionary*. An enemy may also, however, dwell within us; this is indeed one of the basic lessons of psychoanalysis . . . . These are notions that lie at the crossroads of

---

167 William Meissner, *The Paranoid Process*, p. 39.
168 William Meissner, *The Paranoid Process*, p. 39.

what is psychic and subjectively real, and what is external and regarded as objective reality.[169]

DEI's core myth rests upon this paranoid construction of the pseudocommunity of persecutors. Every aspect of the ideology grows from this core myth, and it is this myth that animates the entire racialist interpretive system. We will see in a later chapter that when evidence of this core myth is not forthcoming, such evidence is fabricated in the form of "hate crime hoaxes," which have served opportunists throughout history, from the trials of witches to the forging of documents, such as the anti-Semitic *Protocols of the Learned Elders of Zion*.

6. Creation of an Interpretive System.

The paranoiac constructs a systematized belief system—it is a theory that explains the world and is grounded in a contrived myth.

> [T]he delusions become systematized; that is, the patient does not accept them as unrelated beliefs, but rationalizes them or explains them more or less logically in relation with the rest of his life or with what he observes in the world. A definite delusional system may be built around the idea that the patient is persecuted because of his ideology, philosophy, or religion. He may build a system of beliefs and then attempt to give

---

169 H. Shmuel Erlich, "Enemies Within and Without: Paranoia and Regression in Groups and Organizations," in Lawrence J. Gould, Mark Stein, Lionel F. Stapley (eds.), *The Systems Psychodynamics of Organizations* (New York: Routledge, 2018), p. 122.

this system an apparently plausible scientific, philosophical, or theological structure.[170]

This belief system hardens, and new facts and events are slotted into the framework to reinforce the worldview and expand and elaborate upon it. Inconvenient facts are ignored or shoehorned into the system.

> Once this organized interpretive schema is elaborated, any new cognitive input tends to be assimilated to the system .... Real events are distorted and reinterpreted to fit the overall picture provided by the schema; nonspecific and trivial happenings are endowed with important and relevant significances; contradictory evidences are either rejected or ignored, or transformed to fit the overriding implications of the system.[171]

High intensity of belief and appeals to emotion work to legitimize the delusions. Thus, we see the overt celebration of emotions and, in its extreme forms, loss of emotional control. These types of emotional displays are often witnessed at political rallies as even the most "responsible" of people yield to the uninhibited expression of their beliefs fueled by visceral emotions. Even those we think of as sober, serious people can succumb to this urge.[172] This investment of emotion is seen as a virtue, not a vice.

170 Silvano Arieti, *Interpretation of Schizophrenia* (New York: Basic Books, 1974), p. 36.
171 William Meissner, *The Paranoid Process*, p. 40.
172 Senate minority leader Chuck Schumer unleashed an emotional diatribe on the steps of the Supreme Court building in spring of 2020 in which he threatened two justices of the U.S. Supreme Court, Brett Kavanaugh and Neil Gorsuch. Said Schumer: "I want to tell you, Gorsuch. I want to tell you, Kavanaugh. You have released the whirlwind, and you will pay the price .... You won't know what hit you if you go forward with these awful decisions." The Editorial Board, *The Wall Street Journal*, March 4, 2020. https://www.wsj.com/articles/schumer-threatens-the-court-11583368462

If nothing else, DEI's Big Con has shown how good money can be had by those who commercialize fear, regardless of its source and whether warranted or not. The result of this magnification of imagined fear is predictable, as sociologist Barry Glassner contends.

> The short answer to why Americans harbor so many misbegotten fears is that immense power and money await those who tap into our moral insecurities and supply us with symbolic substitutes.[173]

Wilfred Reilly agrees with Glassner that some people or some groups have an interest in incentivizing a paranoid worldview among African Americans. He argues that "when millions of people are terrified of threats that do not even exist, there is strong evidence that someone is deliberately trying to scare them."[174]

In the case of U.S. race relations, and of majority-minority relations more broadly, we can understand why multiple entities might attempt to do this. Institutions as well as individual persons can profit from pushing the paranoia. As Reilly notes, "An astonishing edifice of power and profit rests upon the assumption that the United States is a racist nation." The strategic goal, then,

---

173 Barry Glassner, *The Culture of Fear* (New York: Basic Books, 2010, 2018), p. xxxvi.

174 Wilfred Reilly, *Hate Crime Hoax: How the Left is Selling a Fake Race War* (Washington, DC: Regnery Publishing, 2019), p. xviii. Reilly provides a list of institutions that to a greater or lesser degree might be interested in perpetuating a climate of paranoia in America's minority population: "In the case of U.S. race relations, and of majority-minority relations more broadly, it is not hard to understand why multiple entities might attempt to do this. An astonishing edifice of power and profit rests upon the assumption that the United States is a racist nation: affirmative action, minority business set-asides, NGO donations, corporate diversity initiatives, and academic departments of post-colonial brother-man are all highly profitable for their beneficiaries. Large non-governmental organizations that promote hate scares, such as the Southern Poverty Law Center (SPLC); the NAACP . . . Black Lives Matter and the Movement for Black Lives; the National Organization for Women (NOW); and the like owe their viability to this assumption."

is to populate the paranoid pseudocommunity with actual persons labeled as persecutors. Without this pseudocommunity of enemies, always poised to strike, the delusions of paranoia lose their force. The threat must be maintained. It must be continual. It must be "permanent." The confession coerced from "persecutors" constitutes the creation of enemies where few actually exist.

From Paranoid . . . to Conspiracy Theorist

This chapter has laid the groundwork for understanding the psychology of paranoia, and I included a portion of Kurt Snyder's testimony as a sufferer of paranoid schizophrenia. Snyder is one of the most famous persons afflicted with this form of paranoia. Snyder received treatment and eventually his symptoms subsided.[175]

But what if Snyder had *not* been treated for his delusions? What if, instead, his delusions had been nurtured and validated?

What if Snyder had sought out others who shared this type of persecutory malady and joined with them in a community of shared conspiracy? A community of believers to build and to nurture a consistent and coherent worldview grounded in paranoia?

> [E]laborate speculative systemization and organization of forces in external reality provides the paranoid with a consistent and coherent world view which supports his need for conviction of rightness, and erases the last semblances of uncertainty in his delusional beliefs. His tolerance for uncertainty or ambiguity is minimal, since it is precisely such uncertainty that poses a

---

175 Kurt Snyder, with Raquel E. Gur, M.D., Ph.D. and Linda Wasmer Andrews, *Me, Myself, and Them* (Oxford: Oxford University Press, 2007).

threat to his existence whose severity parallels the degree of his pathology.[176]

When paranoiacs and their supporters combine to form a community, whose members all subscribe to the same delusional belief system of villains and victims, we call this conspiracism.

Characteristics of Conspiracism

Sunstein and Vermeule offer a keen analysis of conspiracy theory and have identified both psychological and social mechanisms that "produce, sustain, and spread these theories."[177] They observe that a conspiracy theory has a "self-sealing quality."[178] This quality protects the conspiracy theory and makes it "unusually hard to undermine or dislodge [and] renders them particularly immune to challenge."[179]

This self-sealing quality was articulated and given widespread currency by Karl Popper, who asserted that it was a characteristic of pseudoscience. The self-sealing quality is a marker of its pseudoscientific pretensions.

> A school of this kind never admits a new idea. New ideas are heresies, and lead to schisms; should a member of the school try to change the doctrine, then he is expelled as a heretic. ...

---

176 William Meissner, *The Paranoid Process*, p. 40.
177 Cass Sunstein and Adrian Vermeule, "Symposium on Conspiracy Theories. Conspiracy Theories: Causes and Cures," *The Journal of Political Philosophy*, Volume 17, Number 2, 2009, p. 203. The authors here focus in their analysis on conspiracy theories that are "false, harmful, and unjustified (in the epistemological sense)", p. 204. The authors speculate that these types of conspiracy theories result from "crippled epistemology," or the lack of relevant informational sources.
178 Cass Sunstein and Adrian Vermeule, "Symposium on Conspiracy Theories," p. 203.
179 Cass Sunstein and Adrian Vermeule, "Symposium on Conspiracy Theories." p. 204.

It is clear that in a school of this kind we cannot expect to find a history of ideas, or even the material for such a history. For new ideas are not admitted to be new. Everything is ascribed to the master. All we might reconstruct is a history of schisms, and perhaps a history of the defence of certain doctrines against the heretics. There cannot, of course, be any rational discussion in a school of this kind. There may be arguments against dissenters and heretics, or against some competing schools. But in the main it is with assertion and dogma and condemnation rather than argument that the doctrine is defended.[180]

We should recognize that DEI provides a powerful and seductive victim/villain story that many find attractive precisely because of its tight internal logic with its carefully curated facts and stories—both true and fictional. It purports to explain *everything*. This is what Daniel Pipes calls *conspiracism*.[181] "It takes over the lives of the faithful and becomes a prism through which they see all existence."[182]

Polish scholar Michal Glowinski has observed that this *conspiracism* is a key element of totalitarian societies, what he calls the "conspiracist vision of the world" with certain features that are inaccessible to the uninitiated and which reveal "how things really are," who is whom, who is an ally, and who is dangerous and hostile.[183] Converts to conspiracism "speak of it as an epiphany

180 Karl Popper, "Back to the Pre-Socratics," *Conjectures and Refutations: The Growth of Scientific Knowledge* (New York: Basic Books, 1962), p. 149.
181 This view of the world is also called the "paranoid style" or the "hidden-hand mentality." Daniel Pipes, *Conspiracy: How the Paranoid Style Flourishes and Where it Comes From* (New York: The Free Press, 1997), p. 22.
182 Daniel Pipes, *Conspiracy: How the Paranoid Style Flourishes and Where it Comes From* (New York: The Free Press, 1997), p. 22.
183 Michal Glowinski, *Totalitarian Speech*. Stanley Bill (trans.) (Frankfurt am Main: Peter Lang, 2014), p. 97-98, 99.

in which they realize how hopelessly naïve they had previously been."[184] DEI rhetoric is inspirational and motivating. It offers a simple external explanation for what people believe they experience, which psychologists tell us can be a meaningful source of relief. The patient's conviction often comes suddenly, as a closure or sudden clarification, with the familiar statement, "It has all become clear to me."[185]

Conclusion

The arguments of this chapter lead us to draw reasonable conclusions about the body of thought that informs DEI and the community of believers who call themselves "diversity experts." Diversity hustlers engage in the twin activities of victim-signaling and virtue-signaling to create the Big Con of *virtuous victimhood*, which is a resource extraction strategy. The victims aim to extract the maximum amount of resources from perceived villains, and it is in the interest of DEI to identify as many villains as possible. In a novel twist on the con, they *train* as many persons as possible to accept villain status, and diversity hustlers are lavishly compensated for this.

As we shall see in the coming chapters, the literature of DEI, university DEI programs, and the behavior of the "diversity experts" who staff DEI offices in the universities exhibit *all six* of the characteristics of the "paranoid style" of 1) Displacement of Responsibility, 2) Suspiciousness, 3), Grandiosity, 4) Delusional Fixity, 5) Creation of a Pseudocommunity of Persecutors, and 6) Creation of an Interpretive System. In forthcoming chapters, we

---

184 Daniel Pipes, *Conspiracy*, p. 23.
185 Norman Cameron, *The Psychology of Behavior disorders: A biosocial interpretation* (Boston, MA: Houghton, Mifflin and Company, 1947), p. 438.

encounter numerous examples of these characteristics at work. In fact, it is the rare racialist who does *not* exhibit a majority of these symptoms.

These characteristics are so pervasive in the canon of DEI racialism that we can conclude that DEI is a delusional belief system grounded in a shared conspiracy. This alternative theorized world must constantly be recreated and rejuvenated by the critical racialists. It must be given life and be "performed." In this sense, then, DEI is "performative." Its conspiratorial script *must* be acted out by its believers for it to have any reality at all. If persons were to stop collaborating and were to stop performing their learned roles—if they were to stop using the contrived lingo of racialism— the DEI social construct of critical racialism would collapse under the weight of its own manifest absurdities. And it would cease to be credible by those it is designed to dupe.

This performative character of paranoid DEI was captured more than 30 years ago by social psychologist Serge Moscovici, at a time when critical race theory was still in the womb. Moscovici's prescient characterization of the paranoid style described racialism as it would emerge in the decades leading to our unfortunate present, where DEI dogma is seemingly ubiquitous. This is the conspiracy made real, and DEI exemplifies it.

Moscovici notes that in the paranoid conspiracist system . . .

> Appearances are misleading, faces are masks, words are lies, and personal relationships are based on illusions. One must always look for the hand of the demon *ex machina* who insinuates himself, hidden behind his mask, mouthing lies, making deceitful gestures. Such a spectacle acted out in reality would

be absurd. It is not absurd on stage, however. It is a performance stripped down to its essentials; it is the confrontation of elemental forces, which can only end in the definitive victory of one party over the other.[186]

---

186 Serge Moscovici, "The Conspiracy Mentality," in C. F. Graumann and S. Moscovici, *Changing Conceptions of Conspiracy* (New York: Springer-Verlag, 1987), p. 155.

4
FANTASY, FABLES, AND FARCE

WHO NEEDS RESEARCH WHEN
YOU CAN JUST MAKE IT UP?

"I could not escape the feeling of being in the presence of a poorly wrought fairy tale and an enormous con."[187]

— Ta-Nehisi Coates, author and activist

We have a big "knowledge" problem in the universities today. Instead of knowledge, we now have "knowledges," and many of

---

187 Ta-Nehisi Coates, *The Message* (New York: One World, 2024), p. 193.

these knowledges are generated by indigenous folks and people of color, who are off-limits to criticism.

You see the problem here—what do we believe and why?

This doubt in the reliability of knowledge is artificial, of course, a product of post-modernism and a debilitating relativism.

DEI contributes to this undermining of knowledge, even in the sciences, primarily because of DEI's corrosive impact on scholarship. Simply put, we are losing trust in university-produced knowledge(s), because so much of it has been revealed as hokum— the "medicine wheel," the "spirit animal," the "talking stick," the "skin-walker" and a litany of other folk science, tribal pass-downs, and myths elbowing for space on the campus.

This chapter shows how DEI functionaries cluster on the campuses in their own bubbles of academic deception. They are rarely challenged, and this is because they influence the levers of judgment over faculty, students, and staff. They are essentially untouchable. This situation has led to hubris and the commission of various types of fraud in the academy, much of it linked to DEI. You see now how the university was ripe for the Big Con and is still vulnerable to the tools and techniques of the diversity grifters.

DEI indeed has tools at its disposal, and its proponents utilize them. They have many ways to operate a Big Con and to affirm deception, from the simplest of lies to the most elaborate of charades. Three tools in particular serve to generate the doctrinal fakery that legitimizes and maintains DEI's Big Con. We examine these tools in this chapter:

Plagiarism
Navel-gazing
Yarn-spinning

The Plagiarists

First, we have the familiar fraud of plagiarism, that is, copying someone else's work and passing it off as your own. This is one sort of fraud, and it has appeared among the DEI folks more often than is comfortable. Harvard President Claudine Gay, a DEI beneficiary more than a practitioner, was brought low by plagiarism in the winter of 2024. Revelations of academic plagiarism at other schools followed, committed by DEI honchos, who seemed to display a propensity for cut-and-paste "scholarship."

One interesting facet of this growing plague was the casting of the plagiarists themselves as victims. In this narrative, these "victims" were the targets of racists, who had chosen to investigate and expose their dishonesty.

The issue, for these plagiarism apologists, was *not* the revelation of the cheating that had leveraged these persons into visible positions of power and prestige. For these apologists, the issue was *not* lying and plagiarism; the issue for them was rather *who* exposed the cheating. High dudgeon was reserved for her accusers—*who* was it who discovered the cheating and called her out? This was certainly how the complicit media covered it in the case of Claudine Gay, Harvard University's erstwhile president.

You see, Gay embodied the caricature of the "DEI Hire." She was a thinly accomplished minority woman, the daughter of Haitian immigrants, who had been installed as Harvard's president in the summer of 2023. Unremarked upon was the fact that she was the daughter of one of the wealthiest families in Haiti and the Haitian aristocracy and attended Phillips Exeter Academy. Gay's Harvard pedigree was built upon a distortion of affirmative action, as scholar Carol Swain notes:

It was no secret that elite colleges and universities often used affirmative action to give a disproportionate leg up to the offspring of immigrants who dominated their entering classes. Black descendants of slaves or students with my profile of hailing from poverty were in short supply among the entering classes.[188]

It turns out that the Harvard pedigree was also built upon Gay's own failings as a would-be scholar, as she plagiarized other people's work for her 1997 prize-winning dissertation, which Swain contends was largely based on purloined ideas and text from her own prize-winning 1993 book *Black Faces, Black Interests.*[189]

Yes, Gay jumped the line, but at a relatively peaceful time, and this likely appeared as all-upside to the Harvard Corporation and to the Board of Overseers—it gave the university cachet as "walking the walk" of diversity and bought the elite institution a royal helping of Big Con absolution.

But then came the Hamas terror attack on Israel October 7 and Harvard's woefully inadequate response to campus unrest.

To Congress, President Gay was unable to defend her actions and those of her administration. She had served only six months as Harvard's president, when she was forced to resign from Harvard under the double ignominy of her disastrous congressional testimony on rampant anti-Semitism at Harvard and her own

---

188 Carol Swain, *The Gay Affair: Harvard, Plagiarism, and the Death of Academic Integrity* (Nashville: Be the People books, 2025), p. xxi.
189 Dr. Swain, a former tenured professor of political science and law at Princeton and Vanderbilt, authored an entire book on Claudine Gay's plagiarizing of Swain's work, that carefully examines the purloined text at length and relates the story of how one scholar took on the world's wealthiest university to achieve justice. Carol Swain, *The Gay Affair: Harvard, Plagiarism, and the Death of Academic Integrity* (Nashville: Be the People books, 2025).

subsequent plagiarism scandal. Said AP about the disgraced president: "In her case, the outrage came not from her academic peers but her political foes, led by conservatives who put her career under intense scrutiny."[190]

But it wasn't "outrage." It was a call for accountability. And the outrage was the cowardly silence of her "academic peers" as Gay egregiously violated one of the most fundamental of academic principles, displaying that she was a cheating scholar. Sympathetic allies wanted to give her a generous pass.[191]

Walter M. Kimbrough, former president of the historically black Dillard University, offered this assessment of Gay's cheating, consistent with shared paranoia. He displaced Gay's responsibility. The crime, according to Kimbrough, was actually not Gay's cheating. The crime was *noticing* it.

"There are going to be people, particularly if they have any inkling that the person of color is not the most qualified, who will label them a 'DEI hire,' like they tried to label her," Kimbrough said. "If you want to lead an institution like (Harvard) … there are going to be people who are looking to disqualify you."[192]

Gay disqualified herself, of course, but continues to teach on the faculty with her presidential salary of $900,000 intact. The conclusion in all of this is inescapable. For DEI, plagiarism appears as a feature, not a bug, with a phalanx of ready apologists poised

---

190 Collin Binkley and Moriah Balingit, "Plagiarism charges downed Harvard's president. A conservative attack helped to fan the outrage," Associated Press, January 23, 2024: https://apnews.com/article/harvard-president-plagiarism-claudine-gay-3b048da1f2ee17b5edec3680b5828e8f
191 Emma Green, "Why Some Academics Are Reluctant to Call Claudine Gay a Plagiarist," *The New Yorker*, January 5, 2024: https://www.newyorker.com/news/q-and-a/why-some-academics-are-reluctant-to-call-claudine-gay-a-plagiarist
192 Collin Binkley and Moriah Balingit, "Plagiarism charges downed Harvard's president."

to prop up a rickety structure of mutually masked deceit. They would rather maintain the fraud than have transgressions exposed. This seemingly irrational preference to excuse cheating, as well as to engage in cheating itself, is driven by a powerful psychological motivation that appears widespread in DEI personnel and the persons who support them. When virtuous victim signaling is part of a resource transfer strategy—a "con game"—we can expect to see these people conduct "attacks on systems, individuals and social norms from cheating and lying, to bullying and violence."[193] The *system* is to blame, you see, not the person who cannot measure up.

In this case, the illusion of competence must be maintained. And this means tolerating behavior from members of select racial groups, behavior that would be intolerable from others. Even after-the-fact, when a faux scholar is outed as a plagiarist, the troops rally around the miscreant as they did with Claudine Gay. Harvard's Black Alumni celebrated the cheat, in fact. They gave her a "Leadership and Courage" award, thus elevating academic con-artistry to an award-winning virtue.[194]

The increasing number of reports of DEI plagiarism has led to the employment of defensive tactics, including imaginative repackaging of how we talk about plagiarism. A new euphemistic lingo has emerged. In the case of Gay, the exculpatory technique was to refer to her cheating as "duplicative language." Another serious plagiarism charge, this one against the president of the University of Maryland Darryll Pines, was handled likewise. Pines

193 Timothy C. Bates, Ciara Grant, Leila Hobbs, Claire Johnston, Shahrzad Moghaddam, Kate Sinclair, "Virtuous Victimhood as a Dark Triad resource transfer strategy," *Personality and Individual Differences*, 234 (2025), p. 2.
194 Frank Zhou, "Former Harvard President Claudine Gay Celebrated at Black Alumni Society Event," *The Harvard Crimson*, October 1, 2024: https://www.thecrimson.com/article/2024/10/1/claudine-gay-black-alumni-award/

was charged with plagiarizing the text of Joshua Altmann, whose work as a young graduate student in Australia found its way into a 2002 article by Pines. Pines called his own plagiarism "recurrent language."[195] Altmann was not amused by the "recurrent language" euphemism: "I do consider it to be plagiarism, and not worthy of an academic," he said.[196]

Another defensive tactic consists of questioning the motives of the persons who bring the charges of plagiarism, as if the veracity of the charges of cheating are somehow linked to who exposes them. In the case of Pines, the plagiarism was exposed by Luke Rosiak in the online site *Daily Wire*.[197] For some, such as the aforementioned "plagiarism expert" Jonathan Bailey, this introduces a faux problem that has been dubbed the "bad faith investigation."[198] Interestingly enough, Bailey is cited often in education publications as an expert, but he himself issues this disclaimer: "I am not a lawyer. I am just a legally minded Webmaster/Writer frustrated by the plague of plagiarism online and doing something about it."

This plague of plagiarism seems particularly acute in the ranks of those who serve in official campus DEI capacities. In May of 2024, two plagiarists were exposed in the ranks of MIT's DEI corps of Deans—Tracie Jones-Barrett and Alana Anderson.

195 Jonathan Bailey, "Understanding the Darryll Pines Plagiarism Allegations," *PlagiarismToday*, September 19, 2024: https://www.plagiarismtoday.com/2024/09/19/understanding-the-darryll-pines-plagiarism-allegations/
196 Josh Moody, Author Argues Maryland President 'Clearly' Plagiarized, *InsideHigherEd*, October 24, 2024: https://www.insidehighered.com/news/governance/executive-leadership/2024/10/24/author-argues-maryland-president-clearly
197 Luke Rosiak, "University of Maryland President Copied Rocket Science Paper From Aussie Student," DailyWire.com, September 17, 2024: https://www.dailywire.com/news/university-of-maryland-president-copied-rocket-science-paper-from-aussie-student
198 Jonathan Bailey, "With Plagiarism, the Problem is Not DEI, But Academia," *PlagiarismToday*, April 24, 2024: https://www.plagiarismtoday.com/2024/04/23/with-plagiarism-the-problem-is-not-dei-but-academia/

Each woman was alleged to have stolen from the academic work of others for their own dissertations.[199] This came in the wake of Harvard University's embarrassment over the plagiarism of Chief Diversity and Inclusion Officer Sherri A. Charleston (compounding the Claudine Gay fiasco).[200]

The plagiarist problem is triply troubling. In academia, plagiarists sin three times.

- First is the odd mindset of these would-be academics that leads to the conscious violation of standards of an academic community to become a member of that same community. It encourages the view that it's okay, even expected, to cheat one's way to prestige and honor.

- Second is the reality that the person who ascended to that august academic position, based on fake credentials, isn't qualified to be there and brings disrepute on everyone associated with the discipline.

- Third, the cheater casts doubt on others who have *not* cut-and-pasted their way up the ladder, who have worked hard and displayed talent and drive.

---

199 Sophie Mann, "Two DEI deans hired by MIT in wake of 2020 racial reckoning are serial plagiarists who passed off huge chunks of other academics' work as their own, lawsuit alleges," *The Daily Mail*, May 14, 2024: https://www.dailymail.co.uk/news/article-13417237/dei-deans-mit-2020-serial-plagiarists-lawsuit.html

200 Tilly R. Robinson and Neil H. Shah, Top Harvard Diversity Officer Sherri Charleston Faces Plagiarism Allegations, *The Harvard Crimson*, January 31, 2024: https://www.thecrimson.com/article/2024/1/31/sherri-charleston-plagiarism-allegations/

One of the first major cases of plagiarism that highlighted the growing problem of campus cheats was the sad affair of Professor Madonna Constantine of Columbia Teachers College, who displayed all three of these sins. She then reaped more headlines with her own twist, an additional transgression that presaged the Jussie Smollett brand of racialist hoax.

When a Case of Plagiarism makes the Front Page

Madonna Constantine was fired in 2008 from her tenured position as a professor of psychology and education at Columbia University's Teachers College for two dozen instances of plagiarism over five years.[201] She had copied the work of two students and a colleague and presented it as her own in her journal articles. Constantine was a major figure in Columbia Teachers College and was a close partner and co-author with the guru of microaggressions Dr. Derald Wing Sue.[202]

In the midst of the plagiarism investigation prior to her dismissal, Constantine became the center of racial attention for another reason—a "noose."

Constantine claimed that someone had hung a noose on her office doorknob to intimidate her. While she made a great public show over the incident, garnering sympathy, she refused to cooperate with investigators. Some speculate that Constantine

---

201 "More than a year before the noose incident, two Teachers College doctoral students, Karen Court and Tracy Juliao, and a former Professor, Christine Yeh, lodged separate complaints that Constantine had plagiarized their writing." Ashley Thorne, "The Copyist: The Plagiarist and the Noose," National Association of Scholars, February 27, 2008. https://www.nas.org/blogs/article/the_copyist_the_plagiarist_and_the_noose.

202 Madonna G. Constantine and Derald Wing Sue (eds.), *Addressing Racism: Facilitating Cultural Competence in Mental Health and Educational Settings* (Hoboken: John Wiley & Sons, Inc., 2006). Sue would weather the break with Constantine almost unscathed and continue on as the primary scholar in the problematic field of "microaggressions" for the next two decades.

placed the noose herself. If true, it would constitute a case of compounding her serial plagiarism with a "hate crime hoax."[203] One online news source observed that Constantine "planted the noose to divert attention from her embarrassing plagiarism charges."[204] The last of her several lawsuits against Columbia was dismissed in March of 2012.[205]

Constantine crashed spectacularly.

The Navel-Gazers

A second type of fraud (and it's fraudulent only when offering itself as "research") is navel-gazing, which is sometimes passed off as a type of "science" in the broad approach of qualitative research. Navel-gazing characterizes someone who is focused excessively on their own thoughts or feelings: "Essentially, it's introspection taken to the extreme, to the point where the gazer becomes oblivious to the world around them."[206] This is a characteristic of the variety of qualitative approaches that posture as knowledge creation. One of these is the technique of "autoethnography" which relies upon "lived experience" and at times is little more than—you guessed it—navel-gazing.

203 Wilfred Reilly, *Hate Crime Hoax: How the Left is Selling a Fake Race War* (Washington, DC: Regnery Publishing, 2019).

204 Zondra Hughes, "More Hate Crimes That Never Happened," *The Root*, October 24, 2012. https://rollingout.com/2012/10/24/kkk-hoax-5-more-outrageous-hate-crimes-that-never-happened/4/. "When the smoke cleared, authorities determined that Madonna Constantine—even with an angelic name like hers—planted the noose to divert attention from her embarrassing plagiarism charges."

205 "Ex-Professor Loses Bid to Revive Defamation Claim," *New York Law Journal*, March 14, 2012. See also: Doug McIntyre, "Bias is in the eye of the beholder," *Los Angeles Daily News*, February 23, 2019: "It's now widely believed Constantine placed the noose herself or had friends do it to distract from the plagiarism charges." https://www.law.com/newyorklawjournal/almID/1202545491661/?slreturn=20210515190014

206 Candace Osmond, "What is navel-gazing? Origin & Meaning," Grammarist: https://grammarist.com/idiom/navel-gazing/

These stories are published in journals created for the purpose, and they are often aggregated into themed collections.[207] The titles of these compilations capture the thrust of the enterprise: *Presumed Incompetent, Presumed Incompetent II, Toxic Ivory Towers, Racial Battle Fatigue in Faculty, Black Fatigue,* and various titles that all allude to "exhaustion" in one way or another. The stories need not even be true—just "authentic." In aggregate, they constitute a genre of literature that does little except support the Big Con: 1) They invent evidence, 2) They concretize ambiguous comments, 3) They express beliefs in terms of absolute certainty, and 4) They amplify the enormity of the conspiracy that creates a "hostile, malevolent world" that persecutes an "immense talent." These characteristics appear in all racialist autoethnographies in various combinations. Even those who share ethnicity are enemies if they do not adhere to racialism.

Racialists accuse successful faculty of color of complicity in the paranoid conspiracy, of having "internalized" what they call a "white perspective" or "whiteness." As it goes, these enemy "Scholars of Color have internalized racist and sexist beliefs."[208] Supposedly, disloyal colleagues such as Princeton/Vanderbilt scholar

---

207 Gabriella Gutiérrez y Muhs, Yolanda Flores Niemann, Carmen G. González, Angela P. Harris (eds.), *Presumed Incompetent: The Intersections of Race and Class for Women in Academia* (Logan, UT: Utah State University Press, 2012). Yolanda Flores Niemann, Gabriella Gutiérrez y Muhs, Carmen G. González (eds), *Presumed Incompetent II: Race, Class, Power, and Resistance of Women in Academia* (Logan, UT: Utah State University Press, 2020); Nicholas D. Hartlep and Daisy Ball (eds), *Racial Battle Fatigue in Faculty* (New York: Routledge, 2020); Mary-Frances Winters, *Black Fatigue* (Oakland: Berrett-Koehler Publishers, 2020); Ruth Enid Zambrana, *Toxic Ivory Towers: The Consequences of Work Stress on Underrepresented Minority Faculty* (New Brunswick: Rutgers University Press, 2018).
208 Yolanda Flores Niemann, Gabriella Gutiérrez y Muhs, Carmen G. González (eds), *Presumed Incompetent II: Race, Class, Power, and Resistance of Women in Academia* (Logan, UT: Utah State University Press, 2020), p. 8. See also: Karen D. Pyke, "What is Internalized Racial Oppression and Why Don't We Study it? Acknowledging Racism's Hidden Injuries," *Sociological Perspectives,* Vol. 53, No. 4 (Winter 2010).

Carol Swain[209] ally with the "pathology of Whiteness" enemy, broadened to encompass minority faculty who do not subscribe to this paranoia.[210] This ethnic disloyalty to the DEI creed is often characterized by saying that "skinfolk are not always kinfolk."[211]

The paranoid notion of "they're out to get me" animates an uncomfortably substantial number of these faculty. Lots of what they do isn't actual "scholarship" at all, but rather the product of feelings-based essays, narratives, *testimonios*, and such like. Much of their "academic" work consists of what is called qualitative research, and this usually consists of interviewing like-minded folks, typically a group of 10-15 persons selected precisely because of their prior agreement with the researcher's agenda. The sample can be a group of folks who work down the hall.[212] It's a kind of "This I believe, and don't you believe it, too?" sociology.

We can see a commonality in all of this academic pretense. This is the creation of a simulacrum of actual academia in which feelings, emotions, imagination, poetry, and fables constitute a growing body of pseudo-scholarship. All of this work is premised on a contrived enemy that is always "out to get me."

This legitimizes a kind of navel-gazing that showcases the person in whatever narrative offered. Whether it's "collaborative"

209 Carol Swain, "Critical Race Theory Is a Cancer on Our Educational System," June 2, 2021, Unity Training Solutions. https://unitytrainingsolutions.com/carol-swain-commentary-critical-race-theory-is-a-cancer-on-our-educational-system/
210 Cleveland Hayes, "I Feel No Ways Tired: The Exhaustion of Battling the Pathology of Whiteness," Nicholas D. Hartlep and Daisy Ball, *Racial Battle Fatigue in Faculty* (New York: Routledge, 2020), p. 43.
211 Yolanda Flores Niemann, et al, *Presumed Innocent II*, p. 7.
212 Joanna Brewis, The Ethics of Researching Friends: On Convenience Sampling in Qualitative Management and Organization Studies," *British Journal of Management*, Vol. 25 (2014). See also Bernd Marcus, Oliver Weigelt, Jane Hergert, Jochen Gurt, and Petra Gelleri, "The Use of Snowball Sampling for Multi-Source Organizational Research: Some Cause for Concern," *Personnel Psychology*, 70 (2017).

research in which the scholar omits any pretense of objectivity and joins with the folks under observation to create "outcomes," or whether it's a convenient batch of interviews of one's students and colleagues, or whether it's an "all about me" narrative.

All of it invariably swirls around a self-absorbed core, threatened and embattled.

This is how fraudulent ideas pass from pseudo-academia into the mainstream, carrying the slick patina of phony legitimacy. Examples of this faux academic literature are easy to find, once you recognize the pattern. The small number of the same primary sources appears. Where secondary literature is referenced, it is marginal, extremist, and almost always problematic with its reliance upon disreputable non-academic publishers, which are themselves members of the closed conspiracist community.

Here is the template for the process.

A bogus notion of mere wishful thinking is expressed. This idea is used at the basis for an anecdotal essay or "autoethnography" or "counterstory" or a *Testimonio*. Perhaps the idea is presented as the "lived experience" of a group of people selected precisely because they share an opinion. The essay is then published in one of the fake journals, which assume the look, feel, and form of traditional academic journals, including the trope of "peer-reviewed."

The article then becomes the basis for lay opinion that purports to draw upon academia when it actually draws upon a *simulacrum* of academia—that is to say, a fake version of the real thing. Campus workshops, caucuses, and reading groups are organized around the bogus notion, and facilitators advertise themselves as professionals in a vaguely named field.

These "facilitators" and "diversity consultants" then run

workshops in private companies and on university campuses. They present the bogus notion as the product of "scholarship." The circle is completed when poorly credentialed university administrators, who view themselves on-par with faculty, invite these fake independent "scholars" onto the campus to implement their workshops as part of the "co-curriculum."

Sure enough, one of the more popular tropes of this sort is the constant faculty lament of their *exhaustion*.[213] It's become a talking point that's surfaced in the popular press; I've heard senior diversity functionaries express it in meetings on my campus in angry exclamations of "I'm exhausted. *Just exhausted!*" Yes, *exhaustion*.[214]

If you didn't immediately catch on to the self-absorbed, narcissistic nature of the racialist navel-gazer, then this trope of "exhaustion" should clarify it. This is a brilliant bid for political sympathy that addresses no specific issue. The concept is popularized by diversity workshoppers like Mary-Frances Winters, who runs a consultancy called The Winters Group.[215]

A sympathetic piece in *Business Insider* reads like superb satire as it reports results of interviews from top corporate DEI executives and well-heeled consultants, who can't keep up with the business coming their way.[216] They're exhausted because business is

---

213 Amanda Miller Littlejohn, "Black professional women are exhausted. They're finally claiming the time to rest," *The Washington Post*, August 20, 2021: https://www.washingtonpost.com/business/2021/08/20/black-women-professionals-rest/

214 Janice Gassam Asare, "Dear America: Black Women Are Tired," *The Pink Elephant Newsletter*, July 29, 2024: https://www.linkedin.com/pulse/dear-america-black-women-tired-janice-gassam-asare-ph-d--bwwie/

215 Mary-Frances Winters, *Black Fatigue: How Racism Erodes the Mind, Body, and Spirit* (Oakland: Berrett-Koehler Publishers, Inc., 2020).

216 Marguerite Ward, "DEI execs are burning out amid the billion-dollar push to diversify corporate America: 'It's hard to be both the advocate and the abused,'" *Business Insider*, April 9, 2021 https://www.businessinsider.com/dei-leaders-risk-burnout-diversity-equity-inclusion-addressing-systemic-racism-2021-4

thriving. As we have seen in earlier chapters, it's also a victimhood strategy used to extract resources.

Universities actually offer advanced academic degrees based on this type of self-indulgent navel-gazing. In a feat of sublime circularity, degrees are awarded to persons in education programs who craft dissertations comprised of nothing more than their personal ruminations and discussions with classmates about those very programs in which they are enrolled.[217]

The ruminative autoethnography laid the groundwork for the inevitable "duoethnography." Each author interviews the other author, and then the co-authors massage the interviews into an article for publication in a cargo-cult journal that is "peer-reviewed" by the like-minded. Here's an example: "Using duoethnography, the authors document the embodied experience of being Black faculty responding to an expressed need for creating space to organize, express anger, and transmute hurt and pain into community."[218]

The door was opened for this type of self-indulgent exercise with the explosion of qualitative research approaches in the past 25 years that turned inward and focused on the researcher himself as a source of wisdom—you just had to mine yourself thoroughly.[219]

Qualitative studies that yield the desired results are a mainstay of DEI work. The technique is to craft research to "prove" a predetermined conclusion.

---

217 I have collected dissertations of these persons, who have navel-gazed their way to "doctor" status. Most are not practicing faculty—they work as support staff—and I've no desire to embarrass them further by naming them.
218 Stephen John Quaye, Mahauganee Dawn Shaw, and Dominique C. Hill, "Blending Scholar and Activist Identities: Establishing the Need for Scholar Activism," *Journal of Diversity in Higher Education*, 2017, Vol. 10, No. 4, p. 381.
219 Janice Morse, "The Changing Face of Qualitative Inquiry," International Journal of Qualitative Methods, Volume 19, 2020: https://journals.sagepub.com/doi/full/10.1177/1609406920909938

There's no better way to get the rankings you want than to start with the people who agree with you . . . . If the factors you evaluate can only be verified by like-minded individuals, it is not an objective ranking.[220]

A **third** type of DEI fraud is possibly the most egregious. This is the conviction that you can just make things up and pass it off as "research." These are the DEI yarn-spinners.[221] As syndicated columnist and political analyst Jonah Goldberg stated, "If a lie works, it becomes true enough for the task at hand."[222]

Yarn-spinners simply fabricate "evidence" for whatever they need, whenever and wherever it's needed. They solemnly pronounce their "truth." Thus, we have "storytelling," "counternarratives," "composite stories," the fable (a specialty of the late Derrick Bell), and a type of Black Mysticism (a specialty of Ta-Nehisi Coates).

The public arena gives us examples of make-believe supplanting reality. Take the example of the unfortunate Jazmine Barnes case in 2018, in which a little girl was shot and killed by a drive-by murderer. In that case, the original story of a white man in a pickup truck shooting and killing Jazmine was quickly debunked. Two suspects were caught and charged with the crime—both suspects

---

220 Ryan Quinn, "Conservative and Exploring Colleges? The Heritage Foundation Has Ratings for You," *Inside Higher Education*, September 13, 2024: https://www.insidehighered.com/news/diversity/2024/09/13/heritages-new-college-ratings-guide-conservatives

221 Danielle McLeod, "Spin a Yarn: Origin & Meaning": "To *spin a yarn* is an idiomatic phrase that means to tell an unusually long and sometimes imaginative story. Occasionally, these stories can be rather creative in nature and possibly unlikely to have occurred—meaning the phrase is used as a way to cast skepticism on the teller of the tale." *Grammarist*: https://grammarist.com/idiom/spin-a-yarn/

222 Jonah Goldberg, "The Fascist Lie: How the F-word lost its Bite," *The Dispatch*, October 25, 2024: https://thedispatch.com/newsletter/gfile/the-fascist-lie-2/

were Black. But the identity of the killers did not matter. The fraudulent narrative lived on.

The manufactured story of the white killer had become reified and assumed a life of its own. The narrative itself became the evidence for its truth—the narrative served as its own evidence for a nonexistent alternative reality. It became a circular social fantasy.

This false narrative was perpetuated by people like Shaun King, a race hustler extraordinaire. Rather than shame, King doubled-down on his bombast: "[T]hat it turned out to not be the case I don't think changes the devastating conclusion that people had thought something like that was possible."[223]

King's statement exemplifies the paranoid mind at work. The fake narrative always trumps what actually happens. Disconfirmation becomes confirmation—what matters is that it *could have been true*. Even as it wasn't.[224]

A Litany of Racialist Fabulism

Let's look briefly at some of these fabrications of DEI and those who made them up or popularized them:

"White Privilege"—popularized by Peggy McIntosh in the late 1980s and into the 1990s; McIntosh was a comparative literature professor who specialized in the poetry of Emily Dickinson and who today claims to be a "research scientist."

"Racism as prejudice + power"—fabricated by a teaching assistant called Patricia Bidol in 1971 and published in a pamphlet

---

223 Sarah Mervosh and Mihir Zaveri, "A Twist in the Jazmine Barnes Case as a Suspect Is Charged with Capital Murder," *The New York Times*, January 6, 2018.
224 Sarah Mervosh and Mihir Zaveri, "A Twist in the Jazmine Barnes Case."

for use in Detroit schools. Interestingly, Bidol offered an early take on "privilege" in her 1972 dissertation.[225]

"White Fragility"—popularized in the 2020s by a woman named Robin DiAngelo, who claims to be a sociologist and who lifted the term from a person by the name of David G. Allen, who apparently coined it back in the 1990s.

"Racial Microaggression"—conjured by a psychiatrist by the name of Chester Pierce in 1970[226] and given new life in the 2000s by a psychologist called Derald Wing Sue, whose entire program was substantially debunked in 2017 by Emory University psychologist Scott Lilienfeld,[227] in 2018 by Campbell and Manning in 2018,[228] and again in 2021 in a devastating takedown by Cantu and Jussim, who contend that microaggressions constitute an example of "idea laundering."[229]

"Racial Battle Fatigue"—this is a relative newcomer into the lexicon that describes a psychological reaction earmarked by professions of "exhaustion," as in "I'm so exhausted." This is blatant victim-signaling and a brilliant bid for political sympathy that addresses no specific issue.

Each of these is cushioned by pseudo-academic rhetoric about "different ways of knowing," "lived experience," "personal truths," the existence of various "knowledges," belief in the efficacy of "storytelling" and "composite stories," with all of it enveloped in

---

225 Bidol gets far too little credit in the pantheon of critical racialist thought leaders, if such a thing exists. Her 1972 dissertation is rife with many of the concepts wielded later by McIntosh and by the racialist sensation Ibram Kendi.
226 Chester Pierce, "Offensive Mechanisms," in Floyd B. Barbour (ed), *The Black 70s* (Boston: Porter Sargent, 1970), pp: 265-282.
227 Scott Lilienfeld, "Microaggressions: Strong Claims, Inadequate Evidence," *Perspectives on Psychological Science*, 2017 2017, Vol. 12(1), pp. 138-169.
228 Bradley Campbell and Jason Manning, *The Rise of Victimhood Culture* (New York: Palgrave Macmillan, 2018).
229 Edward Cantu and Lee Jussim, "Microaggressions, Questionable Science, and Free Speech," *Texas Review of Law & Politics*, vol. 26, 2021.

a perspective that: "It might *not* be true, but what matters is that it *could* be true."

The technique appears to be to simply fabricate something, the more ambitiously egregious the better, to pass it off as fact, and then to circulate it with evangelical zeal, bluster, and bluff. It demonstrates the power of paranoid thought and action and repetition to achieve legitimacy as a ritualized "truth."

The appeal to prejudice trumps every other consideration, including fidelity to the facts. Popular author and racialist Ta-Nehisi Coates uses this technique freely. Coates also holds the Sterling Brown Endowed Chair in the Department of English at Howard University, appointed in 2021.[230] Coleman Hughes observed the technique in his review of Coates's 2024 book *The Message*.

> Coates is not a journalist so much as a composer—one who uses words not to convey the truth, much less to point a constructive path forward, but to create a mood, the same way that a film scorer uses notes. And the specter haunting this book, and indeed all of his work, is the crudest version of identity politics in which everything—wealth disparity, American history, our education system, and the long-standing conflict between Israel and its Arab neighbors—are reduced to a childlike story in which the "victims" can do no wrong (and have no agency) and the "villains" can do no right (and are all-powerful).[231]

---

230 Wayne A. I. Frederick, "Two Iconic Writers Join Howard's Illustrious Faculty," From the President, Howard University, August 31, 2021: https://president. howard.edu/from-the-president/viewpoints/two-iconic-writers-join-howards-illustrious-faculty
231 Coleman Hughes, "The Fantasy World of Ta-Nehisi Coates," *The Free Press*, October 2, 2024: https://www.thefp.com/p/ta-nehisi-coates-the-message-israel-hamas

Hughes could not have nailed virtuous victimhood more squarely had he tried.

Coates's amateur account of the Israeli-Hamas conflict, based on his 10-day sponsored tour of Gaza is as laughable as it is ignorant and the product of an obvious partisan. It is difficult to determine whether he is a dupe of terrorists or an active fellow-traveler with terrorists. He is certainly all-in on the ideology that informs DEI, which is the extremist notion of "decolonization" as some kind of righteous panacea.[232]

He uses his borrowed prestige to opine on a topic of which he is completely ignorant. To wit: The most startling thing one observes about Coates's three trips—to South Carolina, to Senegal, and to Israel—is that *nothing noteworthy happens*. Literally, nothing of note. The angst-ridden Coates endures solitary meals in local restaurants, picks at his meticulously described food, and he cogitates (occasionally with tears in his eyes). He sees people on the street. He ogles the "enormous guns" of security personnel. His travelogue regales readers with little more than the exploration of his "feelings" and his constant references to his race-obsessed worldview, which gives us repeated fabrications of how he imagines things must have been in some earlier time and some other place.

The Message is autoethnographic memoir, in which his surroundings serve only as scaffolding for his sublime ruminations. Coates gives free rein to his perpetual inner-sophomore. The aura of self-importance, of "genius," suffuses the strained prose of this eternal undergraduate. He is locked into a phase through which most young would-be writers pass, a narcissistic preoccupation

---

232 Eve Tuck and K. Wayne Yang, "Decolonization Is Not a Metaphor,"
Decolonization: Indigeneity, Education and Society 1, no. 1 (2012).

with the uniqueness of one's reaction to an exotic place, when he is just the latest tourist infatuated with the sights and smells.

> This is about the forest again—about the limits of genius, about the need to walk the land, as opposed to intuit and hypothesize from the edge. There are dimensions in your words—rhythm, content, shape, feeling. And so too with the world outside. The accretion of imperfect, discomfiting life must be seen and felt so that the space in your mind, gray, automatic, and square, with angle, color, and curve—the potholes, the dented fenders, the fried bread, the walls of fabric, the heaping plate of rice and fish .... Africans jogging on the beach or a dilapidated gym revealing itself as a beautiful example of civic spirit says something important about the world I was trying to describe but also about me, my fears, and my doubts.[233]

Is there nothing so mundane in his surroundings, nothing so pedestrian in his thoughts that Coates would hesitate to share it on the page, goosing it with *neo-hoodoo* to bestow meaning where none exists outside the shabby reality he depicts? "Neo-HooDoo believes that every man is an artist and every artist a priest. You can bring your own creative ideas to Neo-HooDoo."[234] Practitioners of Ishmael Reed's *neo-hoodoo* display hostility to suggestion that they ought to adhere to anything resembling rigor, logic, or even facts. In this way, the serpentine sentence becomes the vehicle for imaginary constructs—metaphors and allusions and bombastic proclamations.

---

233 Ta-Nehisi Coates, *The Message* (New York: One World, 2024), p. 44-45.
234 Ishmael Reed, "The Neo-HooDoo Manifesto" in *Conjure: Selected Poems, 1963-1970* (Amherst: University of Massachusetts Press, 1972), p. 20-25.

We have a right to our imagined traditions, to our imagined places, and those traditions and places are most powerful when we confess that they are imagined . . . . And we have a right to imagine ourselves as pharaohs, and then again the responsibility to ask if a pharaoh is even worthy of our needs, our dreams, our imagination.[235]

Page upon page of this sort of kabbalistic blather, and you inevitably marvel "What is *wrong* with this fellow?" But if you *do* wonder this, recognize that the problem is yours, not his.

The reasons for the popularity of this hero-narcissist aren't hard to find. Racialism works best on willing audiences of those who wished to be fooled. Coates's storytelling exemplifies the skill of the con-artist, and he spikes his own autofictography with a double-shot of mystification. It's an effective technique described by the scholar of con games, Maria Konnikova.

Give us a compelling story, and we open up. Skepticism gives way to belief. The same approach that makes a blind man's cup overflow with donations can make us more receptive to most any persuasive message, for good or for ill . . . . At their root, magic tricks and confidence games share the same fundamental principle: a manipulation of our beliefs. Magic operates at the most basic level of visual perception, manipulating how we see and experience reality.[236]

---

235 Ta-Nehisi Coates, *The Message*, p. 57-58.
236 Maria Konnikova, *The Confidence Game*, p. 7.

Coates is more fortunate than most navel-gazers in that he has a platform of willing supplicants, ready believers who partner with him in a symbiotic dance of mediocrity.

The First DEI Hire—*Yarn-Spinner Extraordinaire*

The late Derrick Bell was a paranoiac who always wondered if he was good enough. This is precisely the mental state we find in what has become known as the DEI hire. The regime of DEI institutionalizes the imposter syndrome, and Bell was the first prominent DEI hire. He clearly knew this, and the stigma and shame of this status motivated him not to pursue excellence, but rather to pursue self-destruction and the wholesale delegitimization of the legal edifice that had reached out to include him.

Bell was a Harvard Law Professor considered by many to be the founder of critical race theory, and he pioneered this type of yarn-spinning. Bell's brand of fabulism is a modern version of the Aesopian fable.

The traditional Aesopian fable begins with a lesson to teach. Then, a story is woven around it to illustrate the point. One of the most familiar of these Aesopian tales is the "Boy Who Cried Wolf," which illustrates the view that you should not raise false alarms about nonexistent emergencies lest your would-be rescuers decline to be fooled again, when you have an *actual* life-threatening emergency.

Bell pioneered this technique in the pages of the *Harvard Law Review*. His masterpiece book-length compendium of the fabulist form is *Faces at the Bottom of the Well: The Permanence of Racism*, a collection of his fables that includes his much-ballyhooed tale of "The Space Traders."[237] This book was a reprise of the fabulist method he developed and used in his earlier 1987 volume *And We Are Not Saved*.[238] Bell acknowledged his use of the unorthodox method: "Critical race theory writing and lecturing is characterized by frequent use of the first person, storytelling, narrative, allegory, interdisciplinary treatment of law, and the unapologetic use of creativity."[239]

Bell's neo-Aesopian method has found traction. His blending of fact and fiction offered a sublime solution to the central problem and a shortcut to the writing life that those of us who labor in the nonfiction vineyard restrained by reality can only envy. Says Bell:

> In that earlier book [*And We Are Not Saved*], through a series of allegorical stories, [Geneva Crenshaw] and I discussed the workings—and the failures—of civil rights laws and policies. Here, I again enlist the use of literary models as a more helpful vehicle than legal precedent in a continuing quest for new directions in our struggle for racial justice, a struggle we must continue even if—as I contend here—racism is an integral permanent, and indestructible component of this society .... The interweaving of fact and fiction requires writing skill and experience possessed by few law teachers, including this author.[240]

Those who mimic Bell's technique of fabrication take a

---

237 Derrick Bell, *Faces at the Bottom of the Well: The Permanence of Racism* (New York: Basic Books, 1992).
238 Derrick Bell, *And We Are Not Saved: The Elusive Quest for Racial Justice* (New York: Basic Books, 1987).
239 Quoted in Michael Bérubé and Jennifer Ruth, *It's Not Free Speech: Race, Democracy, and the Future of Academic Freedom*, (Baltimore: Johns Hopkins University Press, 2022), p. 138.
240 Derrick Bell, *Faces at the Bottom of the Well*, p. xi and xiii.

short methodological journey to a predictable dead-end. They self-ghettoize themselves into a cramped theater of the intellect, where the same thematic play is enacted night after night—different actors, slightly different script, perhaps different names, but the same exhausted theme. This has provided the wrong kind of inspiration for ongoing generations.

I lament the phalanxes of young black students moving through the university's tiered system of classes, too many of whom are sidetracked into the *cul-de-sac* of racialism. They believe falsely that they must think about, write about, become consumed with their own racial identity steeped in a vat of toxic ideology. Bright young men and women are transmogrified into racialist beings, grandiose and narcissistic, hyper-suspicious and blame-shifting, unable to deal with other persons outside of a paranoid mindset and unable to generate authentic knowledge that carries validity in a larger context outside of their racialist provincialism.

A DEI bureaucracy trains and amplifies this intellectual constriction. It inculcates this paranoia into perfectly normal persons, so that they adopt and display the paranoid behavior. If they were not behaving as paranoiacs already, they soon learn. They begin to reinterpret their "lived experiences" so to ferret out "racism" on the campus, which allegedly is rampant with it. They rarely stop to recognize that this "lived experience" is a highfalutin word for "anecdote," and that they have been trained to internalize victim mentality and to exhibit the victim behavior that campus DEI monitors.

It's not difficult at all to find young people enamored with the ease of the racialist methodology—plagiarism, navel-gazing, and yarn-spinning—that is harnessed to the perpetuation of a central myth connected to social justice. It is seductively easy.

And this is the trap for young intellectuals in their formative years. The idealism of all young people is surely present and easy to discern. The fork in the road is equally discernible. One path is captivating in its simplicity.

This tine of the fork leads down into the abyss of self-referential racialism, to a well-worn thoroughfare of narcissism, grandiosity, posturing and paranoia. "I have something to say!" that is fresh, new, different and authentic. I have a "lived experience" to share and to contribute to the central myth. I have my own mite to tithe, and always huddled around me is a cluster of nodding nabobs to give me validation. I can join the groupmind and ghettoize myself for instant validation by the mediocrities trading their discount "scholarship" back and forth. I can write about "race." I can plagiarize others who have written about race, I can contemplate my predicament in a chin-scratching autoethnography, or I can just make something up—like Derrick Bell.

Wallowing in this septic abyss, I can contribute nothing original to our society or to my own self-worth. All I can do is repeat the myth, treading a tidepool brimming with narcissists. The only accolades available to me are those of like-minded hustlers, who valorize each other as they "do the work." This is the technique of leveraging paranoia and conspiracy thinking by offering fabulous fiction that breathes life into those paranoid beliefs.

There is, however, a different path.

This is the difficult path of knowledge creation that offers *entre* to an expansive canvas upon which to sketch, the gateway to an endless rapturous universe of knowledge discovered and potential knowledge that awaits the ambitious, the talented, the dedicated. A path that is free of the asphyxiating racialism of DEI.

Conclusion

In this chapter, we reviewed the three main tools used by the DEI industry to legitimize itself and to gain societal influence by running the Big Con. Higher education is key to gaining this "legitimacy," as it opens doors to business and government as well as providing for entry and re-entry onto the campuses. A deepening and broadening bureaucratic process cycles racialists into the universities in growing numbers, where they exert power and influence to transform the university into a crucible of indoctrination based on the Con Story of DEI.

The fakery and outright fraud of plagiarism, navel-gazing, and yarn-spinning has proven effective in running the DEI con game, and we've examined many examples here, while other examples abound and await review. Now that you know what to look for, you can likely provide your own examples of the DEI con in your own professional venue.

The next chapter relates the incredible story of the grandest DEI yarn of all. This aspect of the Big Con has earned its own chapter because of its role as a foundation for so many others, on campus and off: The "White Supremacy Culture" list.

If DEI is the biggest con of the 21st Century, then this example of fake scholarship—of *idea laundering*—is its founding document.

I call this document the *Protocols of the Learned Elders of Diversity*.

5

"WHITE SUPREMACY CULTURE"

THE PROTOCOLS OF THE
LEARNED ELDERS OF DIVERSITY

"I came home and I sat in front of the computer. And the article literally came through me onto the computer. It was not researched. I didn't sit down and deliberate. It just came through me."[241]

— Tema Okun, activist

241 Ryan Grim, "Tema Okun on her Mythical Paper on White Supremacy," *Disconnected* podcast, The Intercept, February 23, 2023: https://theintercept. com/2023/02/03/deconstructed-tema-okun-white-supremacy/

In the last chapter, we reviewed many of the fabrications of DEI included in the Con Story, and those who contrived them: "White Privilege," "Racism as prejudice + power," "White Fragility" "Racial Microaggression," "Racial Battle Fatigue." These fabrications are all part of victim-signaling the Con Story of *virtuous victimhood*.

But is all of this believable enough to run a Con against those really smart people in the universities? It all seems so far-fetched, and yet folks in higher education seemed to buy into it. The key is that they believed it, because the Con was *tailored especially for them*.

This is the central problem with any long con—and most certainly the Big Con of DEI. Is the Con Story believable? Is it tailored to the specific vulnerabilities, desires, and fears of the mark? Will the sucker take the bait?

To run the Big Con of virtuous victimhood on the nation's campuses for time-enough to reap the biggest rewards requires the sucker's belief to maintain the fraud. Evidentiary support is obligatory, and the support must come in a form acceptable to academia, at least nominally. It must maintain the attack on the guilty white pseudocommunity as culpable and complicit in some great crime. This is so that the prospect of expensive absolution appears legitimate, attractive, and worth its high price.

We've seen that the DEI narratives of diversity *victim-signaling* and *virtue-signaling* are supported by a network of grifters and narcissistic gurus with articles, books, podcasts, and speeches. The goal of this furious activity is to shoehorn into the academy dubious concepts and outright prejudice through a process that intentionally mimics authentic academia. Their grand lies and contrived concepts all have a common thread—they are the product of *idea laundering*.

This chapter introduces the main technique whereby the Con Story is given its *gravitas* to convince the denizens of the university to fall for it. This is called idea laundering. Then we turn to the most egregious example of successful diversity idea laundering in this century—the "White Supremacy Culture" fraud. This is the case of Tema Okun's fake list of white supremacy behaviors that appears in hundreds of DEI programs and on websites great and small—it's completely made-up by a disgruntled diversity grifter in a fit of pique.

Laundering Bad Ideas into the Academy

Idea Laundering[242] is utterly essential to the success of leveraging DEI's *virtuous victimhood* Big Con into the university. Idea laundering is the process that legitimizes prejudice and opinion as accepted fact and "knowledge." It camouflages social justice activism as "scholarship." Conspiracy theory expert Jovan Byford notes (with scholar Michael Barkun) that it is a way to

> bring conspiracy theories closer to the mainstream of academic enquiry [and] help to sanitize the conspiracy culture in terms of its underlying politics and a provide it with a route to the "territory of semi-respectable beliefs."[243]

This is how the most absurd pronouncements, bombastic

---

242 "Idea Laundering" is a term coined by biologist Bret Weinstein in 2018. It was expanded upon in an important *Wall Street Journal* op-ed by Dr. Peter Boghossian in 2019. Peter Boghossian, "'Idea Laundering': How nonsensical jargon like 'intersectionality' and 'cisgender' is imbued with a false air of authority," *Wall Street Journal*, November 24, 2019: https://www.wsj.com/articles/idea-laundering-in-academia-11574634492

243 Jovan Byford, *Conspiracy Theories: A Critical Introduction* (New York: Palgave Macmillan, 2015), p. 98; Michael Barkun, *A Culture of Conspiracy: Apocalyptic Visions in Contemporary America* (Los Angeles: UCLA Press), p. 83.

declarations, and problematic conclusions are smuggled into the university to support the Big Con of virtuous victimhood.

First, we look here at the method of idea laundering. Second, we see how this process has led to a bushel basket of absurdities finding their way onto the campuses and then taught to under-graduates, both in the curriculum and in the fake co-curriculum.

Idea Laundering

What is idea laundering? It sounds sinister, as in laundering a gangster's dirty money to get it into circulation. This is appropriate, as idea laundering's purpose is to put bad theory, absurd concepts, and nasty prejudice into circulation on the nation's campuses, where this nonsense can gain the approval of academia and then subsist on the prestige thus borrowed illegitimately. Thence, it moves easily into society at-large.

Idea laundering is a stage-by-stage technique to gradually elevate speculation and extremist opinion to the status of "knowl-edge" that is accepted by the university. In this way, charlatans gain ersatz legitimacy for their prejudices. They publish in fake "peer reviewed" academic journals to start a chain of citations that can lift the most egregious of hokum to the perceived status of legitimate knowledge.

It is, of course, a fraudulent process that is specifically designed to acquire faux legitimacy for the kind of hack work we saw in the last chapter—plagiarized articles, navel-gazing essays, and pure fiction passed off as scholarship.

It involves the capture of peer review processes by activists to create the false impression that certain ideologically and rhetorically useful claims have scientific credibility, even when, by conventional scientific standards of rigor, logic, and strong evidence, the claims command no credence . . . .

Some idea is presented or even claimed to be true in a book chapter or article, with little or no evidence. It might even be done reasonably, as speculation, or it might involve a researcher leaping to an unjustified conclusion based on weak evidence. The idea, now published in a peer-reviewed journal, can now be cited by other researchers publishing in other peer-reviewed journals as "evidence" for the validity of the claim. In the total absence of validity evidence, new researchers can then further cite one another's peer-reviewed publications in support of the claim.[244]

Most, if not all, of the progressive concepts supporting DEI are prejudice and opinion masquerading as accepted fact—intersectionality, white fragility, whiteness, white privilege, and such like. They have been laundered through the complex of faux academic journals set up for that purpose. These are called "cargo cult" journals.

Since no reputable journal will accept social justice educators' pretense to scholarship, social justice educators have had to

---

244 Edward Cantu and Lee Jussim, "Microaggressions, Questionable Science, and Free Speech," *Texas Review of Law & Politics*, vol. 26, 2021, p. 242.

take over, or create wholesale, hundreds of academic journals dedicated to social justice scholarship. Publication is easy, since the editors and the peer reviewers are also social justice educators.[245]

These journals and publishers comprise an elaborate scaffolding that generates a vast quantity of hoax literature. This body of literature undergirds the victim/virtue-signaling messaging of DEI and aids in maximal resource extraction from the university. This hoax literature provides a citation-chain that grows constantly. The chain links together a series of earlier essays, anecdotes, stories, and fake social science "studies," all of which offer the same unsupported pronouncements. When they are linked in a series, they constitute a *citation chain* that launders an absurd idea into respectability.

Here is how it works.

Layers of shared opinion are laid down one over the other in "cargo cult" journals created for the task and designed to mimic mainstream scholarship. These articles can be flimsy opinion essays, filled with powerful "decisive assertions."[246] The decisive assertion is conveyed with great confidence and usually with heavy moralizing and emotional content where bombast and fanfare rule the day.

---

245 These are called "cargo cult" journals because they mimic the form and language of authentic journals so that problematic concepts, prejudice, and mere opinion can be passed off as akin to "social science." See David Randall, *Social Justice Education in America* (Princeton: National Association of Scholars, 2019), p. 233-234.
246 Mark Bauerlein, *Literary Criticism: An Autopsy* (Philadelphia: University of Pennsylvania Press, 1997), p. 35.

The fact that the premises remain largely unsubstantiated and the conclusions unproven easily goes unnoticed when scholarship is cloaked in a rhetoric of canniness and certitude.[247]

This cloak of canniness and certitude is where the Big Con begins. It's where absurd slogans like "Diversity is our strength," begin to accrue rhetorical power and add to the diversity Con Story. These initial early works then are cited in subsequent pieces, which themselves are then laid over to become part of the rhetorical edifice. Rarely is anything new introduced, except in anecdotes or "stories."[248] Rather, the same pronouncements are cycled and recycled. It's an echo chamber of opinion designed to look like scholarship, and Jovan Byford observes that the technique is well-traveled in circles of conspiracy.

[Conspiracists are] sceptical towards conventional mechanisms of warranted belief production: peer reviewed journals, judicial investigations, university departments or scientific institutions, and yet they routinely seek to emulate mainstream scholarship and enquiry. The 'high brow' conspiracy theorists will flaunt dubious academic credentials (professor, Dr., MD, etc.) and other markers of institutional respectability. They will publish books with scholarly sounding titles and adopt a style of writing

---

247 Mark Bauerlein, *Literary Criticism,* p. 35.
248 The stories that are offered as "evidence," it must be noted, may be true or metaphorical, or simply fiction contrived for the purpose of the article. This storytelling is key a key to maintenance and growth of the critical discourse community—new stories contribute to the growth of the master narrative of the community, its collective myth. Only certain stories are permitted, those that confirm and illustrate the central myth.

that mimics mainstream academia: they will use the appropriate jargon, graphs, footnotes and extensive bibliographies.[249]

The principle is that if you can get enough people uttering the same opinion in journals set up for the express purpose of publishing that opinion, it can and will be accepted as legitimate in some sense by a larger audience.

This explains the repetitive use of the phrases "lived experience" and "marginalized voices" and "participatory research." Anecdotes—true or contrived—add to the weight of repetitive "evidence."

> At one level, conspiracy theories are an example of suppressed knowledge, because those who believe in conspiracy theories are convinced that only they know the true manner in which power is held and decisions made .... At another level, conspiracy theories explain why all forms of stigmatized knowledge claims have been marginalized—allegedly the conspiracy has utilized its power to keep the truth from being known.[250]

This superficial similarity to genuine academic work gives the cargo cult its power—it is the well-known power of mimesis, a kind of sympathetic magic we find in primitive magic systems, such as voodoo. It is the notion that by crude mimicry of form, by fabricated substance, and by rhetorical abstrusity, one can generate the same respectable, rigorous results as actual science. In the

---

249 Jovan Byford, *Conspiracy Theories,* p. 89.
250 Michael Barkun, *A Culture of Conspiracy: Apocalyptic Visions in Contemporary America* (Berkeley: University of California Press, 2003), p. 27.

vernacular, it is a counterfeit intended to gain the same results as the genuine article. Jovan Byford and Michael Billig observe:

> The conspiracy theorists' endeavour to emulate mainstream scholarship stems from the fact that the conspiracy thesis often addresses "the failed, or would be intellectuals, and amateurs who dream of intellectual success where the professional fails." Conspiracy theory instils in the audience the faith that "a believer can become an expert," a feature that is linked to the participatory approach to conspiracy theory.[251]

You can be "seen" and "heard" and your "marginalized voice" can weave a tale of "lived experience" that must be "validated" by all who hear it.

The Guarantor Method that opens Academic Doors

Laundering an absurd proposition into academic acceptance is not that difficult, even for the most ridiculous of notions. One means of doing this is by using a "guarantor method" to cloak research into respectability. Philosopher Roger Scruton is merciless in his take on this. Says Scruton, the point is "not to explain the phenomenon before him, but to create the *appearance* of a scientific question, the appearance of data, and the appearance of a method that will arrive at an answer.[252]

---

251 Jovan Byford, *Conspiracy Theories: A Critical Introduction* (New York: Palgave Macmillan, 2015), p. 90; Michael Billig, "Anti-Semitic themes and the British far Left: Some social psychological observations on indirect aspects of the conspiracy tradition," I C.F. Graumann and S. Moscovici (Eds.), *Changing Conceptions of Conspiracy* (New York: Springer-Verlag, 1987), p. 132.
252 Roger Scruton, "Scientism and the Humanities," in Richard N. Williams and Daniel N. Robinson (eds.), *Scientism: The New Orthodoxy* (London: Bloomsbury, 2016), p. 135.

The laundering process begins with a partisan concept, such as "whiteness" or "privilege" or a catchy trope that arrives at just the right moment—"White Fragility" or "Antiracism." The concept becomes the subject of a study in which, say, the view of "whiteness" provides beforehand a premise identical to the desired conclusion—the premise and conclusion are linked by a confirming methodology guaranteed to close the circle. The investigation is informed by the prejudice of the hustlers who engage in it, which in many cases constitutes what Bourdieu translator Richard Nice has called the "Magic Circle of Belief."[253] The Circle duly cites and reciprocates citation in the way of all conspiracy theories striving for acceptance.

> At the same time that stigmatization is employed as a virtual guarantee of truth, the literature of stigmatized knowledge enthusiastically mimics mainstream scholarship. It does so by appropriating the apparatus of scholarship in the form of elaborate citations and bibliographies. The most common manifestation of pedantry is a fondness for reciprocal citation, in which authors obligingly cite one another. The result is that the same sources are repeated over and over, which produces a kind of pseudoconfirmation. If a source is cited many times, it must be true. Because the claims made by conspiracy theorists are usually nonfalsifiable, the multiplication of sources may leave the impression of validation without actually putting any propositions to the test of evidence.[254]

253 Pierre Bourdieu, *Outline of a Theory of Practice*, (Cambridge: Cambridge University Press, 1977, 1972), p. viii.
254 Michael Barkun, *A Culture of Conspiracy*, p. 28-29.

The type of work we saw in Chapter 4 abjures any sort of rigor, framework, discipline, or *a priori* control over faux academic projects. Instead, they travel unmolested toward a destination that the activist's worldview inevitably anticipates, undisturbed by pesky disconfirmations, by data that do not fit, by "lived experiences" that do not count, by "voices" that do not confirm.

The Agreeable Rhetoric of Shared Opinion

A guarantor method expresses a circular argument. In such exercises, the *premise* of a research question also serves as the *conclusion*. The method puts distance between the premise and the conclusion and links the two in a scripted exercise of expected validation. The guarantor method *ensures* that the "theory" is confirmed. No other outcome is possible.

Thus, we expect nothing new from this circular exercise. Novelty, of course, is *not* the purpose. Contribution to genuine knowledge is *not* the goal. Rather, the purpose is to generate symbolic capital for the author that contributes to the core of the hustle. It's a rite of passage that communicates that the author has absorbed his lessons and is ready to contribute his personal stories to the diversity Big Con.

Guarantor methods support the decisive assertions of prejudice and opinion in circular exercises that pass as "scholarship." This body of scholarly "diversity work" constitutes a septic well from which lay authors and "public intellectuals" draw for articles, popular books, "workshops," and seminar materials, all of it duly referenced and footnoted with the look and feel of actual knowledge rather than the speculative pseudoscience and fakery it is.

Philosopher Peter Boghossian exposed this skullduggery in a *Wall Street Journal* piece in 2019.

> These academicians accomplish this by passing off their ideas as knowledge; that is, as if these terms describe facts about the world and social reality. And while some of these ideas may contain bits of truth, they aren't scientific. By and large, they're the musings of ideologues . . . .

> Within their academic ecosystems, grievance scholars hire new faculty members with similar moral commitments who've written for the same journals. Eventually, they institutionalize their ideas in the larger academic system. This process, which has been propagating laundered ideas for at least three decades, now has enough "scholarship" behind it to have a significant cultural impact.[255]

While DEI's Big Con of *virtuous victimhood* is propped up by many fraudulent concepts, pseudo-academic pabulum, and paranoia, few examples illustrate the fraud of DEI as thoroughly as what I call the *Protocols of the Learned Elders of Diversity*. This is the "White Supremacy Culture" List that was fabricated in 1999. To my mind, this is the most important example of idea laundering and greatest contribution to the hoax literature of diversity's Big Con of virtuous victimhood.

---

255 Peter Boghossian, "'Idea Laundering': How nonsensical jargon like 'intersectionality' and 'cisgender' is imbued with a false air of authority," *Wall Street Journal*, November 24, 2019: https://www.wsj.com/articles/idea-laundering-in-academia-11574634492

The "White Supremacy Culture" Behaviors List

The "White Supremacy Culture" list was fabricated and published for the first time in 1999 and is now republished repeatedly nationwide. Journalist Ryan Grim summed the List's cancerous growth and its increasingly deleterious impact:

> [S]tarting in the late 2000s, the paper began to be circulated widely in progressive spaces. After George Floyd's murder, it was everywhere, and it started to morph into something different, often wielded by employees during performance reviews, or when pressed about a deadline, or it was otherwise weaponized in the internal battles that continue to engulf institutions, organizations, or even corporations around the country.[256]

This is one of the most absurd documents of this century, a document that has earned a place alongside the great forgeries and frauds of history. A document whose twaddle has been laundered so thoroughly into the fabric of DEI that it has even found its way into mainstream academia, where it serves not only as justification for bizarre racialist beliefs but also as a tool for training so-called "antiracism pedagogy."[257]

The List is a compendium of 15 qualities that purportedly constitute "white supremacy culture." Here they are:

Perfectionism

A sense of urgency

Defensiveness and/or denial

---

256 Ryan Grim, "Tema Okun on her Mythical Paper on White Supremacy," *Disconnected* podcast, The Intercept, February 23, 2023: https://theintercept.com/2023/02/03/deconstructed-tema-okun-white-supremacy/

257 "Practicing Anti-Racism and Anti-Racist Pedagogy: An Overview," University of Michigan, Equitable Teaching Site: https://sites.lsa.umich.edu/equitable-teaching/anti-racist-practices/

Quantity over quality
Worship of the written word
The belief in one "right" way
Paternalism, either/or binary thinking
Power hoarding
Fear of open conflict
Individualism
Progress defined as more
The right to profit
Objectivity
The right to comfort

The List is everywhere, in workshops on campuses, in corporate diversity sessions, in secondary school programs, in New York City education workshops for teachers. Versions of The List appear on government websites, on "anti-racist" non-profit sites, and actually made it onto the Race, Research, and Policy Portal of Harvard Kennedy School's Shorenstein Center.[258] [It has since been quietly removed and one gets the obligatory 404: Page Not Found] The List even briefly appeared on the Smithsonian Website for the National Museum of African American History and Culture in 2020, before someone with risk management sense recognized it as a fraud and took it down. But like a game of whack-a-mole, it springs up again.

The List is a centerpiece of DEI at the University of Michigan. Says Nicholas Confessore in *The New York Times*:

Programs across the university are couched in the distinctive jargon that, to D.E.I.'s practitioners, reflects proven practices

---

258 https://rrapp.hks.harvard.edu/article-authors/818/

for making classrooms more inclusive, and to its critics reveals how deeply D.E.I. is encoded with left-wing ideologies. Michigan's largest division trains professors in "antiracist pedagogy" and dispenses handouts on "Identifying and Addressing Characteristics of White Supremacy Culture," like "worship of the written word."[259]

One of those "handouts" is the Okun List.

At the University of Wisconsin in Madison, too, the List is offered as a resource. It's on the university's website. Check for yourself.[260]

The National Education Association (NEA) has been duped as well, offering a convenient link to Okun's list at *Dismantling Racism Works*.[261]

Boston University's "Diversity and Inclusion" division says that it "works closely with all of the University's 17 schools and colleges to help create a positive and welcoming campus climate." This includes promoting Okun's fraudulent List as "the characteristics of white supremacist culture within organizations and the unconscious bias and standards these institutions adhere to." A link to Okun's List appears on BU's 2025 site.[262]

According to a piece in *The American Mind*, The List is used in Denver Public Schools as well as the infamous Loudoun County

259 Nicholas Confessore, "The University of Michigan Doubled Down on D.E.I. What Went Wrong?" *The New York Times*, October 2024: https://www.nytimes.com/2024/10/16/magazine/dei-university-michigan.html
260 University of Wisconsin-Madison, College of Agricultural and Life Sciences, August 4, 2023, website: https://admin.cals.wisc.edu/learninghub/characteristics-of-white-supremacy-culture/
261 National Education Association, "White Supremacy Culture Resources," NEA Center for Social Justice, December 2020: https://www.nea.org/resource-library/white-supremacy-culture-resources
262 Diversity & Inclusion, "White Supremacy Culture Characteristics." Boston University: https://www.bu.edu/diversity/resource-toolkit/white-supremacy-culture-characteristics/

public school system in Virginia. Authors Hess and Addison note that:

> The materials used by the Denver Public Schools teach educators that "the belief that there is such a thing as being objective," distinguishing between "good/bad" and "right/ wrong," and valuing an "emphasis on being polite" are all distinctive characteristics of white culture. The same is true of the "individualist" mindset that "if something is going to get done right, I have to do it." In Loudoun County, Virginia, one of the nation's wealthiest counties, the *Dismantling Racism Workbook* was used to train teachers this summer highlighted "15 Characteristics of White Supremacy Culture," including a weird admixture of positive and negative stereotypes, including "perfectionism," "progress is bigger, more," "right to comfort," and "defensiveness."[263]

This List does, indeed, appear in a manual called the *Dismantling Racism Workbook*, published by DR Works, a now-defunct organization based in Durham, North Carolina.[264]

This workbook surfaces again and again. The List is referenced at events, in documents, and on university campuses around the country. For instance, the University of Michigan boasts workshops and "antiracist" trainings that utilize the List.

---

263 Frederick M. Hess and J. Grant Addison, "Anti-racist Education is Neither," *The American Mind*, December 18, 2020 (American Enterprise Institute). https://americanmind.org/memo/anti-racist-education-is-neither/

264 The *Dismantling Racism* 2016 workbook can be found at: https://resourcegeneration.org/wp-content/uploads/2018/01/2016-dRworks-workbook.pdf

This resource guide highlights characteristics of white supremacy culture, as outlined by Dr. Tema Okun, that can be pervasive in organizations and institutions. White supremacy is made manifest in many ways, some being more covert than others. The characteristics identified in this resource guide can be rendered invisible due to how they become norms and standards in a variety of settings, academia included.[265]

Who generates this racialist material, where, and why? Is it the result of sophisticated theorizing? Did this White Supremacy Culture List emerge in the findings of an extensive, multi-year social science study?
Where did this List originate?[266]

Escaped from a Lab in Wuhan?

You can be forgiven if you believe that The List was generated from social science studies that utilized academic research methods to create knowledge, perhaps a survey that engaged feedback from thousands of subjects. Or perhaps you believe that this list of "white supremacy culture" emerged from a careful theoretical exposition hedged with the proper caveats and generated by university faculty with standing and a modicum of respect.

265 Frankie, "Identifying and Addressing Characteristics of White Supremacy Culture" University of Michigan, Equitable Teaching Site: https://sites.lsa.umich.edu/equitable-teaching/identifying-and-addressing-characteristics-of-white-supremacy-culture/
266 I've researched where the origins of this list might have been publicized previously, and I've found only three references. One is a piece by Rod Dreher in *The American Conservative* in July of 2020 and, oddly enough, a piece on a "Unitarian Universalist" website called *The Fifth Principle*. Similarly, an independently published book by Anne Schneider called *The Self-Confessed "White Supremacy Culture": The Emergence of an Illiberal Left in Unitarian Universalism*. (2019). If I have omitted mention of astute others, this is my apology.

But you already suspect that it was *none* of these things, don't you?

You've always thought it likely that the entire edifice of DEI is laid on a foundation of fakery and fiction, storytelling and superstition. Your suspicions have been substantially confirmed in previous chapters. Now, this "white supremacy culture" list, the product of "idea laundering," is one of the most egregious examples.

As with all racialist material that postures as "knowledge," the List is traceable to a relative handful of diversity hustlers of the critical race theory variety. The author of The List is Tema Okun,[267] a journeyman academic. Okun has been trading in the lucrative racialist workshop industry since at least the mid-1990s. From this point, I refer to this document as the "Okun List," after its author, a diversity peanut hustler for much of her career, who achieved a degree of notoriety in the 2000s based on her fabrication.

The Okun List is a group of prejudiced assertions that have nothing to do with so-called "white supremacy." It has been laundered thoroughly to give the appearance of a vetted and researched piece in the academic world. It is not academic scholarship. It has simply been assumed into the discourse about "racism."

It's an extreme example—perhaps *the* example—of the decisive assertion slowly climbing the ladder out of intellectual poverty to achieve a place in the academy to support diversity's Big Con.

---

267 Ms. Okun credits others with contributions, such as Kenneth Jones. Someone called Daniel Buford is responsible for certain terms, but the list was fabricated by Okun alone. Buford is a shadowy character. He is described this way by a group that interviewed him: "Reverend Buford is an artist, a minister, formerly at Allen Temple Baptist Church, a community organizer and a social justice activist." From: http://www.generationofoakland.com/reverend-daniel-a-buford/ An interview with Buford is available here as well.

The List Supports the Big Con

According to the diversity Con Story, a system of "White Supremacy" suffuses America's universities and is manifested in "rampant
racism" on the campuses. This system advantages white folk and
disadvantages persons of color in numerous overt and subtle ways.
But university types are generally skeptical, and with no real evidence to justify belief in this supposedly ubiquitous system, something was needed to clinch the deal. The Okun List was perfect to
the task. Here's why: It took a series of common perceptions and
behaviors and simply labeled them "white supremacy" behaviors.

The Okun List was drafted into service to support the Big
Con of virtuous victimhood. It had already gone through the
laundry process and was appearing in "workshop" materials and
was utilized by hundreds of diversity grifters.

The Okun List undergirds DEI, it is distributed nationwide
as "training" material, it is distributed on campus websites as an
"antiracist" resource, and it is propagated by hundreds of DEI
hustlers to explain racism in America. The Okun List is handed
out for DEI "training" at the University of Michigan, and it undergirds the Duke University School of Medicine "diversity" plan.[268]
It is used as the basis for a guide to "student affairs" university
employment for the American College Personnel Association
(ACPA), the principal non-profit "professional" group for "student
affairs" bureaucrats.[269] I've seen The List rolled out in university
workshops at my own institution, Drexel University; in summer

---

268 Mary E. Klotman, Dean, Duke University School of Medicine, "Dismantling
Racism and Advancing Equity, Diversity and Inclusion in the School of
Medicine," Duke University School of Medicine (June 2021): Linked at
Brutalminds.com https://brutalminds.com/?p=2722
269 Dr. Roshaunda Breeden (chair), ACPA Presidential Task Force on 21st Century
Employment in Higher Education, *Report on 21st Century Employment in
Higher Education*, ACPA-College Student Educators International, 2022.

of 2020, "Being Anti-racist" workshops were offered to the campus community and moderated by a dance therapist and a bureaucrat.[270]

And yet, Okun's imagination gave us a list of prejudice and opinion—what a disgruntled diversity worker didn't like after an unsuccessful session, who then jotted down her list of dislikes in a fit of anger.

This document is a racialist fabrication whose rise and durability in the public consciousness parallels that of the most influential, infamous, and perhaps nastiest forgery of the 20th century—*Protocols of the Learned Elders of Zion*.[271] The purpose of the original *Protocols* was to libel the Jewish people as participants in an international Jewish conspiracy to control the world. Forged by Czarist secret police in 1903, the *Protocols* has proven durable as part of the canon of fake conspiracies. The document served as justification worldwide for anti-Semitic pogroms, prejudice, and discrimination for many decades. It is astounding that the original *Protocols* still has influence in dark corners of the world today, even in the United States, as new generations of bigots embrace its racist message.

Now we have a new *Protocols*, one of the most ambitious and egregious fabrications in the history of the modern university, one that props up the Big Con of virtuous victimhood—the "White Supremacy Culture" list.

---

270 The Drexel College of Nursing and Health Professions sponsored these events. See: "Being Anti-Racist: Workshop – Characteristics and Antidotes of White Supremacist Culture," April 6, 2020 and July 7, 2020: https://www.youtube.com/watch?v=AwVoRwLhKH0 and https://www.youtube.com/watch?v=NffkLgD0_oM

271 Stephen Eric Bronner, *A Rumor about the Jews: Reflections on Antisemitism and the Protocols of the Learned Elders of Zion* (New York: St. Martin's Press, 2000).

The List appeared in Tema Okun's 2010 dissertation written for an obscure school of education program at the University of North Carolina-Greensboro. Her work itself is a parody of scholarship, one of the "navel-gazing" exercises we met in Chapter 4. It's a winding personal narrative of her days working with non-profits, variously called "Grassroots Leadership," "ChangeWork," and "DRWorks." Okun's dissertation is what is called, in the lingo, an "autoethnography" of herself as a workshop facilitator. Okun spins a tale of her time with off-campus non-profits and the people with whom she was consorting at the time. I link to it so that you can judge for yourself its quality.[272]

But the List itself went back even further. It first appeared a decade earlier in an article that Okun wrote for Change-Work in 1999.

Origin of the List

In the mid-1990s, Okun was a disaffected corporate trainer. One day, she returned home frustrated from a training session that did not go as she wanted.

In a fit of pique, Okun scribbled furiously a list of all those nettlesome things that she disliked about the people in her sessions, the people who resisted her message. She made up a list of 15 attitudes and behaviors she didn't like. She called this a "quick and dirty" listing and, for some unexplained reason, she called these behaviors a part of white supremacy culture that show up in organizations. Let Okun tell us in her own words.

---

272 https://libres.uncg.edu/ir/uncg/f/Okun_uncg_0154D_10299.pdf

Sometime in the mid 1990s, I arrived home after a particularly frustrating consultation with an organization I was working with at the time. In a flurry of exasperation, I sat down at my computer and typed, the words flowing of their own accord into a quick and dirty listing of some of the characteristics of white supremacy culture that show up in organizational behavior. The paper I wrote in such a frenzy on that afternoon so many years ago lists 15 behaviors, all of them interconnected and mutually reinforcing—perfectionism, a sense of urgency, defensiveness and/or denial, quantity over quality, worship of the written word, the belief in one "right" way, paternalism, either/or binary thinking, power hoarding, fear of open conflict, individualism, progress defined as more, the right to profit, objectivity, and the right to comfort.[273]

Okun just made it up. She fabricated a list of behaviors she didn't like and called it "white supremacy culture." I cannot emphasize this enough. In 2023, *The Intercept's* Ryan Grim interviewed Okun in the podcast *Deconstructed*. Okun reiterated the origin of the list as simply a product of her own musings.

I went to some kind of meeting and I don't remember any details of the meeting, but I went to a meeting and it was a very frustrating and horrible meeting. And I came home and I sat in front of the computer. And the article literally came through

---

273 Tema Jon Okun, *The Emperor has no Clothes: Teaching about Race and Racism to People Who Don't Want to Know*, Dissertation: 2010, University of North Carolina-Greensboro, p. 29.

me onto the computer. It was not researched. I didn't sit down and deliberate. It just came through me.[274]

Indeed, it was like magic. She wrote it down . . . then put it in an article . . . then put it in a workbook . . . then used the workbook as part of her dissertation . . . then published her dissertation as a book with an obscure independent publisher . . . and while she has since shown regret over the "misuse" of the list "out of context," many, many others have promulgated the Okun List ever since as authoritative. This is the classic example of Idea Laundering, without even the respectability of an "idea."

The Okun List went through the idea laundering process, and this is precisely how the List has climbed the ladder of faux respectability and entered the corpus of mainstream discourse.

Here is the process of Idea Laundering as it was applied to the Okun List:

Step One, Okun, an angry diversity worker, generates a "quick and dirty" list of behaviors she doesn't like in successful people.

Step Two: Okun includes this quick-and-dirty list on an "anti-racist" website, and she begins to market it. Others pick up the list and begin to publicize it.

Step Three: Okun enrolls in a middling PhD program in "education" at an obscure satellite campus of a state university system, that is, University of North Carolina – Greensboro.

---

274 Ryan Grim, "Tema Okun on her Mythical Paper on White Supremacy," *Disconnected* podcast, The Intercept, February 23, 2023: https://theintercept.com/2023/02/03/deconstructed-tema-okun-white-supremacy/

Step Four: Okun inserts her list into her "education" dissertation, which makes use of: "storytelling," "counternarrative," "autoethnography," "white supremacy," and such like.

Step Five: She then receives her doctorate from in the field of in 2010.

Step Six: Newly frocked "Doctor" Okun turns her dissertation into a book published by Information Age Publishing Inc. (IAP), a niche publisher founded in 1999 by George F. Johnson and located in Charlotte, North Carolina, just down the road from Greensboro.

Are you surprised that this is the origin of The List? Are you surprised that an angry diversity hustler called Tema Okun cobbled it into an article in 1999 and that it now appears nationwide in materials presented as fact to the nation's schoolchildren, the nation's teachers, the nation's corporations, and the nation's college students?

You likely think that this can't be so. This just is too simple and simple-minded to be true. Surely, someone with a modicum of intelligence and integrity must have questioned the incorporation of fakery into an education program? That a list of supposed "white supremacy behaviors" that is currently disseminated in American secondary schools, that is disseminated at the University of Michigan in DEI trainings, and informs a prominent medical school's "DEI plan," and was even featured on a Harvard website is simply a product of one disgruntled person's imagination?

But this is indeed the truth of the matter.

With perhaps millions of persons primed to confirm their

racialist inclinations, Okun gave them what they needed: a confirmation of a pseudocommunity of persecutors, an externalization of their failures, and an excuse not to engage in success behaviors. Not only was there now a pseudocommunity, but here was a description pin-pointing their villainous behaviors, so that you could identify the villains.

In exploring Okun's list of "white supremacy behaviors," we encounter the pathological preferences of a someone afraid that she cannot measure up in the workspace. Why can't she get people to believe her opinion on racial indignities in her workshops? Why does she encounter all of this resistance? Her own inadequacy is not a permissible explanation, nor is any critique of the doctrine itself. So, to rationalize the problem, she completely externalized it. She contrived her list to fit and explain her own lack of ability. Rather than examine her inadequate doctrine and her inadequate presentation skills, she externalized her frustration to appeal to others saddled with the same psychological malady.

It was "white supremacy."

It is here that we encounter the B-Player ethos. This is the manifestation of *virtuous victimhood* and the lament of grandiose paranoia with its externalization of blame. If you cannot measure up, blame "white supremacy." If you cannot meet objective standards, describe your "oppressors" as engaging in "white supremacy behaviors."

Are these behaviors denied to you? Of course not. You simply prefer to do something else.

In the pantheon of Okun's behavior list, she criticizes what she calls perfectionism. This is, of course, what others call "attention-to-detail" or "competence." It's the quality that reduces the chances of building a tourist submarine that *won't* implode in proximity to the sunken Titanic (with a nod to irony) submerged more than two miles down in the ocean. Who would subscribe to such a thing as a doctrine of "good enough," which appears to be the central message of the Okun List? Generally speaking, these are folks who want to half-step, folks who hope someone else can assist them in the "collective" effort. Folks who want to be relieved of the burden of meeting a deadline, of delivering quality work, of meeting high standards. The result of this B-player approach is exactly what you would expect, and we can call this the "tourist submarine" result.

And that's the ignominious origin story of the "White supremacy characteristics" fraud. It's a "quick and dirty list" of what a diversity trainer didn't like about the people in her workshop. Thus legitimized, the thoroughly laundered "White Supremacy Culture" list enters the mainstream wherever the checks are weak and wherever social justice warriors have a degree of control.

This is the Derrick Bell Method we met in the last chapter. Other prominent examples abound, the best-known Peggy McIntosh's "Invisible Knapsack" privilege list.

McIntosh Hits Privilege Paydirt

In terms of influence and dubious origins, the only fraud that comes close to the Okun List is Peggy McIntosh's "white privilege" trope that was popularized in her essay "The Invisible Knapsack."[275] McIntosh competes with Okun for the title of Most Magnificent Fraud in service to the Big Con of *virtuous victimhood*.

Similar to Okun, McIntosh simply scribbled out a List of her

---

275 https://www.nationalseedproject.org/key-seed-texts/white-privilege-unpacking-the-invisible-knapsack

own, this one a series of questions designed to reveal "privilege." As I have noted elsewhere, Peggy McIntosh was a comparative literature professor who specialized in the poetry of Emily Dickinson and who today bizarrely claims to be a "research scientist." Her 1989 knapsack piece offered her musings about her own ultra-parochial experiences as a college professor at a single-sex college, and she has made a luxurious living off her popularization of the magical concept of "white privilege." McIntosh has, in effect, laundered herself and her privilege "knapsack" into a kind of intellectual respectability.

McIntosh tapped into a well-established psychological phenomenon, namely that most people either want to confess or *must* confess to something. McIntosh gives them something with her brand of reflexive *J'accuse!*[276] The McIntosh method pioneered the introspective journalism of the "This I believe!" sort: "Hey, look what happened to me. Has it happened to you as well? *Bingo!*—we have a theory!"

Robin DiAngelo's shtick is similar, of course. *White Fragility* appeared in her 2004 dissertation as a toss-off line lifted from one of her advisors, but she later cobbled it into a lucrative consulting business.[277]

But in terms of sheer perniciousness, nothing matches the chutzpah of the Okun List. It is the Okun List that perpetuates the virtuous victimhood hoax in such insistent fashion that it

---

276 McIntosh has a literature PhD buttressed by her dissertation on the poetry of Emily Dickinson. In a bid for upscale borrowed prestige, McIntosh now bills herself as a "research scientist." See Wellesley Centers for Women website: https://www.wcwonline.org/Active-Researchers/peggy-mcintosh-phd
277 Journalist Matt Taibbi delivered what is perhaps most trenchant takedown of DiAngelo in his regular column. "DiAngelo isn't the first person to make a buck pushing tricked-up pseudointellectual horseshit as corporate wisdom, but she might be the first to do it selling Hitlerian race theory." Matt Taibbi, "On 'White Fragility,'" *Racket News*, June 28, 2020: https://www.racket.news/p/on-white-fragility

constitutes the lodestone of the diversity con and the yardstick by which all others are measured.

Conclusion

The stunning popularity of Okun's list shows the power of fiction over fact. Okun tapped into the power of pejorative prejudice and fabricated something that many people desperately wanted to hear. She tapped into so much of the pathology that gave rise to DEI.

Her list informs the grift of virtuous victimhood and it confirms the paranoia and narcissism of those easily manipulated, it identifies the paranoid "pseudocommunity of persecutors," and it offers itself in the form of a document with many of the trappings of academia.

This is the denigration of success behaviors by labeling them manifestations of so-called "whiteness." These are not "white supremacy" behaviors. These are A-Player behaviors. Thus, we find that according to the Okun List, race-neutral success behaviors are in fact open to anyone and yet are denigrated as "white" behavior.

From Tema Okun to Peggy McIntosh to Robin DiAngelo, race-baiting with an academic sheen has become widespread in the body politic. It's even acceptable in academia, at least for the moment.

This chapter has shown how the process of idea laundering has filled the diversity project with fraudulent content. The Okun List and the basket of fraudulent concepts that undergird the Big Con continue to have currency. The next chapter shows how the content is administered on the campuses to students, faculty, and staff by the DEI bureaucracy set up to do just that.

6
TRAINING PEOPLE INTO MENTAL ILLNESS

PATHOLOGIZING SUCCESS
AND EXALTING FAILURE

"There is the demand that one confess to crimes one has not committed, to sinfulness that is artificially induced, in the name of a cure that is arbitrarily imposed."[278]

— Robert J. Lifton, psychiatrist and author

Campus DEI training is a substantial part of the indulgence that universities pay to the diversity industry to absolve higher

---

278 Robert Jay Lifton, *Thought Reform and the Psychology of Totalism* (W. W. Norton & Company, Inc., 1961), p. 425.

education of its guilt for "crimes one has not committed, to sinfulness that is artificially induced, in the name of a cure that is arbitrarily imposed." This training is a major component of the Big Con of virtuous victimhood, and it constitutes victim/virtue-signaling, which is essential to maintain the central fiction of the Big Con. Universities invest heavily in DEI training—it gets them off the hook for their imaginary "rampant racism."

Exactly what do these DEI trainings hope to accomplish?

Trainings comprise a vague menu of aspirational outcomes involving "authentic selves" and such like. But we find that not only do DEI trainings *not* accomplish their stated goals, they exacerbate the very problems they are supposed to solve. In fact, they actually introduce racial animosity and divisiveness into the campus milieu. However one wants to measure the so-called racial climate on the campus, that climate deteriorates in the wake of DEI trainings.[279] The idea of unifying around shared values is abandoned in favor of a vague celebration of difference, and it turns out that no one bonds over difference.

Does DEI Training Work?

Studies show that DEI training achieves none of the stated goals. In fact, these training sessions do more harm than good. And whether they do *any* good is questionable. So, what is the impact of training? If we can say that the outcome is suboptimal, what exactly is the outcome of DEI training?

---

279 Ankita Jagdeep, Anisha Jagdeep, Simon Lazarus, Mendel Zecher, Ohad Fedida, Gidon Fihrer, Collin Vasko, Joel Finkelstein, Danit Sarah Finkelstein, Sonya Yanovsky, Lee Jussim, Pamela Paresky, Indu Viswanathan, *INSTRUCTING ANIMOSITY: HOW DEI PEDAGOGY PRODUCES THE HOSTILE ATTRIBUTION BIAS*, Network Contagion Research Institute, Rutgers University, November 2024, https://networkcontagion.us/reports/instructing-animosity-how-dei-pedagogy-produces-the-hostile-attribution-bias/

We can answer this in three ways. **First,** the outcome for *universities* in the public eye is a distorted notion of success—something is being done to resolve the rampant racism on campus and that gives college presidents a box to check. **Second,** for *DEI hustlers,* millions of dollars are extracted from the university as penance. **Third,** for the participants of trainings, the result is a divided campus with more suspicion, more anger, more distrust, more segregation, all of which justifies more trainings. And new cohorts of students graduate each year, ill-equipped to perform as adults in modern 21st-century society.

This chapter examines the sort of DEI training programs that emerge when paranoia and conspiracy theory go untreated and, in fact, serve as the basis to train others into behaviors associated with the mental illness of paranoia. The reality of this training is that it's a significant part of the payout of the grift.

DEI Training on the Campuses

DEI "training" is the vehicle whereby the college community is socialized into the Big Con of virtuous victimhood. It postures as "teaching about race" as it imposes the racialist orthodoxy of villains and victims and trains participants to fulfill their assigned roles as either persecutors or persecuted. This process masquerades as education, presenting unvetted, problematic material as settled fact.

As well, training has become the remedy of choice when a person in a university is accused of some affront.

These days of heightened sensibilities mean that increasing numbers of people on the campuses are choosing to be offended by most anything, from outright hate talk to the imaginary slights of "microaggressions." They dutifully report these transgressions on snitch lines set up just for them, and university "bias response teams" ensure that persons who are anonymously reported are investigated. Many universities opt to "re-train" persons as part of a menu of disciplinary measures.

It sounds reasonably good. As if the only reason that people act in ways that violate university policy is because of a lack of training. It's ludicrous when you think about it. Training is most often administered to students and faculty as part of the DEI indoctrination process. "Re-training" is provided to personnel who run afoul of university policies. It gives the appearance of doing something to remedy the situation and to get onlookers to move along quickly. Problem fixed.

But what does that "training" consist of? What's the content? Who runs it and decides what's included? The folks in charge hope you don't ask. This is because the DEI bureaucracy uses "training" to enforce the paranoid view of the world generally, and of the university especially.

Participants are divided into villains and victims and are given their assigned roles. White participants are assigned guilt for active complicity in a system of "white supremacy" on a campus that is "rampant" with racism. Black students, augmented by various persons of color as the moment demands, are assigned the role of victims and trained how to ferret out racial offenses where none exist and to engage in all of the characteristics of paranoia—narcissism, hyper-suspiciousness, grandiosity, conspiracism, delusional fixity, and acceptance of a pseudocommunity of persecutors.

The conspiracy emerges from the tendency of its hyper-fearful "victims" to see exactly what they want to see in the world, and to discount everything else. Not only are paranoiacs attracted to the training, they find their fears amplified and given credence in these artificial communities of paranoia.

Anti-Racist Task Forces precede the "Training" Boom

Convinced that racism is rampant on the campuses and equally convinced that "white supremacy" permeates the personnel, policies, and procedures, and programs of the institution, university administrations began in 2020 to ratchet up their investment in diversity, equity, and inclusion. To justify major expenditures and policy changes, college presidents established "antiracism task forces" to examine the problem and, indeed, to confirm what was already assumed—that there was a serious racism problem on the campus, and that the diversity industry was needed to fix it.

The go-to instrument for the opportunist college president is the creation of the task force. When a president wants to do something, either to appear concerned or to rubber-stamp something he has in mind, he reflexively appoints a curated task force or hires a consulting firm. This provides breathing space for the administration, gives the appearance of activity, and empowers the president to obtain a rubber-stamp for what he or she wanted to do from the beginning **while simultaneously abdicating personal responsibility.**

With violence roiling the nation's cities in the summer of 2020, the last thing university presidents wanted was unrest coming to the campuses on *their* watch. And so they made common cause with activist faculty and staff to *do something*. Or at least give the appearance of doing something during the nation's so-called "racial reckoning." These task forces sprouted at universities like kudzu—at Kent State, at Williams College, at Villanova, at Indiana, at Michigan, at Drexel, at the campuses of CUNY, and at the med schools of Penn, Yale, and Duke. And so on.

By 2021, the many task forces assembled by the nation's university presidents yielded a trove of diversity and strategic plans that constitute their own genre of literature. While serving as window-dressing for skittish presidents driven to do something, these task forces—without exception—became instruments for activists keen on amassing power, privilege, and personnel in the "diversity" bureaucracy of the university. In this case, presidents appointed task forces to study a "problem" that they refused to define and that they only dimly understood.

Predictably, the task forces found "racism" on their own campuses, because that's what they were tasked to find, of course. In this, they were utterly essential to the Play of the Big Con. They would provide the justification to leverage hundreds of millions of dollars to combat the phantasm of racism.

The racism invariably was "rampant" and begged solution. The task forces gave sweeping recommendations that they knew beforehand they would deliver, which included more power, personnel, and money for new DEI bureaucracies, all covered with façade of the task force.

And if there was a strange familiarity to the dull cadence of rhetoric and its bombastic pronouncements, the reason was clear. As social critic Christopher Rufo put it:

The elements of critical race theory are, in fact, a near-perfect transposition of race onto the basic structures of Marxist theory. "White supremacy" replaces "capitalism" as the totalizing system. "White and black" replaces "bourgeoisie and proletariat" as the "oppressor and oppressed." "Abolition" replaces "revolution" as the method of "liberation."[280]

This was Marxism retooled into a binary racialism, and it was the wedge issue that would pry open the door to the universities for DEI hustlers to seize the bureaucracy. Higher education seemed ready for sackcloth and ashes, and many were ready to believe the Big Con.

It was the perfect storm of willing suckers, combined with skilled con artists ready to dupe them. Obscure hustlers like Robin DiAngelo were thrust into the limelight with reading groups parsing the meaning of her screed *White Fragility*. The modestly gifted scholar Ibram Kendi found himself sanctified as the avatar of "antiracism."

A Time for Mediocre Bureaucrats to Shine

The revenue potential was enormous, and any grifter worth the label could see the opportunity. An entire new bureaucracy would be established, and an essential function of the new DEI offices would be the inculcation of the students, faculty, and staff in the orthodoxy of diversity that had heretofore existed on the margins of intellectually respectable society.

---

280 Christopher F. Rufo, *America's Cultural Revolution: How the Radical Left Conquered Everything* (New York: Broadside Books, 2023), p. 234.

With the new receptivity to the Con Story of rampant racism, DEI would have pride of place on the campuses. Suddenly, diversity, equity, and inclusion would mysteriously find its way into university mission statements without discussion or approval, would become the focus of unspecified training by dubious instructors, and would be encouraged into course content at every turn.

DEI training has several functions. In the successful con of virtuous victimhood, it extracts resources from the university in the form of payments to bureaucrats and to an endless parade of outside consultants and speakers to headline seminars and "antiracist" forums. It transmits the unhealthy orthodoxy of villain/victim in each new cohort of students who pass through the university. It recruits believers into the paranoid binary of the pseudocommunity of persecutors and those who are persecuted. It maintains the fiction of a university community guilty of institutional racial oppression, white supremacy culture, and "rampant racism."

In this way, the so-called racial climate is roiled constantly to perpetuate the very problem that these "diversity experts" are hired to fix.

> [R]ecent years have seen a proliferation of high-level administrators given the task of instituting what amounts to a "shadow curriculum" of student and faculty training, the content of which is the explicit transmission and enforcement of controversial political views about race, gender, sexuality, and power. Even more unsettling has been the cloud of unknowing that has descended over the political imperatives governing faculty and administrative hiring practices.[281]

---

281 Michael W. Clune, "We Asked for it: The politicization of research, hiring, and teaching made professors sitting ducks," *The Chronicle of Higher Education*, November 18, 2024: "https://www.chronicle.com/article/we-asked-for-it

While it may strain credulity, we have already seen how DEI training programs for students, faculty, and staff are animated by paranoia and conspiracy. The entire point of these trainings is to divide the participants into clearly delineated villains and victims. Moreover, they would prefer that you not notice that the material in trainings is carefully curated to include racialist claptrap masquerading as accepted truth.

With respect to DEI, both trainers and the training sessions propagate fabrications, distortions, and absurdities as social reality. They offer problematic assertions accepted as uncontroversial facts. Much of the material used in DEI training is sourced from the racialist hoax literature created for the purpose. Moreover, the material is typically presented in activities designed overtly as thought reform sessions.[282] An egregious example is the work of Diane Goodman.

Goodman is a long-time diversity peanut grifter who describes herself in the usual fashion, as "an educator and consultant on diversity, equity, inclusion, and social justice issues for over three decades." Her major solo work tips us off that she is a racialist who targets certain folks; it is presumptuously titled *Promoting Diversity and Social Justice: Educating People from Privileged Groups.* She is well-traveled on the diversity conference circuit, offering "institutes and sessions at NCORE (National Conference on Racial and Ethnic Diversity in Higher Education), Teachers College Roundtable on Multicultural Psychology and Education, The White Privilege Conference, The Diversity Challenge"

---

282 Among many others, see Maurianne Adams, "Pedagogical Frameworks for Social Justice Education," in Maurianne Adams, Lee Anne Bell, and Pat Griffin, *Teaching for Diversity and Social Justice* (New York: Routledge, 1997), p. 31. See also Katharina Von Kellenbach and Matthias Buschmeier (eds), *Guilt: A Force of Cultural Transformation* (New York: Oxford University Press, 2022). See Diane J. Goodman, *Promoting Diversity and Social Justice: Educating People from Privileged Groups* (New York: Routledge, 2011).

and others.[283] She has signed-on to the author consortium that produces the brainwash manual called *Teaching for Diversity and Social Justice*, which explicitly utilizes the quasi-legal thought reform techniques employed in authoritarian societies worldwide, particularly in today's Communist China.[284]

As noted, much of DEI "training" is designed around psychological experimentation on participants, who rarely—if ever—are provided the opportunity to provide informed consent. Much of this training would not survive scrutiny from the requisite institutional review board as these training sessions routinely violate federal prohibitions against human subject experiments. In much of this, we see a clear disconnect from reality and an irresponsibility by those who run these thought reform sessions, particularly those sessions that involve attacks on student psyches.

All of this is done for a reason, and the major reason is that it's profitable. Diversity grifters often move seamlessly from their private consultancies to the campuses and back again. The payoff for all of this can be fabulous, and central to all of it is the virtuous victimhood Con Story of DEI, with its bombastic victim-signaling designed to shakedown universities for cash.

These are characteristics of what has become known as "Victimhood Culture."[285] Artists of the Big Con and many hundreds of peanut grifters alike use *victim-signaling* to bring in the revenue. Such a culture renders it financially and psychologically advantageous to announce victim status publicly. The entire logic of DEI's

283 Diane Goodman Consulting: Diversity, Inclusion, Equity, Social Justice: https://dianegoodman.com/bio/
284 For a complete dismantling of this brainwash manual, see Stanley K. Ridgley, *BRUTAL MINDS: The Dark World of Left-wing Brainwashing in Our Universities* (New York: Humanix, 2024), pp. 20-40.
285 Bradley Campbell and Jason Manning, *The Rise of Victimhood Culture* (New York: Palgrave Macmillan, 2018).

Big Con is built on this idea of virtuous victimhood. 1) Claiming victim status for profit and payouts (a version of the "protection racket") and 2) asserting *moral immunity* to justify use of "deceit, intimidation, or violence" to receive that payout.

You likely believe that no reasonable person would submit willingly to programs like these, and you'd be correct. This is why these "trainings" are 1) misrepresented to the audiences, 2) utilize deception in the same way that cults utilize deception in recruiting activities, 3) present problematic and outright false material as fact ("white supremacy culture" list), and 4) use coercive psychological techniques to deal with especially troublesome resistors. Says Christopher Rufo:

> They designed their programs to appear neutral while, in reality, they exist to promote left-wing orthodoxy, suppress dissent through the punishment of supposed "bias" crimes, and harness the university to a campaign of social activism.[286]

The Origins of DEI Training

One of the best accounts of the origins of DEI training is provided by Christian Parenti, whose research uncovered the source of one of DEI's most infamous training games. This is the *Privilege Walk*, a short-con designed to dupe students and other participants into revealing personal, sensitive information. In many ways, it is this *Privilege Walk* that exemplifies the interrogatory and accusatory nature of so-called "diversity."

---

286 Christopher F. Rufo, *America's Cultural Revolution*, p. 47-48.

Typically, the Walk's origin is ascribed to Peggy McIntosh sometime in the 1990s. McIntosh, a feminist, anti-racism trainer, and Senior Research Scientist at the Wellesley Centers for Women, is famous for describing "white privilege" as an "invisible knapsack." However, as McIntosh told me in an email: "I did not invent the exercises you refer to and in fact I urge people not to undertake such exercises. They are too simple for complex experiences relating to power and privilege. I don't know where they originated. They seem to answer a craving for instant One-size-fits-all awakenings. I think they are counterproductive."[287]

It was actually the widow of the Frankfurt School neo-Marxist Herbert Marcuse who designed and applied the first privilege walk. Erica Sherover-Marcuse is not a household name, even to those invested in the DEI project, but she was a pioneer in DEI training and developed training programs that became the prototype of the programs we see today:

> In the 1980s, Sherover-Marcuse led workshops on "institution-alized racism," "internalized oppression," and "being an effective ally," and invented the now-famous "privilege walk" exercise, in which participants sort themselves into an oppression hierarchy, then atone for their racial, sexual, and economic privilege.[288]

The privilege walk is typical of the games utilized in DEI trainings that are conducted by undistinguished student affairs

---

287 Christian Parenti, "The First Privilege Walk," nonsite.org, November 18, 2021: https://nonsite.org/the-first-privilege-walk/
288 Christopher F. Rufo, *America's Cultural Revolution: How the Radical Left Conquered Everything* (New York: Broadside Books, 2023), p. 46-47.

personnel. The games are not competitive exercises to the purpose of fun. They are all camouflaged interrogation activities that are designed to elicit information from the participants in a carefully constructed atmosphere of "trust." They are, essentially, short-cons, and the folks who run them are peanut hustlers. For example, here's how the "privilege walk" unfolds.

The privilege walk positions students in a horizontal line (holding hands), and they are told to remain silent. The facilitator then asks a series of curated personal questions. According to each student's answer, the student takes a step forward or a step back. The final result is a visual depiction of students categorized by their answers and designed to illustrate the false premise of "privilege." Also, DEI trainers extract private, often sensitive, information from students. This helps them construct the villains/victims paradigm that is crucial to the Big Con. Unknowing students, usually naïve freshmen, have fallen for the short-con interrogation. They have unwittingly revealed a raft of information to a hostile diversity hustler, whose purpose is to train the students into the roles of oppressors and oppressed.

DEI training has an extensive menu of "games" that are employed on students.[289] While the training sessions also are inflicted on faculty and staff, I refer here primarily to students as they constitute the majority of participants. These games are all examples of peanut hustles. Each follows the formula for a short-con. The peanut hustler—or facilitator—offers a scenario that 1) creates the perception of a benign situation, 2) gains the trust of the mark(s), 3) gets voluntary buy-in to the activity, 4) elicits the

---

289 Privilege Walk, Fishbowl, Racial Inventory, Role Play / Role Reversal, Starpower, Blindfold Exercise, and many others. See "Engagement Games" at *What's Race got to do with it? Social Disparities and Student Success*, http:// www.whatsrace.org/pages/games-pf.html

desired psychological effect(s),[290] 5) extracts the desired private information, 5) closes with a recapitulation of the lesson.

The privilege hustle amplifies the virtuous victimhood message of oppressors and oppressed. Says one progressive critic of the privilege walk:

> [P]rivilege walks quite literally create a divide in the room and in the group. This divide can in turn generate a sense of us vs. them and an accompanying we-could-never-understand-each-other's-experiences-feeling. ... Us vs. them mentality has been used to continue to justify and perpetuate injustices.[291]

The privilege walk is just one of the many and varied short-con games, and the hustles are even ranked according to their "risk."[292]

While this short-con tactic of "games" is reliable for the most part, additional leverage is often needed for resistant audiences. And thus it is that DEI programs are run in the same way that

---

290 This is a key problem with the "games" approach in that it violates federal regulations against human subject experimentation. Powerful emotions can be provoked in these games. Here's one testimonial: "It felt awful. I felt guilty and shameful every time I took a step forward, it was powerful . . . . Shame can be incredibly corrosive and often stops us from seeking out more information or believing that we can change. Shame makes us feel like bad people, not people who are part of bad systems." Meg Bolger, "Why I don't facilitate Privilege Walks anymore and what I do instead," Medium, February 16, 2018: https://medium.com/@MegB/why-i-dont-won-t-facilitate-privilege-walks-anymore-and-what-i-do-instead-380c95490e10

291 Meg Bolger, "Why I don't facilitate Privilege Walks anymore and what I do instead," Medium, February 16, 2018: https://medium.com/@MegB/why-i-dont-won-t-facilitate-privilege-walks-anymore-and-what-i-do-instead-380c95490e10

292 The games are actually grouped into risk categories: Low Risk, Medium Risk, High Risk. See "Engagement Games" at *What's Race got to do with it? Social Disparities and Student Success*, http://www.whatsrace.org/pages/games-pf.html You can get a sense of the scope of the problem by doing a google search of "Diversity Training Games," which turns up hundreds of listings in the diversity industry of "consultants."

any authoritarian governing body must run the messaging of its orthodoxy, when the vast majority of people recognize it as a lie.

Trainings in Paranoia and Conspiracy

The diversity industry accelerated its penetration of the campuses in 2020, and problems began almost immediately. When universities turn over substantial power to DEI bureaucracies dominated by racialist ideologues who advocate a primitive ideology, the result is not difficult to predict and should not be surprising when it comes to pass. A research group at Rutgers University studied the major themes in DEI "oppressive rhetoric" workshops informed by the works of Ibram X. Kendi and Robin DiAngelo. The results were stark.

> Some DEI programs not only fail to achieve their goals but can actively undermine diversity efforts. Specifically, mandatory trainings that focus on particular target groups can foster discomfort and perceptions of unfairness. DEI initiatives seen as affirmative action rather than business strategy can provoke backlash, increasing rather than reducing racial resentment. And diversity initiatives aimed at managing bias can fail, sometimes resulting in decreased representation and triggering negativity among employees. In other words, some DEI programs appear to backfire.[293]

With the content of trainings consisting of "anti-oppressive" material drawn from the reservoir of hoax literature generated

---

293 Ankita Jagdeep, et al, *INSTRUCTING ANIMOSITY: HOW DEI PEDAGOGY PRODUCES THE HOSTILE ATTRIBUTION BIAS*, p. 2.

in the cargo cult complex of racialism, the Rutgers group found that DEI training *increased* racial animosity significantly. The study showed that DEI trainings can "exacerbate intergroup and interpersonal conflicts" and they can "increase hostility towards members of groups labeled as oppressors,"[294] a reaction called *hostile attribution bias*: "Instead of reducing bias, they engendered a hostile attribution bias, amplifying perceptions of prejudicial hostility where none was present, and punitive responses to the imaginary prejudice."[295]

Moreover, the study identified the dynamic put in play by training and shows how the training succeeds in maintaining the problem that DEI was supposed to solve.

1. **Anti-Oppressive Intervention**: DEI training rooted in anti-oppressive rhetoric introduces narratives that lead people to assume that certain groups are inherent oppressors and others as inherent victims.

2. **Increased Racial Suspicion**: Exposure leads to hostile attribution bias, causing participants to see discrimination when there is no evidence that discrimination has occurred, driving racial prejudice, intergroup hostility, suspicion and division.

3. **Authoritarian Policing**: This heightened suspicion triggers authoritarian policing tendencies, leading

---

294 Ankita Jagdeep, et al, *INSTRUCTING ANIMOSITY: HOW DEI PEDAGOGY PRODUCES THE HOSTILE ATTRIBUTION BIAS*, p. 2.
295 James Epps, Phillip C. Kendall, "Hostile attributional bias in adults," *Cognitive Therapy and Research*, Vol. 19, No. 2, 1995.

people to endorse surveillance and purity testing, strict social controls, and escalating responses from corrective to coercive.

4. **Punitive Retribution**: Participants show greater support for extreme punitive measures against perceived oppressors as well as those seen as ideologically impure.

5. **Calls for More Interventions**: The heightened punitive atmosphere feeds back into demands for more anti-oppressive DEI training, creating a self-reinforcing cycle of suspicion and intolerance.[296]

This finding is consistent with this book's contention that DEI trainings recruit students into the scripted villain and victim roles, which then perpetuates the perception of "rampant racism" on the campus and, thus, the "need" for more DEI training, more DEI personnel, more funding. The Big Con reproduces the conditions for its continuation, and the money flows.

Even the nation's military academies are not exempt from the predations of DEI "trainings" or the creation of lumbering bureaucracies to implement policies. A year-long study by the Center for American Institutions at Arizona State University concluded that:

> The massive DEI bureaucracy, its training and its pseudo-scientific assessments are at best distractions that absorb valuable time and resources. At worst they communicate the

---

296 Ankita Jagdeep, et al, *INSTRUCTING ANIMOSITY: HOW DEI PEDAGOGY PRODUCES THE HOSTILE ATTRIBUTION BIAS*, p. 14-15.

opposite of the military ethos: e.g. that individual demographic differences come before team and mission.[297]

DEI programs are part of an extensive shadow curriculum run by student affairs.[298] This operation is called the "co-curriculum," it exists on campuses nationwide, and it has become the primary vehicle for leftist ideological indoctrination. This is a network of seminars, orientations, caucuses, residential life programs that showcase various short-con games that contribute to the central Big Con of virtuous victimhood. These short-cons are run primarily by peanut hustlers—various clerks, enrollment managers, advisors, residence hall staff, and off-campus consultants. DEI's racialist offerings include "difficult dialogues," "courageous conversations," "racial caucuses," "brave spaces," and such like.

I have written extensively about this pernicious shadow curriculum.[299] Others have as well. In a piece on the shadow curriculum that appeared in the October 2021 issue of the *Chronicle of Higher Education*, Professors Elizabeth Corey and Jeffrey Polet observed:

> As nearly every professor knows, when it comes to campus "trainings," there is often no dialogue and no room for dispute .... People with limited academic qualifications are "training" faculty members to develop skills tangential to the

297 Paula Baker, Matt Lohmeier, Karrin Taylor Robson, and John Cauthen, *Civic Education in the Military: Are Servicemembers More Prepared for Micro-Aggression or Macro-Aggression?* The Center for American Institutions, Arizona State University, June 2024: https://cai.asu.edu/civiceducation
298 Martha McCaughey and Scott Welsh, "The Shadow Curriculum of Student Affairs," AAUP website, October 2021. The original article was removed from the AAUP website without explanation, but a screen capture appears here: https://brutalminds.com/?p=3013
299 Stanley K. Ridgley, *BRUTAL MINDS: The Dark World of Leftist Brainwashing in our Universities* (New York: Humanix, 2023), p. 89-105.

academic enterprise, and to pursue ends about which faculty members have no say . . . . Given that many faculty members know the training sessions do not satisfy the conditions of social science or academic integrity, they often merely go through the motions. This pro forma activity wastes countless hours and millions of dollars.[300]

Additionally, Professors Martha McCaughey and Scott Welsh note that these trainers "cross a line when they start to confuse their essential support for the educational, disciplinary mission of the institution for which they work with pursuing a separate, social, moral, or political mission to be carried out within colleges and universities."[301]

In spite of obvious shortcomings and a growing pushback, the DEI bureaucracy stumbles forward in lockstep with the ancillary support staff of student affairs, their message unchanged. This is why the absolution promised by DEI to a guilty university was bound to trigger a reaction. It was predicated on a theory so divorced from reality that it could not be administered without the coercive elements characteristic of totalitarian regimes. And the folks concerned seemed oblivious to this point.

But not everyone is blinded by the chimera of "social justice."

---

300 Elizabeth Corey and Jeffrey Polet, "Indoctrination Sessions have no place in the Academy: For Educators, nothing is self-evident; for Trainers, everything is," *The Chronicle of Higher Education*, October 5, 2021: https://www.chronicle.com/article/indoctrination-sessions-have-no-place-in-the-academy

301 Martha McCaughey and Scott Welsh, "Performing versus Supporting the Educational Mission of Colleges and Universities," Academe Blog: the blog of Academe Magazine, AAUP, November 4, 2021: https://academeblog.org/2021/11/04/performing-versus-supporting-the-educational-mission-of-colleges-and-universities/

DEI Functionaries: *Totalitarians of a Different Sort*

I have found that emigres from Eastern Europe are typically more astute on the subtleties of authoritarian rule. Those who have lived under a totalitarian regime—men such as the Polish intellectual Michal Glowinski—recognize the familiar contours of ideological indoctrination in the universities. In an eerily accurate presaging of college DEI training, Glowinski provides a five-stage model of the DEI training process.

Except that Glowinski doesn't actually deal with DEI.

Instead, he provides the stages and characteristics of how any totalitarian regime treats its citizens to ensure compliance with doctrine. The doctrine of campus DEI is a form of totalitarian discourse. Another way of putting it is "dictator talk." This sort of dictator rhetoric animates DEI training. In the following schema provided by Glowinski, the word totalitarian has been replaced by **diversity**, with sobering results.

1. In **diversity** discourse, persuasive elements are limited, since the point is not to convince the audience, but rather to impose certain views and ways of seeing the world upon them, providing guidelines on how they should think and behave. Persuasion requires argument, while **diversity** speech in its deepest sense conveys what is conceived as a command. Its recipients—both individual and collective—must treat it as such. … [T]hey are quietly and obediently to accept what the discourse serves up to them.

2. In **diversity** discourse, we find a peculiar construction
   of the speaking subject . . . . who is essentially not an
   individual, but rather the depository of "correctness."
   This is the case both when the speaker can arbitrarily
   impose his opinions, while excluding in advance any
   criticism. When the speaker is an insignificant member
   of the rank and file, then his or her task is merely
   to repeat whatever belongs to the official canon at a
   given moment.

3. For **diversity** discourse, unusually clear and
   dichotomous divisions are of fundamental significance,
   treated as absolute and indisputable. Any questioning of
   these divisions would be tantamount to casting doubt on
   the general principles of the discourse. In fact, the most
   important element is the very sharpness of the divisions.

4. The next feature of **diversity** discourse is linked with
   the clarity of the simplest dichotomous divisions.
   One-dimensional value judgments always predominate.
   They are formed in such a way as to be indisputable
   and to exclude any other axiological forms in advance.
   Diversity discourse imposes on the audience a certain
   system of values. Indeed, this is one of its most
   important distinguishing features. . . . One-dimensional
   value judgments permeate everything that appears
   within **diversity** discourse.

5. **Diversity** discourse constructs a certain vision of the world . . . . The vision is constructed as if it revealed certain features of the world that are inaccessible to the uninitiated or superficial glance. Specifically, it reveals how things really are, who is whom, who wants what, who stands behind whom, who is dangerous and hostile. We might say that this discourse—characterized by indisputable "correctness" and authority—forms a conspiracist vision of the world, often irrespective of its genuine subject.[302]

This is the template for training any authoritarian ideology, such as Marxism, communism, or Maoism, or the type found in extremist religious cults. The implication is obvious. DEI training methods are straight out of the totalitarian playbook. This is the template for DEI training on the nation's college campuses, which universities have purchased as their antiracist absolution.

I have provided a copy of Michael Glowinski's template of DEI training on a website, suitable for downloading and distribution to college students, faculty, alumni, and donors to the university.[303]

College DEI Training Workshop

What kinds of training does your university run under the rubric of DEI? What sorts of trainers show up at the front of the room to posture as fake faculty? How can you gauge what's going on?

302 Michal Glowinski, *Totalitarian Speech*. Stanley Bill (trans.) (Frankfurt am Main: Peter Lang, 2014), p. 97-99.
303 Stanley K. Ridgley, "What to Expect in 'Diversity' Training Programs," Brutalminds.com, December 21, 2024: https://brutalminds.com/?p=3023

Recognize that none of it is spontaneous—they have an indoctrination plan for you in mind, and here I provide the warning signs, which begin with an initial vagueness and a generalized solicitation for "trust." This plea for trust is, in fact, the tactic of every successful cult recruitment campaign. Is your college or university running "workshops" that exhibit any of the following characteristics? Let's run down the list.

1. The workshop is sponsored by your office of "student life" or "diversity and inclusion" (that is to say, by administrators, clerks from "student life," and *not* faculty; a "Chief Diversity Officer" is typically involved).[304]

2. The workshop is advertised as "antiracist training" or "antiracist pedagogy" absent explicit description of what "racism" problem exists on the campus and who, exactly, are the supposed racists (this attack occurs in the workshops themselves).

3. The workshop is advertised as designed to educate the community on "systemic racism" or "institutional racism," without identifying how these concepts apply to your school, either whole or in part (again, this attack occurs in the workshops).

---

304 Investigate the backgrounds of the sponsors of the event on your campus and you invariably discover that they are middling bureaucrats with master's level degrees in subjects like "counseling," "education," "student affairs," and such like. If actual faculty are involved, they are typically drawn from the academic discourse communities of education, "public" sociology, and many from the liberal arts.

4. The workshop facilitators may be outsiders with suspect academic credentials (of a magic healing crystals sort) or wholly unmatched to the topic.[305]

5. The workshop materials are provided by un-vetted outside non-profit organizations that embrace a particular problematic ideology.

6. The workshop offers program(s) with benign-sounding names, such as "learning about race," "racial caucuses," "difficult dialogues," "courageous conversations," "intergroup dialogues."

7. The facilitator urges students to "trust" each other, to "make yourself vulnerable," to feel comfortable enough to "disclose" personal information.[306]

8. The actual workshop content is informed by material from fringe academic discourse communities, such as "critical whiteness studies," "critical race theory," "critical pedagogy," or "antiracist pedagogy," which are well-known examples of paranoiac pseudo-scholarship of the DEI doctrine.

---

305 See, for instance, the workshopper Shakti Butler, whose PhD is from the "California Institute of Integral Studies in the School of Transformative Learning and Change."

306 Maurianne Adams, "Pedagogical Frameworks for Social Justice Education," in Maurianne Adams, Lee Anne Bell, Pat Griffin, *Teaching for Diversity and Social Justice* (New York: Routledge, 1997).

9. The workshop content makes declarations about entire races and then attributes to individual students or faculty these group racial characteristics, *irrespective of individual histories* (this is called the fallacy of division).

10. The workshop content features no actual dialogue and instead looks, sounds, and feels like a race-based attack on persons of a particular target race. The facilitator will likely establish what they call "ground rules" for discussion, which means that no disagreement with the central message is tolerated. "We don't want your opinion," is how DEI trainers phrase it.[307]

11. The actual workshop content declares that *all* white students, faculty, and administrators are racist and are oppressors who are complicit in supporting institutional racism or systemic racism. In the vernacular, this is called race-baiting. The words "guilty" and "complicit" appear frequently.[308]

12. The actual workshop offers a primitive binary worldview in which all people are either allies or enemies. To

---

307 Robin DiAngelo and Ozlem Sensoy, "We don't want your opinion: Knowledge Construction and the Discourse of Opinion in the Equity Classroom," *EQUITY & EXCELLENCE IN EDUCATION, 42*(4), 2009.

308 "Complicity" is a useful trope for those engaged in extracting the "white confession." For how this trope is employed, see the work of Barbara Applebaum, a professor at the Syracuse University School of Education. Barbara Applebaum, "Social Justice Education, Moral Agency, and the Subject of Resistance," *Educational Theory*, Volume 54, Number 1, 2004.

cushion this, often only "ally" is used, leaving you to fill in the blank with "enemy."[309]

13. The actual workshop declares that white students must "do the work" necessary to achieve what is sometimes called "critical consciousness," the definition of which is simply agreement with the ideology on offer ("the work" and "do the work" are favorite rhetorical tropes of DEI).[310]

14. "The work" described in the workshop consists of imposing a psychological transformation process onto students, staff, and faculty to adopt the DEI orthodoxy, usually in stages or a step-wise fashion, moving along a "moving walkway."[311] This is sometimes called "racial identity development" and presented as a settled concept.[312]

---

309 Allan C. Mathew, Stephen N. Risdon, Allison Ash, Jason Cha, and Alexander Jun, "The Complexity of Working with White Racial Allies: Challenges for Diversity Educators of Color in Higher Education," *Journal of Diversity in Higher Education*, Vol. 16, no. 1 (2023).

310 For the "do the work" mantra, see Christine Clark, Kenneth J. Fasching-Varner, and Mark Brimhall-Vargas (eds.), "Occupying Academia, Reaffirming Diversity," in *Occupying the Academy* (Lanham: Rowman & Littlefield, 2012), pp. 1-19; and Layla F. Saad, *Me and White Supremacy* (Naperville,Il: Sourcebooks, 2020).

311 "I sometimes visualize the ongoing cycle of racism as a moving walkway at the airport," said the influential critical racialist Beverly Daniel Tatum, whose book of "conversations about race" set the tone for much of the intervening 25 years: Beverly Daniel Tatum, *"Why are all the Black Kids sitting together in the Cafeteria?"* (New York: Basic Books, 1997, 1999), p. 11. The conveyer belt metaphor is embraced by many critical racialists and has its counterpart in Chinese Communist thought reform. See "The Lenient Policy," Appendix 1 in Edgar Schein, *Coercive Persuasion: A Socio-psychological Analysis of the "Brainwashing" of American Civilian Prisoners by the Chinese Communists* (New York: W. W. Norton & Company, Inc., 1961, 1971), p. 287-288.

312 See Janet E. Helms, *Black and White Racial Identity* (Westport: Praeger, 1990).

15. At some point, a "confession" is required of the white workshop participant regarding his or her "privilege" and, perhaps, a demand that the student confess "guilt" and "complicity" in "institutional racism" and, in more extreme versions, complicity in supporting white supremacy.[313]

16. An announced goal is to transform the white subjects into what the ideology calls "allies," which means a full acceptance of the paranoiac racialist ideology. If full acceptance is not given, the student is or can be denounced as racist.[314]

17. The workshop activities end with a call for a continued activism to "do the work" to proselytize the ideology to other white people and to act in ways to further "social justice." [315]

Remember that this activity is conducted almost exclusively by non-faculty, usually DEI personnel augmented by the ancillary staffers of student affairs. This type of "workshop" is, in fact, anathema to the entire enterprise of the university.

---

313 Ricky Lee Allen, "Whiteness and Critical Pedagogy," *Educational Philosophy and Theory*, Vol. 35, No. 2, 2004, 129-130.

314 This type of denunciation is typical in the current Peggy McIntosh workshop.

315 [I]t begins with getting honest with yourself, getting educated, becoming more conscious about what is really going on (and how you are complicit in it), and getting uncomfortable as you question your core paradigms about race. If you are willing to do that, and if we are all committed to **doing the work** that is ours to do, we have a chance of creating a world and way of living that are closer to what we all desire for ourselves and one another [bolding added]. Layla F. Saad, *Me and White Supremacy* (Naperville, Il: Sourcebooks, 2020), p. 5.

Faculty worthy of their privileged positions do not abuse the trust students place in them. We resist the temptation to collect disciples, encourage cults of personality, recruit agents for ideological missions, or teach a political agenda as a settled truth. More than providing answers, we teach students how to form and pursue questions. This is because faculty members, situated as we are within disciplines, are keenly aware of the constantly shifting state of what we colloquially refer to as knowledge . . . . Faculty members help students develop intellectual abilities, not a particular political ideology.[316]

The foregoing list of workshop characteristics exemplifies the rogue mission of malefactors in the university, which is more indoctrination than anything else. It's certainly not education. If a university imposes anything akin to the racialist ideology described in the above list of workshop characteristics, then students, faculty, and staff who have been subjected to this material and the coercive techniques of "thought reform" have a valid complaint to the school's respective Office of Diversity (or similarly named office) and a complaint to the Institutional Review Board (IRB) of the institution. Legal action could well be successful if the university does not grant relief. These types of activity fall under the anti-discrimination policies of many, if not most, universities today. This gives rise to the odd possibility that the student facing harassment must report the violation to the university office that is guilty of the violation.

---

316 Martha McCaughey and Scott Welsh, "The Shadow Curriculum of Student Affairs," *Academe* (AAUP), October 2021: https://brutalminds.com/?p=3013

Conclusion

This chapter has demonstrated that DEI training universally follows a coercive template that was perfected by authoritarian societies and is performed to convey the regnant orthodoxy. It is the template followed by cults in inculcating new recruits.

Moreover, the vast majority of DEI trainings are conducted by unqualified or minimally qualified clerks, enrollment managers, residence live staff, off-campus diversity consultants, or in-house diversity grifters. Most claim to have an advanced degree, but when probed we find that almost all are products of America's abysmal schools of education with the ubiquitous masters in student affairs or masters in higher education.

The Big Con of diversity that's playing universities now includes a full package of DEI initiatives. Part of the absolution package purchased by universities from the diversity industrial complex includes an enormous bureaucracy that conducts diversity activities on the campuses, such as trainings, snitch lines, and involvement in crafting policies to restrict academic freedom.

While indoctrination in training sessions by mediocre student affairs personnel are a problem, an even bigger problem is the reporting and enforcement mechanisms set up by the bureaucracy—Snitch Lines and Bias Response Teams.

7
DEI'S ENGINE OF DECEIT

SNITCH CULTURE, BRTS, AND RACIAL MICROAGGRESSIONS

"Everybody can use the political police against everybody else—quickly, without delay or undue formalities . . . Everybody shared the power to bring down and destroy anybody else."[317]

— Jan T. Gross, sociologist and historian

In 2018, Greg Lukianoff and Jonathan Haidt published a book

---

317 Jan T. Gross, "A Note on the Nature of Soviet Totalitarianism," *Soviet Studies*, Vol. 34, No. 3 (July 1982), p. 375, 376.

on higher education that became a *New York Times* bestseller. The *Coddling of the American Mind* was hailed as the high-toned sequel to Allan Bloom's surprisingly popular *Closing of the American Mind* in 1987.

In *Coddling*, Lukianoff and Haidt identified a psychological change in the young people moving in cohort fashion through our colleges and universities. They speculated that beginning around 2013, young people seemed to become more fragile and sensitive to the routine vicissitudes of life. They were beginning to speak in a quasi-therapeutic lingo of emotional self-absorption: mindfulness, self-care, triggers, safe spaces, cry rooms, microaggressions, "being seen," and such like.

This Orwellian corruption of the language is a marker for nascent totalitarianism: "The language—the public domain as such—is appropriated by a small group of citizens and distorted to fit the ideological orthodoxy of some political movement."[318] The authors labeled this "safetyism" to capture the overwhelming sense of threat that apparently had come over America's college students, a fearful disposition akin to what one might have found in a medieval village, circa 900 AD. This jittery posture has given rise to stark comparisons to illustrate the absurdity.

World War II's Greatest Generation is recognized for its crowning magnificence of storming the beaches of Normandy under withering enemy fire in 1944 to defeat National Socialism, while today's generation of medicated, skittish, and mentally fragile students is ensconced in "self-care suites" to help them weather the devastating mental trauma of Donald Trump's presidential election

318 Jan T. Gross, "A Note on the Nature of Soviet Totalitarianism," *Soviet Studies*, Vol. 34, No. 3 (July 1982), p. 376.

in 2024—Georgetown University's rooms came stocked with milk and cookies, coloring books, and a Lego station.[319] Lukianoff and Haidt believe that this vulnerable posture of college students toward an increasingly threatening world is genuinely new, and universities bear a large share of the blame for infantilizing an entire generation of today's youth.

> What is new today is the premise that students are fragile. Even those who are not fragile themselves often believe that others are in danger and therefore need protection . . . . Many university students are learning to think in distorted ways, and this increases their likelihood of becoming fragile, anxious, and easily hurt.[320]

We saw in Chapters 3 and 6 the strange racialist doctrine of paranoia and conspiracy that permeates DEI trainings. Trained to perform in scripted ways, students invariably begin to exhibit the outlier behavior of paranoiacs. Not all students, but enough to catch the attention of researchers like the authors of *Coddling*.

DEI trainings prepare students to behave according to a paranoid script, which emphasizes hyper-suspicion, narcissism, and externalization of blame. This paranoia is reinforced by a system dedicated to support the scripted campus paranoia, called the Bias Response System (BRS), or some variation. Thus, campus DEI

---

319 Chris Nesi, "Georgetown U. provides 'self-care suites' for coddled students stressed about Election Day—complete with milk and cookies and coloring books," *The New York Post*, November 5, 2024: https://nypost.com/2024/11/05/us-news/georgetown-providing-self-care-suites-for-students-on-election-day-complete-with-milk-and-cookies-and-coloring-books/

320 Greg Lukianoff and Jonathan Haidt, *The Coddling of the American Mind* (New York: Penguin Press, 2018), p. 7, 9.

offices maintain snitch lines that students are encouraged to use to report incidents of "bias" of the sort that DEI offices train the students to spot. Closing the loop, the reports are handled by what are called Bias Response Teams (BRT), which answer the solicited complaints.

This chapter shows how DEI offices have established anonymous snitch lines, where anyone can report on anyone for a DEI-approved transgression, and how bias response teams engage the gears of the university's various offices, including law enforcement, legal counsel, and in-house juridical processes. This mechanism is ostensibly intended to improve the "racial climate" of the institution, which is measured by the DEI office itself. A "bad" racial climate invariably means that more must be done, and it's the DEI office that must do it.

If this sounds ominous, it should. It resembles the book-burning firemen of Ray Bradbury's dystopian novel *Fahrenheit 451*, ready to squelch free expression at a moment's notice.[321] The anonymous reporting system, with a follow-on enforcement mechanism, is a proven method of governance—for totalitarian systems. While universities put the best face on snitch lines and BRTs, they have been employed so often and by so many in history that we needn't guess at the results, or at the behavior of those they affect. The evidence here awaits our review to come. Let's explore.

The Emergence of a *Culture of Denunciation*

University DEI offices don't operate in a vacuum and their power and influence extend throughout the campus. Their bureaucrats have established outposts in virtually every corner of the campus,

---

321 Ray Bradbury, *Fahrenheit 451* (New York: Ballantine, 1953).

and where they have not done so, they aspire to. The policies generated and the university administration that supports those policies corrode campus life. They can and do cast a pall over all who study and work there. With the addition of Snitch Lines, a "culture of denunciation" can emerge. The snitch line, or mechanism of denunciation, has a long and unsavory history.

A system of anonymous reporting of your neighbors' transgressions enables even the lowliest of peasants or workers to marshal the power of the state's coercive apparatus in service to the envious, the aggrieved, the mentally fragile, the revenge minded. We know what happens in authoritarian societies that incorporate snitch lines and response teams, whether the Soviet KGB, the East German Stasi, or Communist China's Ministry of State Security (MSS).

Authoritarian regimes that impose a coercive ideology on the societies they govern are keen to turn the people against each other. It's a tenet of unpopular regimes that the people must be recruited to participate in their own oppression. And they should do so enthusiastically. By tapping into some of the basest of human emotions—bitterness, envy, spite—the conformity of behavior can be enforced to ensure that orthodoxy is followed.

During the Soviet dictatorship from 1917-1991, the communist government assiduously cultivated a culture of denunciation, in which neighbor reported on neighbor, children reported on parents, and students reported on each other. Russians had a word for the anonymous denouncer—the *Stukach*. Here in the West, we call him the stool pigeon or the snitch.

Denunciation—the act by which one citizen tells the authorities about wrongdoing on the part of another citizen, implicitly or explicitly calling for his punishment—has always been a touchy subject. In the first place, there is the inevitable uneasiness about motive: is the denouncer the patriot that he claims to be, or is he acting out of self-interest and a wish to settle personal scores?[322]

The snitch line cedes power to society's most envious to harness the entire police apparatus of the state in service to petty grudges. It permits the disaffected, maladjusted, and aggrieved to report their neighbors and colleagues. It can serve as a vehicle for venal self-interest, and this is in fact how it has served the closed societies that have employed it. It's a way for the system to draft the entire population to identify the troublemakers, the heretics, the "resistors."

This was the culture of fear that permeated the Soviet Union throughout its history, and which still impacts Communist China today. Denouncers could do this anonymously and be assured that the secret police (secret police variously called OGPU, NKVD, KGB) would investigate. The operational dynamic, the system of incentives, is the same for any anonymous reporting system. It's the kind of thing that the inquisitor Torquemada would have employed, even relished. What totalitarian wouldn't delight in maintaining a direct line for loyalists to rat on their neighbors for their "heresy," to settle scores, to mete out punishment citizen-to-citizen, using the state as an instrument for revenge? "During

322 Sheila Fitzpatrick, "A Little Swine," *London Review of Books*, Vol. 27, No. 21, November 3, 2005: https://www.lrb.co.uk/the-paper/v27/n21/sheila-fitzpatrick/a-little-swine

the Spanish Inquisition ... there was no need to rely on a secret police system, because the population as a whole was encouraged to recognize the enemy within the gates."[323]

Our own campus not-so-secret police is DEI, the product of soft totalitarianism. Let's look at what happens when an anonymous snitch and enforcement system is established on university campuses.

The Campus Snitch

The college campus Snitch Line is a simple and powerful way for authoritarians to sow suspicion among the people and turn neighbor against neighbor. The snitch line most often is a form on the school's website that a student can fill out, choosing to provide his name or not. A telephone contact is also provided. If an accuser provides a name, confidentiality is ensured.[324] The links on the majority of these sites are open for your exploration, and I encourage you to do so and assess for yourself the potential for abuse.

First, it places enormous power in the hands of students (faculty and staff can also avail themselves of the snitch line). A disaffected student can harness DEI's substantial investigatory power in service to his envy, to his desire to "raise awareness," to his imagination that he is somehow aggrieved. We've already seen how DEI "training" incentivizes persons to take on the

---

323 Sheila Fitzpatrick, "A Little Swine," *London Review of Books*, Vol. 27, No. 21, November 3, 2005: https://www.lrb.co.uk/the-paper/v27/n21/sheila-fitzpatrick/a-little-swine

324 Here's a link to an Ivy League school that takes its bias reporting seriously. Cornell University's Diversity and Inclusion SITE is here provides a bias reporting link. Diversity and Inclusion, Bias Reporting at Cornell: https://diversity.cornell.edu/our-commitments/bias-reporting-cornell   The incident reporting form is here: https://cornell.guardianconduct.com/incident-reporting

characteristics of the paranoid personality—to heighten suspicion, to take offense, to interpret every interaction racially, to internalize a sense of grievance, and to report anonymously these suspected grievances to a DEI office. The training also tells students whom to hate, by creating an imaginary race-based pseudocommunity of persecutors. This is the secret of the power of the snitch line, the harnessing of institutional power to private grievance.

> The real power of a totalitarian state results . . . from its being at the disposal of every inhabitant, available for hire at a moment's notice. The absence of the rule of law in a totalitarian régime is also reflected in the fact that every citizen has direct access to the coercive apparatus of the state, unmediated by lengthy and complicated procedures.[325]

At the receiving end of the snitch line, enormous power is placed in the hands of those charged with investigating grievances, whether KGB or DEI. These investigatory organs are labeled, for the most part, bias response teams. The university may deploy one of these "teams" to investigate the report, often not even letting the target know that he or she is under investigation.

What better way to police society and ensure ideological reliability than to set up an anonymous snitch system? It's even easier when a bureaucracy employs a seemingly innocuous "hotline" to report . . . well, to report most anything.

Given what we know about how DEI trains students into behaviors associated with the mental malady called *paranoid personality disorder*, we can surmise the kinds of people using the

---

325 Jan T. Gross, "A Note on the Nature of Soviet Totalitarianism," p. 375.

snitch line and the kinds of reports submitted. The incentive structure is in place, and it motivates those who have been trained into
mimicking the mental illness behaviors of paranoid personality
disorder to report members of the pseudocommunity of persecutors for imaginary transgressions.

Investigation and Enforcement

The operational arm of *snitch* programs on campuses is how anyone
can make an anonymous complaint and be assured that a team of
"professionals" will mobilize to investigate the report. Or, at the
very least, "review" it to ensure the right college department is
involved in resolving the crisis. The composition of these response
teams varies from school to school, and if a college or university has
a BRS set up, it will usually name the personnel. At Georgetown,
for example, here is the lineup of folks entrusted with the function:

> The Bias Reporting Team includes trained professionals from
> across Georgetown, including the Center for Multicultural
> Equity & Access, LGBTQ+ Resource Center, Women's Center,
> Office of Residential Living, Office of Mission & Ministry, the
> Office of Institutional Diversity, Equity, & Affirmative Action
> (IDEAA), the Office of Equity & Inclusion (Georgetown
> Law), and the Office of Diversity and Inclusion (School of
> Medicine).[326]

At Mary Baldwin University, the bias response team is com-
posed of the representatives from the following offices:

---

326 Bias Reporting, Georgetown University website: https://biasreporting.
georgetown.edu/

- Office of the Chief Diversity Officer
- Office of Inclusive Excellence
- Office of the Chaplain
- Office of Student Engagement
- Academic Leadership
- Title IX
- Student Counseling Center
- LGBTQ+ Services

Other offices or individuals such as the General Counsel or the Office of Integrated Communications are consulted on a case-by-case basis.[327]

At Washington University in St. Louis, the website is friendly and inviting and apparently objection-free:

Washington University in St. Louis values diversity, inclusion and human dignity, and strives to foster an environment in which all community members are respected and able to take part in academic, co-curricular and social activities.

Following these values, the university developed a system through which students, faculty, staff and community members who have experienced or witnessed incidents of bias, prejudice or discrimination involving a student can report their experiences to the university's Bias Report and Support System (BRSS) team.[328]

327 Reporting Bias, Mary Baldwin University: https://marybaldwin.edu/meet-mbu/dei/reporting-bias/
328 Bias Report and Support System, WashU Center for Diversity and Inclusion: https://cdi.washu.edu/support/bias-report-support-system/

Again, Washington University's system opens the door to anonymous accusers whose imaginary demons can be blamed on clearly identified villains on campus, villains that they have been trained to identify by race and ethnicity.

At Cornell University, which maintains a Bias Assessment and Review Team (BART), the website provides this listing of the BART group:

BART Co-Chairs:

- Shura Gat, Associate Dean of Students and Director of the Gender Equity Resource Center

- Christina Liang, Director, Office of Student Conduct and Community Standards

Bias Assessment and Review Team:

- Joseph Canzano, Operations Lieutenant, Cornell University Police

- Devan Carrington, Associate Athletics Director for Student-Athlete Support, Development and Inclusion

- Janna Lamey, Senior Assistant Dean for Graduate Student Life

- Kyle McGee, Assistant Director of Sorority and Fraternity Life and MGFC Advisor

- Christine Nye, Associate Director, Office of Student Conduct and Community Standards

- Julie Paige, Director, Off-Campus and Cooperative Living, Housing and Residence Life

- David Reetz, Director, Counseling and Psychological Services, Cornell Health

- Scott Voss, Assistant Director of Conduct and Care, Housing and Residence Life

- Kathleen Wilhite, Assistant Director of Sorority and Fraternity Life and IFC Advisor[329]

Cornell assures that this group "is neither an investigative nor a disciplinary body. Actions will generally be educational in nature and can include conflict coaching or mediation dependent upon the reporters [*sic*] decision regarding anonymity."[330]

At Wake Forest, the process is administered by a review group. Members of that group and their positions appear here: Stephanie K. Carter-Atkins (Executive Director, Residence Life and Housing), Aishah Casseus (Director of the Title IX Office/504 Coordinator), Matthew Clifford (Associate Vice President, Campus

---

329 Diversity and Inclusion, Cornell University website, Bias Reporting for students: https://diversity.cornell.edu/our-commitments/bias-reporting-cornell/students
330 Diversity and Inclusion, Cornell University website.

Life and Dean of Students), Shelley Sizemore (Director, Women's Center), Erica Still (Associate Dean for Faculty Recruitment, Diversity & Inclusion, Associate Professor of English).

What is a "bias" incident at Wake Forest?

A **bias incident** is an act or behavior motivated by the offender's bias against facets of another's identity. Bias occurs whether the act is intentional or unintentional. Bias may be **directed toward an individual or group**. Bias may contribute to creating an unsafe, unwelcoming environment.

When the Wake Forest review group receives a report, this happens:

University Police will assess the situation for danger of imminent harm.

A team led by the Dean of Students and the Office of Diversity & Inclusion **will review the report and reach out** to you to provide care, offer support, and learn more about the incident. If needed, the Dean's team will direct the report to the appropriate office for investigation.[331]

The Key to Snitch Line Success—Gin-up some *Rampant Racism*

The public idea behind the snitch lines and BRTs is to address so-called bias incidents quickly to satisfy the DEI office and, of course, to communicate to the aggrieved reporter that your lived

---

331 Report Bias, Wake Forest University, https://reportbias.wfu.edu/

experience is important and that "you are seen" and "you are heard." But for the DEI bureaucracy that administers the mechanism, it is essential for the gathering of evidence to affirm the need for that very bureaucracy. The complaints are collected, collated, and compiled in racial climate "reports." At times, expensive outside diversity consultants are brought in to assess this amorphous racial climate, and to provide the necessary expensive "training" to improve the climate, which is always found wanting.

But what if the snitch line doesn't provide the necessary critical supply of "racism"? You know, the phantom racism running "rampant" at Princeton, examples of which no one could provide. To reiterate:

> If Princeton's racism was as conspicuous as alleged, one would expect the ultimatum's authors to be able to dash off some vivid, revealing examples. Instead, they refer with unsatisfying generality to "micro-aggression" and "outright racist incidents," leaving readers uncertain about what, precisely, they have in mind.[332]

Racism is largely absent on college campuses, and this would appear to be good news, unless your DEI salary depends on racism running rampant. If you and your fellow bureaucrats are heavily invested in a Big Con whose operation depends on this not-so-rampant racism, you have a problem.

---

332 Randall Kennedy, "How racist are universities, really?" *The Chronicle of Higher Education*, August 12, 2020: https://www.chronicle.com/article/how-racist-are-universities-really

How will your racial climate survey yield the necessary glumness if, as Harvard Law Professor Randall Kennedy contends, universities are likely the least racist places in America.[333]

The solution is two-fold.

First, you must inflate the numbers of racist incidents on campus and collect them via a snitch line set up for the purpose. The comb used to ferret out racism becomes increasingly fine-toothed, which allows for the collection of imaginary incidents called racial microaggressions.

Second, when racism is in short supply, you fake it. This is bizarrely referred to as "raising awareness" of the problem, a problem that is so nonexistent that fakery is necessary to make people aware of it. This is commonly called the "hate crime hoax," and it has become so pervasive on the campuses as to crowd out coverage of actual displays of racism, on those rare occasions when they appear. The hate crime hoax is examined in Chapter 8, and the ignoring of actual incidents of racialist anti-Semitic hate on campuses is examined in Chapter 11.

Here, we examine how DEI functionaries rescue their enterprise with the confection of the "racial microaggression." The fraud is so bold, the concept so ubiquitous on the campus, and its importance to the success of the Big Con so essential that the next section examines it in-depth to place it within the framework of DEI's engine of deception.

---

333 "Some charges of racism are simply untenable. Some complainants are careless about fact-finding and analysis. And some propose coercive policies that would disastrously inhibit academic freedom." Randall Kennedy, "How racist are universities, really?" *The Chronicle of Higher Education*, August 12, 2020: https://www.chronicle.com/article/how-racist-are-universities-really

The Elegant Fakery of Racial Microaggressions

The term "racial microaggression" was allegedly invented by Chester Pierce in the 1970s. This is what everyone says, and a case could be made for it. You can read his seminal piece in a collection of essays edited by Floyd Barbour called *The Black Seventies*.[334]

But in fact, it was Emil Kraepelin who articulated the central idea of the "microaggression" more than a century ago and who described its expression. He did so in detail and at length, and his description stands the test of time.

> The demeanour and the glances of the passers-by, a movement of the hand, a shrug of the shoulders, have a mysterious meaning for the patients; it is sometimes painful and tormenting, sometimes elevating and beneficent. People wish in that way to insult him, blame him, make him contemptible, warn him, encourage him, impart to him some or other important information. A phrase accidentally caught up, a remark at the neighbouring table contains a hidden allusion; "They thought that I did not understand it," said a patient. The conversation of the party at table points dimly to a secret understanding; the patient "notices that there is something there, but doesn't know what it is."[335]

Kraepelin referred to the mental disorder that, today, we broadly call paranoia. This is the key to the microaggression agenda—the filling of a benign external environment with ghosts and dangers,

334 Chester Pierce, "Offensive Mechanisms" in Floyd Barbour (ed), *The Black Seventies* (Boston: Porter Sargent Publisher, 1970), p. 265-283.
335 Emil Kraepelin (Mary Barclay, trans), *Manic-depressive Insanity and Paranoia* (Edinburgh: E & S Livingstone, 1921), p. 217.

threats and enemies. This concept is race-based and emerges naturally from the core of the DEI enterprise.

The college student is encouraged to give rein to their imagination, to identify in every benign situation the hidden relationships of power and privilege that bedevil them. They should fix his gaze on imagined enemies identified by skin pigment, and to report them. It is this state of hyper-awareness and constant vigilance of the paranoiac that leads them to seize upon every imagined or real slight and to escalate it into a major transgression, which can be punished with appropriately harsh sanction.

Columbia Teachers College social psychologist and "certified hypnotherapist" Derald Wing Sue is the chief proponent of this ingenious tool. He identified the term this way:

> Racial microaggressions are brief and commonplace daily verbal, behavioral, or environmental indignities, whether intentional or unintentional, that communicate hostile, derogatory, or negative racial slights and insults toward people of color.[336]

Sue publishes virtually the same article repeatedly, usually with different batches of his graduate students, based on smoke and mirrors and "lived experience." His career appears to have suffered not at all from his long-time collaboration with the notorious plagiarist and noose hoaxer[337] we met earlier, Madonna Constan-

336 Derald Wing Sue, et al, "Racial Microaggressions in Everyday Life: Implications for clinical practice," *American Psychologist*, May-June 2007: https://www.cpedv.org/sites/main/files/file-attachments/how_to_be_an_effective_ally-lessons_learned_microaggressions.pdf
337 Ashley Thorne, "The Copyist: The Plagiarist and the Noose," National Association of Scholars, February 27, 2008: https://www.nas.org/blogs/article/the_copyist_the_plagiarist_and_the_noose

tine.[338] Sue's career *ought* to suffer with the addition of his current partner, Professor Lisa Spanierman of Arizona State University, a rogue psychologist who advocates quasi-legal psychological experiments on white male students in the classroom to convince them to work for "social justice."[339]

So Derald Wing Sue is not alone. He is merely the most exalted, most successful, and longest-lived of the microaggression diversity hustlers. He has built a professional career with the oppression mantra, especially as it relates to "racial microaggressions." He and his young colleagues have generated a stream of journal articles and at least one textbook, many of which are repetitive. It is as if the same journal article appears repeatedly with only the names within it changed. This should be expected when you elevate a single anecdote to the status of a "case," attribute major importance to it, then wrap a "peer-reviewed" article around it while wagering that the charged character of your subject matter increases the odds of publication.

Often, Sue's articles are little more than conversations with a handful of people recruited specifically to confirm preconceived conclusions. In this way, relaxed standards of publication have unleashed a barrage of articles that appear eerily similar to each other. So similar, in fact, that Sue and his colleagues have been confused on at least one occasion when they successfully published highly similar articles in two different publications, with some passages appearing verbatim in both journals, and with the titles

---

338 The Root Staff, "More Hate Crimes that Never Happened," *The Root*, October 24, 2012: https://www.theroot.com/more-hate-crimes-that-never-happened-1790893864
339 I've written about Spanierman here. This post contains her seminal experimentation article referenced in the above text: https://brutalminds.com/?p=1474

almost identical. In essence, another instance of diversity plagiarism, this time an author plagiarizing himself. Sue and colleagues were compelled later to issue a "clarification."[340]

Much of Sue's rhetoric in these articles consists of *ex cathedra* statements, asserted with authority. They are made with strength and conviction, often with bellicosity. Karl Marx himself anticipated this kind of rhetoric: "One must admit that this is a very impressive method – for swaggering, sham-scientific, bombastic ignorance and intellectual laziness."[341]

Not to single out Derald Wing Sue as an especially bad example of microaggression posturing—he is neither better nor worse than many others engaged in this sort of thing, and there *are* many others. One of the most flamboyant and aggressive is Monnica Williams, who is a character in her own right and who vigorously defends the microaggressions project. Williams provides us with a glimpse into the mystical side of microaggressions.

---

340 "We wish to clarify the relationship between 'Racial Microaggressions in the Life Experience of Black Americans' by Derald W. Sue, Christina M. Capodilupo, and Aisha M. B. Holder (*Professional Psychology: Research and Practice*, 2008, Vol. 39, No. 3, pp. 329–336) and 'Racial Microaggressions Against Black Americans: Implications for Counseling' by Derald W. Sue, Kevin L. Nadal, et al. (*Journal of Counseling and Development*, 2008, Vol. 86, No. 3 pp. 330–338). The first study investigated racial microaggressive dynamics, processes, and their detrimental consequences for African Americans, whereas the second study explored the universe of hidden demeaning racial microaggressive themes. In the second article, which did not mention the sample overlap, a few descriptive sentences from the first article, primarily in the Method-section, were repeated verbatim and without citation from the earlier study. We apologize for these oversights." This "clarification" appears as an add-on at the end of the article in *Professional Psychology: Research and Practice*.
341 Letter from Karl Marx to Ludwig Kugelmann, June 27, 1870, cited in Conway Zirkle, *Evolution, Marxian Biology, and the Social Scene* (Oxford: Oxford University Press, 1959), p. 90. Marx was referring to the method of identifying any occurrence as evidence for a theory's validity; in this case, Marx criticized the use of the Darwin-inspired "struggle for life" as a blanket label for "every concrete struggle" and thus justification for what Marx called the "Malthusian population fantasy." The irony of this method, which he himself engaged masterfully, may have been lost on the supremely confident Marx.

The Sleeping Octopus, the Cosmic Sister, and Race-baiting

Monnica Williams is a board certified licensed clinical psychologist and tenured Professor at the School of Psychology at the University of Ottawa, and like too many passengers hanging onto a full train departing from Matunga station in Mumbai, Williams is someone who subscribes to the pseudoscience of racial microaggression theory. She earns a good living from its propagation. She has nothing new to offer, mind you, but she knows exactly what she doesn't like about the persons criticizing the microaggressions project.

Williams dismisses the criticism of more senior and accomplished psychology colleagues such as Jonathan Haidt and Scott Lilienfeld and sociologists Bradley Campbell and Jason Manning by noting that they are "all white males" and asserts that this is the reason that they "came to the wrong conclusions about the causes and impact of microaggressions."[342] Williams displays the easy confidence of a 1930s German National Socialist patiently explaining why Albert Einstein's theories are the product of "Jew physics."[343] Her race-baiting masquerades as research.

342 Monnica Williams, "Are Racial Microaggressions on College Campuses Harmful?" *Psychology Today*, Nov. 12, 2017. https://www.psychologytoday.com/us/blog/culturally-speaking/201711/are-racial-microaggressions-college-campuses-harmful

343 Other epithets of that time were "Jewish Physics," "Jewish Science," "Jewish world-bluff," and the product of "Jewish Spirit." See Walter Isaacson, *Einstein: His Life and Universe* (New York: Simon & Schuster, 2007), p. 270, 289. Said a young Adolf Hitler in a newspaper piece, "Science, once our greatest pride, is today being taught by Hebrews," p. 289. See also Steven Gimbel, *Einstein's Jewish Science: Physics at the Intersection of Politics and Religion* (Baltimore: Johns Hopkins University Press, 2012). See Werner Heisenberg, *Encounters with Einstein* (Princeton: Princeton University Press, 1983), p. 111. See Robert Jungk, *Brighter than a Thousand Suns* (New York: Harcourt, Brace & World, Inc, 1958, 1956), p. 33. See David C. Cassidy, "Heisenberg, German Science, and the Third Reich," *Social Research*, Vol. 59, No. 3 (Fall 1992), p. 652. For "Jewish Spirit," see Alan D. Beyerchen, *Scientists Under Hitler: Politics and the Physics Community in the Third Reich* (New Haven: Yale University Press, 1977), p. 132-133.

For context, here is Ms. Williams's entire dismissal of those who criticize her pseudoscientific posturing of "microaggressions."

> Microaggressions, which tend to be covert and subtle, may be more likely to escape the notice of those without such lived experiences and consequently be misinterpreted as oversensitivity on the part of the victim. This may explain why researchers such as Lilienfeld, Haidt, Campbell, and Manning, who are all white males, came to the wrong conclusions about the causes and impact of microaggressions. It's also worth noting that none of these scholars conduct much, if any, diversity research, and so their their [*sic*] ideas should be seen as opinions and not expert consensus.[344]

The use of this race-baiting invites speculation as to why it's implicitly endorsed by a reputable publication such as *Psychology Today*. Unremarked in *Psychology Today* is that Ms. Williams accepts race-based experiential knowledge as somehow imbued with a mystical authority.

This was suggested in her remarks at a 2018 conference called the Sleeping Octopus Assembly on Psychedelics (SOAP), for which Ms. Williams received a *Cosmic Sister's Women of The Psychedelic Renaissance* speaking grant. The purpose of Ms. Williams's speaking grant is described this way in a press release from "Cosmic Sister."

---

344 Monnica Williams, "Are Racial Microaggressions on College Campuses Harmful?" *Psychology Today*, See also, Monnica T. Williams, "Microaggressions: Clarification, Evidence, and Impact," *Perspectives on Psychological Science,* Vol 15, 1, 2020, pp. 3-26

Cosmic Sister's Psychedelic Feminism educational advocacy projects, Women of the Psychedelic Renaissance (WPR) and Cosmic Sisters of Cannabis (CSC), support outstanding women as they step into the spotlight and speak out.[345]

Another colorful description of the conference activities describes the passing around of something called a "talking stick." The award-winning headline reads "Psychedelic Feminism Grants Hand Talking Stick to Women of Cannabis and the Psychedelic Renaissance."

When Ms. Williams was handed this talking stick—there is no description of the stick itself, of its size or its ornamentation or any special powers—she gave this familiar summary to the crew assembled at the Sleeping Octopus Assembly on Psychedelics, consisting of the oppression theme of "invisible structures" and the Manichean worldview.

> The results of oppression are clear in the disparities faced by people with multiple marginalized identities, such as Black women, but the mechanisms are carefully hidden from view. To that end much of my work is intended to make the unseen seen.[346]

The irony here of making the "unseen seen" at a conference promoting mind-altering psychotropic drug use is likely

345 "Psychedelic Feminism Grants Hand Talking Stick to Women of Cannabis and the Psychedelic Renaissance," AMHERST, Mass. (PRWEB) July 10, 2018. https://www.prweb.com/releases/2018/07/prweb15611319.htm
346 Monnica Williams, "Racial Trauma, the War on Drugs, and Psychedelic Medicine," *Sleeping Octopus Assembly on Psychedelics*, (Pittsburgh: July 13-15, 2018). http://www.zoehelene.com/monnica-williams

unintended. Certainly, the antics of the Sleeping Octopus conference indicate that magic thinking and mysticism is never far from the work of those engaged in cargo cult writing. Whether the views of Cosmic Sister Monnica Williams are part of the psychology "expert consensus" at the University of Ottawa is a question for her department colleagues, who doubtless await their turn at the Talking Stick so that they might interrogate their Cosmic Sister on the matter.

Racial Microaggressions on Campus

Such is the world of microaggressions that informs the DEI university project. Since 2020 at least, university DEI offices have attempted to legitimize "microaggressions" as a category of bias reporting. The addition of microaggressions inflates the numbers of bias incidents on campus. For example, take Cornell University's latest *FY24 Reporting Bias System Annual Report: Summary of Activity July 1, 2023 - June 30, 2024.* The report aggregates the reports of "bias" collected by its Bias Assessment and Review Team.

I provide a portion of the table in the accompanying graphic, which provides a tabulation of "bias incidents" for fiscal years 2020 to 2024.[347] The important point to note is that after 2021, Cornell added a "microaggression" category to its tabulation. The addition of the microaggression category immediately inflated the number of "bias incidents" to anywhere from 30 percent to more than 50 percent of all reported incidents for a given year. The perception of Cornell's "racial climate" suffered accordingly, and this is certainly convenient for the perpetuation of the Big Con on campus.

---

347 *FY24 Reporting Bias System Annual Report: Summary of Activity July 1, 2023 - June 30, 2024,* Cornell University: https://diversity.cornell.edu/sites/default/files/uploaded-files/FY24%20Bias%20Report.pdf

Classification of Bias	FY20	FY21	FY22	FY23	FY24
Bias Motivated Speech					
Without Microaggressions	76	82	61	39	89
Add Microaggressions			14	53	44
With Microaggressions	N/A	N/A	75	92	133
Bias Motivated Conduct					
Without Microaggressions	38	42	8	9	28
Add Microaggressions			7	17	23
With Microaggressions	N/A	N/A	15	26	51

The "racial microaggression" affirms the paranoia inculcated into students and into overly credulous staff and faculty and, presumably, substantiates a fraudulent negative "racial climate" that must be addressed with ever increasing numbers of personnel, training, and expenditures.

The perpetuation of the Big Con requires a negative or worsening racial climate, and the racial microaggression provides the grist to generate that climate.

The Campus "Racial Climate" . . . _nudge-nudge, wink-wink_

You can be forgiven if you're hazy on what, exactly, is a racial climate. The term is intentionally vague yet suggests urgency and criticality, which is ideal for a concept at the core of increased budget demands, particularly demands coming from offices immune to criticism.

Racial climate became important as the victim-signaling fraud of "rampant racism" on the college campuses fell apart. It evaporated quickly when cool minds did a second take and saw that, in fact, racism *wasn't* "rampant" on the campuses. Far from it. So the DEI movement needed a replacement and needed it fast to maintain momentum. That replacement became the ubiquitous racial climate.

"Racial climate" looks more and more like a superb short-con for victim/virtue-signaling, doesn't it? Racial climate has long been a staple of the diversity hustle, which explains its popularity in DEI campus circles. "Research" on this flimsy concept goes back decades to its seminal papers.[348] The paper cited here features co-authors Jeffrey Milem and Mitchell Chang. Interestingly, their article on "Making Diversity Work on Campus" has indeed reaped reward for the authors themselves as Milem today draws a $318,383 annual compensation as the Dean of the Graduate School of Education at UC Santa Barbara, and Chang ascended to the heights of diversity largess, pulling in $348,232 annual compensation until late 2024 as Interim Vice Provost of Equity, Diversity and Inclusion at UCLA. Chang also contributes to the work of Shaun Harper's Race & Equity Center. You see how this Circle of Friends operates.

---

348 Jeffrey F. Milem, Mitchell J. Chang, and Anthony Lising Antonio, "Making Diversity Work on Campus: a Research-Based Perspective," Association of American Colleges and Universities, 2005: https://www.uwp.edu/explore/offices/EDI/upload/Making-Inclusive-Excellence.pdf   See also: Sylvia Hurtado, Jeffrey Milem, Alma Clayton-Pedersen, Walter Allen, "Enacting Diverse Learning Environments: Improving the Climate for Racial/Ethnic Diversity in Higher Education," *ASHE-ERIC Higher Education Report*, Vol. 26, No. 8, 1999. Washington, D.C.: The George Washington University, Graduate School of Education and Human Development: https://eric.ed.gov/?id=ED430514

This notion of racial climate all hinges, of course, on something called "compositional diversity," which is the claim that there should be some base level of proportional ethnic representation that, once achieved, means that something good will happen. "Emancipation," perhaps.

Other factors influence the climate, of course, but it always comes back to stark numbers, even as naming the exact desirable racial/ethnic percentages is assiduously avoided. Vague, unassailable, and with ancillary crossover appeal to the climate-change faction, this victim-signaling instrument of racial climate was malleable enough to serve as the perfect shill to keep the con in business.

The racial climate on a campus could be positive or it could be negative. But for effective victim-signaling, it's clear which climate the DEI bureaucracy needs to keep the grift in business. A negative racial climate indicates the need for more DEI personnel and services and an expanding role with increased budget. But where does the assessment of this mysterious racial climate come from? The elegance of this system is that the source of information on the campus racial climate is the DEI office itself that administers the racial climate survey. As you learned already, it also trains the survey respondents into racial illiteracy.

If you're employed by a DEI office, how can *you* ascertain the racial climate on your own campus so that you, too, can victim-signal for a higher budget?

You could construct your own survey, or you could solicit outside help in a bid to appear objective. For instance, you can order a racial climate survey yourself from the University of Southern

California's Race and Equity Center and its National Assessment of Collegiate Campus Climates (NACCC).[349]

This NACCC is a part of the sprawling Race and Equity Center at the University of Southern California. The Center offers a multifarious range of diversity consulting services. It is led by Professor Shaun Harper, formerly of the University of Pennsylvania. The Center's division called NACCC specializes in racial-climate surveys. The cost for the 2023 student survey was $12,000, and we can safely assume that the price continues to climb (in 2022, it was $10,000). Given the list of 160 schools the Center has serviced thus far, you can calculate the total jackpot yourself.[350]

The Harper group offers three different surveys, one each for students, staff, and faculty. Here's what you get for the money spent on one of the group's student surveys: A report that assesses the racial climate on the campus (it's likely in bad shape) that is "measured" along six dimensions: 1) Mattering and Affirmation, 2) Racial Learning and Literacy, 3) Appraisals of Institutional Commitment, 4) Cross-Racial Engagement, 5) Encounters with Racial Stress, and 6) Impact of External Environment. Each of these is explained, sort of, as to how they comprise the "climate." The report also provides recommendations and "strategies" to improve, and it helpfully suggests that *another* division of Harper's own group can come to the rescue.

Harper's USC Equity Institute offers "virtual modules" of instruction to assist in implementing the Institute's recommendations and strategies. These modules are listed by name and number

349 USC Race and Equity Center: https://race.usc.edu/colleges/naccc/
350 USC Race and Equity Center: https://race.usc.edu/wp-content/
    uploads/2022/12/ALL_Participating-Institution-List-as-of-10.15.pdf

so the school can quickly and easily sign up at a cost of $40,000 for eight 2-hour zoom sessions.[351]

Especially interesting is the lineup of consultants that Harper has assembled to deliver his virtual training. It reads like a second tier who's who of the diversity consulting world—Nolan Cabrera, Stephen John Quaye, Shaun Harper himself, the Chief Diversity Officer of the University of Michigan Tabbye Chavous, whose annual Michigan DEI salary tops out at $417,000, and many others.

The USC Center[352] was founded in 2017 by DEI guru Harper,[353] who also runs his own diversity consulting business. If you pay your $12K to Shaun Harper's outfit, it's a good bet that the results will reflect what you expect. The Russians have a saying that captures the spirit of this sort of self-reinforcing arrangement: **"рука руку моет"** or "One hand washes the other."

This comfortable setup is also apparent with the various groups dedicated to working for "racial justice" and improving the campus "racial climate."

For instance, the Student Affairs Administrators in Higher Education (NASPA) conducted a survey published in 2023 designed to assess these very issues.[354] Who did they ask? They queried a curated list of 65 "student activists" involved in working

---

351 See the NACCC 2020 racial climate survey conducted for St. Louis University, which lists the areas that the school must improve, alongside recommended modules offered by the Harper group. You can review the survey results here: https://race.usc.edu/colleges/usc-equity-institutes/#cost-and-enrollment
352 USC Race and Equity Center: https://race.usc.edu/
353 J. Brian Charles, "Can Shaun Harper Save DEI?", *The Chronicle of Higher Education*, June 20, 2024: https://www.chronicle.com/article/can-shaun-harper-save-dei
354 NASPA is a far-left off-campus non-profit membership group that caters to "Student Affairs" staff activists nationwide. In fact, NASPA offers training, journals, and books on how to engage in activism to undermine and transform the university: www.naspa.org

on racial justice issues; the student activists themselves would provide the definition of racial climate and determine its importance for the survey, even as the sample featured for the most part one person per school (65 activists from 55 schools).

NASPA also surveyed 176 vice presidents of Student Affairs and senior diversity officers, essentially surveying its own membership. For this segment of its survey, NASPA partnered with another group. This partner was the National Association of Diversity Officers in Higher Education (NADOHE). The school officials, all of them involved in the DEI bureaucracy, were asked what they perceived as "factors that influence efforts to advance racial justice and racial climate on campus."[355] You likely already know the responses.

It's appropriate that the NASPA final report should speak for itself here in a wish list of decisive assertions for the nation's universities. In the final assessment, the report states that students and administrators advocated for structural changes to achieve the following series of goals:

1. Racial/ethnic diversity exists at all levels of the institution.

2. Spaces and engagement opportunities within campus and the surrounding community are well supported, welcoming, and accessible.

355 Jill Dunlap, Alexa Wesley Chamberlain, Alexis Wesaw, and Amelia Parnell, "Advancing Racial Justice on Campus: Student and Administrator Perspectives on Conditions for Change," NASPA, 2023: https://www.naspa.org/report/advancing-racial-justice-on-campus-student-and-administrator-perspectives-on-conditions-for-change

3. Reporting mechanisms for bias incidents are in place and individuals are held accountable for causing harm.

4. Commitments for change are tied with actions validated by students.

5. Progress is measured, transparently reported, and ongoing.[356]

It is well worth downloading and digging into the report itself to understand the many linkages among the various DEI constituencies that profit from a "negative racial climate." Or, rather, a *report* of a negative racial climate. It perhaps comes as no surprise that this NASPA report was funded by the Bill and Melinda Gates Foundation.

So, does all of this DEI focus on the "climate" actually do anything to, say, justify the large bureaucracies and hefty budgets devoted to manipulating it? One think tank asked that question, researched the answer, and published a report in 2021.[357] Given all our foregoing discussion, the answer is not surprising.

The Heritage Foundation's 2021 report "Diversity University: DEI Bloat in the Academy," examined the DEI commitments of 65 universities and compared the numbers of DEI personnel employed with the numbers of faculty employed and with other

356 Jill Dunlap, Alexa Wesley Chamberlain, Alexis Wesaw, and Amelia Parnell, "Advancing Racial Justice on Campus: Student and Administrator Perspectives on Conditions for Change," NASPA, 2023, p. 44: https://www.naspa.org/report/advancing-racial-justice-on-campus-student-and-administrator-perspectives-on-conditions-for-change

357 Jay P. Greene, PhD, and James D. Paul, "Diversity University: DEI Bloat in the Academy," *Backgrounder*, Heritage Foundation Center for Education Policy, No. 3641, July 27, 2021: https://www.heritage.org/education/report/diversity-university-dei-bloat-the-academy

offices required by the federal government. It also measured the size of the DEI bureaucracies against the schools' own climate survey results. The results are grim:

> DEI bureaucracies appear to increase administrative bloat without contributing to the stated goals of diversity, equity, and inclusion. Employing dozens of DEI professionals—in the form of chief diversity officers, assistant deans for diversity, and directors for inclusive excellence—may be better understood as jobs programs subsidizing political activism without improving campus climate.[358]

The Heritage report is exceedingly generous in its characterization of higher education DEI as a "jobs program." Yes, it's that. But the description doesn't fully capture the interweaving of the psychology of victims/villains with the need of administrators to acquire virtue in a public display of absolution by putting dozens of diversity "experts" on the payroll.

We can best understand it as an elaborate con-game in which DEI personnel employ a racialist resource extraction strategy. This "racial climate" component is a brilliant short-con that helps to maintain the atmosphere of racial emergency on campus. The racial climate short-con fits into the DEI engine of deception this way:

DEI offices are invested in a negative result on their surveys, and the key to ensuring an unhealthy campus "racial climate" is to:

1. inculcate in the student body the fiction that the campus is rampant with racism and white supremacy,

---

358 Jay P. Greene, PhD, and James D. Paul, "Diversity University: DEI Bloat in the Academy,"

2. set up a Bias Response System to solicit complaints about the rampant racism,

3. cultivate the notion of the racial microaggression to guarantee a base level of complaints, especially if no actual racism is forthcoming,

4. hire an outside firm at a costly fee to report that the "racial climate" is bad or worsening,

5. demand more funds for personnel and programming and pay the outside firm to battle this negative "racial climate" (with lots of positive valence lingo like "inclusivity" and "belonging.").

This is the fuel that reproduces ersatz "racism" on the campus to perpetuate the DEI *virtuous victim* con game. The negative "racial climate" report, based largely on numbers inflated with imaginary "microaggressions" justifies the hustle.

The DEI Hustle meets Resistance

DEI's Snitch and BRT regime accelerated almost unopposed on the campuses beginning in 2020. The bureaucracy was firmly in control of the campus agenda and enthusiastically entrenching itself. But opposition emerged. The opposition came from off-campus.

In the early 2000s, it seemed that only The Foundation for Individual Rights and Expression (FIRE) was explicitly addressing the problem of speech and bias reporting and actively supporting persons on the campuses whose rights were violated. In 2018, Speech First was founded to address the DEI problem and complemented the work of FIRE. The American Council of Trustees and Alumni had been founded in 1995 to mobilize and inform trustees and donors of university activities, potentially for action in the preservation of American higher education.

The Chronicle of Higher Education has labeled today's emerging opposition to DEI and concurrent support of civil rights laws as a "New anti-DEI bureaucracy."[359] Other groups that constitute the constellation of the "anti-DEI bureaucracy" include Turning Point USA, Free Speech Alliance, Alliance Defending Freedom, Moms for Liberty, Leadership Institute, Young America's Foundation, and surely others that may be unintentionally omitted. Whether or not the collection of social movement groups mobilizing against the powerful forces that impose the range of DEI activities deserves the pejorative of "bureaucracy," we see that they grow more influential by the day, winning stunning court battles and emboldening student and parents to demand reform.

Speech First has aggressively taken on the issue of Bias Response Teams in the universities. The group is devoted to "restoring freedom of speech on college campuses because we believe that by exposing students to different and challenging ideas, they will emerge stronger, smarter, and more resilient." The group advocates for college students in several ways, including litigation, and education. Speech First's language is combative, which is refreshing in this era of simpering capitulation, and puts

---

359 Maggie Weeks, "The New Anti-DEI Bureaucracy," *The Chronicle of Higher Education*, June 21, 2024: https://www.chronicle.com/article/the-new-anti-dei-bureaucracy

"colleges and universities on notice that shutting down unwanted speech will no longer be tolerated."[360]

Here, the focus is on campus snitch lines and bias response teams. In 2017, FIRE published its first major expose on bias reporting on the campuses and found 232 BRSs. FIRE predicted the number would increase, and the organization was right. Speech First has done yeoman's work in exposing the underbelly of college BRTs nationwide. In 2022, the group published a major report on BRTs. The study examined a total of 821 higher education institutions and found 454 Bias Reporting Systems, almost doubling the number from just five years earlier.[361]

The good news is that this number may have reached a high-water mark.

Conclusion

When asked to explain the purpose and operation—the *necessity*—of the bias response teams, we see that DEI folks invariably offer explanations that make no sense or that redound to the benefit of the personnel involved. They claim with sobriety that these are benign operations to ensure compliance with university regulations. They sanitize it so that it doesn't appear *too* threatening: the DEI team is performing noble work to ensure that the university is functioning as intended, with a commitment to the "values" of diversity, equity, and inclusion. Snitch lines and Bias Response Teams are essential to that work.

The notion that a university snitch line and a bias response

360 Speech First website, 2024: https://speechfirst.org/about/
361 Cherise Trump, "Free Speech in the Crosshairs: Bias Reporting on College Campuses," Speech First, 2022: https://speechfirst.org/wp-content/uploads/2023/04/SF-2022_Bias-Response-team-and-Reporting-System-Report_Final.pdf

team might have negative impact on the college community that employs the mechanism does not appear on college sites. It's simply not on the table for discussion. This surely occurs to critical thinkers who espy the con-mechanism of **Train students —> solicit complaints —> collate complaints to report a worsening racial climate —> leverage the worsening racial climate to institute more training, bigger budget, and more personnel.** This is the narrative of the Big Con, and its contours should be crystallized for you by now.

Does the idea of a group of race hustling "bias professionals" investigating you based on anonymous complaint(s) give you the creeps? It should. The folks behind this collegiate abomination are on the payroll. Their work in monitoring an amorphous "racial climate" demands that they find *racism* to justify their jobs and the expenditure of enormous sums of tuition money. We've seen that the "racial microaggression" is the golden ticket to pump up the perceived "racism" on a campus, achieve a negative climate rating, and maintain a constantly expanding racialist bureaucracy.

The destructive social power of the snitch line combines with the Bias Response System to generate the "racial climate" needed to perpetuate the Big Con of *virtuous victimhood*. The "climate" is assessed by the persons who are responsible for remedying a climate that is deficient in ways determined, again, by the DEI office. Expensive outside diversity consultants can be brought in to assess the climate of a college. When problems are found—and they're *always* found—that same climate assessor can provide an expensive suite of programs to address the issues.

This con is so effective because it's the proven dynamic of all totalitarian ruling systems.

Here, on the campuses, it's a form of soft totalitarianism, a means whereby members of the university community can settle scores and satisfy their perceived aggrievement. While the con game of DEI may enrich some folks and meet the psychological needs of others, it does real damage to those innocent students, faculty, and staff caught up in the web of paranoia, suspicion, and anger.

> This ability to get anybody arrested was the great equalizer of Soviet citizens. It was a weird power, power to destroy but not to protect. Nobody was able to provide for their own security, while anybody was able to ruin anybody else's life. Hence, also, social atomization under totalitarianism. Because, in the end, what brings social atomization is less the outlawing of voluntary associations than the mutual fear and distrust induced in people's minds when the social control mechanism in their society is such that they can only cause harm to one another and are defenceless against such attempts by others.[362]

But you are not defenseless. In fact, once you understand the pernicious nature of the DEI operation, you are empowered.

Recognize that when someone charges you with a "microaggression" or, worse, a "racial microaggression," that this is a fake charge imagined by the accuser. It arises out of a particular persecutory mindset that approaches or is already consumed with paranoia. Moreover, it is increasingly becoming a reflexive trope wielded as need arises when someone "feels" uncomfortable. Reject explicitly the notion of "microaggression," which has no basis in

---

362 Jan T. Gross, "A Note on the Nature of Soviet Totalitarianism," p. 376.

genuine academia and which was contrived off the cuff in 1970 by a fellow named Chester Pierce in an article called "Offensive Mechanisms." It's maintained today by Derald Wing Sue, Lisa Spanierman, and Cosmic Sister Monnica Williams.

The charge of "racial microaggression" is race-baiting and a violation of most discrimination policies at universities. You can countercharge your accuser with making a false accusation, and I encourage you to do so. And I encourage you to press your university for relief and to take it into the public realm if such relief is not forthcoming. This is the path to disrupt the diversity engine of deceit that keeps the Big Con in play.

In this chapter, we saw the engine of deceit used by DEI offices to maintain their power and their sinecures. Essential to this is the necessity to create "racism" on the campus where little if any actually exists. We saw that the confected "racial microaggression" is one way to inflate numbers of bias incidents and to advertise a negative racial climate. The second method is as ingenious as the first.

If racism is in short supply, just *make it up*.

And this has led us to the ubiquitous "Hate Crime Hoax," which we examine in the next chapter.

8
HATE CRIME HOAX

THE "INNER TRUTH" OF DEI
TURNS OUT TO BE A LIE

"Consider a college campus boiling with racial and gender sensitivity, with courses in victimization, organizations for victims, a constant barrage of victimization propaganda—but no immediate and palpable victims. "Anti-racist" vigilantes with no racists (or misogynists and homophobes) to hang had better get busy and make some, and as we see, they often do."[363]

— Laird Wilcox, researcher of political fringe movements

---

363 Laird Wilcox, *Crying Wolf: Hate Crime Hoaxes in America* (Olathe KS: Laird Wilcox, 1994).

The last chapter revealed the "racial microaggression" as the chief institutional vehicle whereby the illusion of "rampant racism" is generated on college campuses so that DEI offices can maintain the façade of doing the work of antiracism. And, of course, this is key to continuing the voluminous funding necessary to maintain a sprawling bureaucracy, conduct trainings, and operate snitch lines and BRTs.

The *other* method for generating a negative racial climate is a fraudulent and illegal exercise called the "hate crime hoax."

A hate crime hoax is a faked racist incident on the campus, in which a student or students (and on occasion faculty and staff) contrive a racist scenario and then report it to the police or to the Bias Reporting System as an actual act of racism. Hate crime hoaxes can consist of fake nooses, fake assaults, fake hate-letters, fake vandalism.

The hate hoax is a familiar phenomenon at the university, and these usually are revealed to be publicity stunts to draw attention to racial problems—to "raise awareness"—that either don't exist or that are so infrequent and inconsequential as to require people to fabricate them.

Given that such contrived hate hoaxes are rarely punished, the utility of such an approach should be obvious. Why are they rarely punished? Because the hate hoax is in a good cause, usually attributed to the activism of "raising awareness." This fits snugly into the Big Con of *virtuous victimhood* in that maximum leeway is given to the perpetrators and their motives. We should remember that perpetrators are considered "victims" in the DEI framework. Contrast this treatment with that afforded to those accused of "racial microaggressions," in which *no leeway at all* is given, and the accused is guilty by virtue of the accusation itself.

In the case of the hate hoax, virtue is ascribed to the hoaxer as well. In fact, the right kind of "student activism" is considered virtuous, particularly activism in pursuit of "social justice."[364] This is the explanation given for this kind of performativity, and the "raising awareness" trope creaks under more weight than it was ever meant to carry.

> It's no great surprise that a bright, socially-conscious individual would realize quite on his or her own that there's nothing like some racist graffiti or some other "hate crime" to invigorate the militants, and what the hell, it's for a good cause—right?[365]

One of the logical expectations of DEI on campus has been the rise of these hate crime hoaxes, given the incentive structure that encourages the contrivance of fake racist incidents by students and sometimes faculty and staff. Why would people do such a thing? One scholar of the subject is Wilfred Reilly, and he replies straightforwardly: "The basic answers would seem to be fame, profit, and the advancement of a political ideology."[366]

> As we have seen in case after case, hoaxes are often perpetrated: to collect on the insurance, to win an election, to cover up the perpetrator's own crimes or disobedience to her parents, to get attention, or in a deliberate attempt to bolster the Continuing

---

364 Ann Christiano and Annie Neimand, "Stop Raising Awareness Already," *Stanford Social Innovation Review,* Spring 2017: https://ssir.org/articles/entry/stop_raising_awareness_already#
365 Laird Wilcox, *Crying Wolf.*
366 Wilfred Reilly, *Hate Crime Hoax,* p. 1.

Oppression Narrative. People who attempt to damage American race and class relations for such reasons are not heroes but criminals, and they should be prosecuted.[367]

But often universities do not prosecute these persons. In fact, they often engage in gaslighting.

When Universities Gaslight

Gaslighting involves a university delivering positive treatment of a fraudulent incident, which can create suspicion where none is warranted, waste scarce law enforcement resources on nonexistent threats and crimes, and wantonly damage the reputation of the university—all of this is really a *good* thing.

Whole societies can and have been gaslighted, in which entire populations are forced to "live a lie," as Vaclav Havel contends in his famous essay the "The Power of the Powerless." Says Havel, "It is a world of appearances trying to pass for reality."[368] Propaganda suffuses such societies, repeating the official messages that compel citizens to speak, act, and believe in ways contrary to what they experience and know to be true. Pretense becomes the norm, and communities are manipulated to distrust their own cognitive reasoning about the world they inhabit. An old Soviet joke captures this elevation of pretense to policy regarding the dysfunctional Soviet economy: "We pretend to work, and they pretend to pay us."

Institutions can be instruments of gaslighting, and sometimes they create entire bureaucracies to further the fraud. Bureaucratic

367 Wilfred Reilly, *Hate Crime Hoax*, p. 250.
368 Vaclav Havel and Paul Wilson (trans), "The Power of the Powerless," *International Journal of Politics*, Fall-Winter 1985-86, Vol. 15, No. 3/4, p. 30.

gaslighting is the process of convincing people to doubt their own experiences—what they see, hear, smell, touch, and taste.[369]

In the case of colleges captured by ideology, it's a process to convince them that their perception of their world is a product of "false consciousness" and should be replaced with the propaganda of ideology contrived by a tiny minority of radicals and enforced by the bureaucrat equivalent of doctrinal camp guards.

Official narrative portrays something bad as good. In this case an actual crime is acceptable, even honorable, if it raises awareness. In fact, universities routinely behave as if the revealed hoax *was an actual campus hate crime*, and they devote campus resources (training, always training) to address the faked problem.

But patience with hate hoaxes wears thin.

At Rhodes College, in Tennessee, for example, a "bias incident" was reported that December 11, 2024, racist notes were scattered over an area of the campus devoted to celebrating black fraternity and sorority life. An investigation showed that the person who originally reported the incident, in fact, had done it. The person had planned to blame someone else. The College was unamused and elected to take a surprisingly tough stance: "This matter has caused enormous pain to our community, and we are taking the appropriate steps to hold this individual accountable, including all legal avenues that may be available to us," Rhodes College said in a statement.[370]

369 I have written extensively on this. See Stanley K. Ridgley, "The $36 Million Question College Presidents Won't Answer," *American Greatness*, December 22, 2022: https://amgreatness.com/2022/12/22/the-36-million-question-college-presidents-wont-answer/

370 David Royer, "Rhodes College says racist messages found on campus fabricated" News Channel 3, Memphis, December 18, 2024: https://wreg.com/news/local/rhodes-college-says-racist-graffiti-found-on-campus-was-fabricated/

Raising awareness? Perhaps the actual awareness that's now being raised is of a small, malevolent group of persons, perhaps mentally disturbed, willing to lie and commit fraud to gain attention. This is reasonable, given what research tells us. In a 2016 article, journalist Jamaal Abdul-Alim expressed alarm that it was a rapidly increasing problem.[371] As early as 1994, investigative journalist Laird Wilcox pinpointed this short-con as the province of student peanut grifters.

> What I see happening with hoaxes is a kind of "market" process: the frequency of hoaxes increases with their utility in accomplishing desired ends. When the "market" or payoff for victimization goes up, the temptation to create victimization where none exists is very strong and the temptation of exaggerate minor cases of alleged victimization is even stronger.[372]

Psychologists explain best the make-believe world in which individual persons afflicted with paranoia, isolation, hyper-suspicion want to call attention to themselves. They want to externalize their problems, to blame others for failure, to point the finger at a fraudulent white supremacy culture. It can contribute to a sense of grandeur, of mattering, of being seen, and to the central myth of social justice to receive psychic pleasure.

Perhaps the best-known hate hoax in general circulation is the staged attack on actor Jussie Smollett in Chicago on January 29, 2019. It captures all the elements of a hate hoax of the

---

371 Jamaal Abdul-Alim, "False Reports of Hate Crimes Beset College Campuses," *Diverse*, May 8, 2016: https://www.diverseeducation.com/demographics/african-american/article/15098498/false-reports-of-hate-crimes-beset-college-campuses
372 Laird Wilcox, *Crying Wolf*.

sort we describe here—a racial component that plays to negative stereotypes easily believed by undemanding audiences, the reflexive racialist default guaranteed to elicit sympathy (the victim-signaling), and the tearful outlay of sympathy and call for justice (virtue-signaling). In this, no set-up is too unbelievable, no fraud is too great.

The actor claimed that in the early morning of Tuesday at 2 a.m., the coldest night of the year in the midst of a polar vortex when the temperature plunged to -20 degrees Fahrenheit below freezing, two "white" men wearing ski masks attacked Smollett, doused him with bleach, and strung a noose around his neck, while shouting "This is MAGA country." [Fake noose attacks are a particular favorite of black hate-hoaxers[373]] Smollett claimed he was out to buy a Subway sandwich.

Smollett was convicted in December of 2021 of staging the entire event, having hired two Nigerian bodybuilders (the brothers Abel and Ola Osundairo) to attack him. If any more shame could be had by Smollett, it's that his sordid escapade had no social justice overtones at all: "Police officials concluded that Smollett orchestrated a hate crime against himself because he was 'dissatisfied with his salary' on the Fox series "Empire."[374] Smollett appealed his conviction to the Illinois Supreme Court, and it was overturned in November 2024 on a technicality.[375]

Unfortunately, the Smollett style of faked hate crime is not unique. It is, in fact, a growing phenomenon, especially on college

---

373 Michelle Malkin, "MALKIN: Handy History of Fake Noose Stories," *The Toronto Star*, February 23, 2019.

374 Will Thorne, "Robin Roberts Calls Jussie Smollett Hoax a 'Setback for Race Relations," *Variety*, February 21, 2019: https://variety.com/2019/tv/news/jussie-smollett-robin-roberts-good-morning-america-interview-1203145056/

375 "Jussie Smollett: Timeline of a hoax, jail time and an overturned conviction," BBC, November 21, 2024: https://www.bbc.com/news/newsbeat-47317701

campuses. This goes back to the initial DEI lie of "rampant racism" on the campuses and the insertion of "racial microaggressions" to fill the gap. Again, if actual racism on the campus is near-nonexistent, then the lie threatens to collapse unless something can be done to gin-up racism.

The 2024 documentary film *Demand for Hate* examines the phenomenon,[376] which apparently has grown significantly since snitch lines and BRTs have been institutionalized on campuses. This coincides with the creation of DEI trainings to boost anonymous reports of imaginary grievances or reports of grievances so trivial that the mere fact of reporting them indicates the student's severe lack of maturity, toughness, and ability to negotiate the routine difficulties of life. When we hear reports of a severe mental health crisis on the campuses, university administrations should dedicate resources to how DEI contributes to that crisis.

Today's Hoax Deluge

Campus hate crime hoaxes today have become so numerous that they could fill an entire book. Dr. Wilfred Reilly, an associate professor at Kentucky State University, has, in fact, written such a book.

As chronicled by Reilly, campus reactions to these hoaxes are usually hysterical, and the claims themselves waste valuable law enforcement resources in futile hunts and investigations. The hoaxer is often someone seeking attention for himself or for his cause.

---

376 *Demand for Hate*, The Daily Caller, May 17, 2024: https://www.imdb.com/title/tt32321835/

When a student makes a false claim of bias at a typical elite American university, the faculty will be supportive; the student body will have been conditioned to see "hate" everywhere; hundreds of willing and aggressive radical allies will spring from the ground like soldiers from dragon's teeth; and the risk of punishment from on-campus judicial procedures (assuming the hoaxer is ever exposed) will be low.[377]

All these faked crimes display a common and disturbing element that largely confirms our hypothesis about the power of paranoia and ritual performativity of critical racialism—after the big reveal of the hoax, the community invariably rallies around the perpetrator. Says Reilly: "The campus community [behaves] exactly as though the falsely alleged incident actually happened, even after it was proven to be fake."[378]

After one egregious hoax at The University of Chicago in 2014, the school newspaper *Chicago Maroon* opined that "The revealing of the hoax should not de-legitimize the issues of racism that have been raised or mitigate the seriousness with which they should be addressed."[379] In other words, the incident may have been faked, but it revealed a kind of "inner truth."

This inner-truth attitude toward hoaxes and forged material is designed to maintain the myth of a conspiracy in the face of disconfirmations. It is commonplace among those who espouse conspiracy theories, and it's this "inner truth" that perpetuates the myth of the virtuous victim and, thus, enables the *virtuous victimhood* con-came to continue.

---

377 Wilfred Reilly, *Hate Crime Hoax*, p. 59.
378 Wilfred Reilly, *Hate Crime Hoax*, p. 75.
379 Wilfred Reilly, *Hate Crime Hoax*, p. 75.

Devotion to the "Inner Truth"

This devotion to an inner truth was especially true of those who embraced the notorious anti-Semitic forgery called *The Protocols of the Learned Elders of Zion*, which we reviewed earlier. It was authored to perpetuate a conspiracy theory of Jewish world domination. The document was known to be a forgery, even by leading members of the Nazi Party in Germany, 1933-1945, but this of course did not matter with respect to so called inner truth.

> Although most leading Nazis realized that *The Protocols of the Elders of Zion* was a spurious document, they found it useful in promoting belief in the international Jewish conspiracy of which they were already convinced. *Authorship and other details were irrelevant, they averred, if the book expressed "inner truth."*[380] [italics added]

The critical racialist script is performed ritualistically *as if* the staged incident(s) were actually real. The conspiracy theory's *inner truth* says there must be racial incidents, and if there *are* none, then incidents must be created so that the conspiracy theory is "confirmed." Nazi Party chief Alfred Rosenberg stated as much when he said of the *Protocols* that the issue was "less the so-called authenticity of *The Protocols* than the inner truth of what is stated."[381]

---

380 Randall L. Bytwerk, "Believing in 'Inner Truth': The Protocols of the Elders of Zion in Nazi Propaganda, 1933–1945," *Holocaust and Genocide Studies* 29, no. 2 (Fall 2015), p. 212. [Emphasis added]
381 Rosenberg quoted in Randall L. Bytwerk, "Believing in 'Inner Truth': The Protocols of the Elders of Zion in Nazi Propaganda, 1933–1945," *Holocaust and Genocide Studies* 29, no. 2 (Fall 2015), p. 215.

In other words, to both Shaun King (of Jazmine Barnes infamy) and to Alfred Rosenberg, it doesn't matter if it's not true; what matters is that it *could* be true. Inner truth, you see.

Hate crime hoaxes are not limited to the campuses, as Reilly points out. They are increasingly common occurrences in the larger American society. Reilly estimates that at least 15 percent of all reported hate crimes are hoaxes. This figure is drawn from data provided by the University of Wisconsin at LaCrosse in 2016, which reported that of 192 bias incidents, 28 were hoaxes.

The 15 percent at Wisconsin is a conservative number, given that the big-basket of "legitimate" hate crimes include such things as a report of a "Campus Crusade for Christ poster."[382] While the hoaxes themselves are abominable, it is the readiness to believe them that interests us here. This is paranoiac behavior—the readiness to believe and to say virtually anything that fits within their belief system and to disbelieve and to counter anything that doesn't mesh with it. The readiness to believe the *inner truth* of the racialist doctrine.

What makes this so fascinating is not simply the racialist readiness to believe, based on nothing but a primitive ideology. Rather, it is the additional characteristic of wholesale discounting of vast swaths of reality, so that what they perceive *as* reality is in fact just a tiny slice of it. This tiny slice constitutes their entire world.

---

382 Wilfred Reilly, *Hate Crime Hoax*, p. xxiv.

This constricted model of "reality" is dictated, circumscribed, and hermetically self-sealed from disconfirmation. Nothing can shake it. This paranoid belief system accepts and rejects facts arbitrarily, and anything outside the ideology does not exist or is rationalized in ways that "confirm" the ideology, much as primitive astronomers explained the movements of the heavenly bodies with auxiliary rescue hypotheses to protect Ptolemaic astronomy from disconfirmation.

By now, a normal person likely speculates as to why hate hoaxes are manufactured on campuses. Why do people act this way? Why do people manufacture racism and fake hate crimes where none exist?

Part of the answer can be found in the unscrupulous moral calculus embraced by some hustlers in victim culture. This has been a factor in the racial peanut grift for decades.

> In terms of cost-benefit analysis, the actual payoff for victim-hood can be very high and the risk of discovery of a hoax very small. This issue of "secondary gain" plays an important part in racist and anti-Semitic hoaxes, and the search for an answer to this troubling phenomenon is well served by the question, "Who benefits?"[383]

The rest of the answer can be found in the role of DEI. The DEI hierarchy and its enforcement machinery enables hoaxes of this sort. It actually *encourages* them.

The DEI snitch line, the propagation of the myth of the racial microaggression, the willingness of DEI functionaries to believe

---

383 Laird Wilcox, *Crying Wolf.*

any report of racism, no matter how fraudulent and shaky, and the unwillingness of administrations to prosecute racialist fakers has created campus climates where racialist fakery is not only perpetrated ... but rewarded. All of this combines to ensure the belief in the myth of the virtuous victim.

Let's look in-depth at an example of how nominally smart, professional persons can abandon all sense of critical reason where this "inner truth" is involved.

Fraud at Smith

From 2013 to 2023, Kathleen McCartney was the handsomely paid president of Smith College at more than a half-million dollars annually, and she presided over a small, but richly blessed institution with a $2 billion endowment, a college that lists more than $400 million yearly income,[384] and a $1.95 tagline: "Audacity, Agency, Authenticity."[385] It's anybody's guess what this tagline actually means, other than to suggest that not much of that $400 million is spent on first-class marketing for the school.

President McCartney has a history. Unlike her exorbitant salary, it is unenviable.

That history is her ignominious stumbling over racial issues at her school during the decade of her tenure, which has yielded a reputation of obsequious pandering in a series of apologies for her verbal missteps.[386] Nowhere in her responses over her decade

---

384 Her annual salary in 2021 was $515,461 Available at: https://nonprofitlight. com/ma/northampton/trustees-of-the-smith-college
385 www.smith.edu
386 Michael Powell, "Inside a Battle Over Race, Class and Power at Smith College," *The New York Times*, March 1, 2021. Available at: https://www. nytimes.com/2021/02/24/us/smith-college-race.html This article chronicles McCartney's presidential escapades as she awkwardly navigated through a series of *faux pas* that demonstrated anything but leadership ability.

of imprimatur did McCartney exhibit even a thimbleful of the "Agency" or "Authenticity" that Smith College claims for itself. And her "Audacity" consists in throwing her own working-class employees under the bus out of fear of a vocal, well-heeled minority on her campus. That is to say, no "audacity" at all.

It's a grim story.

Smith is an idyllic school, graced with Colonial, Greek Revival, and Victorian architecture and located in bucolic North-hampton, a Massachusetts community invested with a powerful pedigree. Smith's school website is professional and features the obligatory images, carefully filtered through matrices of equity and inclusion. The text on the site offers a rhetoric of obligatory boilerplate language that every college and university that desires to stay in business must publish.

The Potemkin façade at Smith was, until recently, tattered but relatively intact. Then, a scandal rocked this traditional small college with its royal-sized endowment and its president tacking furiously with the political wind. This misfortune involved President McCartney and decision-making that left most normal people baffled.

The first incident involved a hate crime hoax filed by a black student called Oumoe Kanoute. She lodged the hoax accusation against working class employees at this $78,000 per year school in summer of 2018.

Who is Oumoe Kanoute? She was no affirmative action student brought in from the projects to fill a diversity matrix. Smith presumably enrolled her because she is smart and savvy. And she is the very definition of privilege. In fact, if privilege could ooze, she'd ooze it from every pore.

Kenoute attended Westminster School, a private preparatory academy in Simsbury Connecticut, an institution with a $130 million endowment and that costs each student $67,145 per year with room and board.[387] She graduated in 2017.

On the Smith campus in summer of 2018, on July 31, she violated school regulations and ate her lunch in an area restricted to young children who were participants in a summer camp. She parked herself in a deserted lounge in a closed dorm. A janitor, upon seeing a stranger in a deserted dormitory, followed his instructions and called security. Kanoute was identified by a well-known and unarmed campus police officer, and she was politely informed of her rule violation, and the officer left.

But she remained.

That night, Kanoute forgot all about her Westminster School education, which calls on its graduates to exhibit "grit of character" and "grace of mind." Kenoute posted a vicious Facebook screed, claiming that she had been singled out in some way when, in fact, she had singled herself out by trespassing in an area restricted to those persons with a personal background check (which the summer camp required for persons with access to the camp children). With preciosity, Kenoute whined:

> It's outrageous that some people question my being at Smith, and my existence overall as a woman of color.[388]

---

387 Available at: https://www.westminster-school.org/admissions/affording-westminster

388 Michael Powell, "Inside a Battle Over Race, Class and Power at Smith College,"

This post "hit campus like an electric charge," says *The New York Times's* Michael Powell. And the response from the administration was what we have come to expect.

President McCartney immediately capitulated to the hoaxer. Without knowing any of the facts, McCartney went into personal damage-control mode, eager to avoid her own cancellation.

McCartney leaned into her go-to tactic—the groveling apology. Reported *The New York Times*: "I begin by offering the student involved my deepest apology that this incident occurred. And to assure her that she belongs in all Smith places."[389] She then drew herself up to her full presidential status and brought the power of her office to bear. She came down on the innocent working-class employees who had long-served the college.

The janitor who made the initial call was put on paid leave, or so he said. Smith now denies this. Jackie Blair, a cafeteria worker who played no role whatever in the incident, was harassed and misidentified by Kanoute on Facebook, with a photo and name posted.

By this time, President McCartney was all-in, rendering judgment on the affair. An investigation had not even begun, but the moral grandstanding had become a parade. Jodi Shaw, a student affairs employee at the time, who later resigned, recalled it this way:

> Before even investigating the facts of the incident, the college immediately issued a public apology to the student, placed the employee on leave, and announced its intention to create

---

389 Michael Powell, "Inside a Battle Over Race, Class and Power at Smith College,"

new initiatives, committees, workshops, trainings, and policies aimed at combating "systemic racism" on campus.[390]

These workshops are a standard tool of the DEI bureaucracy to implement campus thought reform. They are non-academic, typically deployed without the participation of the faculty, and they are driven by an ideology alien to the American experience.

McCartney did indeed institute the obligatory racialist training sessions. Given her missteps in previous years, she likely did not want to be seen as unenthusiastic about the incident, even if it turned out to be a hoax, which it did. Presidents have a single-minded focus on professional survival, and if it means that justice, honor, truth, and the working lives of Smith's loyal working-class employees must be sacrificed, then that's just what it means. Even if they did nothing wrong.

McCartney's working-class employees were innocent of wrong-doing, and it was McCartney's own investigation that determined their innocence. Three months after the hysterical response, the college itself found nothing wrong in the actions of its employees.[391]

But still, President McCartney would not support her own loyal employees, who had performed their duties flawlessly.

390 Jodi Shaw letter of resignation published in Bari Weiss, "Whistleblower at Smith College Resigns over Racism," *Common Sense with Bari Weiss*, February 19, 2021. Available at: https://bariweiss.substack.com/p/whistleblower-at-smith-college-resigns
391 Emma Whitford, "Smith Finds No Bias in Incident That Roiled Campus," *InsideHighered.com*, October 30, 2018 Available at: https://www.insidehighered.com/news/2018/10/30/investigation-finds-no-policy-violations-when-police-were-called-black-student

President McCartney thundered, "It is impossible to rule out the potential role of implicit racial bias"—even though the investigation she commissioned left no basis for ruling it *in*. At one point, Smith College even encouraged the cafeteria worker, Jackie Blair, to attend "restorative justice" sessions to facilitate a "willing apology." She quite reasonably asked, "Why would I do this?" After all, she noted, "This student called me a racist, and I did nothing."[392]

Smith College, for its part, posted an FAQ on the affair on August 1, 2018, which was last updated at this writing in late 2024.[393] The complete 35-page, single-spaced investigation report is available there as well.

The authoritarians claimed their innocent victims, and the ideology of racialism that empowered false accusations remained unchecked. Life at Smith went on, McCartney left her lavishly compensated position in 2023, and she was replaced by Sarah Willie-LeBreton, a trained applied sociologist and committed racialist and collectivist. Says the website, "[S]he has a demonstrated record of addressing social inequality and fostering community." Her own chosen descriptive quote on the Smith site is: "The promise of education is not just the creation of knowledge, but the model of how to share it for our mutual liberation and the collective good."[394] Her two books indicate her location deep in the academic ghetto of racialism: *Acting Black: College, Identity,*

392 Frederick M. Hess and R.J. Martin, "A janitor and security guard did their jobs; Smith College branded them racists," *Inside Sources*, February 26, 2021. Available at: https://insidesources.com/a-janitor-and-security-officer-did-their-jobs-smith-college-branded-them-racists/
393 Available at: https://www.smith.edu/news/campus-police-call
394 https://www.smith.edu/about-smith/presidential-announcement

and the Performance of Race and *Transforming the Academy: Faculty Perspectives on Diversity and Pedagogy.*

And Kenoute? She's apparently not changed for the better as a result of her hate hoax at Smith. She immediately moved on from Smith to become a research assistant intern in a lab at the Columbia University School of Social Work, which apparently trains persons to become professional racialists: "This lab focuses on innovative ways to conceptualize, and measure racism . . . . [I]t immerses people in a virtual reality of racism to help them understand the complexities of racism."[395] At last check, she's moved on yet again, with nary a word about her earlier racialist shenanigans at Smith.

In the end, it's a headline from the UK's *Daily Mail* that provides a snapshot of the Smith hate hoax, and this is how we ought to remember Kenoute:

> Student was not victim of racism for "eating while black" at $80k Smith College and made up details that ruined the lives of four campus workers and led to controversial anti-bias training that employee resigned over.[396]

---

395 https://www.linkedin.com/in/oumou-kanoute-b30668186/ This link has since been deleted and the LinkedIn profile changed to "Oumoe K." She has scrubbed most of the racialist references from her profile, and there is certainly no mention of the incident at Smith that so nettled her at the time.
396 Harriet Alexander, "Student was not victim of racism for 'eating while black' at $80k Smith College and made up details that ruined the lives of four campus workers and led to controversial anti-bias training that employee resigned over," February 24, 2021, *DailyMail.com*. Available at: https://www.dailymail.co.uk/news/article-9297475/Black-student-not-victim-racism-eating-black-80k-Smith-College.html

Racial Microaggression—*You, too, can stage your own Hoax*

The problem faced by DEI racialists in the universities is the dearth of actual racism on campus. With no racism to battle, DEI is stripped of its very purpose for existence, demonstrated to be superfluous. It's unneeded.

If you're a bureaucrat in a bureaucracy that is financially superfluous, this is a precarious place to be, particularly in an industry in financial peril, like higher education. This is all the more pressing when the highest paid campus DEI mandarins are lavishly compensated. Take the University of Michigan's Chief Diversity Officer Tabbye Chavous and her $417,000 salary. Or UC Berkeley's Vice Chancellor for the Division of Equity and Inclusion Dania Matos and her $331,098 salary.

With little to no actual racism to police, it's easy to see the incentive for DEI offices to create fake racism to justify the bureaucracy. DEI offices encourage minority students to seek offense at every turn and to cast themselves as victims of imagined "microaggressions." They can then use the anonymous snitch line discussed in Chapter 7 to unleash a bias response team for an investigation.

Public Intellectual Coleman Hughes demonstrated his experience with the "racial microaggression" in high school and at Columbia University. He related how he was instructed to feel oppression and to take offense reflexively.[397]

Hughes is criticized by racialists in the predictable way that all pseudo-sciences defend themselves—what Karl Popper called "soothsaying." Pseudo-sciences, such as Marxism, reflexively

---

397 Coleman Hughes, *The End of Race Politics: Arguments for a Colorblind America* (New York: Thesis, 2024).

explain away disconfirmations of the doctrine by confecting what Popper identified as the "rescue hypothesis."[398]

> The Marxist theory of history, in spite of the serious efforts of some of its founders and followers, ultimately adopted this soothsaying practice. In some of its earlier formulations (for example in Marx's analysis of the character of the "coming social revolution") their predictions were testable, and in fact falsified. Yet instead of accepting the refutations the followers of Marx re-interpreted both the theory and the evidence in order to make them agree. In this way they rescued the theory from refutation; but they did so at the price of adopting a device which made it irrefutable. They thus gave a "conventionalist twist" to the theory; and by this stratagem they destroyed its much advertised claim to scientific status.[399]

Likewise, the racialism that Coleman Hughes describes is high fakery in the academic world. The critical racialists—represented on campus as DEI apparatchiks—explain away the Hughes position with a pop-psychological convention. They call this "internalization" of the oppressed mentality. In actuality, they have simply contrived a word to label a major disconfirmation of the theory that undergirds DEI. At the same time, imaginary transgressions are given credence and amplified to coach young

---

398 "Some genuinely testable theories, when found to be false, are still upheld by their admirers—for example by introducing ad hoc some auxiliary assumption, or by reinterpreting the theory ad hoc in such a way that it escapes refutation. Such a procedure is always possible, but it rescues the theory from refutation only at the price of destroying, or at least lowering, its scientific status." Karl Popper, *Conjectures and Refutations* (New York: Basic Books, 1962), p. 37.
399 Karl Popper, *Conjectures and Refutations* (New York: Basic Books, 1962), p. 37.

minority students that they are, indeed, oppressed and that the white majority is the culprit.

Le Grand Hoax

We finish with the mother of all campus hate hoaxes, which only achieved closure late in 2024. It illustrates the power of a story to harness the emotions of people already deeply invested in believing an overarching false narrative of victims and villains. It shows how university leadership can become suckers, too, and cost their institutions millions of dollars when they too-readily believe the virtuous victim narrative.

The year 2006 saw the unfolding of one of the most sensational campus hate crime hoaxes of all time—the Duke Lacrosse scandal, which involved rape accusations, and claims of racism against "privileged" oppressors. It pitted rich against poor, white against black, gown against town, male against female. It was the classic oppressor *versus* oppressed that the nation had been waiting for.

On March 13 of that year, the Duke lacrosse team held an off-campus party for which they hired three female strippers to perform. The party went off as expected but then took a bad turn. One of the dancers, Crystal Mangum, alleged afterward that she had been raped.

Thus, all the elements of the *virtuous victimhood* scam were in place. The setup was perfect for a Bonfire-of-the-Vanities Great White Defendant, the kind of case where careers could skyrocket and where the downside was so minimal as to be nonexistent. Or so it was thought.

In this case, three well-to-do white kids at a prestigious university in the South versus a poor, black woman forced to abase herself for their pleasure and then, raped for her trouble. A local prosecutor with political ambitions, Mike Nifong, jumped on it. Duke's President Dick Brodhead caved immediately and suspended the lacrosse team and fired coach Mike Pressler (forced resignation) on April 5, 2006. In the vernacular, Brodhead hung his students out to dry.

Faculty got in on the action. A gaggle of Duke professors, called the Group of 88, attacked the young men in an ad in the school newspaper. Actual charges of first-degree sexual offense, kidnapping and rape were brought against three players—David Evans, Collin Finnerty, and Reade Seligmann—but it wasn't long before the case fell apart completely.

The NC attorney general Roy Cooper dropped all charges. Duke quickly settled lawsuits with the three students for $20 million apiece. It also settled with the fired coach for a substantial sum.

The DA Nifong, on whose narrow shoulders most of the blame was heaped, became the classic fall guy. He received the lion's share of punishment for his part in the con: "guilty of fraud, dishonesty, deceit or misrepresentation; of making false statements of material fact before a judge [and] bar investigators, and of lying about withholding exculpatory DNA evidence, among other violations."[400]

But why talk about this years-old case?

Because any doubts in the case were resolved in December 2024 with the confession of the dancer who made the original

---

[400]"Former Duke Prosecutor Nifong Disbarred," ABC News, February 10, 2009: https://abcnews.go.com/TheLaw/story?id=3285862&page=1

accusation. From the North Carolina Correctional Institution for Women, where she is currently in prison after being convicted of murdering her boyfriend in 2013, Crystal Mangum said she made it all up.[401] It was a hate crime hoax.

Aside from Nifong, it seemed that no one paid a price for the hoax, especially not the campus louts who rushed to judgment to crucify innocent students based on their belief in the virtuous victimhood narrative.

What of Duke President Dick Brodhead, a modern-day Pontius Pilate who had bought into the con of Great White Defendant and had sacrificed his own students on the altar of the screaming crowds. He paid no price whatever and offered, eventually, a lame apology for his actions that cost the university more than $60 million in settlements. Bizarrely, he also intimated that he, too, was a duped victim of the unscrupulous prosecutor Mike Nifong.[402]

What of the Group of 88 faculty? Their lack of judgment and reckless behavior appear not to have hurt their careers in the least. I was especially distressed to see one of my own former Duke professors had signed the indictment of the innocent students. He, like the others, continue unblemished careers, moving on to other schools and leaving behind their unpleasant and best-forgotten turpitude.[403]

401 Dom Fenoglio , Ranjan Jindal , Sophie Levenson and Abby Spiller, "Crystal Mangum admits to fabricating 2006 Duke lacrosse scandal accusations," *The Chronicle*, December 12, 2024: https://www.dukechronicle.com/article/2024/12/duke-mens-lacrosse-scandal-2006-crystal-mangum-admits-fabrication-rape-18-years-later-apologizes-kat-depasquale-evans-finnerty-seligmann-brodhead-pressler-nifong

402 Duke Today Staff, "Duke President Shares Lessons Learned, Regrets About Lacrosse Case," *Duke Today*, September 29, 2007: https://today.duke.edu/2007/09/rhb_lawconf.html

403 KC Johnson, "Whatever Happened to the Group of 88?" *Minding the Campus*, May 23, 2010: https://www.mindingthecampus.org/2010/05/23/what_ever_happened_to_the/#comments

The Duke Lacrosse scandal serves as a cautionary tale of the power of the Big Con, especially grounded in the *virtuous victim-hood* Con Story.

Hate Hoaxes are so routine nowadays that social media compiles the best-of in lists at the end of the year. For instance, 2024 saw almost two dozen campus hoaxes make the headlines.[404] One of them is particularly ingenious and illustrates how enterprising individual peanut grifters can milk the *virtuous victim* Con Story online, through GOFUNDME campaigns.

In one smart short-con, Roda Osman, a Somali Muslim grad student at UT-Austin, raised $40,000 off a racially motivated brick attack on herself that actually never happened. Well-acquainted with the short-con, Osman appears to be a regular peanut grifter familiar to the local police with "a history of running online fundraisers on questionable grounds."[405]

Conclusion

Hate crime hoaxes are indeed a scourge on the nation, especially on the campuses where administrations are especially likely to fall for them, where they often go unpunished, and where they artificially heighten the sense of racial tensions. The hate hoax is an important augmentation of the racial microaggression to help create the perception of a negative campus climate. When racism is in great demand, but short supply, you have to make it up, and there's no sign that universities have learned their lesson as far as

404 The College Fix staff, "There were 21 campus hate crime hoaxes uncovered in 2024," The College Fix, December 27, 2024: https://www.thecollegefix.com/there-were-21-campus-hate-crime-hoaxes-uncovered-in-2024/

405 College Fix Staff, "HOAX: 'Black feminist theory' PhD student raised $40K on false assault claim, police say," January 22, 2024: https://www.thecollegefix.com/hoax-black-feminist-theory-phd-student-raised-40k-on-false-assault-claim-police-say/

cracking down on those who lie and commit racialist fraud to the detriment of their entire university communities.

Rather than confect a what-to-do list about the ubiquitous hate hoax, I leave it to the country's foremost academic expert on the subject to prescribe a multi-pronged solution. Wilfred Reilly cuts to the root of the issue and addresses it.

> To boil principles down to essentials, this is what we need to fight the hate crime hoaxes that are dangerously undermining relations between Americans of different races: (1) understand that many hate crimes are hoaxes, (2) actively and aggressively punish individuals discovered to have faked bias crimes, (3) stop making excuses for these criminals, and (4) stop the flow of benefits with which we currently reward these crimes. Hate crime hoaxes only feed the cynical false narrative of ethnic conflict and oppression that is destabilizing society.[406]

As long as the incentive structure is in place to generate fake racism, we should continue to expect hate crime hoaxes. When universities crack down on the hoaxers, then—and only then—will the pandemic of fakery subside. The only roadblock for a thorough crackdown are the obstacles maintained by the functionaries employed in the DEI bureaucracy. These bureaucrats are the folks who benefit from the hoaxers.

This noxious incentive structure is the topic of the next chapter.

---

406 Wilfred Reilly, *Hate Crime Hoax*, p. 254.

9
THE NEW DEI COMMISSARS

SURVEILLANCE FOR POLITICAL PURITY

"The philosophers of the Enlightenment, whose belief in the possibility of law-based democratic states gave us both the American and French Revolutions, railed against what they called obscurantism: darkness, obfuscation, irrationality. But the prophets of what we might now call the New Obscurantism offer exactly those things: magical solutions, an aura of spirituality, superstition, and the cultivation of fear."[407]

— Anne Applebaum, *The Atlantic*

407 Anne Applebaum, "The New Rasputins: Anti-science mysticism is enabling autocracy around the globe," *The Atlantic*, January 7, 2025: https://www. theatlantic.com/magazine/archive/2025/02/trump-populist-conspiracism-autocracy-rfk-jr/681088/

It isn't an accident that DEI bureaucrats seem to be everywhere on the campus, urging everyone to "do the work." Even as it remains a mystery exactly what this work is.

The summer of 2020 triggered the expenditure of multiple millions of dollars to construct Soviet-style bureaucracies on campuses populated with oddly credentialed persons with a sweepingly vague mandate and obscure success indicators for the positions created for them. Every college and university that wanted to insulate itself from the inevitable unrest that would plague hesitant leaders, appointed "Chief Diversity Officers" and a phalanx of DEI political officers to populate the hierarchy.

These Diversity Officers even have their own off-campus political non-profit organization. The group, called the National Association of Diversity Officers in Higher Education (NADOHE), ensures political and doctrinal uniformity among the rank-and-file of diversity officers nationwide.

Rather than the typical bureaucracy you find at, say, the local DMV or at the post office, DEI's university scaffolding is insidious and pervasive. This is because it markedly resembles a tool of political control and guidance used successfully by the Soviet Union and similar authoritarian states. This was/is the "commissar" method.

This chapter examines the role of Chief Diversity Officer and the people who occupy the expensive and sprawling DEI bureaucracies they govern. We look at the "work" that they apparently are always doing, we look at the expanding scaffold of political control employed by the bureaucracy, and we look at the exorbitant salaries and bloated budgets extorted from universities as part of DEI's resource-extraction strategy.

DEI Commissars of Control

In the Soviet Union, from 1917-1991, the communist party utilized a method of political control of the military that went by various labels. We call it here the commissar method. This commissar method featured the insertion of a political officer—a *zampolit*—into every military unit to ensure political reliability of the regular officers and to conduct ideological training for the troops. If you want to see a realistic dramatization of what a political officer looks like and how he behaves, you can see this in the 1989 action film *The Hunt for Red October*.

The film was based on a Tom Clancy novel about the defection to the United States of a Soviet Admiral with a high-tech Russian submarine and its entire crew. The only potential glitch in the plan was the presence of the political officer, or *zampolit*, who was tasked to monitor the political loyalty of the sub commander. The *zampolit* was eliminated soon into the film, at the 18:22 mark.

In Communist China, too, the commissar system was adopted to monitor and control political activity in the universities. Scholars were censured for hewing to "bourgeois theories and methods of research."[408] It looked like this:

> Since liberation, the responsible representatives of Party and state in the universities have come to evaluate the lectures given by a professor not in terms of his 'creativity' or his ability for independent scholarly research, but according to his willingness to submit to 'discipline'. 'Discipline' means that the professor lectures in class exactly according to the outline or

---

408 Theodore H. E. Chen, *Thought Reform of the Chinese Intellectuals* (Hong Kong: Hong Kong University Press, 1960), p. 96-97.

lecture notes previously approved by the leadership'; he is not allowed to use any lecture material not previously approved.[409]

Likewise, today, diversity officers are assigned to most units within the university to monitor, to advise, and to report on compliance. American Enterprise Institute senior fellow Mark Perry notes that DEI people have spilled onto the campus proper.

> "What's happened over the last five to 10 years is it's spread out in decentralized ways," Perry told Fox News. "At the University of Michigan, each college, school, or department on campus will have a diversity officer, including the library, the arboretum, school of nursing – the college of engineering at Michigan has about 10" diversity officers.[410]

These functionaries are assigned even within academic units, where diversity functionaries have attempted to exert control over faculty behavior, over faculty hiring, and over the curriculum. They are called "Academic Diversity Officers," and the overwhelming majority ostensibly report to the deans or other heads of their units but also maintain a relationship to a hierarchy overseen by a chief diversity officer or some similarly named functionary, most times a vice provost or vice president. Christopher Rufo has characterized this commissar system and its functioning thusly:

409 Wu Ta-k'un, "Let the professors lecture independently," *Jen-min jih-pao* (JMJP), August 19, 1956, cited in Theodore H. E. Chen, *Thought Reform of the Chinese Intellectuals* (Hong Kong: Hong Kong University Press, 1960), p. 97-98.
410 Joe Schoffstall, "Top DEI staff at public universities pocket massive salaries as experts question motives of initiatives," Foxnews.com, March 30, 2022: https://www.foxnews.com/politics/top-dei-staff-at-public-universities-pocket-massive-salaries-as-experts-question-motives-of-initiatives

They created a circular, self-reinforcing system that created its own demand and installed a new, universal class of "diversity officials" across the institutions, which seeks to break down the old protections of individual rights, colorblind equality, and private property and replace them with a substitute morality and system of government based on the principles of critical race theory.[411]

Even some faculty members believe that these DEI commissars should assume pride of place in the midst of faculty business. This faculty business consists of hiring and promotion and curriculum-building. Michael Berube and Jennifer Ruth crafted an entire book to support DEI participation as members of an "academic freedom" committee to police faculty behavior.[412] As I noted in my review of the book:

> The authors call for the establishment of Orwellian "academic freedom" committees to police the faculty on campuses nationwide. On each campus, select faculty would join with "professionals hired by the university to DEI [diversity, equity, and inclusion] positions" to form these committees that will police the speech, teaching, and research of professors. "We propose that faculty and professionals with expertise in the relevant areas be the primary drivers of any committee or

---

411 Christopher F. Rufo, *America's Cultural Revolution: How the Radical Left Conquered Everything* (New York: Broadside Books, 2023), p. 249.
412 Michael Bérubé and Jennifer Ruth, *It's Not Free Speech: Race, Democracy, and the Future of Academic Freedom*, (Baltimore: Johns Hopkins University Press, 2022).

review panel. The professionals hired by the university to DEI positions would retain significant influence."[413]

Involving the "professionals" of DEI in the business of the faculty is a long-term goal of DEI cadres. Berube and Ruth attempt to "redefine" academic freedom to make it more tractable to the control of mediocre bureaucrats who increasingly pervade university bureaucracies. They siphon away faculty autonomy and curricular control even as you read this.

Those of us on campus recognize that these DEI offices are uniformly staffed with modestly educated hirelings steeped in the social justice ideology learned in academically shallow programs such as online diversity certification, educational leadership, or higher education administration. These are the folks who administer secret campus courts, conduct investigations based on anonymous claims, run bias response teams, conduct racial re-education struggle sessions, all while evading accountability and crouching behind benign pronouncements of inclusion, accessibility, equity, and social justice.

If Berube and Ruth and the middling bureaucrats have their way, what might this DEI "involvement" look like?

To know what this type of power looks like when exercised, we can look to where the system has been implemented and bureaucrats are busy "doing the work." And what the intellectuals subjected to middling bureaucrats have to say about it.

In their eyes the intellectuals were persons to be reformed and

---

413 Stanley K. Ridgley, "The Critical Race Tribunals," *Academic Questions*, Winter, 2022: https://www.nas.org/academic-questions/35/4/the-critical-race-speech-tribunals

they the reformers with the right—which they often exercised—to call any faculty member out of the classroom any time and demand of him a satisfactory 'self-examination' before permitting him to return to his teaching duties. It was also said that the personnel department of the university, controlled by Communists, was virtually an 'independent kingdom' in the university.[414]

Examples of the predation of Diversity Commissars abound. Here's one from Michael Clune, an English professor at Case Western Reserve:

I will give an example from my own work as chair of several faculty search committees over the past two years. At a mandatory training session, I was told by the university's diversity officer that I was to use candidates' diversity statements as a means of ascertaining candidates' racial identity. Yet at another training session, I was told that I was *not* to base hiring decisions on knowledge of candidates' racial identity.

Chairing a search-committee meeting in which faculty members were openly discussing candidates' race, I wondered aloud if what we were doing was illegal. I then received a stern email from the diversity dean telling me that it was unacceptable to raise the question of the legality of the university's practices. I then asked what those practices were. How, in fact,

414 Theodore H. E. Chen, *Thought Reform*, p. 159-160.

does the university want us to take account of race? I never received a reply.[415]

Cadres in the University

What does it take to be a commissar in the ranks of DEI? Is there some sort of expertise based in the DEI office? Are there tasks, conditions, and standards to be met? That's iffy. One college president put it this way: "In colleges, what you hire now is administrators ... Now, because they are appointing all these diversity officers, what are their degrees in? Education. It's easy. You don't have to know anything."[416]

That may be a harsh assessment, but if it's true, it suggests that other qualifications are in play for appropriate diversity personnel—the same qualifications that suited the Red Guards of Mao Zedong's Cultural Revolution, who did not wield power for their academic expertise, nor their compassion, nor their intellect. **They wielded coercive power for their blind loyalty to a simple-minded ideology that slotted people into prescribed categories as either villains or victims.** They employed that coercive power to punish enemies brutally, killing several million and torturing hundreds of thousands more over an entire decade.

The political cadres of Mao Zedong's Cultural Revolution are one of its most memorable visual elements. Red Guards wore PLA green pants and jacket, a wide leather belt, and the "prized bright

415 Michael W. Clune, "We Asked for it: The politicization of research, hiring, and teaching made professors sitting ducks," *The Chronicle of Higher Education*, November 18, 2024: https://www.chronicle.com/article/we-asked-for-it

416 Stanley K. Ridgley, "Hillsdale's Larry Arnn is over the target," *American Greatness*, July 20, 2022.

red armband."[417] The thousands of Red Guards, many or most of them teenagers, deployed throughout Chinese cities and would conduct nightly search raids of private homes, destroying paintings, cultural icons, and especially books. Communist propaganda stressed the need to root out and eliminate the "Four Olds—old thought, old customs, old culture, and old morals."[418] What goes on in a "search raid?" One young Red Guard explains:

> People have been hiding all sorts of things. Counterrevolutionary materials, pre-Liberation Reactionary artworks, gold, jade, silver, jewelry—the trappings of Feudalism-Capitalism-Revisionism are everywhere.[419]

The search teams, comprising 6-8 guards, were not cordial when conducting a raid:

> Despite the heat they were all wearing white cloths over their mouths and noses, and dark clothes. The one who seemed to be the leader carried a long metal spring with a rubber tip. He struck it against the table with a loud crack. "Liang Shan!" he said. "Is there anything Feudalist-Capitalist-Revisionist in your house?"[420]

If this formulaic hyphenated litany sounds familiar, that's because today's critical and antiracist pedagogues mimic the thuggish trope. The late novelist bell hooks (the penname of Gloria

---

417 Liang Heng and Judith Shapiro, *Son of the Revolution* (New York: Vintage Books, 1984, 1983), p. 68.
418 Liang Heng and Judith Shapiro, *Son of the Revolution*, p. 68.
419 Liang Heng and Judith Shapiro, *Son of the Revolution*, p. 70.
420 Liang Heng and Judith Shapiro, *Son of the Revolution*, p. 72.

Jean Watkins) was notorious for repeating the dull cadences of Red Guard rhetoric. She was a well-known DEI guru, and in her many essays on education, hooks would insert a mantra-like trope that she repeated for authoritarian effect. She incanted this mantra with variations on the theme, and at times employed it in what can only be interpreted as a conscious bid for a kind of Red Guard excess:

> Successful curriculum changes that promoted inclusion and diversity threatened the existing status quo, and the uphold-ers of imperialist white-supremacist capitalist patriarchal biases . . . . [and again, just six sentences later] In reality, the focus on diversity revitalized learning by changing education so that it would not reflect and uphold the biases inherent in imperialist white-supremacist capitalist patriarchal thinking.[421]

The very clunkiness of this trope appears contrived to call attention to it, and hooks was too keen a writer to have missed its resemblance to the stilted ideological style of Red Guard thugs conducting their search raids. She apparently believed that its ritualistic repetition had utility for her ultimate objective, which outweighs aesthetic considerations. And as if to say "yes, I really mean it," hooks added yet another iteration of her mantra at the close of her short essay, with her lament of "work that reinforces the hegemony of imperialist white-supremacist capitalist patriar-chy." For good measure, hooks adds a coda to reference "dominator

421 bell hooks, "Learning Past the Hate," *Teaching Critical Thinking* (New York: Routledge, 2010, 2019), p. 105.

culture."[422] The cumbrous phraseology contains the magic hope of drafting large numbers of people into the maelstrom of ritual.

Why would hooks employ such barbarisms? It came to her quite naturally. She was an admirer and acolyte of the Brazilian educator Paulo Freire, whose derivative "philosophy" was drawn directly from the educational theory of Mao Zedong. The lineage is explicit, and this is the doctrine that informs the university cadres of DEI.

She is important, because of her status as a guru of DEI, a crafter of doctrine, and a respected member of the pantheon of DEI worthies. She has inspired many thousands of DEI cadres, just as have a clique of other DEI gurus whom we will meet in Chapter 10.

Cadres, you say?

The cadres of DEI are in place on the campuses, and that is a fact with which we must deal. It's a measure of how far higher education has declined that bureaucrat hirelings motivated by their paranoia and lucrative con-game of virtuous victimhood should occupy any sort of professional position that impacts the lives of students, staff, *or* faculty. Their numbers are legion, and they increase every year. One report found that in 65 top public universities, nearly *3,000 people* listed as having DEI responsibilities.[423]

Nationwide, university DEI bureaucrats and their enablers are moving steadily to acquire power over the last bastion of clear

---

422 bell hooks, "Learning Past the Hate," p. 110.
423 Jay P. Greene, PhD, and James D. Paul, "Diversity University: DEI Bloat in the Academy,"

thought and free inquiry in the universities—the faculty. In this effort, they have established a new specialized sub-class of diversity officers, called Academic Diversity Officers. These are diversity apparatchiks embedded within separate units of the university.[424]

[S]ome institutions have established the chief diversity officer (CDO) role. More recently, with the CDO role as a model, a new position is emerging on some campuses: the academic diversity officer, or ADO. ADOs work alongside CDOs to ensure that diversity, equity, and inclusion practices are prioritized and executed in specific schools and colleges, disciplines, and department units.[425]

Thus, DEI doctrine is disseminated at the faculty unit level, and faculty are monitored for their compliance with DEI *diktats*. Some faculty are reported if found uncooperative or insufficiently enthusiastic. Universities actually attempt to apply hip-pocket judicial processes to discipline faculty if they run afoul of the DEI edifice. Later, we examine a number of cases that universities likely wish they'd not brought against faculty.

So DEI apparatchiks are embedded around the campus, keeping an eye out for policy violations. We've seen before what happens when unqualified political apparatchiks are inserted into

424 Jeffrey K. Grim, Laura Sánchez-Parkinson, Marie Ting, Tabbye Chavous, "The Experiences of Academic Diversity Officers at the University of Michigan," *Currents: Connecting Diversity Scholarship to Practice and Society*, Vol. 1, No. 1, 2019: https://quod.lib.umich.edu/c/currents/17387731.0001.111?view=text;rgn=main#top
425 "The Role of the Academic Diversity Officer," *Higher Education Today*, American Council on Education, undated: https://www.higheredtoday.org/role-academic-diversity-officer/

the university into powerful monitoring and enforcement roles. In China, political cadres staffed with "progressives" were placed in positions of authority over faculty to ensure ideological reliability.

> Of all the aggravating frustrations, the hardest must have been the necessity of accepting the supervision and "leadership" of cadres whom the Communists trusted as progressive persons "rich in revolutionary experience" and well indoctrinated in the dogmas of Marxism-Leninism, but who, in their academic achievements, could not even qualify as students in the colleges and universities where they held sway. These symbols of the authority of the Party and the state not only browbeat the intellectuals in their thought reform and political indoctrination but even told them how they should carry on their professional activities.[426]

Likewise, the call for DEI personnel to monitor faculty hiring, teaching, and curricular input resonates with latter-day campus authoritarians who fancy themselves college educators.

What about the Grift? How's the Pay-out?

This book's contention is that DEI is an effective Big Con, a successful resource extraction strategy called *virtuous victimhood* that has resulted in a take that tallies in the *billions* of dollars. DEI commissars are the most visible beneficiaries of the grift. Certainly, the wealth and power at the top of the DEI hierarchy can be phenomenal, especially for the universities that go all-in

---

426 Theodore H. E. Chen, *Thought Reform,* p. 96.

to purchase their absolution. The University of Michigan is the primary example of this.

At a time when higher education faces numerous financial and enrollment challenges, DEI at Michigan remains flush with cash.

Michigan Goes All-In

Michigan launched its DEI program in 2016 with great fanfare, unveiling it as DEI 1.0. Its first Vice Provost for Equity and Inclusion and Chief Diversity Officer was Robert Sellers.

By the time Sellers stepped down in 2021, he was raking in a chill $431,000 annually. Keeping Michigan DEI literally in the family, Sellers was replaced by his wife, Tabbye Chavous-Sellers, in May of 2022. *Her* annual compensation is $417,000. Chavous-Sellers sits atop a Michigan DEI edifice that has spent $250,000,000 on diversity programs since 2016. The hemorrhaging of cash from this major university could have continued indefinitely but for an expose from the an unlikely source—*The New York Times Magazine*. The only brake on this gusher of cash from a revenue-strapped university was, apparently, public scrutiny.

In October of 2024, *The New York Times Magazine* published an expose on Michigan's out-of-control DEI budget.[427] The article aired an immense load of dirty DEI laundry and got the attention of the Michigan regents, who roused themselves to their oversight duties.[428] On December 5 at their regents meeting, they voted to eliminate the requirement for faculty to offer "diversity statements"

427 Nicholas Confessore, "The University of Michigan Doubled Down on D.E.I. What Went Wrong?", *The New York Times Magazine*, October 16, 2024:
428 Michigan's Board of Regents, University of Michigan website: https://regents.umich.edu/regents/

in hiring, promotion, and tenure.[429] This was a major reform for Michigan that ended a particularly odious practice akin to the loyalty oaths required of people in authoritarian regimes.

It was earlier, in January 2023, that President Santa Jeremy Ono had rolled out a new set of Michigan values, including DEI alongside other, reasonable and actual "values." Here they are: Integrity, Respect, Inclusion, Equity, Diversity, Innovation. Given the gross hemorrhaging of cash to the tune of a quarter of a billion dollars since 2016, Michigan probably ought to add "frugality" and "effectiveness," for these are not to be found in the Michigan vocabulary: "Fifty-six percent of that amount went to salaries and benefits for D.E.I. staff across the university's three campuses, according to an internal review conducted last spring by Michigan's central D.E.I. office."[430]

Michigan's DEI administrators scrambled to mount a defense against the damning revelations. Chief Diversity Officer Chavous-Sellers responded:

> The New York Times published an article on DEI efforts at the University of Michigan that was filled with misinformation, disinformation and, sadly, sexism .... I want to state up front that those of us who do DEI work—both at U-M and nationally—welcome thoughtful, critical questions about our work

---

429 Nicholas Confessore and Steve Friess, "University of Michigan Ends Required Diversity Statements," *The New York Times*, December 5, 2024: https://www.nytimes.com/2024/12/05/us/university-of-michigan-dei-diversity-statemements.html

430 Nicholas Confessore, "University of Michigan Weighs Changes to Its Diversity Program," *The New York Times*, December 4, 2024: https://www.nytimes.com/2024/12/04/us/university-of-michigan-dei.html

grounded in accurate data and evidence. Such inquiries make us more reflective, innovative, and effective.[431]

But of course, we already know that DEI offices refuse to answer pointed questions as a part of their embattled doctrine of conspiracy, as demonstrated explicitly at Princeton. My own experience in dealing with extremist DEI proponents confirms this, albeit anecdotally. They do not welcome questions at all, and the standard procedure is to simply categorize questioners as "diversity resistant." DEI staff view those pesky questions and those who ask them as part of their problem.

In the Michigan case, Chavous-Sellers demonstrated a bold unawareness of the rickety academic standing of DEI by accusing the NYT author of "confirmation bias." As we saw in Chapter 4, confirmation bias is an actual method widely used by DEI "scholars" to perpetuate the central myth of DEI. Said Chavous-Sellers:

> While I am not a journalist, as a professor it reminded me of the novice student writing a class paper who starts with a preconceived thesis on a topic, then looks only for the "evidence" that confirms the thesis, ignoring all evidence to the contrary. In my field (psychology), this is called confirmation bias. (And even new college students rarely exhibit this as egregiously as it was in this article).[432]

431 Tabbye Chavous, "CHAVOUS: A Battle for Truth – Setting the Record Straight on DEI at U-M," University of Michigan website, October 18, 2024: https://odei.umich.edu/2024/10/18/a-battle-for-truth-setting-the-record-straight-on-dei-at-u-m/
432 Tabbye Chavous, "CHAVOUS: A Battle for Truth – Setting the Record Straight on DEI at U-M,"

We've already seen how confirmation bias is an essential DEI tool in training students to maintain a negative campus racial climate—confirmation bias is the bread-and-butter of racial microaggressions. Nonetheless, Chavous-Sellers and the rest of the UM team slogged on with herculean damage-control that was buttressed by a hortatory message from a fellow-traveler, NADOHE's president:

> [T]o declare that diversity programs "went wrong" is not only inaccurate, but it fundamentally misunderstands what the work entails and what its goals are. The pursuit of equity and inclusion for a pluralistic democracy that thrives and works for all is aspirational, and it is an ongoing process that requires constant reassessment, recalibration, and renewal.[433]

A public already on alert for the Big Con narrative cocked a skeptical eye, as did the unamused Board of Regents, as we've seen. This incredible rapid-fire spate of events in October and December of 2024 revealed the first cracks in a once-formidable DEI edifice. An appropriate coda was provided with the firing of a Michigan DEI administrator—the head of "academic multicultural initiatives"—over her anti-Semitic remarks.[434]

Even so, the cash-flush Big Con continues at the majority of colleges and universities nationwide.

---

433 Paulette Granberry Russell, "Message to Members: We Know Our Value," NADOHE, October 21, 2024: https://www.nadohe.org/statements/we-know-your-value
434 Stephanie Saul and Vimal Patel, "D.E.I. Official at University of Michigan Is Fired Over Antisemitism Claim, Lawyer Says," *The New York Times*, December 12, 2024: https://www.nytimes.com/2024/12/12/us/university-of-michigan-dei-administrator-antisemitism.html

The Big Con Cash Roll-Call

A look at the University of California University System, for example, reveals the enormous sums of money involved. Here is a list of the beneficiaries, the top diversity officers at 10 of the California system's universities:

Berkeley—Dania Matos, Vice Chancellor for Equity and Inclusion $325,000 (2021)

Davis—Renetta Garrison Tull, Vice Chancellor for Diversity, Equity and Inclusion $323,810 (2023)

Irvine—Dyonne Bergeron, Vice Chancellor for Equity, Diversity & Inclusion $346,146 (2023)

UCLA—Mitchell Chang, Interim Vice Provost for Equity, Diversity and Inclusion $348,232 (2023)

Merced—Delia S. Saenz, Vice Chancellor for Equity, Diversity and Inclusion $304,944

Riverside—Mariam Lam, Vice Chancellor for Diversity, Equity and Inclusion $299,524

San Diego—Becky Petitt, Vice Chancellor for Equity, Diversity and Inclusion $342,272

San Francisco—Renee Navarro, Vice Chancellor for Diversity and Outreach $357,204

Santa Barbara—Jeffrey Stewart, Vice Chancellor for Diversity, Equity, and Inclusion $404,712

Santa Cruz—Anju Reejhsinghani, Vice Chancellor for Diversity, Equity, and Inclusion $299,031

Office of the President—Yvette Gullatt, Vice Provost for Equity, Diversity and Inclusion $362,010

The pay at other schools around the country is comparable. According to the 2021 Heritage study and other sources, DEI salaries can be enormous. Georgina Dodge, the vice president at the office of diversity and inclusion at the University of Maryland, which employs 71 DEI personnel, makes $358,000 a year; Menah Pratt-Clarke, vice provost for inclusion and diversity at Virginia Tech, which has 83 DEI personnel, receives over $351,000 annually; Sean C. Garrick, vice chancellor for diversity, equity and inclusion at the University of Illinois, which has 71 DEI employees, earns nearly $330,000 annually[435]

Of special note is the University of Virginia. The *virtuous victimhood* Big Con of resource extraction is incredibly successful as UVA pays more than **$1 million in salary and benefits** to its top two DEI sinecures. The senior associate dean of the Darden School of Business and global chief diversity officer, Martin N.

---

435 Jay P. Greene, PhD, and James D. Paul, "Diversity University: DEI Bloat in the Academy,"

Davidson, earns the most in a DEI role, at **$452,000**, or **$587,340** with benefits. The second-highest paid DEI executive is Kevin G. McDonald, the vice president for diversity, equity, inclusion and community partnerships, who takes home **$401,465**, or an estimated **$520,000** with benefits.[436]

By comparison, Virginia's governor Glenn Youngkin is paid $175,000, which begs the question as to what, exactly are these two UVA mandarins of DEI *doing* that is valued at $1 million. We find that *in toto*, DEI's Virginia operation extracts **$20 million yearly** and pays out to 235 DEI college functionaries. The top 10 highest-paid DEI functionaries receive almost $3 million in salary and benefits.[437]

Finally, the assiduous researchers at openthebooks.com put Ohio State University under the spotlight and discovered exactly what you'd imagine.

> Ohio State University spent $13.3 million on pay for 201 employees with DEI-related roles last year. That's the equivalent of full tuition for over 1,000 in-state students at its main Columbus campus.

> The highest paid DEI officials are James L. More, vice provost for diversity and inclusion and chief diversity officer at OSU, and Keesha Mitchell, associate vice president for the Office of Institutional Equity, practically tied at just under $300,000 each.

436 Adam Andrzejewski, "University of Virginia Spends $20 Million On 235 DEI Employees, With Some Making $587,340 Per Year," Openthebooks.com, March 4, 2025: https://www.openthebooks.com/substack-university-of-virginia-spends-20-million-on-235-dei-employees-with-some-making-587340-per-year/
437 Adam Andrzejewski, "University of Virginia Spends $20 Million On 235 DEI Employees,"

Another 29 people make between $100,000 and $269,000, with titles such as associate dean for diversity, inclusion, and outreach ($269,260), another associate vice president for the Office of Institutional Equity ($226,644), assistant vice provost for diversity and inclusion ($171,889), academic director for diversity and inclusion ($170,435), assistant dean and director of diversity, equity and inclusion ($145,923), among many more.[438]

Perhaps smarting from criticism of the sumptuous salaries and benefits ladled out to DEI functionaries, some schools are scrubbing DEI and EDI from their lingo, replacing the tainted DEI brand with something more benign. Schools aren't trimming the salaries and personnel; they're simply relabeling the offices.

UCLA, for instance, has renamed its *Office of Equity, Diversity and Inclusion* to the *Office of Inclusive Excellence*. This new name aligns well with the admirably opaque "Inclusive Excellence" mantra of the National Association of Diversity Officers in Higher Education (NADOHE), more about which in a moment. As of this writing, UCLA is recruiting a new vice provost for inclusive excellence at an expected salary range between $320,000 and $440,000.[439]

438 Openthebooks, DEI Blitz Reaches Buckeye Nation," Openthebooks.com, December 30, 2024: https://openthebooks.substack.com/p/dei-blitz-reaches-buckeye-nation

439 Shiv Patel, "UCLA announces new Office of Inclusive Excellence to replace current EDI office," *The Daily Bruin*, October 17, 2024: https://dailybruin.com/2024/10/17/ucla-announces-new-office-of-inclusive-excellence-to-replace-current-edi-office

The Diversity Officers Klatsch—*Where DEI "Professionals" Assemble*

Diversity officers in higher education have their own off-campus non-profit called NADOHE. It is in this professional organization that the sausage is made regarding policies and procedures that CDOs take back to their campuses. Unfortunately, this organization is rife with the ideology discussed in previous chapters. The NADOHE is where DEI doctrine is propounded in its most extreme forms. But the public image of NADOHE is pristinely benign and the group likes it that way.

> NADOHE is the preeminent voice for chief diversity officers. It leads the national and international conversation on diversity, equity, and inclusion in postsecondary education. Ultimately, it investigates, influences, and innovates to transform higher education so inclusive excellence thrives at the core of each institution worldwide.[440]

In point of fact, we know that these diversity officers are steeped in the oppressor/oppressed doctrine, with its core of "all whites are racist," and that the public pronouncements of this group are simply cover for its nasty racialism.

The NADOHE continues to be permeated with this noxious doctrine, all the while offering on their website photos of smiling diversity officers, commiserating and sharing the "sacred" space where "exhausted" CDOs can opine about being "understaffed, under-resourced and under-appreciated." We need look no further than the speaker lineup of its conferences to confirm that the racialist doctrine of DEI is intact.

The 2023 conference was opened with a keynote by the racialist ideologue Ijeoma Oluo, whom we met in Chapter 3 with her embrace of the DEI fundament—"all whites are racist." The conference closed with remarks by Nolan Cabrera, a professor at the University of Arizona. We met Cabrera briefly in Chapter 7 as one of the consultants who participates in Shaun Harper's Race & Equity Center's "learning modules" at $40,000 a pop to help improve campus "racial climate."

The 2024 NADOHE conference closed with remarks by Dr. Derald Wing Sue, Columbia Teachers College faculty and the guru of racial microaggressions, whom we met in Chapter 7.

In this environment, the air is thick with ideological fever, the bureaucrats have no clue what they are supposed to do (other than "the work"), and while half of them know they are running a con, the other half are paranoid true believers fighting against "white-man hegemony."[441]

It's a febrile environment, so how do diversity people conceive of their "work"? Let's listen in.

CDOs define their duties—their "work"

An amorphous mystification surrounds diversity staff and their functions. This mystification is captured by constant references to "the work" and the necessity to "do the work." Articles in DEI journals speak interminably about the "work," how "exhausting"

---

441 Alexis J. Stokes, Sherri H. Benn, Luz Janet Mejias, Angela Spranger, Caryn Reed-Hendon, J. Camille Hall, Ria DasGupta, and R. Adidi Etim-Hunting, "A Framework for the Sustainability of WOC DEIA+ Practitioners," in Carol Henderson (ed), *Chief Diversity Officers in Higher Education Today* (New York: Routledge, 2025), p. 86.

the work is, and how overworked and under-resourced their offices are. But when we wade into the description of the skill set of the CDO, we find a recital of generic nebulous functions with no connection to actual metrics. The flight from specificity is endemic to DEI offices.

We find lots of organizing, facilitating, community engagement, institutionalization, strategizing, leading with love, and—a favorite—"establishing an ethic of care on campuses." The work is never described with the specificity necessary for someone to actually accomplish tasks for which a person can be held accountable. Here is hired vice chancellor for equity and inclusion Dania Matos, for instance, ladling a dollop of diversity-speak when she was hired at Berkeley: "Honoring the ideals of diversity, equity, inclusion, belonging and justice is about perpetuating beauty in the center of injustice," Matos said in an interview with *Berkeley News*. "To do that we must confront our enduring legacy of slavery and the structural inequities that founded this nation with actionable solutions that lead to transformative change."[442]

Matos lamented the tough work of battling oppression and racism at one of the most left-wing campuses in America:

> I am up against a lot of systems of power that are bigger than myself. It takes a little bit out of you. When you're battling injustices, systemic oppression, racism, sexism—all those things—your heart breaks into a million pieces. I have to

---

[442] Ivan Natividad, "Dania Matos will 'lead with love' as Berkeley's new head of equity, inclusion," *UC Berkeley News*, July 2, 2021: https://news.berkeley.edu/2021/07/02/dania-matos-will-lead-with-love-as-berkeleys-new-head-of-equity-inclusion/

pick all those pieces up and put my heart back together every single time.[443]

One imagines that the task of mending a broken heart at Berkeley is made infinitely easier at a $325,000 annual salary. This emotionalism combined with on-the-job vagueness is likely intentional and, given that this is an elaborate con, perhaps unavoidable.

What's most concerning in this report are the results of a survey that describe these diversity officers' three highest priorities. If we view these priorities through the lens of the Big Con, we detect not one whit of actual potential accomplishment, but rather a reiteration of menu items tiresomely familiar by now.

1. diversity, equity, and inclusion strategic planning and implementation;

2. capacity building for resources, tools, and programming aimed at institutional transformation for equity, inclusion, achievement, belonging, and justice;

3. organizational leadership.

Let's move now from the tedious bureaucratese of official diversity reports to the personal descriptions provided by actual diversity officers—their attitudes about themselves and about their work.

---

443 Tom Tillison, "UC Berkeley's new Vice Chancellor of Equity details emotional toll of her $325,000 salary job," AmericanWire, December 14, 2021: https://americanwirenews.com/uc-berkeleys-new-vice-chancellor-of-equity-details-emotional-toll-of-her-325000-salary-job/

The Exhausted, the Embattled, the Oppressed— *Caveat Lector*

We now enter a strange place that is not for the literarily squeamish, which is why I offer the warning *caveat lector*—let the reader beware. The discourse of diversity officers reveals a cadre of persons uncomfortable with words, awash in narcissism and paranoia and mysticism, keenly conscious of their academic illegitimacy, fearful of being found out, and protective of their sinecures. These are unsung heroes, and if no one else will sing about them, they'll sing to each other.

They talk about their "superpowers," they advocate a more "holistic" measure of work to exclude most anything connected with work—publishing, material production, and professionalism in general. They advocate naps in "sacred spaces" in a program run by someone called The Nap Bishop in response to all that "doing the work," which never seems to be described. This is a world of navel-gazing, mysticism, autoethnographies, and *testimonios*.

A bizarre testimonial on DEI "work" is provided by a group of women who call themselves the "Queen's Collective" of diversity officers. When people of a particular psychological type combine, it generates reinforcement of certain behaviors, and this is an example of a self-referential paean to their own importance. It is all too typical, and it illustrates the B-player mentality, sliding into C-player territory and couched in some of the cringiest prose imaginable.

It's only fair that diversity folk ought to stand or fall based on their expositions in their own words. In this section, I offer selections from the ruminations of actual diversity officers from a volume called *Chief Diversity Officers in Higher Education Today: Narratives of Justice, Equity, Diversity, and Inclusion.*

> We choose not to subscribe to the societal and academic pressure that says your value is in your production. Rather we remind each other that we are valuable just as we are, and we can redefine productivity in a holistic way that acknowledges contribution beyond publication and material output. ... We forged a mentoring network that reflected the values and characteristics we honor. This mentoring network empowered the group to celebrate our diversity and codified what being a woman of color in this work means to us. We've done so by acknowledging our "whole" self and redefining productivity.[444]

This is heady, spirit-draining stuff. Perhaps more time should be set aside for Chief Diversity Officers to nap and to recharge from all the work that apparently doesn't include publication and other material output? Do you think that's an unkind statement, unfair and judgmental?

It turns out that more naptime is *exactly* what the Queen's Collective wants. And they advocate it in a quasi-therapeutic lingo that is a trademark of DEI functionaries:

> Hence, our renewed sense of urgency in changing what contribution to the work and productivity looks like for practitioners. We are continuously constructing and fostering spaces that empower others to embrace their authentic selves. However, it

---

444 Alexis J. Stokes, et al, "A Framework For The Sustainability of WOC DEIA+ Practitioners," p. 95, 97.

is rare to encounter individuals—intentionally creating similar spaces for us as professionals. Organizations such as the **Nap Ministry**, is an example of how many Black professionals are creating spaces for respite and self-care amidst being overworked and overextended. The **Nap Ministry** creates "sacred spaces where the liberatory, restorative, and disruptive power of rest can take hold" (Organization of Multitudes section). The Queen's Collective aims to provide that safe space for ourselves. With global uncertainty, instability within the university and political landscape, and a constant attack on DEIA+, we have cultivated and nurtured a community where the protective barriers shielding our egos crumbled away, allowing our genuine selves to emerge and be fully present within the group. [Boldface added][445]

The work ethic of this Queen's Collective appears to be: I want to be paid for who I am, I don't want to be judged because I don't produce value based on commonly accepted metrics, I refuse to define what I mean by "doing the work," and I want to take more naps because I'm "overworked and overextended."

Again, lest you believe this is an uncharitable assessment—that these DEI officers want to work less, nap more, and be paid for just being there—let's look for a moment at this Nap Ministry endorsed by the diversity officers of the Queen's Collective.

The visual that dominates the Nap Ministry website is a photo of a black woman taking a nap on a bench swing in a brick

---

445 Alexis J. Stokes, et al, "A Framework For The Sustainability of WOC DEIA+ Practitioners," p. 95.

courtyard.[446] Is a more insulting illustration to encompass a group of people possible?

This Nap Ministry is run by someone called Tricia Hersey, who describes herself as a performance artist, writer, theater maker, activist, theologian, and daydreamer. She calls herself the Nap Bishop. Here is Hersey's *shtick*, embraced by the Queen's Collective of women of color diversity officers:

> Our *"REST IS RESISTANCE"* framework and practice engages with the power of performance art, site-specific installations, and community organizing to install sacred and safe spaces for the community to rest together. We facilitate immersive workshops and curate performance art that examines rest as a radical tool for community healing. We believe rest is a form of resistance and name sleep deprivation as a racial and social justice issue.[447]

If nothing else, we can spare grudging admiration for a grifter who has monetized naptime as a revolutionary act and turned it into a consulting business wholeheartedly endorsed by diversity officers. Let's take a closer look:

> **Collective Napping Experience:** Our signature program that installs sacred spaces for the community to nap together. We curate the experience with yoga mats, blankets, pillows, curated soundtrack, rest altar, poetic meditations, and a post-nap-talk, all guided by Tricia Hersey, The Nap Bishop. It is a transformative

---

446 https://thenapministry.wordpress.com/about/
447 https://thenapministry.wordpress.com/about/

and healing experience that rejuvenates and opens the mind to the possibilities of *"REST IS RESISTANCE."* We have transformed parks in Chicago, yoga studios, conferences, art galleries, living rooms, and community organizations into **sacred** nap spaces to gather and harness the power of rest.[448] [boldface added]

You likely noticed the misuse of the word sacred. Yes, it's out of place with respect to a secular program; it leads us to believe that the actual meaning of the word is lost on these folks, and they simply want to borrow religious profundity as a garnish for their efforts. But back to the ruminations of the Queen's Collective:

When one considers the powerfully ubiquitous nature of White-man hegemony . . . . [and conducts] examination of the intersectionality of race, gender, and gender roles under the auspices of hegemony and the use of the Black female experiences as an analytic category, challenges the research lenses that construe reality through White male identity.

[W]e aim to disrupt the hegemonic scope of knowledge production to account for the compounded complexities of gender intersecting race in the work of justice. It is essential for our stories as women of color in the DEIA+ space to be told.[449]

This mash-up is the result of shallow digging, and if you'd like to continue digging, I assure you that it doesn't improve. This

---

448 https://thenapministry.wordpress.com/about/
449 Alexis J. Stokes, et al, "A Framework For The Sustainability of WOC DEIA+ Practitioners," p. 86, 87.

is standard for the field. If nothing else, it communicates clearly why some voices have been "marginalized," and with good reason. The mystification continues. Here's another:

> I was once told that I possess a superpower, similar to the cultural superpower of heroes in comic books. I harnessed the power to get people to elicit their stories while simultaneously shifting their preconceived perception .... This "power" has been the narrative in my life and has happened for as long as I can remember. It was as if I had a natural gravitation towards all things diversity, equity, inclusion and belonging (DEIB), and I could never let it go nor 'bite my tongue' in the mist [*sic*] of advocacy.[450]

To understand the DEI hustle, it's important that the actual words and thoughts of these persons are presented. You can make of them what you will. They constitute a stew of ideology and deceit and victimhood culture, their bizarre musings couched in writing of the purpliest sort:

> The proximity I had achieved, the profound transformations I had under gone, all guided by my innate power, imbued this situation with heightened significance. I found myself grappling with a pressing question: Could the internal drive channeled by my superpower inadvertently lead me to a cause that had morphed into a fleeting trend, exploited by academia and corporations? As I delved into the intricate web of complexities

---

450 R. Adidi Etim-Hunting, "Feeding my 'Superpower' or Embracing my Spirit," in Carol Henderson (ed), *Chief Diversity Officers in Higher Education Today* (New York: Routledge, 2025), p. 16.

within this internal conflict, paradoxically, my engagement with the work deepened further.[451]

This is the mindset of the New Commissars. It constitutes a mystical, magical world of "doing the work," which no one can describe, to swat at racist phantoms of "white supremacy culture" and invisible systems of oppression.

Conclusion

As we can see, diversity officers are a motley crew. Some of them are malignly motivated, some are paranoid believers drawn to a simple doctrine, some are superpowered mystics who believe in the act of "napping" as a form of "resistance," while others see the chance to amass a boodle riding the Big Con to retirement.

This crew finds solace in their professional group, NADOHE, where their paranoid creed of villains and victims is reinforced by exchanging tales of woe and listening to racialist speakers like Ijeoma Oluo and Derald Wing Sue.

My own view is that NADOHE's racialist creed, its bizarre pantheon of heroes and theorists, the paranoia of its rank-and-file, and its shakedown of universities in a clever resource extraction strategy indicates a deep psychological malady that is reproduced by DEI groupthink.

This is a toxic psychological environment that maintains the collective delusion. The delusion means different things to different people. For a small coterie of believers, it may actually mean eventual emancipation of a sort and so they strive to reeducate students, staff, and faculty.

---

451 R. Adidi Etim-Hunting, "Feeding my 'Superpower' or Embracing my Spirit,"p. 26.

For others, the longer the delusion of white supremacy culture can be propped up, generous payments from universities will continue to flow to them. For a small group of self-styled sophisticates—called a vanguard in vulgar Marxist terms—DEI is simply part of a larger game in play, one in which social justice can be imposed across a spectrum of routine progressive causes—climate change, transgender rights, extremist feminism, gender ideology, decolonization, anti-Semitism in the guise of the "boycott, divest, and sanction" movement, and so on. If progressive allies are best positioned to penetrate the bureaucracy through the vehicle of DEI, then that's what they'll do.

There is no shortage of persons who strive in the diversity vineyard to craft and tweak the doctrine that animates the bureaucrats. These are the top-tier racialists, who keep the doctrine current for the rank-and-file, to ensure that it has the ingredients of hate, envy, and greed in the right proportions, and to ensure that it serves up enough "guilt" to convince the suckers who pay for absolution.

This group of people constitutes the Gurus of Grift.

10
THE GURUS OF GRIFT

PEANUT GRIFTERS TO BIG CON ARTISTS

"[O]ur minds are built for stories. We crave them, and, when there aren't ready ones available, we create them . . . . When we don't understand what or why or how something happened, we want to find the explanation. A confidence artist is only too happy to comply—and the well-crafted narrative is his absolute forte."[452]

— Maria Konnikova

For a successful con to work, the con-artist must spin a great Con

---

452 Maria Konnikova, *The Confidence Game,* p. 6.

Story. It must have *gravitas*. Someone must identify the "mark" and craft a story tailored to dupe the mark into either parting with cash or to lead him into behavior to satisfy a need. Someone must craft the Con Story, give it intellectual cachet, to invest it with credibility. Someone must serve as inspiration for the phalanx of grifters and con men.

That someone is the racialist intellectual who weaves together a bit of fact and lots of fiction. This is the guru of grift.

These gurus of grift ply their trade at the topmost tier of the DEI tale-spinning hierarchy, where compensation is lavish and responsibilities nil.

These are hustlers *extraordinaire*, and they provide the veneer of legitimacy and even a bit of faux intellectualism that is essential to the success of DEI on campuses. These masters of the con provide the story, its essential details, and the plausibility for the intellectual classes of the university to buy into the fraud. They provide the story for others to repeat, ad infinitum, so that it gains unquestioned legitimacy by virtue of repetition alone.

These DEI yarn-spinners constitute the mandarin class of hustlers. They generate the ideas and stories that comprise the Con Story of *virtuous victimhood*. Big Con-artists and many hundreds of peanut grifters alike use *victim-signaling* to bring in the cash in what we know as "Victimhood Culture.[453] This culture renders it financially and psychologically advantageous to announce victim status publicly and sell absolution to the college rubes they dupe.

The entire logic of DEI's Big Con is built on this idea of virtuous victimhood. 1) Claiming victim status for profit and payouts (a version of the protection racket) and 2) Asserting *moral*

---

453 Bradley Campbell and Jason Manning, *The Rise of Victimhood Culture* (New York: Palgrave Macmillan, 2018).

immunity to justify use of "deceit, intimidation, or violence" to receive that payout.

Rise of the Racialist Mandarins

A new breed of racialist public intellectual has ascended to the public stage to gain stupendous popularity, luxurious wealth, and, in some cases, superstardom—Kendi and DiAngelo, Oluo and Bell, Dyson and Coates, hooks and Harper. These are some of the best-known of the prosperous DEI gurus who command top dollar on the lecture circuit and who sign six-figure book deals.

They are the creators of the DEI's toxic neo-Maoism that infests higher education and serves as the informing orthodoxy of Diversity, Equity, and Inclusion.

The racialist public intellectual is a member of a category of thought leaders that constitute the "ideas industry" of the 21st century.[454] The DEI public intellectual is a spinoff within this ideas industry. In fact, some wags have called their lucrative vineyard the diversity industry, which is synonymous with the mantra of "diversity, equity, and inclusion."

The diversity industry is that confabulation of people and activities that believes that America is afflicted with systemic racism. This malady is allegedly responsible for yielding any and all suboptimal outcomes for that coalition of people designated "persons of color."[455]

---

454 Daniel W. Drezner, *The Ideas Industry: How Pessimists, Partisans, and Plutocrats are Transforming the Marketplace of Ideas* (Oxford: Oxford University Press, 2017).
455 This contrivance "people of color" strikes me as a convenient means of coalition building where no actual confluence of interests exists. If you can get persons of various ethnicities to sign on to the critical racialist ideology with a kind of "me too" slogan or trope, then symbolic capital is generated for the core constituency.

DEI's idea people contend that education is one way of correcting this systemic problem, which they believe is captured in the umbrella moniker white supremacy. They also believe, as we now know, that it constitutes a fabulous Con Story that can wring extraordinary riches from university administrations riven with guilt.

This chapter chronicles the rise of the Racialist Intellectual, whose high-priced meal ticket depends on fooling people that "rampant racism" is a real, tangible, serious problem in America, especially on the college campuses. Following this coterie of racialist intellectuals is a tag-along of would-be gurus, consultants, and bureaucrats who constitute the cadres of DEI.

The Chimera of White Supremacy

So-called white supremacy has become the proxy of choice to describe everything that critical racialists don't like about themselves—about their lot in life, about outcomes they lament as "inequitable," about their place in America, which they apparently believe is stuck somewhere around 1950. For these racialists, it is forever Selma and Tulsa. It is forever Rosa Parks and Emmet Till.

We saw in earlier chapters how white supremacy has become the mass externalization of blame that explains all of their suboptimal outcomes. Pushing this discourse is a new class of persons that came to prominence in the first quarter of the 21st century. Tagging behind these gurus of the new dispensation is a phalanx of folks armed with minimal education, a handful of brittle ideas, and assorted twitter accounts. They test the winds of popular passion. They surf the latest wave of emotion—often the emotions of hate, bitterness, and envy. Many speak with an insecure bombast and militant certitude that is characteristic of true believers. They are engulfed by a simple idea that, to them, explains a complex reality.

The calculated con of the racialist public intellectual is tarted up in *faux* academic lingo of equal parts fantasy and guile and celebrated by audiences of guilt-ridden urban yahoos, whether on Long Island, in Harlem or in the Bronx or in the Upper West Side or in Martha's Vineyard or in Silicon Valley or in Jackson Hole. These are fellow travelers who dwell in an intellectual ghetto constructed for them by the disciplined con artists of DEI. They remain prisoners trapped by their own vanity and the prospect of easy riches. The search for like-minded companionship led them into the ghetto, where their vanity keeps them imprisoned.

I've traced the lineage of DEI's origin to learn its canon, to understand its themes and its core mythos, and to recognize the thinkers and scholars who populate the racialist pantheon. This led naturally to a study of the great popularizers of racialist ideas, which in turn led into an oily world of consultants, pseudo-academics, diversity grifters, and race hustlers peddling the same mash-up of ideas that seems to have captured the minds of so many on the campuses. This chapter presents the phenomenon of DEI's Gurus of Grift.

Top Tier Hustlers . . . "Grovelers" and "Grifters"

Race hustlers in the top tier are those whose influence extends across all the campuses and on into the larger society. Many have already appeared in this book. They include Ibram Kendi, Ta-Nehisi Coates, Robin DiAngelo, Shaun Harper, Peggy McIntosh, Tema Okun, Derrick Bell, bell hooks, Derald Wing Sue, Michael Eric Dyson, and such like. These are the persons who spin the theories, create the buzzwords, coin the aspirational slogans, and provide the faux research on which the edifice of the DEI grift is built.

We examined the major contributions of Tema Okun and Derald Wing Sue in previous chapters and the deleterious effects of the Okun List and the fraud of racial microaggressions. Let's next look at a quartet of the most influential of these Top Tier grifters and understand their con game. They are Robin DiAngelo, Ibram Kendi, Ta-Nehisi Coates, and Ijeoma Oluo,

Robin DiAngelo—*Guilt Groveler Extraordinaire*

Robin DiAngelo's name is synonymous with self-abasement and self-aggrandizement. She has monetized guilt groveling and given it *cachet*, no mean feat.

For instance, in a speech at Boston University, she said: "I'd like to be a little less white, which means a little less oppressive, oblivious, defensive, ignorant and arrogant."[456] This is one of her standard self-abasing tropes, which she repeats in interviews endlessly.

Some have called what Ms. DiAngelo does a "grift" and consider DiAngelo a kind of Johnny Hooker of the diversity industry. Like Hooker, from the popular 1973 Hollywood film *The Sting*, DiAngelo took her shot at the bigtime to goose some life into her 2018 book-length social fantasy *White Fragility*, which reached #1 on the New York Times bestseller list and sold more than a million copies.

456 Dana Soriano, "White privilege lecture tells students white people 'dangerous' if they don't see race," The College Fix, March 6, 2019: https://www.thecollegefix.com/white-privilege-lecture-tells-students-white-people-dangerous-if-they-dont-see-race/

The nationwide racial outcry that has followed the killing of George Floyd has supercharged the Diversity and Inclusion industry, and DiAngelo may be its greatest success story. While she has likely made over $2 million from her book, the speaking circuit is where she is cleaning up. One of the speakers' bureaus that represents her told the *Free Beacon* that a 60-90 minute keynote would run $30,000, a two-hour workshop $35,000, and a half-day event $40,000.[457]

DiAngelo reportedly charges up to $15,000 per session—a March 2019 appearance, for example, cost the University of Kentucky $12,000, as well as a $5-a-minute phone-call fee. Recent virtual events run up to $175 a ticket. The eight to ten private events DiAngelo says she speaks at each month likely net her at least $1.5 million annually.[458]

Oddly enough, DiAngelo has a sparse original research record, unless we count her substantively disastrous human subject psychology experiment, which is described in her 2004 dissertation: "Whiteness in Racial Dialogue: A Discourse Analysis." This is where she first used the term "white fragility," which she apparently lifted from a person by the name of David G. Allen, who served on her committee.[459]

For Robin DiAngelo's fans, it makes not one whit of difference that she could be a creation of P. T. Barnum's "humbugs,

457 Charles Fain Lehman, "The Wages of Woke: How Robin DiAngelo got rich peddling 'white fragility,'" Free Beacon, July 25, 2020: https://freebeacon.com/culture/the-wages-of-woke-2/

458 Charles Fain Lehman, "The Wages of Woke: How Robin DiAngelo got rich peddling 'white fragility,'"

459 I patiently dismantle DiAngelo's seminal work here. Stanley K. Ridgley, "Minute 14 for Robin DiAngelo," American Greatness, August 1, 2020: https://amgreatness.com/2020/08/01/minute-14-for-robin-diangelo/

delusions, impositions, quackeries, deceits, and deceivers," and surely no better than a Melanesian weather doctor casting chicken bones in the dust and intoning about the impending yam harvest. But for normal people, hers is a fascinating and cautionary tale of how a provincial striver can cobble together a dramatic career out of academic fakery to ride the madness of the crowd to riches and fame. She succeeded by combining the fakery of critical racialist ideology with the general tendency for soft minds to express guilt and to confess to most anything. She created a new shuck-and-jive, and she has reaped millions of dollars for her Vaudeville act.

But DiAngelo has discovered that her exaggerated self-abasement does not protect her from being devoured by the Diversity machine. She appears to have ritualized her humiliation so deeply that her behavior has become mechanical and reflexive. The scenario of her scrounging in her purse for $30 to pay reparations to a black television producer will follow her the rest of her life.[460]

She acknowledges that she is constantly striving to escape her very identity. She is ashamed of what she is, and she has made it her mission to wheedle others to share her shame. But that is not how others see her. We see her as mentally broken, crippled by an ideology that she embraces with such enthusiasm that her behavior is a caricature of humanity.

DiAngelo has been destroyed by the very racialists she courted with her weak, simpering brand of sycophancy. While she was one of the most successful of racialist grifters (and the darling of DEI when *White Fragility* was at the top of the charts back in 2020), she lost cachet because she was seen as transgressing on the

460 See Matt Walsh's docu-comedy *Am I Racist?* Released in September 2024.

African-American racialist grift. She was white, you see. It has made no difference how much DiAngelo grovels.

> Since DiAngelo is herself white she has to do a certain amount of self-abasement to earn the trust of her audiences. She does so by assuring them that she is aware that just by standing on a stage and speaking she is "reinforcing whiteness and the centrality of the white view."[461]

Ibram Kendi—*Space Aliens!*

Ibram X. Kendi is the author of *How to be an Antiracist*, published in 2019 to great acclaim, and which naturally carries a gushing book blurb by the fake sociologist Robin DiAngelo.[462] Unlike DiAngelo, however, Kendi is an engaging writer, and he spins a good yarn. I say "spin" and "yarn," because I have no idea whether what he writes is true. I don't know if it's false, either. It's probably all "true" in the sense of, well, it *could* be true, even if it isn't.

So Kendi pronounces, performs, and pimps a brand of know-nothingness, and the urban yahoos nod and affirm, for Kendi's know-nothingness is *their* know-nothingness. It's a carapace of ignorance that protects the grift from hard questions and the ultimate realization that they are being had.

For my part, I would not consult Ibram Kendi on anything regarding American history, as he is simply not reliable as historian. On the other hand, if I believed in *hoodoo*, I'd surely consult

---

461 Douglas Murray, *The Madness of Crowds: Gender, Race, and Identity* (London: Bloomsbury Continuum, 2019), p. 173.
462 Robin DiAngelo describes herself as a "sociologist," which she is not.

the mystic Kendi for a prediction on the quality of the impending yam harvest.

Professor Kendi formerly called himself Henry Rogers before his transmogrification into a racialist guru, qualified to offer immediate commentary on incidents involving race, regardless of time, location, persons involved, and most important—*regardless of what actually happened or whether he has personal knowledge of the incident.*

The business-savvy Kendi is now subsidized with large corporate contributions, among them a $10 million drop by former Twitter CEO Jack Dorsey[463] to fund Kendi's "Center for Antiracist Research."[464] Kendi's public *persona* as a writer has made him a millionaire by way of his books. His speeches? A single talk can net him $20,000 for a virtual engagement lasting just 60 minutes. This is fabulous largesse for today's hustler, a "conjure man" *par excellence*.[465]

Kendi may be a hustler with a fake name. He may be an academic lightweight, as Columbia University linguist John McWhorter once called him in an interview: "I think he's a preacher walking around promulgating undercooked simplistic ideas."[466] He may have a proclivity to intone tautological maxims worse than those of Chung Mee, the drug lord in the Tom Hanks film *Volunteers.*

---

463 Margarite Ward, "Twitter CEO Jack Dorsey donates $10 million to Ibram X. Kendi's center on antiracism at Boston University," *Business Insider*, August 20, 2020.

464 https://www.bu.edu/antiracism-center/

465 Hoodoo Sen Moise, *Working Conjure: A Guide to Hoodoo Folk Magic* (Newburyport, MA: Weiser Books, 2018).

466 "Calling out Ibram X. Kendi," Glenn Loury and John McWhorter, *The Glenn Show*, November 27, 2020, 36:25: https://www.youtube.com/watch?v=3qanSigtOO4&t=2125s

Chung Mee: "We must all do what we must do, for if we do not, then what we must do does not get done."[467]

Ibram Kendi: "Racism is a collection of racist policies that lead to racial inequity, that are substantiated by racist ideas."[468]

But one thing Kendi does well is to practice the *hoodoo* of our universities' con-artists and rake in millions from the yokels who buy into it. Moreover, he does this while pretending to proletarian roots he does not have, and this pretense is all you really need know about Kendi. Here is Kendi's set-up:

> I am one generation removed from picking cotton for pocket change under the warming climate in Guyton, outside Savannah. That's where we buried my grandmother in 1993. Memories of her comforting calmness, her dark green thumb, and her—

Wait, *what? You* never worked "picking cotton for pocket change." No, *you* didn't do that, Ibram.

Now, pause and consider the technique for a moment and what Kendi accomplished with it, what *you* might accomplish with it. I, too, can use the one-generation-removed formula. How can *I* suggest to my readers the idea that I'm courageous and connected to great deeds, when the former is doubtful and the latter probably untrue? How can I do this with a factual statement, which really

---

467 Chung Mee in *Volunteers*, 1985. https://www.imdb.com/title/tt0090274/ characters/nm0361719
468 "How to be an Antiracist," Aspen Ideas Festival, 2019 https://www.youtube. com/watch?v=TzuOlyyQlug&t=2170s 34:30 Mark

accomplishes nothing *except* to plant a thought in the reader's mind? Just this way. Let's say you're reading my book, with interest I hope. Suddenly, I tell you this:

> "I am one generation removed from hitting the beaches at Normandy under withering machine-gun fire."

With this odd sentence, I link my own experience with that of the Greatest Generation, "hitting the beaches at Normandy" when I actually did no such thing and when I probably don't have the guts to do such a thing, which is why we call the folks who *did* do such a thing the Greatest Generation.[469]

However, as someone who *actually did* labor 10-hour days in the fields under the hot sun for "pocket change" in my teens, I feel a resonance with Kendi's chosen trope for a reason that I likely share with other folks, but not in a way that Kendi could ever relate to. His donning of victim sackcloth smacks of parody, and his racialist proletarian chic is laughable.

"Picking cotton for pocket change." Who is he trying to fool?

Consider this. Kendi, as an adult, expressed the belief that he believes that white people are actually "aliens."[470] He also provides a powerful self-description of what happens when primitive man meets a simple doctrine, with himself playing the role masterfully: "I sat there in my dorm room, sweating, mesmerized, scared. It felt like I have climbed up and consumed forbidden fruit." This was Kendi's reaction to reading the creation myth of the Nation

---

469 My own father would have "hit the beaches at Normandy," except he was recuperating in a London hospital from a war wound that he suffered in the Italian campaign.

470 Ibram X. Kendi, *How to be an Anti-Racist* (New York: One World, 2019), p. 134.

of Islam, a fantastical hate-filled fable that inspired Kendi's search for bizarre explanations for the state of the world. Kendi believed these myths as an adult, and this ought to give pause to anyone inclined to buy into Kendi's own special sauce.

But DEI racialists wolf this stuff down.

The mistake is to believe that Kendi offers some sort of redemption, that he has anything new, fresh, or different to offer. Says journalist Kelefa Sanneh in a *New Yorker* profile of Kendi in 2019, "As he studied African-American history he came to believe that the basic story was even simpler than he had thought. American history, he discovered, was a 'battle between racists and anti-racists.'"[471]

Again, the primitive binary tarted-up for a guilt-minded audience in the 2020s. Kendi offers a world spectacularly simple-minded in its reduction of American history to the single factor of race, which he splits into a world of evil *versus* good—the racists *versus* the anti-racists. It's incredibly appealing to a certain type of person for the same reasons that such persons are attracted to cults, and many have bought into this primitive philosophy of life. Its simplicity removes the ambiguities of a world that many persons cannot negotiate.

Others sign on to the Kendi agenda out of fear of being labeled a "racist" by Kendi and his coterie of Kendinistas. This latter process has turned out to be lucrative exercise.

Boston University's Ibram X. Kendi, whose book has jockeyed with DiAngelo's on the bestseller list, charges $150 for tickets

---

471 Kelefa Sanneh, "The Fight to Redefine Racism," *The New Yorker*, August 12, 2019. https://www.newyorker.com/magazine/2019/08/19/the-fight-to-redefine-racism (Accessed: April 7, 2021)

to public events and $25,000 for a one-hour presentation, his representatives told the *Free Beacon*.[472]

Most recently, Kendi has suffered a loss of cachet in spite of his antiracist credentials. His mismanagement of his Center for Antiracist Research at Boston University forced the layoff of many staff and a retrenchment of the ambitious goals he had set.[473] The center has closed, and Kendi has moved on to Howard University to start anew. He is increasingly overshadowed by the up-and-coming diversity hustler Shaun Harper at the USC Race & Equity Center as well as the resurgent graphic novelist Ta-Nehisi Coates.

Peggy McIntosh—*Research Scientist*

My initial inclination was to relegate Peggy McIntosh to second-tier status in this compendium of racialists. She is surely worthy of mention, give her name's synonymy with "white privilege." But after her splash onto the public scene in the late 1980s with her popularization of the term, she gradually faded with no additional significant contributions to the critical racialist canon.

McIntosh still plies her trade as a workshop facilitator with her own non-profit. She does substantial business trade from her name and her notoriety as a one-trick-pony who claims now to be a "research scientist." This last is responsible for my inclusion of her in the pantheon of influential racialist ideologues, along with her

472 Charles Fain Lehman, "The Wages of Woke: How Robin DiAngelo got rich peddling 'white fragility,'"
473 Stanley K. Ridgley, DEI Downsizing at Ibram Kendi's Outfit: Kendi's Boston Center for Antiracist Research takes a 'New Direction,'" September, 2023, Brutalminds.com: https://brutalminds.com/?p=1611   The post contains commentary on stories from the *Boston Globe* and *Semafor*.

unusual contribution to research methodology—the "hypothetical anecdote."

It is rare to find a person with a literature PhD, specializing in the poetry of Emily Dickenson, and who runs racialist workshops, who will claim to be a "research scientist" and do so with apparently straight face. Is this a grift, or is it mere self-promotion?

Let's look at her one-trick "white privilege" from 1988, which still survives in our discourse like some academic zombie.

Anecdotal evidence is generally frowned upon in the social sciences, of course (or at least anecdotal evidence with which we disagree). But McIntosh appears to have invented a new methodology that drops anecdotal evidence to a new low of disrespect. She did this in her 1989 piece called "White Privilege and Male Privilege: A Personal Account of Coming to See Correspondences Through Work in Women's Studies," which became known as "The Invisible Knapsack."[474] McIntosh acknowledges openly in the initial paragraphs of her essay that her notions of "privilege" emerged from her personal experiences teaching in a "Women's Studies" program. These experiences led her to believe that there exists a social malady she labeled "male privilege"—"a phenomenon with a life of its own."

McIntosh moved on to identify what she called white privilege: "White privilege is like an invisible weightless knapsack of special provisions, assurances, tools, maps, guides, codebooks, passports, visas, clothes, compass, emergency gear, and blank

---

474 Peggy McIntosh, "White Privilege: Unpacking the Invisible Knapsack" and "Some Notes for Facilitators," This essay first appeared in *Peace and Freedom Magazine*, July/August, 1989, pp. 10-12, a publication of the Women's International League for Peace and Freedom, Philadelphia, PA. https://www.nationalseedproject.org/key-seed-texts/white-privilege-unpacking-the-invisible-knapsack

checks." It launched what might be called the *J'accuse* genre of pop social science, in which carefully curated anecdotes serve as the centerpiece.

To her credit, McIntosh acknowledges that her work is not "scholarly" and consists of a compendium of "daily experiences within my particular circumstances." That is to say—anecdotes. But what makes this article so interesting is its use of what can be called the *hypothetical anecdote*. Here's how it works.

To illustrate her point that there exists an invisible knapsack of privilege, filled with the copious metaphorical baggage she lists, she compiles a test of sorts—a list of elastic hypothetical conditions that if met confirms the existence of the malady that she describes [some versions of the essay have 26 questions, some 46, and some 50].[475] I use the word "hypothetical" to be charitable. The list is contrived to lead the reader to a particular conclusion. It is, in fact, the very definition of confirmation bias—a list of "conditions" designed to elicit personal anecdotes to confirm the existence of what is assumed.

The reader is invited to fill in the blanks to create magically the conclusion that McIntosh assumes beforehand. It isn't surprising that a scholar trained in English literature would commit methodological blunders such as this one, particularly as it likely arises from deeply held convictions about what one wants to believe. This is typical, in fact, of unscientific thought. In his extensive survey of the literature on confirmation bias, Raymond Nickerson concludes that:

---

475 https://admin.artsci.washington.edu/sites/adming/files/unpacking-invisible-knapsack.pdf

Our natural tendency seems to be to look for evidence that is directly supportive of hypotheses we favor and even, in some instances, of those we are entertaining but about which are indifferent .... The point is that we seldom seek evidence naturally that would show a hypothesis to be wrong and to do so because we understand this to be an effective way to show it to be right if it really is right.[476]

It's no exaggeration to suggest that McIntosh's essay constitutes an exercise on how to engage in confirmation bias and the illusion of objectivity. Her conditions are elastic. They're downright colloquial, as if penned by an undergraduate, probably one studying "public sociology." Here is what I mean—in her list of conditions that solicit reader input, McIntosh uses the qualifying terms "most of the time," "pretty sure" [five times], "pretty well assured," "widely represented," "I can be casual," "remain oblivious," "I can easily buy," "I can be sure," "I can easily find." The lack of precision and social scientific rigor here is stupendous.

In fact, it becomes an elaborate exercise in wishful thinking or of an explanation born of magical thinking, what one might expect from a "senior research scientist" with a Ph.D. in English Literature.

"Privilege," indeed.

Ijeoma Oluo—Small Town Girl Makes Good

Some of the books and articles in the "autoethnography" genre offer fine reading and tell elaborate and emotion-laden stories. It's

---

476 Raymond Nickerson, "Confirmation Bias: A Ubiquitous Phenomenon in Many Guises," *Review of General Psychology*, Vol. 2, No. 2, 1998, p. 211.

time wasted, but perhaps if escapist fare is your pleasure? Racialist guru Ijeoma Oluo writes this way.

This kind of writing isn't difficult for folks like Oluo, who time-served at Western Washington University for a political science degree and then offered years of repeated iterations of the same article for the defunct website *Jezebel*, pieces that characteristically sweat with the kind of urban superstition that motivates groupies to evoke cries of "*Grrrrrl*, you *rock!*"

Oluo has leveraged her political science bachelor's degree into a kind of journalism. In her initial public offering, aside from the lesbian coloring book she self-published in 2015,[477] Oluo elected to trod the path worn by so many tiresome, hectoring young folks who believe themselves in possession of something crafty and keen, but which is actually the umpteenth iteration of simulacra whose original is completely forgotten. She gifted us with a book in 2018, a peanut hustle called *So you want to talk about race*, and it is testimony to the corruption of the literati that it reached #1 on *The New York Times* bestseller list.[478]

Oluo parlayed that book into guru-status and followed it up with a racialist screed that was impeccably timed, published just six months after the death of George Floyd—*Mediocre: The dangerous legacy of white male America.* The book catered to an audience eager to populate a pseudocommunity of persecutors, and it edged onto *The New York Times* bestseller list.

No, *Mediocre* is not an Oluo autoethnography, although Oluo does incorporate personal tales of woe scattered amidst

---

477 Ijeoma Oluo, *The Badass Feminist Coloring Book* (CreateSpace Independent Publishing Platform, 2015).

478 Ijeoma Oluo, *So you want to talk about race* (New York: Seal Press, 2018, 2019).

disquisitions on Buffalo Bill, Colin Kaepernick, her dreams of Bernie Sanders, and Mormon migrants. The *Times* ran a gushing review of *Mediocre*, gushing precisely because it was penned by fellow racialist Brittney Cooper,[479] a Rutgers University professor best-known for her homicidal exhortations that anticipated the assassin Luigi Mangione: "The thing I want to say to you is we got to take these mother---kers out."[480]

Like so many before her, Oluo has cobbled together a personal brand and a sparkling public career that offers us a mess of pottage, complete with book tour and speaking gigs. This furious literary activity crafted a persona for Oluo that suited her for keynote speaking at the national conference of the diversity folks. Oluo indeed opened the 2023 NADOHE conference. A long way from her humble beginnings at Western Washington University from which she graduated in 2007.

When she is on the stump—as long as the main topic is kept vague and her fawning hosts don't probe too deeply—her dry, world-weary attitude and the contrived *l'esprit d'escalier* anecdotes are guaranteed to beguile white liberals and elicit snorting approval from her target audience of simpering urbanites. In her book, she adopts an anecdotal style coupled with fact-free universalization of her own limited experiences living in Seattle. This is the inevitable style of the lightly educated, who caters to the base psychological

---

479 Brittney Cooper, "In America, Is Power in the Hands of Too Many 'Mediocre' Men?" *The New York Times*, December 1, 2020: https://www.nytimes. com/2020/12/01/books/review/mediocre-ijeoma-oluo.html
480 Cooper is a Rutgers University Associate Professor of women's and gender studies and Africana studies. She was invited as the closing Keynote Speaker for the 2022 ACPA National Conference. Jackie Salo, "'We got to take these motherf--kers out': Rutgers professor calls white people 'villains,'" *New York Post*, October 29, 2021. https://nypost.com/2021/10/29/rutgers-professor-calls-white-people-villains/ For the entire interview with Cooper, see: https://www.theroot.com/the-root-institute-2021-unpacking-the-attacks-on-criti-1847711634

needs of the equally lightly educated. She's a superb plebian mega-phone for the perpetually aggrieved.

Critical Racialist Performance

Oluo runs the grievance *shtick*. She has mastered it, and if I were searching for examples to illustrate the process of successful personal branding in one of my workshops, Ms. Oluo would suffice. In her public appearances, she affects a style—the caricature of the fatigued black woman, exhausted from dealing with worrisome white folks.[481] *So* exhausted.[482] This is her version of what we see so much in the cramped and crowded field of racialist performance.[483]

She populates her stories with stick figures who behave just as we expect they will. It likely never occurs to her that these people who populate her tales are carefully curated into her circumscribed world, the theater in which the same play is enacted ritualistically *ad infinitum*, the tiny cast of characters playing their scripted roles. The play is limned in exquisite detail, while everything else is abstract. The writer Stephen Spender might well have been describing Oluo—*anticipating* her—when he wrote in the 1940s of the average person's tenuous "grasp on reality." Said Spender:

> [N]early all human beings have an extremely intermittent
> grasp on reality. Only a few things, which illustrate their own

481 Suzette Hackney, "Black women say they're exhausted after election, but won't give up activism," *USA Today*, December 10, 2024: https://www.usatoday.com/story/news/investigations/2024/12/10/column-black-women-tired-resilient-election-activism/76688762007/
482 Amanda Miller Littlejohn, "Black professional women are exhausted. They're finally claiming the time to rest," *The Washington Post*, August 20, 2021: https://www.washingtonpost.com/business/2021/08/20/black-women-professionals-rest/
483 Janice Gassam Asare, "Dear America: Black Women Are Tired," The Pink Elephant Newsletter, July 29, 2024: https://www.linkedin.com/pulse/dear-america-black-women-tired-janice-gassam-asare-ph-d--bwwie/

interests and ideas, are real to them; other things, which are in fact, equally real, appear to them as abstractions. Thus, when men have decided to pursue a course of action, everything which serves to support this seems vivid and real; everything which stands against it becomes abstraction. Your friends are allies and therefore real human beings with flesh and blood and sympathies like yourself. Your opponents are just tiresome, unreasonable, unnecessary theses, whose lives are so many false statements which you would like to strike out with a lead bullet as you would put the stroke of a lead pencil through a bungled paragraph.[484]

This is the Oluo method. She is a popularizer of certain ideas grounded in her parochial "lived experience," and in this there is nothing extraordinary about her. This type of thing has an enthusiastic audience, and it taps into the same mentality that comedians cater to—the elevation of transient experiences into cartoonish lampoonery. In Oluo's case, however, we are in the presence of something special—the elevation of the *non*-experience magically woven into fake tales of oppression.

Oluo's method, whether she knows it or not, follows a tradition that came of age in the early 2000s, when Berkeley sociologist Michael Burawoy gave legitimacy to "public sociology," an open-door policy that admitted various vagabond projects into

---

484 Stephen Spender in *The God that Failed* (New York: Bantam Books, 1959, 1949), p. 230. Spender was a poet and essayist who came of age in the 1930s and spent much time in Spain while that country's civil war raged, during which time his intellectual development accelerated in the crucible of conflict. He came to know the mentality of the fanatically committed, and he grew familiar with the psychology that drives fanatical commitment, primarily because he himself was committed to the cause and to the narrative that supported the cause. The cause is hyper-focused, and all else becomes abstract.

the sociology club without paying the steep price of admission. This gave the "anecdote" new luster in academia, and it is here where Oluo finds a comfortable home. The anecdote is her chief currency, but it isn't called anecdote, of course. It goes by a handful of aspirational coinages: "autoethnography," "*testimonios*," "lived experience," "counter-narrative." Oluo practices a kind of ersatz sociology that leverages her anecdotes and spontaneous observations into a methodology.

There is nothing inherently risible with the anecdote *qua* anecdote; the problem arises with exaltation of the anecdote, coupled with demands that it be accepted as scholarship like that found in proven knowledge-generating social science. It's not difficult to understand why this might be so, why folks such as Oluo aspire to public sociology status. It short-cuts the way around the inconvenience of rigor, standards, merit, and even mild criticism to slip through the side door for a seat at the table. Always with the realization that anecdote-driven twaddle doesn't really belong there. So, it comes coupled with a pretentious didacticism in a continuous quest for significance and legitimacy.[485] Public Sociology is to Sociology as Snake-handling is to Religion.

Modern social media provides a wealth of examples of the performances of racialist public intellectuals, and certainly Oluo

---

485 See the extensive literature on Significance Quest Theory. The quest for significance is the fundamental desire to matter, to be someone, to have respect. Psychological theorists have long realized that this quest constitutes a major, universal, human motivation variously labeled as the need for *esteem, achievement, meaning, competence, control*, and so on. See Arie W. Kruglanski, Michele J. Gelfand, Jocelyn J. Belanger, Anna Shreveland, Malkanthis Hetiarachechi, and Rohan Gunaratna, "The Psychology of Radicalization and Deradicalization: How Significance Quest Impacts Violent Extremism," *Political Psychology*, Vol. 35, Supplement 1: *Advances in Political Psychology* (February 2014), p. 73. See, as well, Edward Orehek and Arie W. Kruglanski, "Personal failure makes society seem fonder; An inquiry into the roots of social interdependence," *PLOS ONE*, August 3, 2018, https://doi.org/10.1371/journal.pone.0201361.

is visible on various platforms as any cursory web search confirms. Oluo's performances consist of tales of what happens to her. Even this is not quite right. They consist of tales of what she believes happens to her. Truth? Who knows.

Here is one extended example of Oluo performing vaudeville in a formulaic format, talking about publication of her book in the immediate aftermath of the 2016 presidential election. Her interviewer, Charles Mudede, provides classic straight-man cues for what is essentially a maundering Oluo monologue. Let's listen in:

> I think there was like this real panic that drove people to the book now I think it's more utility. I think that people are starting to realize now that we've kind of accepted that a large portion of our population is trash, that they're not doing enough to balance all that trash, and that they're aiding and abetting in the trash and now it's about finding it in their day-to-day life and I think I'm so happy to have built something that is helping people find where they are aiding and abetting white supremacy and at least start down certain paths of, you know, trying to rectify that.[486]

After establishing that Oluo believes that presumably half of the population of the United States is "trash," Oluo and Mudede hit all of their marks in what turns into a yuk-fest at times—"cultural appropriation," "white supremacy," "black hair," "privilege," and the like.

---

486 Ijeoma Oluo with Charles Mudede: So You Want to Talk About Race, Town Hall Seattle, October 3, 2019: 10:07. Accessed: October 12, 2020. https://www.youtube.com/watch?v=8CkJVThLCOI

There is something uncomfortably embarrassing about two obviously intelligent persons gleefully shackling themselves into their ideological straitjackets and then pontificating within the narrow bounds that constitute their shared mental cell, oblivious to the larger world outside. The cell door is unlocked. All they need do is open the door and walk out.

But they don't.

Oluo shares the paranoiac's delusion that history is a series of events that happen to *them*. She has led and apparently still seems to lead a comfortably uninteresting life, but like a paranoiac, she squeezes meaning from the mundane. Oluo appears as the kind of person, regardless of ethnicity, who sniffs out reasons for offense, takes umbrage at a glance, a raised eyebrow, an overheard conversation. You know the type. Everyone knows the type. It's what DEI "trainings" are all about.

On it goes like this. Oluo, the feted author and celebrity racialist, spinning lackluster tales of non-events filled with an asphyxiating oppression. Take, for example, the oppression in the Seattle airport, which is called Seatac. Oluo relates the tale from her book in which she strides the Seatac terminal on her way to her next high-paid speaking gig; she's searching for something to eat, and she is just gob-smacked by the atrocity of a sign advertising something called the *Africa Lounge*. Oluo features this venue, a kitsch-filled airport eatery, in her book as an example of cultural appropriation.

In her event with Mudede, this cultural appropriation is the topic of conversation for interminable minutes as Oluo strikes a passionate chord with an audience that likely cannot fathom what, exactly, the hoo-hah is all about.[487] Anecdotes like this one—and it's anybody's guess whether they're true or not, but that doesn't matter because they *could* be true—offer the paranoiac's raw material for interpretation according to the conspiracist's grand plan. Brick-and-mortar oppression in the Seattle airport selling burgers and fries.

Is Oluo's world so bereft of actual oppression that she is left to contrive yarns out of the nothingness that all of us experience in everyday life in one way or another, with the major exception that her experiences are that of the lush, racialist show business life, and so she gives every mundane incident and non-incident the heft of conspiracy and great moment?

Let's look at this hapless *Africa Lounge*, which I will surely patronize if I'm ever unlucky enough to lay over in Seattle, and I encourage you to do likewise. Here I confess that I left a positive review on the review site "Yelp" for the *Africa Lounge* without ever having visited.[488] But if you believe everything the DEI folks say about reality, all that matters is that I *could* have visited it and that I *could* have eaten there. We return to Ms. Oluo in the airport, in Seatac.

In her telling, Oluo must suffer the indignities of an oppressive Seattle airport as she travels to her expenses-paid lecture series

---

487 I recall fondly one of my trips to Izhevsk, Russia—this one in 2012—during which I saw briefly through the window a sign for an establishment called "American Café." Not having the opportunity to visit it, I can only surmise that it carried the same kitsch-filled ambience of the FAQ café just off Red Square in Moscow. The FAQ successfully provided a bohemian ambience of America's 1950s beat cafés, and it was there that I met the information director for the Russian Communist Party, who has since gone on to respectability and remains a good friend. The FAQ café, accessed down stairs to its basement location, featured James Dean posters on the walls, low-slung coffee tables. Was it "authentic"? Who knows? Who cares?
488 See review dated October 12, 2020. https://www.yelp.com/biz/africa-lounge-seattle

to collect $10,000 fees. It is here she discovers a restaurant not to her liking, the *Africa Lounge*. In her conversation with Mudede, it becomes the source of much forced merriment. Unlike other folks—in fact, unlike almost *everybody else* who dwells in the world of airport travel—she takes umbrage at the very existence of a place like the *Africa Lounge*, and it's not even clear why it leaves her in such high dudgeon.

She is not, after all, from any of the many African nations or many different African cultures that make up that continent of 1.2 billion people. Her dad is Nigerian, and if her dad has a problem with *Africa Lounge*, Oluo doesn't mention it, but then *Africa Lounge* apparently offers a generic African experience, not a Nigerian experience. Her buddy Mudede is from Zimbabwe, sure, but here he postures as a lay expert on Africa because, as he says, "I am African," which has no more meaning than someone claiming to be "European" rather than Serbian or British or Greek or Finnish. Her audience is presumably supposed to take umbrage now that they have learned of the *Africa Lounge* and its burgers and fries.

All of this may seem like a joke, but to Oluo it's not. She latches on to this *Africa Lounge*, and she can't let go.

One suspects that she talks so much and in such contrived vexation about trivialities because it serves as her own proxy for actual proletarian strife and striving, which as far as anyone knows, she has never experienced. She magnifies the mundane, shines a spotlight on the superficial, and flogs the imaginary to its feet for a lap around the outrage track before it dissipates into its own effervescence or before the audience wises-up, the latter of which isn't likely to happen since this is an easy audience that pleases easily, applauding every errant throat-clear.

The discussion continues interminably, Oluo oblivious to the fact that she and *only* she is affected so deeply by the kitsch of a modern airport as she bemoans her burden of dining on burger and fries while sitting on a zebra-print stool. She transforms her grotesquely trivial and self-indulgent reaction into a significant cultural fact of chin-scratching magniloquence. But no . . . it's just a restaurant in an airport. You cannot but stumble over this passage mentally when you read it. G. K. Chesterton emerges to explain Oluo's problem, even as she is oblivious:

> Are there no other stories in the world except yours; and are all men busy with your business? . . . How much larger your life would be if yourself could become smaller in it . . . You would break out of this tiny and tawdry theatre in which your own little plot is always being played, and you would find yourself under a freer sky, in a street full of splendid strangers.[489]

In another of her personal incidents, which arises only because of her cachet as a racialist public intellectual inspiring the assembled cadres of diversity officers, Oluo takes offense at the venue of one of her lucrative talks, this a lecture to a meeting of the Wisconsin Library Association—*librarians!*—probably no more sympathetic crowd to be found outside the confines of Seattle, unless it's Portland.

If only you and I had such "problems." An all-expense-paid

---

489 G. K. Chesterton, *Chesterton Collected Works, Volume 1: Heretics, Orthodoxy, The Blatchford Controversies* (San Francisco: Ignatius Press, 1986), p. 223. Published originally in 1908.

trip to Wisconsin to speak an hour to a fawning audience where she's booked to speak for somewhere between $10,000 and $20,000.[490] She has a problem, a *big* problem with the venue. She complains that it's a themed safari resort in Wisconsin. Her distaste prompts her to a principled refusal to stay at the "safari" resort, but it extended neither to refusal to speak at the venue, nor to refusal of her five-figure payday. Here is her commentary:

> It's called Kalahari and it's a themed Safari Resort in Wisconsin, you know, in case you're missing the Safari you can find it in Wisconsin and, yeah, I'm just like how, how did whole committees, like, oh yeah this sounds fine, like, and, you know, make this decision and then you get too close to the event and someone's, like, mmm, excuse me, you know, and, you know, it was, like, the one black person that's, like, do I have to say it, oh god do I have to be the one to say I don't want to go to a safari.[491]

Oluo exemplifies the *modus operandi* of the racialist public intellectual who inspires and informs DEI. The poser whose know-nothingness is thorough and whose mind is clear of all but the framework of racialism, free to live a life of racialism opining on *any*thing that happens … without knowing *any*thing about *any*thing that happens. In this case, she is *just* opining, because nothing *does* happen.

In this way, we are treated to a trickle of Oluo's interpretations of imagined events. Or, in Oluo's case, *non*-events, because nothing

---

490 See Keppler Speakers. https://www.kepplerspeakers.com/speakers/ijeoma-oluo
491 Ijeoma Oluo with Charles Mudede: So You Want to Talk About Race, Town Hall.

is really happening or at any rate, nothing very interesting. In a method similar to the racialist Robin DiAngelo, she has assembled a career that parlays a life of limited parochial experience into a jet-set life of speaking gigs and book signings.

This exaltation of the insignificant is classic paranoia combined with classic vaudeville. Do I believe that Oluo is a paranoiac? Not at all. She is a smart, savvy racialist hack, who understands what her audience demands, and she puts on a show that is extremely satisfying. And well-compensated.

"'White Supremacy,' anyone? That'll be $15,000."

Ta-Nehisi Coates

> When students starting out on campuses across the US wonder whether making insincere claims and catastrophizing minute events can be rewarding, they can look to [Ta-Nehisi] Coates and know that it is.[492]

Few writers boast ignorance as a credential—Ta-Nehisi Coates is one of them. And few persons could get a book into print on the Israeli-Hamas conflict, based on a single 10-day visit to Gaza hosted by terrorist-sympathizers, but Ta-Nehisi Coates did just that. The result is his 2024 bestseller *The Message*, most of it his ruminations about himself and his superimposition of crude racialist theory onto a conflict he only dimly understands while timeserving on what has to be one of the dullest travelogues ever penned.

---

492 Douglas Murray, *The Madness of Crowds: Gender, Race, and Identity* (London: Bloomsbury Continuum, 2019), p. 166.

My own expectations of Coates are low, and they have continued to drop with each iteration of a new memoir by this young fellow, who believes he has much to say that is grounded in his "lived experience." That is to say, the uber-mundanity that is his signature theme that he contrives as he moves his career along (witness his brief terror-tourism in Gaza).

Coates has been a reliable practitioner of a racialist writing methodology pioneered by the late Harvard Law Professor Derrick Bell.[493] You simply manufacture a point you want to make, then weave an oppression story around it that caters to an audience's prejudice, add a dash of discount-rack mysticism and . . . *presto!* As is his habit, Coates has never hidden his ignorance of that which he writes about, but rather boasts of his ignorance, considering it a virtue.

As with Kendi, Coates is at best a pedestrian writer. He is most at home with the comic book form, and he has always centered himself in his narcissistic memoirs. The Kendi-Coates method is to begin with a primitive racialist theory and then conjure up a superficial understanding of major events through this racialism. Racialists call this their "lens." Facts are not simply curated selectively in this method—facts are irrelevant and filtered out[494] if they are inconvenient. Sadly, this is not parody. It is the author's idea of chin-scratching sagacity. You can decide for yourself, of course, and enough readers prefer his goulash of prejudice, ignorance, and *hauteur* to make Coates the shrewdest of grifters, if nothing else.

---

493 See Derrick Bell, *And We Are Not Saved: The Elusive Quest for Racial Justice* (New York: Basic Books, 1987) and *Faces at the Bottom of the Well: The Permanence of Racism* (New York: Basic Books, 1992).
494 Ta-Nehisi Coates, *The Message* (New York: One World, 2024), p. 205-206.

I speak of Coates's writing because, well, that's his self-professed occupation. And no matter how much I speak of Coates's writing, be assured that he has spoken more, is speaking more, and *will* speak more. "Former *Atlantic* writer Ta-Nehisi Coates has charged between $30,000 and $40,000 for public lectures."[495]

He fervently believes that he is a fabulous writer with a "gift," and he interminably talks about his love affair with words that began as a youngster, about writing, about himself, about the gift he has embraced, and about the young would-be writers he would recruit as disciples. He teaches such writing at Howard University as Sterling Brown Chair in the Department of English and writer-in-residence.

This self-referential style is off-putting, not least because he never delivers on the promises of depth, breadth, wit, soul, heart, detail, romance. Nothing of the sort. Perhaps this has to do with his abhorrence of complexity. Rather, he shoehorns the glorious reality around him into the same pair of frayed rhetorical loafers he's worn since, well, his last memoir. And the memoir before that.

Quite disturbing is the influence that Coates wields, as purportedly a man in-the-know, combined with his unrelieved ignorance. Folks on the campuses look to him. Reading groups discuss his books. And what do they learn? Well, in *The Message*, he manages the feat of pronouncing on the unrest in Israel and its neighbors from the perspective of a tourist ushered around by a Palestinian group called the Palestine Festival of Literature.[496] He is never far from the provincialism that permeates all of his writing, and he exhibits two of the three methodological pathologies

495 Charles Fain Lehman, "The Wages of Woke: How Robin DiAngelo got rich peddling 'white fragility,'"
496 Ta-Nehisi Coates, *The Message*, p. 122.

we discussed in Chapter 4—navel-gazing and yarn-spinning. All his work is characterized by these pathologies. But as I have noted, there seems always a large and receptive audience for this artifice. It's the same audience that is swayed by the *Protocols of the Learned Elders of Zion*, of *The Man who cried I am*, *The Secret Relationship between Blacks and Jews*, *The Turner Diaries*.

Once an author acknowledges up-front that he takes liberties with the facts, that he has an innate suspicion of even the *possibility* of an objective truth, and that he believes that he conveys an "inner truth," then the entire body of his work becomes suspect. At least for those who think critically. And when the author is a committed racialist, given license by a credulous public to salve his vanity at their expense, he is prone to serve up what his audience wants in the way of racialist porn. His work is candy for believers, convenient confirmations of the racialist myth. No one outside of his committed circle is convinced of anything because of the dubiety of it all, while those who are already locked in the circle nod stupidly and slap the page at the abstract platitudes marching predictably in paragraph formation.

Is it true? Did it happen this way? Do these people even exist, or are they "composite characters" created to make a point? Ta-Nahesi, have you omitted anything that might substantially transform your conclusions? Let's sit back, awash in these ruminations.

> In some sense, my trip to the Land of Palestine was a journey backward toward that instinct I'd lost, an ancestral gift I'd forgotten. The gift is not in the blood but in the stories, the axioms, the experiences garnered from centuries of living on

the outskirts of a dubious democracy. When I went off to become a professional writer, I was brimming with my own skepticism—not of the country but of the gift, which seemed so diffuse and random, a kind of folk wisdom that stood in abeyance of the empirical. Perhaps the most important fact in this skepticism was that I had no living models . . . . . If I was skeptical of the gift, I was never skeptical of the people. I came to think of my trade—long-form magazine or new journalism—as a kind of scientific process that, when correctly applied, must necessarily reveal the truth. And for a time I saw the practitioner of that science as an individual, as individual, as singular, as standing alone, applying the process, searching for truth.[497]

Coates actually offers us this line: "I don't think I ever, in my life, felt the glare of racism burn stranger and more intense than in Israel."[498] Egads! What occasioned this growl of anger?

It was this "incident" he describes here:

I got back to the hotel that afternoon exhausted as usual so exhausted, in fact, that I didn't even see the man standing at the hotel's front door. Or maybe I did see him and did not quite register his role until he blocked my path. "Are you a guest here?" he asked. He addressed me with a kind of well-mannered hostility, like an English inspector who keeps calling his suspect 'sir.' I was fixated on the gun holstered on his hip. I reached into my pocket, flashed my key card, and walked

---

497 Ta-Nehisi Coates, *The Message*, p. 205-206.
498 Ta-Nehisi Coates, *The Message*. p. 204.

inside. I moved through the lobby, shook [*sic*], and got to my room as fast as I could.[499]

The undergraduate inside Coates cannot help himself. He *imagines* a long-past racist American society and then transposes this imagined society onto a foreign country today, in a city of archaeological treasures and in a country victimized by suicide bombers. The jittery Coates—"shook," he says—transports himself in his mind to another land, to another time as he imagines it, so that he can then mine yet another mundane happenstance.

This is his way. He searches for metaphorical pegs on which to hang his hat. One suspects that he is saying what he always *intended* to say before he ever set foot in Gaza or in Israel, and that the incidents he describes (if these happenstances can even be called incidents) are just that—incidental to his canned grand narrative. Indeed, when you strip away Coates's strained prose that desperately flogs life into his unexceptional terror-tour ("enormous guns" and the like), you quickly realize that next to nothing actually happens to Coates.

Coates is a terror-tourist, duped thoroughly over the course of a 10-day sojourn that brim-fills him with the hubris to write knowledgeably about Middle East Jewish-Arab hostilities unencumbered by the "complexity" that he mocks as unnecessary to an understanding of what he considers the simplest of conundrums.

Throughout, he puts himself at the center and then furiously navel-gazes, attaching dramatic meaning to the most mundane of scenarios that barely qualify as scenarios. For instance, he espies guard dogs protecting a settlement.

---

499 Ta-Nehisi Coates, *The Message*, p. 204.

I toured a settlement and seen [*sic*] something that appeared drawn from the world of Mad Max. At the boundary of this settlement, every thirty feet or so, I would see a guard dog rise, growl, and loudly bark. I looked closer and saw a leash attached to each of these dogs. The leashes extended perhaps ten feet up, where they met, at a perpendicular angle, a master cord stretched across the space. The effect was a kind of fencing, a wall made of guard dogs. I felt myself in the presence of a terrible Chimera—a wall of hell hounds that seemed to me drawn from my Montgomery nightmares.[500]

At this point, the obvious thing for a journalist to do escapes Coates entirely. Perhaps a question or two? Does Coates approach anyone in the settlement to ask the most relevant questions that an actual journalist might ask? Something like: "Say, you have some robust guard dogs here. Did something bad happen here to warrant this wall-of-hell-hounds set-up?"

But Coates walks on by, because, well, it would interrupt what Coates had planned to say all along. This "Chimera" was just a set-up.

Reading Coates, it's difficult not to reflect upon his ruminations in the context of a professional historian's caution against precisely this kind of slapdash "history." James H. Sweet is Vilas-Jartz Distinguished Professor of History at the University of Wisconsin-Madison. As Sweet points out, "If history is only those stories from the past that confirm current political positions,

---

500 Ta-Nehisi Coates, *The Message*, p. 192-193.

all manner of political hacks can claim historical expertise."[501] He spells out what he means.

In a 2022 piece, Sweet described how the Ghanaian Afro-tourism industry manufactures slavery tales to cater to African-American tourists, black-washing actual Ghanaian history to omit the full African complicity in the slave trade. Without such complicity, it's difficult to see how the trade would have survived, let alone flourished. Sweet observes how a small fishing village in Ghana called Elmina, one of the largest Atlantic slave-trading depots in West Africa, has morphed into slave tourism.

> Elmina Castle is now as much an African American shrine as a Ghanaian archaeological or historical site .... The Elmina tour guide claimed that "Ghanaians" sent their "servants" into chattel slavery unknowingly. The guide made no reference to warfare or Indigenous slavery, histories that interrupt assumptions of ancestral connection between modern-day Ghanaians and visitors from the diaspora. Similarly, the forthcoming film *The Woman King* seems to suggest that Dahomey's female warriors and King Ghezo fought the European slave trade. In fact, they promoted it. Historically accurate renderings of Asante or Dahomean greed and enslavement apparently contradict modern-day political imperatives.[502]

Meanwhile, in another part of his own book, Coates scoffs at this type of tourist set-up when it involves Israel.

501 James H. Sweet, "Is History History?: Identity Politics and the Teleology of the Present," *Perspectives on History*, Volume 60:6, September 2022: https://www.historians.org/wp-content/uploads/2024/07/Perspectives_60N6.pdf
502 James H. Sweet, "Is History History?"

THE GURUS OF GRIFT

"It all felt so fake," says Coates as he coldly reflected on his experience in Israel at the City of David. "I could not escape the feeling of being in the presence of a poorly wrought fairy tale and an enormous con." But Coates offers us no such skepticism of his African sojourn, which is less an active exploratory sojourn than a vigorous mental self-approbation of the sort that is informed not one whit by his actual presence in the shabby Senegalese city of Dakar.

I am reminded of those Western intellectuals who made pilgrimages to the Soviet Union and to Communist China in the 1930s and the 1950s to bear witness to the building of socialism, but who saw and reported only what they wished to see and what they thought they saw.[503] They transformed shabbiness into splendor, because that's what ideology demanded. What could an honest account of reality possibly contribute to the midwifing a new world into existence? Why this nettlesome fidelity to fact? Coates will have none of it, and he transforms the squalid environs of Dakar into a kaleidoscope of imagined roots and beautiful people, culminating in a dramatic walk to the shore's edge where he dips his hand into the water:

> I bent down and when I felt the water rush between fingers, a joy came with the cold of the wave, and I heard the ghosts singing. I don't know if I've ever experienced a deeper sense of triumph in my life .... And looking out on that rocky beach, I felt the whole of the land speak to me, and it said, *What took you so long?* What indeed.[504]

---

503 Paul Hollander, *Political Pilgrims* (New York: Oxford University Press, 1981).
504 Ta-Nehisi Coates, *The Message*, p. 43-44.

In rare candor, Coates acknowledges that all this springs from his imagination, and he chest-thumps over it all: "We have a right to our imagined traditions, to our imagined places, and those traditions and places are most powerful when we confess that they are imagined."[505] It's not difficult to consider Coates believing that this nonsense is profound in some way, perhaps because, again . . . he made it up.

In the end, it is Coates who provides only one quote worthy of citation, a sentence that captures in one glorious trope his own shortcomings as a writer, as a willfully blind observer, and as an unfaithful truthteller while also communicating the enormity of the DEI project for all of us.

For at least this once, Coates doesn't throw red meat to his paranoid fan-base, but speaks to all human beings who are armed with the critical faculties to know this hustler for who he is: "It all felt so fake . . . . I could not escape the feeling of being in the presence of a poorly wrought fairy tale and an enormous con."[506]

Conclusion

You have just met the best and the brightest. These are the *crème de la crème* who sit upon the mountaintop of racialism, the idea people, the popularizers of DEI.

DiAngelo, Kendi, Coates, and Oluo constitute a representative slice of the type of opportunistic pseudointellectualism that props up DEI. They are augmented by Derrick Bell, Tema Okun, Derald Wing Sue, and Michael Eric Dyson with their various attempts to provide justification for aggressive prejudice. Their

---

505 Ta-Nehisi Coates, *The Message*, p. 57.
506 Ta-Nehisi Coates, *The Message*, p. 193.

racialist works appear in cargo cult journals, and fringe publishers happily publish their books and manuals—Verso, Polity, Seal, Stylus, IAP, Haymarket Books, and such like.

They provide the fool's gold patina for raw racialism.

Many lesser lights attempt to break into the pantheon of the diversity industry. They constitute a choir, and their hymn is always the same—persons like Melissa Harris-Perry, Cheryl Fleming, Layla Saad, Cheryl Matias, Ricki Lee Allen, Zeus Leonardo, Lisa Spanierman.

They provide the depth, such as it is, of this wing of the social justice project. They aren't even the most hateful of the gurus. That dishonor belongs to the likes of Johnny E. Williams of Trinity, George Yancy of Emory, Britney Cooper of Rutgers, and others.

The dramatis personae we met in this chapter are damaged people. They are motivated by outsized egos and overblown theory and unparalleled self-righteousness. Their ideas of history are what happens to them, regardless of how mundane or commonplace—everything from Africa Lounges to unremarkable dinners in Dakar to Buffalo Bill to diversity training thought reform to fakery of Space Aliens to fables of Space Traders to simpering obeisance in every interaction with minority folk to concocting imaginary "microaggressions" for every paranoid occasion. Ideas hinge on non-events, wildly cherry-picked factoids and their slotting into a latticework of racialism.

If nothing else, I wanted to convey the emptiness, the intellectual vapidity, the fraudulence of the entire racialist enterprise through the eyes and words of the primary racialists who generate the ideas that motivate DEI on campus. With their fevered brows, empty hearts, and fat bank accounts, these are the vacuous persons who exemplify racialism and inspire many thousands of others to reject magnanimity of spirit, the evidence of their own senses. And who embrace the bitterness of envy and mysticism.

11
OCTOBER 7—THE NAKEDNESS OF DEI

"DIVERSITY FOR THEE, BUT NOT FOR ME."

"In a study we did with 741 DEI officers, we examined their social media—Twitter feeds—and we observed shocking levels of antisemitism coming from people with a professional obligation not to do that. It's as if we studied doctors and found that they were smokers. It's not something you'd expect from people in an occupation and, yet, DEI staff are active promoters of antisemitism in their social media feeds and it's not surprising that they also facilitate it on campus."[507]

— Jay Greene, PhD, Senior Research Fellow, The Heritage Foundation

---

507 "ICYMI: Stefanik Calls Out DEI Offices' Failure to Protect Jewish Students on College Campuses," Press Release, Congressional Hearing, House Education and the Workforce Committee Subcommittee on Higher Education and Workforce Development, March 7, 2024: https://stefanik.house.gov/2024/3/icymi-stefanik-calls-out-dei-offices-failure-to-protect-jewish-students-on-college-campuses

The track record of DEI in higher education consists largely of histrionics, contrived outrages, and bullying of students and faculty—all of which have roiled the campuses throughout the 2020s. It's been a melodramatic and narcissistic journey for the bureaucrats who "do the work," and they've imposed a hyper-sensitivity expressed in a carefully scripted self-righteousness that asphyxiates campus discourse.

But on the upside, the universities seem primed to grapple with any expression of intolerance, hostility, difference, and bias, even those of the imaginary sort. By 2023, three years of intense public therapy of diversity, equity, and inclusion *surely* meant that the higher education atmosphere was hyper-attuned to the slightest transgression. Offenses would be vigorously policed; they would not be tolerated. This would be a new era, the DEI cadres told us.

But then came October 7, 2023.

On that day, the state of Israel suffered a devastating surprise attack by more than 3,000 terrorists from the Hamas organization in the Gaza strip that left 1,400 Israelis dead, most of them civilians—victims of rape, mutilation, beheading, burning, and other horrific torture, with another 250 kidnapped and subjected to repeated rape, torture, execution.

What would be the American university response to the actual threats against Jewish students, faculty, and staff given the colleges' unctuous commitment to DEI?

Those of us inured to the DEI sepsis affecting the campuses wondered how this politically contrived organ would respond.

Whither DEI?

Surely the colleges that so vigorously investigated imagined micro-aggressions and who policed pronoun usage and who demanded that faculty pay fealty to diversity and inclusion in loyalty oaths would respond robustly. With the full-throated vocal pronouncements and college websites filled with "antiracism," we might expect a rapid and effective response to any transgression, and this time it would be justified as *authentic* hatred and *real* violence roiled the campuses.

From university administrations, we would expect a chorus of condemnation of terrorism against the only democracy in the Middle East, against a staunch U.S. ally that shares Enlightenment values. We would expect university presidents to leap at the chance to proclaim an "anti-Semitic reckoning" and take what ought to be a bold stand against barbarism.

Right?

In fact, October 7 presented and continues to present the starkest clash between civilization and barbarism of anyone's lifetime, and thus it presents a clear moral choice. It's an easy choice for those with moral clarity, uncontaminated by legalistic hair-splitting and defensive on-the-stand quibbling.

But that's not what happened.

It turns out that DEI was a lie all along, and the hypersensitivity of the campuses was revealed as highly selective. How *could* the university respond, given its commitment to coarse DEI ideology?

The reality of this DEI was that it was set up to cater only to particular groups of people against the effects of "white supremacy culture" according to a critical racialist template of "oppressors" and "oppressed." The ideology of DEI that was contrived to deal with fantasy "racisms" and imaginary "microaggressions" was ill-prepared to deal with the reality of hate that erupted on the campuses across America.

DEI staffers were adept at running workshops and hectoring innocent students about their implicit biases, but they proved incompetent to deal with the real world of real hate experienced by real people threatened with death because of their ethnicity. And it turned out that the DEI folks didn't want to do so in any case. The DEI creed told them not to.

You see, in this case, the Jewish victims were *not* DEI-approved. This meant that Jews weren't even victims at all. So, the DEI bureaucrats felt no obligation to deal with the explosion of anti-Semitism. And university administrations apparently did not expect them to deal with it. In fact, the DEI ideology stated this explicitly, and so did careless DEI apparatchiks in moments of rare honesty.

Shoulder-to-shoulder, university administrations showed themselves to be on the side of the barbarians, as witnessed by the incredible exposure of Columbia University administrators who mocked Jewish members of the university community in a series of back-and-forth text messages during a campus event organized to highlight the threat to Jews on campus. Said one congressional committee in a press release on the firings:

> The text messages, which include numerous offensive messages that have not previously been reported, show senior Columbia College administrators mocking and disparaging the

university's Jewish community, and trafficking in antisemitic tropes regarding Jews and money. The texts accused Jewish students of coming from a "place of privilege," dismissed their concerns, disparaged officials responsible for Jewish student life, and insinuated that efforts to address the explosion of antisemitism on Columbia's campus were merely a fundraising ploy.[508]

Further, the tepid statements of university presidents inspired *no one* that they would be protected from the barbarians and bullies who had emerged and were already hard at work on their own campuses as the weeks and months ticked by after the Hamas atrocities in Israel. The palms-outward splayed-fingers nonresponses of those presidents emboldened the enemies of civilization as the violence, threats, and intimidation of Jewish students, staff, and faculty intensified.

In the weeks after October 7, the nation's campuses fairly exploded with hate-filled racialist demonstrations that resembled those of 1930s Nazi Germany and two centuries of Russian pogroms rather than what one finds in a 21st century liberal democracy.[509] Victims were left to fend for themselves on campus after campus in the face of threat and physical assault—at Penn, at Columbia, at MIT, at Harvard, at Berkeley, at Yale.

The thinly veiled anti-Semitism emerged into the open in an orgiastic display seen on television screens nightly. Rogue faculty encouraged these public hate-fests that hid their virulent

508 Press Release, "Columbia Administrators' Texts Reveal New Depths of Apathy and Disdain Towards Jewish Students," Committee on Education and the Workforce, July 2, 2024: https://edworkforce.house.gov/committee/welcomemessage.html

509 "Pogroms," Holocaust Encyclopedia: https://encyclopedia.ushmm.org/content/en/article/pogroms

anti-Semitism behind the fig-leaf of "anti-Zionism." At Columbia, faculty members Joseph Massad, Katherine Franke and Mohamed Abdou were practically joyful over the Hamas attacks.[510] Abdou was reported to have said on social media: "I'm with Hamas & Hezbollah & Islamic Jihad."

Faculty from around the nation dropped their professorial demeanors to cheer on the mass mutilation, murder, and rape of Israeli civilians: **Asad Abukhalil**, Professor of Political Science at California State University, Stanislaus; **Osman Umarji**, a Lecturer at the School of Education at the University of California, Irvine; **Bikrum Gill**, Assistant Professor in the Department of Political Science at Virginia Tech; **Sean Malloy**, an Associate Professor of History and Critical Race and Ethnic Studies (CRES) at University of California, Merced; **Danny Shaw**, Adjunct Lecturer of Latin American and Caribbean Studies and Race, Ethnicity, Class and Gender at the City University of New York; **Rabab Abdulhadi**, Professor and Founding Director of the Arab and Muslim Ethnicities and Diasporas (AMED) Studies Program at San Francisco State University; **Nina Farnia**, Assistant Professor at Albany Law School, and many more.[511] [boldface added]

"Diversity, equity, and inclusion" was exposed as grossly discriminatory, emasculated, and ineffective. The new god of DEI was revealed as the lie that it always was, but which few had the temerity to call out.

With one major and well-publicized exception.

---

510 Stephanie Saul, "Who Are the Columbia Professors Mentioned in the House Hearing?" *The New York Times*, April 17, 2024: https://www.nytimes.com/2024/04/17/nyregion/jospeh-massad-katherine-franke-mohamed-abdou-columbia-university.html

511 Center on Extremism, "Some U.S. Professors Praise Hamas's October 7 Terror Attacks," Anti-Defamation League, November 21, 2023: https://www.adl.org/resources/article/some-us-professors-praise-hamass-october-7-terror-attacks

Policing Imaginary "Microaggressions" *versus* Threats of Mass Murder

President Ben Sasse of the University of Florida emerged as the unlikeliest of heroes in American higher education. The former Nebraska Senator had been appointed as the president of Florida's flagship university by Governor Ron DeSantis in October of 2022. After the October 7 attacks, President Sasse issued a ringing condemnation of anti-Semitism and left no one in doubt of his position that he would deal with those who vandalize, threaten, and assault. But this was, as noted, the exception.

Other university presidents found it incredibly difficult to respond with moral clarity to Hamas barbarism. Instead, they temporized. Those presidents who had spoken with such passion against the largely imaginary "racism" on their own campuses and the need to dismantle systems of oppression found themselves mute and emasculated in the face of hate and actual threat to their Jewish students, faculty, and staff.

They had found it much easier to swat at the phantom of campus "racism" and to engineer a bloated bureaucracy of DEI functionaries than to confront the real hate on the campuses. This was a hate for which they, themselves, were largely responsible and for which they continue to be responsible. Some presidents issued tepid both-sides equivocations, needing to satisfy perceived constituencies, rather than clearly condemn evil, to unequivocally denounce inhumanity.

Instead, they offered abstract denunciations of "violence" of all kinds. Such ritual denunciations constitute a reflexive *pro forma* statement crafted by lawyers and suitably ineffective for any occasion. Strangely, some presidents injected the barbarous neologism "Islamophobia" into the mix alongside anti-Semitism, when virtually no instances of this Islamophobia were exhibited on campus. Instead, quite the opposite—an international "Day of Jihad" was announced for October 13 by the supporters of Hamas, a day on which Jews should be killed indiscriminately.

The threat to Jewish students on the campuses nationwide had manifested almost immediately, as if someone had fired the start-pistol of hate. It was real, virulent, continuous.

And DEI was nowhere to be found.

DEI in Hiding

Where were the DEI folks, who so scrupulously tally and investigate anonymous reports of imaginary microaggressions? The folks who measure the fraudulent "racial climate" on the campus through suspect means and who intone the mantra of "diversity, equity, and inclusion" while Jewish students are hiding in libraries,[512] are physically assaulted on the streets and in the quad, are threatened with mass murder, and whose property is set afire in the dormitory endangering hundreds of students?

Some feebly suggested that DEI offices were ill-equipped to deal with—wait for it—*religious* discrimination. That's what they called the racial animus against Jews on the campus. *Religious* discrimination. While this may sound strange to the normal ear, it makes crude sense to the DEI cadres and the simple doctrine that fuels their world view.

Jews are *white*, you see. In the DEI fantasy world, this makes

---

512 Katherine Donlevy and Steven Vago, "Cooper Union barricades Jewish students inside library as pro-Palestinian protesters bang on doors," *The New York Post*, October 25, 2023: https://nypost.com/2023/10/25/news/cooper-union-barricades-jewish-students-inside-library/

them *oppressors* and therefore ineligible for the rigorous protections afforded to students identified as the *oppressed*. No better visible reason has emerged to highlight the racialist doctrine that informs higher education DEI.

This racialist doctrine went on public display in early December of 2023 with the nationally televised congressional testimony of three DEI immersed college presidents.

Shame of the Universities

The shame of the universities is represented most memorably by the spectacle of three college presidents—of Harvard, Penn, and MIT—testifying before congress as violent anti-Semitic protests roiled their campuses. Calls for a ceasefire in the Gaza war between Israel and the terrorists of Hamas, quickly metastasized into violent anti-Zionist and anti-Semitic expressions.

In their big moment testifying in Washington, these presidents attempted to explain their lack of response to the rampaging demonstrations of anti-Semitic hate. They were advised and coached by their corporate lawyers to carefully parse their words and to equivocate when in doubt. They offered a slick package of obfuscation. They finessed their answers to a noncommittal fine point. They exposed themselves as morally vacuous empty-suit bureaucrats, over-reliant upon lawyers and unable to express themselves.

Claudine Gay, Elizabeth Magill, and Sally Kornbluth scarred their institutions for years with their inability to articulate the simplest condemnation of terroristic barbarism. Theirs was an example of how far our higher education institutions have sunk, and perhaps our society if one wants to draw larger implications.

Or at least that portion of society populated with what might be wryly called the educated elite.

But even more distressing was the moral corruption exhibited by these institutions' top leadership, the boards of trustees and overseers that provide nominal oversight of these august institutions. Penn, at least, showed self-awareness as it cut ties with Magill (she "resigned"), relegating her to a sinecure in the law school in the wake of her smirk-plagued testimony, while Penn's board chairman quit as well.[513]

But no such rectitude was remotely visible at Harvard. In fact, the tempest that swirled around the hapless president Claudine Gay continued for weeks into December of 2023 after her disastrous congressional testimony. Her poor performance before congress shone a spotlight on the hapless Gay, only to reveal a modestly accomplished scholar guilty of plagiarism and defiantly unrepentant for her academic malpractice.

This was the person the Harvard Corporation had selected six months earlier to lead the most distinguished university in the world, and Claudine Gay was found wanting to an alarming degree, unable to articulate a clear and moral response to a softball question. In the weeks that followed her testimony, the situation worsened with the revelation that she was a serial plagiarist of her published academic work, with instances in about half of her meager output. She was forced to issue corrections to her articles, including to her Harvard dissertation.

The Harvard Corporation doubled and tripled down on its

513 "Penn President Liz Magill, board chair resign amid outrage over response to antisemitism," NBC Philadelphia, December 11, 2023: https://www.nbcphiladelphia.com/news/local/university-of-pennsylvania-penn-president-liz-magill-resigns-amid-outrage-over-response-to-antisemitism/3715039/

support for the hapless Gay. These Corporation mandarins—a unanimous eleven of them—rallied round their gal. They actually created a neologism to characterize her plagiarism so to avoid the "P" word. It was, they insisted, only "duplicative language" that had not been properly cited.[514] Presumably this *nouveau* technique would open the door to every Harvard freshman to use this time-saving method.

The slow drip of disrepute continued, and more allegations of academic misconduct surfaced until Gay ignominiously resigned. But Gay doesn't need your sympathy. She returned to teach in the Harvard faculty after her demotion with her presidential salary intact—nearly $900,000 per year.[515]

> Not a shabby wage for someone who apparently had taken a few dozen shortcuts years earlier on her way to crossing the finish line to grab her doctorate sheepskin . . . . This is one heck of a benefit we can attribute to the DEI program at Harvard.[516]

Columbia University Exposed

Inevitably, perhaps, the spotlight returned to Columbia University. In many ways, Columbia was the center of the maelstrom of campus unrest, and the university's anti-Semitic house of cards that suddenly collapsed in early August of 2024.

---

514 Jennifer Schuessler, "Harvard Finds More Instances of 'Duplicative Language' in President's Work," *The New York Times,* December 21, 2023: https://www.nytimes.com/2023/12/20/us/harvard-claudine-gay-plagiarism.html

515 Selim Algar, "Harvard's Claudine Gay set to keep her nearly $900K annual salary despite resigning as university president," *The New York Post,* January 2, 2024: https://nypost.com/2024/01/02/news/claudine-gay-set-to-keep-800k-salary-despite-resigning/

516 Carol Swain, *The Gay Affair: Harvard, Plagiarism, and the Death of Academic Integrity* (Nashville: Be the People books, 2025), p. 7-8.

Three deans who had been suspended all resigned.[517] In a week, they were followed by the resignation of Columbia President Minoche Shafik, whose disastrous tenure will be forever marked by her inability to maintain even a modicum of control of the university in the face of outside and inside bad actors bent on imposing their own violent agenda on the institution.[518] She was the third Ivy League president to leave in disgrace in the aftermath of their testimony before congressional hearings on campus anti-Semitism.

The rot goes deep at Columbia and calls into question the entire leadership structure as well as the ability of that institution to govern itself. For instance, two professors on the school's rules committee, which is charged with determining how the school handles incidents like the encampments, actually *participated* in the encampment. Professors Joseph Slaughter and Susan Bernofsky both supported anti-Israel demonstrations on the campus. Slaughter is a professor of English, while Bernofsky is a "professor of writing" in the "faculty of the arts." Bernofsky, especially, has evinced hostility toward exposure of her activities and of anti-Semitic expression on campus.

> After *Free Beacon* editor-in-chief Eliana Johnson broke the news that Shafik was resigning—before it had been officially announced—Bernofsky also wondered aloud how "the

---

517 Sharon Otterman, "3 Columbia University Deans Who Sent Insulting Texts Have Resigned," *The New York Times*, August 8, 2024: "3 Columbia University Deans Who Sent Insulting Texts Have Resigned," *The New York Times*, August 8, 2024.

518 Josh Moody, "Columbia President Minouche Shafik Resigns Unexpectedly," *Insidehighered.com*, August 14, 2024: https://www.insidehighered.com/news/governance/executive-leadership/2024/08/14/columbia-president-resigns-unexpectedly

ed-in-chief of a garbage right-wing online-only rag got to break the news on this story. Same rag that got 3 Columbia deans fired this summer," she posted, referring to the administrators who resigned last week over their vitriolic text messages about Jewish panelists. "Who's their mole?"[519]

Bernofsky's concern appeared to be only that the fired deans were exposed by the news outlet, not that the deans had expressed clearly anti-Semitic tropes and had been called to account. Other, more sober faculty at Columbia, those who work in the more rigorous disciplines, questioned this obvious conflict of interest of the presence of Bernofsky and Slaughter on the rules committee: "There's going to be plenty of disruption," said Jacob Fish, a professor in Columbia's school of engineering. Slaughter and Bernofsky, he added, should not be giving "any kind of advice to the administration."

Itsik Pe'er, a professor of computer science, said he was "concerned" that Slaughter and Bernofsky would "bias" the rules committee. And Elliot Glassman, an adjunct professor in the school of architecture, likened the two committee members to "wolves guarding the henhouse."

"This predetermines the outcome," Glassman said. "I just want to focus on making great buildings without worrying about disturbances."[520]

Columbia's retrenchment has been slow, and one has a right

519 [510] Aaron Sibarium, "'A Huge Conflict of Interest': Two Professors on Columbia's Top Disciplinary Body Participated in Encampment, Photos Suggest," *Washington Free Beacon*, August 14, 2024.
520 Aaron Sibarium, "A Huge Conflict of Interest"

to consider that it is not entirely sincere, given that most of those expressing anti-Semitism remain in their posts. One who does not remain, however, is erstwhile law professor Katherine Franke. She left Columbia ("resigned") in January of 2025 under a cloud.[521] She erred by going after Jewish students, whom she claimed had been harassing Palestinian students. She continues her claims of wrongdoing on the part of the university.

Where is DEI? Missing in Action

One of the most notable absences in the midst of the campus unrest, which was clearly manifested as racialist anti-Semitism, was DEI.

Diversity's vaunted "bias response teams" were inoperative against a tsunami of racist anti-Semitism. Hundreds of DEI bureaucrats were shown to be morally bankrupt—their primitive doctrine hobbled them in dealing with the complex reality that most people actually experience.

At the University of Michigan, long a bastion of DEI and a mainstay in keeping it on life support, the bureaucracy floundered. Said *The New York Times'* Nicholas Confessore in an investigative piece:

> As the campus arguments grew more rancorous, Jews, Palestinians and their supporters all laid claim to Michigan's promise of inclusion. The school's formidable bureaucracy seemed both paralyzed and heavy-handed, scorned by many students and divided against itself.[522]

521 Ryan Quinn, "Pro-Palestinian Columbia Professor Departs After Investigation," Inside Higher Ed, January 10, 2025: https://www.insidehighered.com/news/faculty-issues/academic-freedom/2025/01/10/pro-palestine-columbia-professor-departs-after
522 Nicholas Confessore, "The University of Michigan Doubled Down on D.E.I."

The DEI position has always been a primitive construct—whites are *de facto* oppressors, and "bipoc"[523] persons are de facto victims of white supremacy and systemic racism. This gymnastic distinction is absolutely necessary to the DEI ideology, which labels Jews as *white* and therefore incapable of being the victims of racism and certainly not racism from primarily "persons of color."

But that fraud has rapidly collapsed as increasing numbers of Jewish liberals have been mugged by the nasty reality of DEI in the raw. The process of coming 'round has not been easy or elegant. It's been cathartic for Jews in a way that resembles that of an earlier generation of intellectuals who renounced their devotion to the grotesque doctrine of communism.[524]

DEI's staunchest supporters wrestled with the conundrum, always afflicted with tortured *ad hocism*. Many were left paralyzed, their doctrine failing them. For example, one DEI afficionado was left unable to utter an opinion except to declare herself speechless on the issue of how and why DEI is constitutionally unable to address anti-Semitism, precisely because the racialist doctrine does not, theoretically, include Jews as an oppressed minority. Far from it, as one DEI functionary at the University of Michigan declared. In a moment of rare candor and stunning ignorance, she was fired for her intemperateness:

> She was accused of saying in a conversation at a conference in March that the university was "controlled by wealthy Jews."

---

523 BIPOC—"black, indigenous, people of color"

524 Richard Crossman (ed), *The God that Failed* (New York: Harper, 1950); Douglas Hyde, *I Believed* (London: Reprint Society, 1952); Howard Fast, *The Naked God: The Writer and the Communist Party* (Westport: Praeger Publishers, 1957); Peter Collier and David Horowitz, *Destructive Generation: Second Thoughts about the Sixties* (New York: Encounter, 2005).

She was also accused of saying that Jewish students were "wealthy and privileged" and not in need of her office's diversity services, and that "Jewish people have no genetic DNA that would connect them to the land of Israel."[525]

Professor Jenni Small reflects on her own intellectual vertigo, occasioned by the misbehavior of those whom she believed to be allies:

> To ignore rising antisemitism on college campuses, a pressing social issue on which I am ostensibly somewhat of an experienced thinker (even if I wouldn't call myself an expert), would be ridiculous. Unfortunately, I am not exactly sure what to say. I am also frustrated, angry, upset, and exhausted over what feels like being let down by many of the progressive allies to whom I've given my support over many years. On the other hand, I still value the DEI framework and critical theories, but I am not sure if I feel good about that valuing. Does it pit me against other Jews? I simply do not feel ready to give up on ideas and principles that have undergirded so much of my work just because some of the people who also claim to abide by them aren't living up to the moment in the way I want them to.[526]

This is what happens when the reality in which most of us live collides with the wishful thinking of "theory." Colloquially, this is called being "mugged by reality."

525 Stephanie Saul and Vimal Patel, "D.E.I. Official at University of Michigan Is Fired Over Antisemitism Claim, Lawyer Says," *The New York Times*, December 11, 2024: https://www.nytimes.com/2024/12/12/us/university-of-michigan-dei-administrator-antisemitism.html
526 Jennie L. Small, "Antisemitism and DEI: Two Ways of Looking at the Current Crisis in Higher Education," *JCC Connexions*, Vol. 10, No. 1, February 2024: https://naspa.org/blog/antisemitism-and-dei-two-ways-of-looking-at-the-current-crisis-in-higher-education

OCTOBER 7—THE NAKEDNESS OF DEI

Suddenly, the grand historical narratives that ring with gran-
diloquence don't resonate as well when one's own life and one's
own relatives become potential victims of the doctrine. Partisans
of DEI discover that they are outsiders. More ominously, they
discover that they are "oppressors" not oppressed, irrespective of
vandalism, bloody noses, and threats.

> Truthfully, when I think about this issue, I feel like I have two
> separate minds: the one of the Jewish parent of a Jewish college
> student and the one of the higher education critical scholar
> and researcher. On the one hand, I want my daughter—and
> all Jewish college students—to be safe and feel included and
> heard on their campuses. On the other hand, I know that
> college administrators come to their work with both their best
> intentions and their own biases, cannot control everything on
> their campuses or certainly off-campus, and probably struggle
> to understand the vastly complex history of Israel and the
> varying ways Jewish students do and do not identify with it.[527]

Kudos are due to Small in her admission of doubt, the crack
in the seamless façade of "theory" that animates the "critical
scholar." When the messy details of what people actually do, even
the behavior of one's "allies," impinge upon one's daily life in the
form of consequences, the mind is concentrated. This is something
the liberal, and certainly the left-radical, rarely contemplates,
balancing as they do the contradictions between the exigencies of
reality and the demands of the dream.

---

527 Jennie L. Small, "Antisemitism and DEI,"

> [T]he spectacle of these dialectical tight-rope acts of self-deception, performed by men of good will and intelligence, is more disheartening than the barbarities committed by the simple in spirit. Having experienced the almost unlimited possibilities of mental acrobatism on that tightrope stretched across one's conscience, I know how much stretching it takes to make that elastic rope snap.[528]

This is how DEI apparatchiks contort the reality of what we see and experience into a grotesquerie sourced from their primitive doctrine. This forms the narrative of the Big Con that we are expected to believe. This is what happens when the contradictions of the Con narrative become apparent to those most affected by those contradictions—the immense cognitive dissonance becomes so disorienting and unresolvable that belief in the Con narrative is eventually abandoned.

* * *

The cognitive dissonance occasioned by the campus unrest of 2024 extended to the institutional level, to the DEI offices themselves. In fact, the DEI offices seemed paralyzed. Tasked with remedying campus bias, DEI bureaucrats showed a remarkable lack of vigor when actual acts of bias occurred on campus perpetrated against Jews—racism, vandalism, racist graffiti, hate speech, arson, blockades, and even assault. Ready to roll out "bias-response teams" at the slightest whiff of an imaginary racial microaggression, DEI came under fire when it refused to act to bring its constituencies

---

528 Arthur Koestler, "The Initiates," in Richard Crossman (ed), *The God that Failed* (New York: Harper, 1950), p. 63.

under control. The students that DEI considered "victims" were persecuting a minority unprotected by the DEI office. DEI personnel were exposed as generally and overwhelmingly anti-Semitic. This was known as far back as 2021, when a report was published showing exactly that.[529]

The fig-leaf of "it's not anti-Semitism, it's anti-Zionism" grew smaller by the day. Likewise, public statements of universities seemed divorced from the fast-moving events they purported to address. They seemed prepared by a PR team as evergreen pronouncements, suitable for roll-out on any occasion. Pronouncements that denounced "violence in all its forms." Pronouncements that bizarrely injected "Islamophobia" into the midst of what appeared obviously to be a higher education pogrom of Jews. The formula went something like this:

1. We're committed to supporting X

2. We've launched an investigation to ascertain the facts

3. We've instituted additional "training"

4. We reaffirm our commitment to X and look forward to serving our university community with care, mindfulness, and inclusivity.

This formula became ever more tiresome and less acceptable

529 Jay P. Greene, PhD, and James D. Paul, "Inclusion Delusion: The Antisemitism of Diversity, Equity, and Inclusion Staff at Universities," The Heritage Foundation Backgrounder, December 8, 2021: https://www.heritage.org/education/report/inclusion-delusion-the-antisemitism-diversity-equity-and-inclusion-staff

to a public weary of the dissembling and constant coverups of DEI's Big Con.

The Weariness of Genuflections to George, a Martyr-Saint

The solemn intoning of "George Floyd" doesn't carry the old zing that it used to, even as his death was used by those who profit from pushing a fake narrative of police singling out black men for killing.[530] In fact, Hamas' horrific terrorism of October 7 constitutes an atrocity of many orders of magnitude greater than what happened to Floyd, awful as it was.

The wanton mutilation, murder, and rape of Israeli civilians October 7 by a terrorist group and the subsequent months of actual persecution of Jewish students, faculty, and staff on America's college campuses rightly overshadowed the ginned-up "rampant racism" fraud.

And thus the greatest fear of DEI cadres has been realized.

This fear is that the DEI trump card, which had opened full the spigot of so much largesse and enabled the propagation of blather to be treated seriously by profoundly unserious administrations, no longer works. It is now seen as 1) the bald anti-white pseudoscience it is, 2) the power grab of mediocrities running a grift, and 3) the financial money-pit that is draining budgets.

Finally, and what is most important as the topic of this book, DEI's paranoid fantasy is recognized as the source code of the indoctrination of students into a hothouse of hateful

---

530 See Heather Macdonald's *The War on Cops*, which debunks the persistent mythology of cop-on-black crime.

ideology—calls to violence often engineered by campus faculty and staff. That violence we have seen too much of on the campuses.

The source of this hatred is no secret. It is being taught assiduously, and the sources are well-known. The fount of this primal urge to lash out is the French Algerian Frantz Fanon, whose screeds *The Wretched of the Earth* and *Black Skin, White Masks* are required reading for the acolytes of hate and envy. Fanon provided the violent blueprint for Third World revolutionary revanchism, and the Brazilian Maoist Paulo Freire provided the more palatable public version, suffusing his rhetoric with attestations of "love" and affection for Maoist cultural re-education and rectification in his series of so-called pedagogy books, beginning with 1970's *Pedagogy of the Oppressed*. This fealty to dead scribblers such as Fanon and Freire, bell hooks and Derrick Bell, Marx and Mao has normalized campus hatred.

Today's kick-line of grifters we met in the last chapter, who receive millions of dollars for purveying hate and violence, weigh heavy on the campuses with their lavish praise and defense of the supporters of barbarism. This agitation for violence and its normalization goes on, even as DEI officers deny their culpability, even as DEI staffers proclaim that their services are for *all* students, when they clearly are not.

For instance, the Chief Diversity Officer at Western Carolina University denies that his office discriminates against certain students.

"If a student comes to my office or any of my colleagues' offices, regardless of the background of that student, we will provide services to that student," Nazario-Colón says. "There is no administrator in higher ed who would say oh, I can't help you my job description says that I cannot work with you or my job description doesn't serve you."[531]

But of course, this is a standard DEI lie and has been for many years. Stanford University's DEI Counseling and Psychological Services DEI program has explicitly ignored anti-Semitic incidents on the campus:

> The DEI committee supported this decision, saying that because "Jews, unlike other minority group(s], possess privilege and power, Jews and victims of Jew-hatred do not merit or necessitate the attention of the DEI committee." ... Stanford's DEI committee's justification—that Jews possess privilege and power—is a theme that comes right out of the *Protocols of the Elders of Zion.*[532]

The University of Michigan fired a DEI functionary, Rachel Dawson, in December of 2024 for making remarks almost identical to those of the Stanford folks. Dawson, whose annual salary for administering the Office of Academic Multicultural Initiatives was $191,660, allegedly said that Jews don't need DEI services because they "control the university," and are "wealthy and privileged."

531 Adrienne Lu, "Who Leads America's DEI Offices? Here Are Their Stories," *The Chronicle of Higher Education*, April 19, 2023: https://www.chronicle.com/article/who-leads-americas-dei-offices-here-are-their-stories
532 Ira Bedzow, "DEI Training Needs To Take Antisemitism Seriously," *Forbes*, November 24, 2021: https://www.forbes.com/sites/irabedzow/2021/11/24/dei-training-needs-to-take-antisemitism-seriously/

Abdication of responsibility at the University of Michigan is a habit. The US Department of Education reported a four-year pattern of failure to address anti-Semitism at the university, beginning in 2020.[533] Seemingly for good measure, the report noted the same pattern at City University of New York.

There is a reason for the sameness of the rhetoric, and it is grounded not in reality but in the groupthink that dominates the minds of the persons involved in DEI. Anti-Semitism is a long-time feature of DEI and not an exception. It is driven by the same oppressor/oppressed creed that dominates DEI's lens on the world.

> [M]any instances of anti-Zionist harassment on campus are perpetrated by members of identity groups served by DEI programs. In addition, many DEI staff themselves harbor virulently anti-Israel sentiments, as demonstrated in a 2021 report examining the social-media postings of DEI staff at major universities. Drawing heavily on ideologies undergirding most DEI programs, these postings portrayed Israel as a racist, settler-colonial state, linked the plight of Palestinians to the struggles of oppressed minorities in America, and implied that it was the duty of antiracist activists to support the liberation of Palestine "from the river to the sea," a rallying cry for the elimination of the Jewish state.[534]

---

533 Andy Rose, University of Michigan, CUNY failed to respond to hostile incident complaints in October 7 aftermath, federal report finds," CNN, June 17 2024: https://www.cnn.com/2024/06/17/us/university-of-michigan-antisemitic-incidents-report/index.html

534 Tammi Rossman-Benjamin, "Why DEI Programs Can't Address Campus Antisemitism: They're too political to help Jewish students," *SAPIR*, August 7, 2023: https://sapirjournal.org/antisemitism/2023/08/why-dei-programs-cant-address-campus-antisemitism/

One former DEI Director was appalled at the blatant, pervasive anti-Jewish hate on her campus, centered in the office to which she was hired. She was astounded at the degree of hatred for Jews on her campus at De Anza College.

> I was told in no uncertain terms that Jews are "white oppressors" and our job as faculty and staff members was to "decenter whiteness." . . . At its worst, DEI is built on the unshakable belief that the world is divided into two groups of people: the oppressors and the oppressed. Jews are categorically placed in the oppressor category, while Israel is branded a "genocidal, settler, colonialist state." In this worldview, criticizing Israel and the Jewish people is not only acceptable but praiseworthy.[535]

Full Circle to the Dictates of Ideology—*When Ideologues Act on Hate*

This takes us back to one of this book's initial contentions—that many persons infected with ideologies of violence and revenge for group ills either real or imagined act in accord with what the ideology instructs them to do, especially when persons in authority support them, encourage them, defend them, and even fund them in some cases.[536] Needless to say, if you can convince reasonably smart students at, for instance, far-left Bryn Mawr College that

535 Tabia Lee, "I was a DEI director—DEI drives campus antisemitism," The New York Post, October 18, 2023: https://nypost.com/2023/10/18/i-was-a-dei-director-dei-drives-campus-antisemitism/
536 Bryn Mawr College, for instance, provides a "Racial Justice Impact Fund" that pays students for "collaboration with established community organizations already engaged in restorative and transformational justice work." https://www.brynmawr.edu/inside/offices-services/career-civic-engagement-center/funding-opportunities/funding-academic-year-opportunities#SupportforActivists

"racism" is a serious problem at Bryn Mawr and that they must unite to battle "inequities on campus and create opportunities for dialogue and collaborative problem-solving to address ongoing experiences of racism and systemic oppression on campus," then you can convince them of anything, regardless of how idiotic.

At Michigan, at Columbia, at UCLA, at Berkeley—at what point do students drunk on hatred and ideology, encouraged by fellow-traveling faculty and staff, step over the line from propaganda and protest to the ultimate acts of violence?

At what point do persons decouple from reality, salute the dead scribbler who inspires them, and act against their fellow human beings, as did the Red Guards in China's Cultural Revolution, as did countless violent protesters on campuses from Penn to Pittsburgh, MIT to Emory?[537] At what point do persons give license to their basest instincts under the guise of their special insight into the relations of "power and privilege" and the "contradictions" in society?

At what point are people transformed from the hapless suckers for a con-game into serving as full-time dupes for violent doctrine?

At what point do persons act exactly as did the assassin Luigi Mangione, who gunned down a man in the back on a New York street December 4, 2024 in the name of anti-capitalism?

Where is that tipping point?

The connection is apparent for those willing to make it. But many persons avert their gaze for fear of recognizing themselves

537 Matt Egan, Elisabeth Buchwald and Samantha Delouya, "'I have become traumatized.' Jewish students describe campus antisemitism," CNNBusiness, February 29, 2024: https://www.cnn.com/2024/02/29/business/antisemitism-college-harvard-upenn/index.html

in the mosh pit of ideology, imprisoned by the writings of long-dead essayists, and acting out the violent fantasies of their favorite public intellectual.

Suckers for the Big Con Take that Final Step

The most disturbing element in the aftermath of Luigi Mangione's assassination of Brian Thompson, aside from the real grief and anguish of the victim's family, was the outpouring of sympathy for the murderer after he gunned down the insurance executive in the early morning. That sympathy, expressed on social media and on television news repeatedly, by journalists and academic hacks alike, is based on shared ideology. They approve of Mangione's act because of what he believed about the world.

Consider this for more than the few moments it takes to read. Not only is little to no compassion reserved for the victim's family, but a smug bravado attaches itself to the full-throated support for Mangione, the "hot assassin."[538] Some people injected shop-worn ideology into the mix, flogging the trusty lingo of "class consciousness" to explain support for Mangione. A sociology professor repeated the oft-stated claim that the murder was important as a conversation starter and used it to leverage the familiar recitation of discontents that animate them.

> [E]veryday targeted attacks and systemic neglect accumulate to harm and render disposable historically and strategically

---

538 Heather Mac Donald, "Luigi Mangione and the American Abyss," *City Journal*, December 23, 2024: https://www.city-journal.org/article/luigi-mangione-unitedhealthcare-ceo-brian-thompson

marginalized communities, such as class under-resourced, BIPOC, women, and trans and queer people.[539]

The people who support Mangione enlist the same thought processes as those inspired by Fanon and Freire and the gurus of DEI. For those motivated by a hate-based creed, it's necessary to act in accord with what it instructs rather than what you know empirically to be true, and it's necessary to extract payment in blood from those your creed tells you are villains.

This is why DEI is so dangerous. It's not just a lucrative grift built on deception or a meeting place for the disaffected and disturbed to share tales of paranoia and personal woe. Nor is it a "sacred space" for mystic diversity officers to swap stories.

It's a call to act. For some, it can be a call to kill.

Here again is the connection to the doctrinaire assassin Luigi Mangione—hatred inspired by ideology that leads to calls for violence in a cause believed to be righteous by many. Mangione was driven to kill a person whom his creed told him was guilty. Likewise for those inspired by the perverse doctrines of "settler colonialism" and "decolonization." Persons who imbibe deeply of a simple, primitive ideology are inclined to behave in simple, primitive ways.

This outpouring of antisemitic hatred is the direct result of DEI's insistence that Jews are oppressors. What started with

---

539 Megan Thiele Strong, "Support for Luigi Mangione Reflects Working Class Weariness of Top-Down Violence," *Common Dreams,* December 28, 2024: https://www.commondreams.org/opinion/luigi-mangione-support

rhetorical attacks has morphed into defending and calling for violent attacks. It's inevitable for an ideology that demeans an entire group of people while accusing them of perpetrating massive injustice. When you stoke that kind of division and anger, you unleash fires you can't control.[540]

This kind of virulent hatred goes unacknowledged by DEI offices, which is unsurprising, as it threatens their Big Con, even as their official pronouncements employ coded tropes that enable them to continue unmolested on the campus. Even as their backchannel support of anti-Semitic activists continues to roil the campuses.

Conclusion

If ever there was doubt that university DEI offices are engaged in a hate-filled ideological crusade, the campus diversity response to the October 7, 2023 attacks in Israel stripped away that doubt. Nestled just below the surface for many years, the anti-Semitism emerged with chest-thumping bravado, with DEI urging on the protesters drunk on "decolonizing" and even dropping the pretense of masking their Jew-hatred with attacks on "Israel's foreign policy." Suddenly, the entire agenda of campus DEI was revealed, an agenda in the making since DEI arrived on the campuses.

Stanley Goldfarb is a former associate dean at the University of Pennsylvania Perelman School of Medicine, and he witnessed first-hand the rapid metastasizing of Jew hatred at Penn upon the arrival of DEI.

---

540 Tabia Lee, "I was a DEI director—DEI drives campus antisemitism," *The New York Post*, October 18, 2023: https://nypost.com/2023/10/18/i-was-a-dei-director-dei-drives-campus-antisemitism/

[T]he campus groups most associated with DEI are now leading the anti-Semitic charge .... Campus DEI bureaucracies
are stoking this hatred, too.[541]

The overwhelming preponderance of evidence against DEI
offices and their problematic staff as centers of anti-Semitism gives
rise to the question of *Why is this allowed to continue?*
The next and concluding chapter demonstrates that the many
victims of DEI's egregious actions have no intention of allowing it
to continue. And universities will pay a heavy price if they *do* allow
it to go on.

---

541 Stanley Goldfarb, "How DEI Inspires Jew Hatred: Diversity bureaucracies stoke anti-Semitism on campus," *City Journal*, November 2, 2023: https://www.city-journal.org/article/how-dei-inspires-jew-hatred

12

CONCLUSION—A NEW ERA?

DEPROGRAMMING, DISMANTLING,

DEFUNDING DEI

"Assumptions once made, even though proved faulty and out of keeping with reality, tend to be repeated over and over and not to be corrected in the face of new evidence."[542]

— Else Frenkel-Brunswik, Austrian social psychologist who studied authoritarian personalities and the psychology of antisemitism

---

542 Else Frankel-Brunswik, "Environmental Controls and the Impoverishment of Thought," in Carl Friedrich (ed), *Totalitarianism* (Cambridge: Harvard University Press, 1954, 1964), p. 185.

By now, you know the outlines of the project called DEI, and you know why it constitutes the Biggest Con of the Century and how it threatens to destroy the Enlightenment University. Moreover, you know the lines commonly used to mask the fraud:

"DEI is just teaching about race."

"DEI is teaching the history of slavery."

"DEI means ensuring a level playing field."

"DEI means ensuring that everyone gets a fair shot."

"Diversity is our strength."

It's none of this. Or if it is, it's only an afterthought or peripheral result. By now, you understand that DEI is a grift and an ideological program to fundamentally change higher education, stripping from the university the very concepts of merit, accomplishment, logic, reason, progress, and the scientific method from pride of place. DEI aims to replace it with prejudiced pseudoscientific nonsense, a primitive binary ideology of racial hate, and the folklore of "medicine wheels," "talking sticks," and "indigenous knowledges."

When exposed to this, surely the supporters of DEI recoil at the reality.

But no, when exposed to conclusive evidence of what DEI is all about, supporters and fellow travelers of DEI invariably balk. Supporters double-down on their support of DEI. They substitute their own internal good-feeling definition of DEI, even as evidence of DEI's systematic attack on the university and its students and faculty is provided in the words of Gurus themselves, in their articles, in their books, at their conferences, and on the campuses.

We see a mindboggling intransigence on the part of DEI supporters. I've faced this intransigence myself. Smart liberal folks, who pride themselves on their critical thinking skills (as do all academics), tell me repeatedly that the negative conception of DEI presented in *DEI Exposed* is "highly exaggerated" or "caricatured." This is puzzling, if not downright bizarre, as the material presented in this book is drawn directly from DEI sources. It is literally what *they* say about *their* activities. Thus, we see the truth of the quote that launched this chapter: "Assumptions once made, even though proved faulty and out of keeping with reality, tend to be repeated over and over and not to be corrected in the face of new evidence.[543] And with each iteration of the fraud, each recapitulation of "teaching about race," each recitation of "Diversity is our strength," the nugget of untruth buries itself deeper in a psyche that is frightened that it may have been duped.

It is as if the Big Con must be maintained in the face of every challenge, regardless of how devastating and delegitimizing.

So how to conclude an exposé about DEI, about a Big Con that is still in play with a massive bureaucracy of performers that is still in place?

A bureaucracy that employs thousands of bureaucrats who draw luxurious salaries for dubious activities, with many of them unsuited to do any sort of productive work, and all of them invested in "doing the work" of diversity? That is to say, convincing themselves that they are worthwhile. That what they *do* is worthwhile. That they're valuable just for who they are—redefining "productivity" to match what they want to do, taking lots of naps, lamenting their exhaustion, training students into mental illness, and drawing half-million-dollar paychecks.

---

543 Else Frankel-Brunswik, "Environmental Controls and the Impoverishment of Thought," in Carl Friedrich (ed), *Totalitarianism* (Cambridge: Harvard University Press, 1954, 1964), p. 185.

You see the problem, of course. It's the people, ultimately, who must be removed from the universities.

But where might they go? What might they do? Where can they draw spectacular salaries for overt systematic race-baiting while pretending to be university people?

The conundrum, of course, is that these people won't go without a fight, and that is the fight that is underway right now.

One way that this can happen is through the aggressive expansion and response of the many good organizations whose combined efforts have stanched the hemorrhaging in the university and curtailed the negative impact of DEI predations on students and faculty. In fact, the legal options available to students and faculty are many and powerful, and as I have said many times, universities respond best to muscle, not argument. The prospect of losing millions of dollars along with a cascade of bad publicity gets results, although it may seem that the denizens of universities can be the slowest learners that I have ever seen.

In the corporate world, companies respond to the prospect of bad publicity as well.

The DEI rollback has been gaining momentum as company after company has eliminated or significantly trimmed its participation in DEI activities. Bureaucracies have been reduced and "trainings" have been scaled back or eliminated.[544] Filmmaker Robby Starbucks has played a larger than life role in almost singlehandedly forcing companies to relook their discriminatory policies. His weapon has been public exposure or the promise that companies that engage DEI against its employees will be given a

544 Julie Kratz, "Is DEI Over? Robby Starbuck Wants You To Think So," Forbes, Dec 03, 2024: https://www.forbes.com/sites/juliekratz/2024/12/03/is-dei-over-robby-starbuck-wants-you-to-think-so/

full public vetting. The multi-million-sized market of consumers can then work its magic. I have contended here that DEI cannot survive the revelation of its racialist core, and Mr. Starbucks has shown that. The business magazine *Forbes* enlisted someone named Julie Kratz to profile Starbuck's efforts, which have been impressive.

> He actively targets companies through public pressure campaigns and negotiations, aiming to eliminate what he considers "woke" policies. His past targets include: Target, Amazon, Lowe's, Tractor Supply, Ford, Toyota, Harley-Davidson, Indian Motorcycle, Polaris, Stanley Black & Decker, DeWalt Tools, Craftsman, Caterpillar, Boeing, John Deere, Coors and Jack Daniel's.

Kratz's ultimate gaslight is that DEI is in good shape in corporate America. It remains strong and popular, she says. Kratz lists herself as "An Indiana University Kelley School of Business professor, certified unconscious bias and psychological safety trainer, master coach." As you suspected, she runs her own side-hustle diversity consulting business that provides "Allyship and inclusion resources to make sure everyone feels SEEN, HEARD, and BELONG-ING at work."[545] Ms. Kratz is a peanut hustler, who hung out her shingle years ago and illustrates the central point of this book, that diversity consultants slip into the colleges and "teach about diversity" as part of the Big Con. She just joined IU as an adjunct instructor in 2025.

Despite Kratz's graveyard whistling on behalf of DEI, Robby

---

545 https://www.nextpivotpoint.com/

Starbuck's efforts have snowballed as corporate America examines the waste, fraud, and mismanagement that inevitably comes with establishing bolt-on DEI programs that, at root, accuse employees of being racists.

Universities offer a stickier wicket.

Complex psychological factors are in play—large numbers of paranoid and paranoid-behaving bureaucrats, imperious college presidents protected by sleepy boards of trustees, decision-makers protected from personal liability for social justice boondoggles that hurt the institutions they govern, foolish insurance companies that shield universities from their racialist civil rights violations (which cost them millions of dollars), racialist extremists running unchecked on the campuses and motivated by a social justice ideology that encourages them to support terrorism, to threaten, to attack, and—now—to murder people. The factors examined in this book.

How might it play out when people fight back against smug and imperious college bureaucrats, drunk on DEI virtue? Let's look at one college's bout at pursuing its love of social justice and how it ended up paying millions in damages to its victims. It was a victory for the good guys at the expense of a smug little college called Oberlin.

The case of Oberlin demonstrates one of the most puzzling aspects of the new DEI campus regime. Why do college presidents heap so much legal exposure onto their colleges when all the red flags and alarm bells of impending litigation are warning them off.

In case after case, what is obvious to the man on the street is apparently opaque to the obtuse president of Anywhere U. Why do so many presidents decide stupidly in matters of import and for which they are still, nonetheless, compensated handsomely. As you know by now, the question that baffles them most is this:

"Where's the racism?"

If you want to see a college president tap-dance to avoid accountability, go ahead and ask: "Who are the racist people, and what are the racist policies, programs, and procedures on your campus you claim is 'rampant' with 'racism?'" Enjoy the public relations messaging, but don't expect a real answer. They *can't* answer, because finding actual racism on a college campus is as likely as sighting Bigfoot. And just about as credible (unless it's against Jewish people, of course, usually encouraged by college administrations)

Now, college leaders are even more likely to circle the wagons against accountability, largely due to fears of litigation. Thanks to the resolution of a legal case in Ohio, this has become a *$36 million* question. Oberlin College paid up on a $36.6 million judgment to a local family bakery for libeling their business as "racist."[546]

The sad and completely unnecessary case of *Gibson's Bakery v. Oberlin College* is likely to reshape the conversation about so-called antiracism efforts on university campuses for years to come, even as colleges fund expensive bureaucracies, commission task forces, and hire well-heeled bureaucrats to solve a problem that is almost nonexistent at their institutions.[547] Especially as the insurance

---

546 Sophie Mann, "'It took a tremendous toll': Bakery owner says it's 'bittersweet' after Oberlin College is ordered to pay $36million for falsely accusing family-owned bakery of racially profiling black students and wishes her husband and father-in-law were alive to see justice," *The Daily Mail*, December 18, 2022: https://www.dailymail.co.uk/news/article-11551561/Bakery-owner-speaks-Oberlin-College-ordered-pay-36M-false-racial-profiling-claim.html

547 Gibson Bros., Inc. v. Oberlin College, 2022-Ohio-1079: https://www.supremecourt.ohio.gov/rod/docs/pdf/9/2022/2022-Ohio-1079.pdf

companies that shield colleges against their stupidity may be wising up.

To Catch a Thief

The incident that led to the judgment occurred in November 2016, when a black Oberlin student shoplifted a bottle of wine from the bakery, was chased and caught by one of the owners, all of which resulted in a scuffle. The thief and his two accomplices, who intervened for their friend to pummel the clerk protecting his business, were all arrested. Within 24 hours, Oberlin moved swiftly into action. *Not* to upbraid the students, nor to apologize to the bakery and to the owner's son, Allyn D. Gibson, whom the trio attacked.

Instead, Oberlin supported a coalition of students, faculty, and administrators to attack the bakery publicly for "racism." The college stopped doing business with the bakery.

Then Oberlin fueled a very public hate hoax. Oberlin's Dean of Students and Vice President Meredith Raimondo was on the protest front lines armed with a bullhorn and leaflets, which constituted much of Oberlin's culpability in the defamation of the Gibson family business.

The college's narrative was not simply false. It was grossly and libelously false. As a bonus, it featured some of the worst optics in public relations history—well-heeled faculty, coiffed administrators, and privileged students bullying a small, fifth-generation family business, all while pushing a fake racialist narrative onto an inconvenient reality.

The Oberlin case shows what happens when "gaslighting" becomes higher education policy, when a college is colonized and captured by ideology. In this case, the college created a false narrative, and it expected its community members to behave according to its Soviet-style script: "We'll pretend that Gibson's Bakery is racist, you can pretend to be outraged, and everyone else will just go along."

It didn't work. Normal people would have none of it. The college discovered that its gaslighting would *not* be tolerated in the small town of Oberlin—outside the intellectual provincialism of the college. Even as the college argued futilely in court for years, it would eventually pay a fabulous price for its self-righteous bullying and defamation.

And thus, it was that something wondrous and magical happened in 2022: The good guys won.

It took six years and much court wrangling, but justice was served. The story ended happily with the judgment and actual payment of many millions in damages.

Even happier was that Oberlin found that its four insurance companies would not pay for the damages awarded by the court, and Oberlin sued them. Two companies were dismissed from the case, and Lexington and United Educators settled with the college in 2024.[548] United Educators is a primary insurer for colleges like Oberlin and lists its mission as helping them "identify, prevent, respond to, and recover from adversity and risks, enabling them to advance their mission."[549] It was founded in 1987 and is owned by the 1600 member schools it insures.

Whether Oberlin has learned its lesson in responsible

---

548 Dave O'Brien, "Oberlin College settles with its insurers in Gibsons Bakery judgment lawsuit," The Chronicle-Telegram, May 24, 2024: https://chroniclet.com/news/392195/oberlin-college-settles-with-its-insurers-in-gibsons-bakery-judgment-lawsuit/
549 United Educators Brochure: https://www.ue.org/48fbee/globalassets/global/ue-meeting-your-liability-insurance-needs.pdf

behavior is anybody's guess, but certainly the higher education community has taken note of insurers that may be monitoring college behavior more closely to assess risk accordingly.

The Oberlin case is encouraging. It establishes important precedents that can positively transform higher education.

- "Racism" is now part of the lexicon of so-called campus "hate speech."

- Baseless accusations of so-called "racism" can no longer be delivered with impunity.

- Colleges and universities are liable for the irresponsible actions of their bureaucrats, who huddle under the rubric of "social justice."

- Colleges and universities that embrace ideological positions and act cavalierly in ways that are contrary to the U.S. Constitution, to U.S. civil rights laws, and to Office for Human Research Protections (OHRP) regulations that protect vulnerable persons from psychological manipulation are on notice that their *carte blanche* has ended.

Whether college presidents are chastened, we'll discover soon enough. What seems clear is that the era of universities paying big bucks in damages in service to "woke" causes may be drawing to a close. One of these causes is discriminatory overreach by haughty DEI functionaries.

The case of Dr. Zack K. De Piero vs. Penn State is one such strange case.

In this case, Penn State University is so manifestly wrong, given the evidence already presented, that the school should have immediately fired several of its own staffers responsible for DEI at the school. No such thing happened. Instead, the university "doubled down" in the journalistic vernacular.

De Piero resigned from Penn State in August of 2022 for its racially discriminatory "DEI Training," which over a period of time displayed overtly racialist themes, with the facilitators using racialist language and behavior. De Piero sued, and the case is progressing. According to court records, Judge Wendy Beetlestone indicated

> ... how the DEI Director emailed all employees "calling on white people" to "feel terrible" about their "own internalized white supremacy" and to "hold other white people accountable." She also noted that the Assistant Vice Provost for Educational Equity "'led the faculty' in a breathing exercise in which she instructed the 'White and non-Black people of color to hold it just a little longer—to feel the pain.'"[550]

Said legal expert Jonathan Turley about such cases:

> These lawsuits are mounting against universities, which continue to burn through funds to defend these controversial statements .... In the case of Penn State, the school appears set on trying a case that will only increase the costs and negative

---

550 Jonathan Turley, "Penn State Loses Major Motion in Race Discrimination Case,"

coverage for the school. It is often the case that administrators lack the courage to challenge DEI programs or material. The alternative of spending potentially millions on litigation and damages can be viewed as rational rather than risking personal backlash for reversing course.[551]

Yes, it's rational, given the incentive structure in place. Certainly, it's rational for presidents who use the wealth of their institutions to shield them from accountability for their decisions. They align the institutions with their personal survival, and they rely upon the deep pockets of their institutions to pay their way out of problems they create.

When I spoke with Dr. De Piero, he was still marveling at Penn State's obtuse take on the situation, as if oblivious to the turpitude of the staff it hired and still pays. Said De Piero:

> I doubt that the elite wings of academia will self-right their sinking ships unless some precedent-setting cases like mine wind up striking the fear of God into re-thinking some of their misguided, wasteful, and discriminatory practices. But maybe that's not enough. Maybe it will also take the hammer of a principled and common sense-driven presidential administration that challenges institutions' accreditation or public funding. With sky-high tuition costs, low student enrollment numbers, and an increasingly bloated bureaucracy, you have to wonder whether many schools understand how to fix this mess. If I had to bet, there won't be much change: The true

---

radicals will just find another acronym for DEI and continue doing what they've been doing with a bit more subtlety.[552]

Many other examples indicate that adamant universities, their presidents, and their entrenched bureaucrats intend to defend every inch of turf won for DEI since the flush days of 2020. But we are entering a new era, where the possibilities seem endless and the prospects of real reform are within our grasp.

A new presidential administration took the reins of US government January 20, 2025, and the change in mood in higher education was palpable, ranging from fear that the Big Con might be coming to an end to exultation for the very same reason. What does the Donald Trump presidency mean for the potential reform of higher education and its restoration to its former excellence?

Educators have only a vague idea what impact the new presidential administration will have on education. The menu of possibilities is long: Student loan reform, investigation of accrediting agencies and their coercion of colleges on DEI, the potential taxing of college endowments, research grants, racial discrimination in student enrollment, the status of illegal aliens enrolled in colleges, the status of federal research funding for colleges that do not obey federal laws, transgender policies, holding colleges and universities strictly accountable for the safety of their students. Speculation is rampant, and even the major education publications recognize that unpredictability is the norm, at least until specific policy recommendations are forthcoming.

The situation began to clarify almost immediately in the first week of the Trump presidency, but the process of reform had

---

552 Personal communication with the author, January 15, 2025.

already begun, almost immediately after the election of the 47th U.S. President. This was the "Trump effect."

The DEI Party Is Over

The election of Donald Trump to the presidency on November 5, 2024, sent shudders through higher education, and the mandarins knew instinctively the game was up. Critics and supporters alike acknowledge that there is a real phenomenon called the "Trump Effect." This aura of power emanates from the man in successive waves and extends outward to modify the behavior of actors both public and private in successive arenas of social activity. In a process of "preemptive compliance," institutions and powerful persons, seeking to avoid scrutiny by the new administration, began to alter their behavior in ways that might shield them from new policies and existing policies that they cross.[553]

Universities had a grace period of about two months to get affairs in order, because as higher education expert Adam Kissel put it: "Colleges and universities, as well as other institutions, are on notice that the DEI party is over."[554]

Universities seemed keen to resolve the issue of anti-Semitism and how they had failed to protect their own Jewish students. This issue, which had brought low the careers of negligent college presidents in 2024, cast a shadow over higher education. Universities, which had shown intransigence in dealing with lawsuits that had resulted from their own mishandling of the campus unrest, suddenly became amenable to settlements with Jewish students

553 Jessica Blake, "Trump Takes Aim at DEI in Higher Ed," Insidehighered.com, January 23, 2025: https://www.insidehighered.com/news/government/politics-elections/2025/01/23/how-trumps-order-targeting-dei-could-affect-higher-ed
554 Jessica Blake, "Trump Takes Aim at DEi in Higher Ed,"

harmed during those protests. A spate of settlements concluded just before the new president was inaugurated January 20.

> [A] wave of universities—including the University of California system and Brown University—have settled Title VI complaints under the Department of Education alleging they failed to respond to campus antisemitism. The settlements allowed universities to close the proceedings before Trump took office.[555]

Notably at Harvard University, the school settled two antisemitism lawsuits one day after Trump took office.

It turns out that skittish university administrators had been right to worry. The 26 executive orders that the new president signed in the first 24 hours of his administration promised a rapid restoration of American society unlike that of any previous administration.

A New Era of Civil Rights Law

First came Executive Order 14151, Ending Radical and Wasteful Government DEI Programs and Preferencing.[556] This focused on the DEI machinery in the federal government, and within hours the bureaucratic gears began grinding to a halt.

At the Federal Trade Commission, Chairman Andrew Ferguson was blunt in announcing enforcement of the directive:

---

555 Dhruv T. Patel and Grace E. Yoon, "One Day After Trump Takes Office, Harvard Settles Two Antisemitism Lawsuits," *Harvard Crimson*, January 21, 2025.
556 Exec. Order No. 14151, Fed. Reg. (January 20, 2025): https://www.whitehouse.gov/presidential-actions/2025/01/ending-radical-and-wasteful-government-dei-programs-and-preferencing/

DEI is a scourge on our institutions. It denies to all Americans the Constitution's promise of equality before the law. It divides people into castes on the basis of immutable characteristics, and treats them as caste members rather than as individuals. It stokes tensions by elevating race and other immutable characteristics above merit and excellence. It promotes invidious discrimination. And it violates federal and natural law. The Biden-Harris Administration reveled in this pernicious ideology. They encouraged it, and it has festered within the federal government for four years.[557]

This paved the way for Executive Order 14173 the next day, titled "Ending Illegal Discrimination and Restoring Merit-Based Opportunity."[558]

This was the blow from the top that universities knew was coming. With the stroke of his giant marker, President Trump reaffirmed civil-rights laws that protect all Americans from "discrimination based on race, color, religion, sex, or national origin."[559] He explicitly named higher education as a transgressor of these laws in their embrace of "dangerous, demeaning, and immoral race- and sex-based preferences under the guise of so-called "diversity, equity, and inclusion" (DEI) or "diversity, equity, inclusion, and accessibility (DEIA) that can violate the civil-rights laws of this nation."

---

557 Press Release, "FTC Chairman Ferguson Announces that DEI is Over at the FTC," Federal Trade Commission, January 22, 2025: https://www.ftc.gov/news-events/news/press-releases/2025/01/ftc-chairman-ferguson-announces-dei-over-ftc

558 Exec. Order No. 14173, Fed. Reg. (January 21, 2025): https://www.whitehouse.gov/presidential-actions/2025/01/ending-illegal-discrimination-and-restoring-merit-based-opportunity/

559 "Title VI of the Civil Rights Act of 1964," Civil Rights Division, US Department of Justice: https://www.justice.gov/crt/fcs/TitleVI

Thus, the gauntlet was thrown down to universities more forcefully than they had perhaps ever faced. It was a clear signal that a Dionysian era of lavish lifestyles, mismanagement, progressive experimentation, abrogation of human rights, discrimination, profligacy, and outright fraud was ending. The battle would be long, difficult, and painful for many, but the battle would be fought.

Universities had to decide—*quickly*—whether they would side with their own inept staff and the raft of awful decisions of the preceding years, or whether they would trim their sails in the cause of justice and America's founding principles.

Section 2 of the EO was enough to send bureaucrats scurrying to safe-spaces for milk and cookies.

> Sec. 2. Policy. It is the policy of the United States to protect the civil rights of all Americans and to promote individual initiative, excellence, and hard work. I therefore order all executive departments and agencies to terminate all discriminatory and illegal preferences, mandates, policies, programs, activities, guidance, regulations, enforcement actions, consent orders, and requirements. I further order all agencies to enforce our longstanding civil-rights laws and **to combat illegal private-sector DEI preferences, mandates, policies, programs, and activities.**[560] [boldface added]

560 Exec. Order No. 14171, Fed. Reg. (January 21, 2025): https://www.whitehouse.gov/presidential-actions/2025/01/ending-illegal-discrimination-and-restoring-merit-based-opportunity/

Of keen concern for colleges is Section 5, which zeroes in on all institutions that receive federal funds. This particularly concerns "all institutions of higher education that receive Federal grants or participate in the Federal student loan assistance program." Of especial concern is whether schools are complying with the 2023 Supreme Court decision that outlaws racial discrimination in admissions: Students for Fair Admissions, Inc. v. President and Fellows of Harvard College, 600 U.S. 181 (2023).

This means that colleges and universities are subcontractors. This in turn means that even private universities must attend to the business of adhering to US Civil Rights laws or forego the lavish emoluments of federal funding—research grants, students relying upon federal loans, and such like. Both public and private universities must consider whether the price of their social experimentation in abrogating the civil rights of its students and faculty is worth the price of losing federal monies.

Even further, universities with endowments of more than $1 billion face additional scrutiny of their potentially illegal DEI activities. The education department has been instructed to select and examine the policies for compliance of nine universities that fit the criteria.

The Department of Education, in fact, is moving with efficient haste to reform itself in response to the new administration's emphasis on civil rights.

- Dissolution of the Department's Diversity & Inclusion Council, effective immediately . . . ;

- Dissolution of the Employee Engagement Diversity Equity Inclusion Accessibility Council (EEDIAC) within the Office for Civil Rights (OCR), effective immediately;

- Cancellation of ongoing DEI training and service contracts which total over $2.6 million;

- Withdrawal of the Department's Equity Action Plan;

- Placement of career Department staff tasked with implementing the previous administration's DEI initiatives on paid administrative leave; and

- Identification for removal of over 200 web pages from the Department's website that housed DEI resources and encouraged schools and institutions of higher education to promote or endorse harmful ideological programs.[561]

The new administration is certainly aware of the deception that is inherent in DEI programs and people. It will monitor persons and groups "advancing a divisive DEI agenda, including programs using coded or imprecise language to disguise their activity."

A third executive order in the initial slate of EOs impacting higher education was aimed at the scourge of anti-Semitism

---

561 Press Release, "U.S. Department of Education Takes Action to Eliminate DEI," Department of Education, January 23, 2025: https://www.ed.gov/about/news/press-release/us-department-of-education-takes-action-eliminate-dei

manifested on our campuses throughout late 2023 and into 2024.[562] Many of the activists who acquired visas to study in the United States decided it was a good idea to become political agitators against the country that had welcomed them, disrupting American higher education and threatening other students in service to a foreign agenda. Said the president in a fact sheet on his order:

> To all the resident aliens who joined in the pro-jihadist pro-tests, we put you on notice: come 2025, we will find you, and we will deport you. I will also quickly cancel the student visas of all Hamas sympathizers on college campuses, which have been infested with radicalism like never before.[563]

Finally, as I emphasized earlier, the possibility of taxing the largest university endowments at a 35 percent rate surely focuses the minds of those allocating and handling funds.[564] No, the tax itself would not "hurt students," as some say. If students are hurt, that pain will be inflicted by the decisions of administrators who levy students with additional invoicing to make up the difference, rather than trim the immensely bloated bureaucracies of deans, assistant deans, assistant provosts, and vice presidents, who contribute only peripheral value, if any, to the educational process.

562 Exec. Order No.14188 Fed. Reg. (January 29, 2025): https://www.whitehouse.gov/presidential-actions/2025/01/additional-measures-to-combat-anti-semitism/
563 *Fact Sheet: President Donald J. Trump Takes Forceful and Unprecedented Steps to Combat Anti-Semitism*, The White House, January 30, 2025: https://www.whitehouse.gov/fact-sheets/2025/01/fact-sheet-president-donald-j-trump-takes-forceful-and-unprecedented-steps-to-combat-anti-semitism/
564 Phillip Levine, "What Trump Means for College Budgets," *The Chronicle of Higher Education*, January 22, 2025: https://www.chronicle.com/article/what-trump-means-for-college-budgets

Hard choices are afoot, and presidents may be forced to earn those million-dollar paychecks. And trim them substantially.

In fact, the flush era of largesse is on the cusp of ending—the flow of ever-increasing tuition dollars, easy federal student loans that universities play no part in insuring, federal research dollars flowing in, and tax-free endowments swelling year-by-year. The steady increase in numbers of supernumeraries to provide invented "student services" will likely be the first extravagance curtailed, perhaps with a welcome cutback in "student success" vice presidents with half-million-dollar salaries.

But the DEI consortium will not go quietly.

Already, the DEI lobby is mobilizing to resist, and these are the folks and organizations you met in this book. Shaun Harper, of the Race & Equity Center at USC, emerged to trot out the menu of "arguments" we've seen already.

"These leaders will be worried about losing their federal funding, which is exactly what DEI opponents want," Harper said in an email to *Inside Higher Ed*. Heterosexual, Christian white men will likely feel supported and affirmed by Trump's anti-DEI orders, as "too many of them have been tricked into misunderstanding DEI initiatives to be unfair, universal attacks," he added. But in the meantime, Harper said that minority students will face increased harassment, discrimination and violence and will "be left stranded without justice."[565]

In other words, Harper presents the arguments we've debunked in this book—1) critics of DEI just "misunderstand

565 Jessica Blake, "Trump Takes Aim at DEI in Higher Ed,"

DEI initiatives" and 2) racism is rampant on the campuses, with minorities facing "harassment, discrimination, and violence." As we have seen, the only persons realistically facing systemic "harassment, discrimination, and violence" are Jewish students, who DEI folks have stated don't deserve protection.

The National Association of Diversity Officers in Higher Education, too, responded vigorously. No surprise there, as it is this group of supernumeraries that operates and benefits from the Big Con and that faces imminent dismissal. The president and CEO of NADOHE Paulette Granberry Russell strummed the familiar absurdist chords as she told *Inside Higher Ed* that:

> By attacking the important work of diversity, equity and inclusion offices at educational institutions, the order seeks to dismantle critical support systems for historically underrepresented students. This would limit workforce preparation and stifle efforts to address systemic inequities. This order depicts diversity, equity and inclusion as divisive when, in reality, these initiatives aim to ensure opportunity for all.[566]

Granberry Russell bizarrely claimed that Trump's EO "is already causing uncertainty and fear" when it is racialist DEI programs that are responsible for the climate of fear and uncertainty on the campuses—the lack of university leadership, as we have seen, has permitted this state of affairs. Granberry Russell continued: "I hope that university leaders will recognize that executive orders

---

566 Jessica Blake, "Trump Takes Aim at DEI in Higher Ed," Insidehighered.com, January 23, 2025: https://www.insidehighered.com/news/government/politics-elections/2025/01/23/how-trumps-order-targeting-dei-could-affect-higher-ed

should not dictate the values and priorities of higher education institutions."

And neither should grasping, extremist off-campus non-profit groups undermine college values with their programs to "boldly transform higher education." If universities had stayed true to their mission throughout this dark period of DEI, the government would have no need to remind them to obey Civil Rights law. A major course correction is overdue, and it's already underway.

It All Comes Back to Money

Money is surely on the agenda, because higher education is the repository of vast wealth.

Universities are tax-exempt institutions and many boast fabulous endowments of billions of tax-free dollars. Their coffers continue to swell with tuition dollars, tuition that inexorably increases. The public also provides many billions of dollars *in toto* to fund the research enthusiasms of faculty. This money has proven not only a lever of scientific advancement for the improvement of our society and the prosperity of our people, but unfortunately is also the source of irresponsibility and wild squandering of wealth.

The new presidential administration puts that wealth in play as a source of revenue for the government and as a source of leverage on institutions that many see as having betrayed the trust given them in the form of self-governance with minimal oversight.

For instance, the *Chronicle of Higher Education* ran a sky-is-falling opinion piece by Phillip Levine, a professor of economics at Wellesley College, that declared "How Trump Could Devastate Our Top Colleges' Finances." Levine ponders if a 35 percent tax on college endowments, an idea floated by new Vice President J.

D. Vance, might threaten a raft of higher education activities.[567] Simultaneously, on the site *Inside Higher Ed*, an article considered the potential upside of a Trump presidency:

> The incoming administration is expected to roll back regulations for colleges and universities, which should provide some benefits. Institutions also could see a boost if the administration changes union or compensation rules. Plus, the protection of certain tax credits could benefit colleges that provide health insurance and promote charitable giving.[568]

The Trump administration has evinced no love of DEI. "Supporters of DEI initiatives spent most of 2024 on the defensive," said a *Wall Street Journal* article, and 2025 should be even better as the new administration ramps up its efforts. Certainly, DEI in government and business will face welcome challenges to eradicate the type of "training" programs that have scourged and hampered businesses and, in some cases, attacked employees for noncompliance with racialist policies.

"The pendulum is swinging back and swinging back very hard against DEI," said Mike Davis, a former Senate lawyer who runs the Article III Project, a conservative legal advocacy group,

---

567 Phillip Levine, How Trump Could Devastate Our Top Colleges' Finances, *The Chronicle of Higher Education*, January 13, 2024: https://www.chronicle.com/article/how-trump-could-devastate-our-top-colleges-finances
568 Jessica Blake, Colleges Expect Less Red Tape Under Trump, More Input on Policies, Insidehighered.com, January 14, 2024: https://www.insidehighered.com/news/government/politics-elections/2025/01/14/colleges-could-see-less-red-tape-under-trump

who is a close outside adviser to Trump. "Until DEI is eradicated from society there's still work to be done."[569]

One headline perfectly captured the bleak mood for DEI: "Diversity, equity and inclusion programs at some of the country's biggest companies fell apart in 2024. Anti-DEI efforts will most likely only ramp up in 2025."[570]

And on the college campuses, it is clear is that the future of DEI is superbly bleak, even as administrations rush to change the names of offices and reassign diversity officers to new roles—basically camouflaging efforts to keep it afloat as long as possible.

Christopher Rufo, the public intellectual mentioned prominently in this book promises to be a major advisor to the new administration on education policy as it relates to DEI.

> Rufo said he has succeeded in demonizing CRT and DEI in the public's mind. Now he wants to uproot what he sees as an administrative state that keeps the policies in place across universities, government and businesses. ... [He] says current diversity practices justify discrimination and devalue individual merit. "An organization can prioritize excellence or diversity, but not both simultaneously," he said.[571]

Certainly, the federal government will coordinate its efforts

569 Theo Francis and Chip Cutter, "Corporate America Drew Back From DEI. The Upheaval Isn't Over," *The Wall Street Journal*, December 28, 2024: https://www.wsj.com/business/corporate-dei-policy-changes-pull-back-33fdab87
570 Curtis Bunn, "DEI programs weathered a myriad of attacks this year, with more to come in 2025," NBCNews.com, December 29, 2024: https://www.nbcnews.com/news/nbcblk/anti-dei-program-effort-2025-states-companies-universities-trump-rcna184580
571 Douglas Belkin, Christopher Rufo Has Trump's Ear and Wants to End DEI for Good, *The Chronicle of Higher Education*, November 25, 2024: https://www.wsj.com/us-news/education/christopher-rufo-education-trump-dei-bb9e7178

with the legislation of state governments, which have performed yeoman's work in prying DEI off the campus with legal action and threats of funding cuts. *The Chronicle of Higher Education* publishes regularly what I call a victory map that tracks the rollback of DEI, and as 2024 drew to a close, showed efforts in 30 states underway.

Many state legislatures utilize a model legislation template prepared by scholars at the Manhattan and Goldwater Institutes. The legislation offers a king's ransom of policy prescriptions that

> would prohibit colleges from hiring diversity, equity, and inclusion officers; bar trainings that instruct staff to identify and fight against systemic racism; eliminate requirements for employees to commit to diversity statements; and could disallow even institutional commitments to social justice and recommendations that students be addressed by their preferred pronouns.[572]

The authors contend that "university DEI offices are the nerve center of woke ideology on university campuses." They are surely correct. They continue: "DEI officers form a kind of revolutionary vanguard on campuses; their livelihood can only be justified by discovering—i.e., manufacturing—new inequities to be remedied."[573]

Another fantastically robust document that charts a path to reform is published by the America First Policy Institute and guided by Dr. Jonathan Pidluzny, the director of the firm's Higher

---

572 Christopher F. Rufo, Ilya Shapiro, Matt Beienburg, "Abolish DEI Bureaucracies and Restore Colorblind Equality in Public Universities," Issue Brief, Manhattan Institute, January 18, 2023: https://manhattan.institute/article/abolish-dei-bureaucracies-and-restore-colorblind-equality-in-public-universities
573 Christopher F. Rufo, Ilya Shapiro, Matt Beienburg, "Abolish DEI Bureaucracies and Restore Colorblind Equality in Public Universities,"

Education Reform Initiative. The document, "Reversing the Woke Takeover of Higher Education: Strategies to Dismantle Campus DEI," provides a specific framework of reform. Combined with the work of the Manhattan Institute, the AFPI's efforts chart a course for rapid and meaningful change.

> States that make higher education reform a priority along these lines will see the effort repaid severalfold in the coming years and decades. University systems will do much more to advance the public interest when they prioritize training students for professional success, driving scientific research forward, and equipping citizens with the civic literacy—and shared under-standing—necessary to reinvigorate a civil public dialogue.[574]

The pendulum has, indeed, begun its slow arc back to sanity and sobriety. But this is no mere mopping up operation. DEI still has incredible vitality, and you know why—millions of dollars, entrenched bureaucrats desperate to hold onto their sinecures, sympathetic administrators, and thousands of clueless allies work-ing for "social justice."

The Battle Continues

While state legislatures and the federal government are powerful players in rectifying the inequities in our society wrought by ideo-logues, the private groups mentioned throughout this book still

---

574 Jonathan Pidluzny, "Reversing the Woke Takeover of Higher Education: Strategies to Dismantle Campus DEI," America First Policy Institute, Higher Education Reform Initiative, August 2023: https://americafirstpolicy.com/issues/research-report-reversing-the-woke-takeover-of-higher-education-strategies-to-dismantle-campus-dei

have major roles to play in continuing to root out racialist DEI from our universities.

Students and faculty can obtain immediate relief.

This is a tocsin for all those persons affected by these training programs to speak out, to write, and to launch no-holds-barred discussions of DEI's toxicity. Only by shining a bright spotlight on the doctrine can the unctuous skin be peeled back, its flawed structure and substance revealed, and its purveyors exposed as the grasping sociopaths that they are.

Is sociopath too strong a word?

Is there nothing redeeming about the DEI enterprise? After all, thousands of DEI professionals are "doing the work" of this both in higher education and in corporate America, even in the government. Are their motives uniformly suspect?

For their own part, in their self-conception, as they perceive themselves . . . no, they are pure. And they certainly do not view themselves as con-artists.

They themselves say that they are motivated variously by compassion, by love, by a yearning for "social justice." They employ the entire better-world litany that is familiar to anyone versed in the imagined utopias of leftists, who always are heavy on critique and light on specifics. It is difficult to measure the psychic reward—campus cultural capital—for embracing an amorphous utopian cause, but we must assume that this reward is real. I suspect that one may acquire genuine satisfaction paying public lip service "for social justice," even without actually doing anything tangible to help another human being.

I don't doubt that many of these people believe what they say in the workshops they deliver and what they write in their articles.

Perhaps their *testimonios* are sincere. They are doing the work of racialism, and they are proud of what they do, because what they do is in the name of DEI. It's a circle of virtue.

Some of these persons are, at bottom, good-hearted. They have a positive, often wildly exalted self-image, which they confer upon themselves and on each other by their moral commitment to social justice activities. This exaltation of self is commonplace in academia and not just in the DEI hierarchy. It's even more common among those who dwell in the world of conspiracy and of paranoia. While it's a product of narcissism, sure, I suspect that it is also defensive in large part as a counter to imposter syndrome and a real contribution to self-esteem.

> One should not discount the emotional aspect of conspiracy theories either. Conspiracism derives much of its appeal from the emotion it awakens in the audience. The conspiracy theory seduces not through its arguments, but by the intensity of the judgement inherent in its Manichaean narrative of praise and blame, good and evil. The most important and the most obvious benefit that conspiracy theories bring to those who believe in them is, however, the feeling of self assurance and superiority towards the non-initiated. The resulting conviction that one is in possession of an unprecedented insight into the working of the world is a huge generator of esteem, because it offers compensation for 'what might otherwise be insupportable feeling of powerlessness.'[575]

---

575 Jovan Byford, *Conspiracy Theories: A Critical Introduction* (New York: Palgave Macmillan, 2015), p. 141-142; Michael Barkun, *A Culture of Conspiracy: Apocalyptic Visions in Contemporary America* (Los Angeles: UCLA Press, 2006), p. 35.

These are the kind of people who love the mass of undifferentiated humanity . . . but who despise individual persons. The kind of people who believe that the needs and wants of the individual person must be sacrificed to the larger imperatives of the "common good."

This "common good" is always defined by a tiny minority. Consequently, no "common good" has ever won a majority of votes, anywhere. Which is why the "common good" is always imposed by coercion. Perhaps a person, like Brian Thompson, must be sacrificed so that we can "start a conversation" about healthcare and the common good?

DEI is one such "common good."

This likely doesn't sound normal to you. And that's been a main purpose of *DEI Exposed*—it indeed exposes the entire project as suffused with abnormality. We understand the DEI Big Con in terms easily grasped by anyone who recognizes that something's not right with the entire enterprise. We have uncovered the machinery of the Grift, the Big Con. We learned about the diversity grifters and their elaborate con game designed to extract resources from the university.

It's called *Virtuous Victimhood*, and it features the combination of active victim-signaling and virtue-signaling from grifters posturing as group-victims and eager to receive recompense. The key to the Con is to find a wealthy Mark, to convince that Mark that he's guilty of some grievous group sin against the group victims, and then to squeeze the Mark to pay reparations. The Con is aimed at the universities and requires a convincing Grifter, a gullible Mark, a credible Con Story, and an extensive hoax literature of "ideas" to give the entire enterprise a patina of legitimacy of the sort to suck in university types.

I see this as an incredibly corrupt operation, a perfect combination of the illicit and the fantastical to create a dystopian social fantasy on the campuses guaranteed to deliver suboptimal outcomes. At bottom, this emergence of elaborate fantasy worlds is yet another reaction against the Enlightenment and the Scientific Revolution. Some people cannot handle Enlightenment—that is to say a world where the wiggle room for hokum has been reduced.

Some people want a simpler, safer, enchanted world instead of an unsettled and hostile world where absolute truth threatens us, but the possibility of "many truths" provides a way out. These people will always follow someone who promises them that fantasy of a simple world with simple answers, perhaps explanations that relieve them of the personal responsibility that comes with freedom.[576]

The talents and dispositions of these plotters lie not in the advance of human understanding and knowledge and the improvement of the human condition. Rather, they aim to fracture society. They strive to elevate their magical schemes to parity with modern science and to concoct strange notions of racialist cause-and-effect. Their goal is to impose the new barbarism on an unsuspecting and barely resistant university community. If they win the university, our larger society will follow quickly and meekly to turn back the clock to an earlier, simpler time when fear ruled, and people kept their heads down and their mouths shut.

---

576 See Erich Fromm, *Escape from Freedom* (New York: Henry Holt and Company, 1941, 1969). See also E. R. Dodds, *The Greeks and the Irrational* (Boston: Beacon Press, 1957), original published in 1951. See chapter VIII, "Fear of Freedom."

DEI is an anti-Enlightenment project and has been from the start. It stands against logic, reason, scientific method, progress, and humane values. We earlier saw a quote from the *The Atlantic* by historian Anne Applebaum that captures the dark spirit of DEI, what she called the New Obscurantism of darkness, obfuscation, and irrationality. Ms. Applebaum is likely unsympathetic to this book's thesis, and she was describing what she believes to be the rise of right-wing European political movements. Unfortunately, she misses the anti-Enlightenment obscurantism right under her nose, the DEI commissars who offer "magical solutions, an aura of spirituality, superstition, and the cultivation of fear."[577] These are the conspiracist folks who eagerly introduce indigenous "ways of knowing" into the university, and who ruminate sagely on the "medicine wheel" and "talking stick."

DEI is also in the first twilight shadows of its existence because of its internal contradictions that render it laughable—the doctrine is profoundly unserious and rooted in pseudoscience and prejudice. We welcome this retreat from chaos and a return to sanity; it's accelerated to the point that today those who imposed on us this destructive monstrosity are running from accountability.

We are obligated to expose today's cool and convenient amnesia of DEI's social engineers, those who inflated DEI and who shoehorned it onto the campuses, who squandered scarce education dollars, who racially attacked hundreds of scholars and students. We should not allow it to go unstudied, unpublicized and unpunished. Books like the one you hold, books that explain the madness and call the culprits to account, are a welcome addition to the corpus of societal restoration and renaissance.

---

577 Anne Applebaum, "The New Rasputins"

This is an incredible story that doesn't yet have a happy ending, but as the progressive chattering class is wont to say, "the arc of history is bending in the right direction."

GLOSSARY

DEI DIVERSITY SPEAK, A-Z

ACPA

The American College Personnel Association (ACPA) was founded in 1931. It is a professional organization for student affairs personnel in colleges and universities. It serves as a repository for far-left ideology that is expressed in journals, books conferences, and various "institutes" sponsored by the group. Members believe themselves to be "college educators," like the faculty and that their mandate extends campus-wide in a process they call "millieu management". The ACPA aims to "promote leadership at all levels through a racial justice and decolonization lens."[578]

---

578 https://myacpa.org/

Antiracism

Antiracism is the euphemistic label for a highly politicized conspiracy theory that is grounded in psychopathological paranoia, and which constructs a racialist Manichean world of villains-and-victims. All of this is buttressed by a cargo cult of fake scholarship. In its manifestation in the university, it constitutes one of the greatest academic frauds of the last century. Some universities have crafted bureaucratic policies informed by this pseudoscientific folderol, and they call this construct an "Antiracist university."

antiracism

Small-*a* antiracism describes a position that persons adopt with respect to working against prejudice, hate, and illegal discrimination based on race or ethnicity.

Antiracist Pedagogy

Antiracist Pedagogy is the popular *nouveau* name for Maoist/Freirean coercive thought reform that employs psychological behavior modification techniques inside and outside the classroom. Fundamentally, it's amateur psychotherapy employed in the university to impose a pre-Enlightenment ideology on students, faculty, and staff.

The label "Antiracist" itself is a rhetorical ploy used to achieve positive valence and disarm critics while propagating a paranoid conspiratorial view of the world. The centerpiece of this crude coercive method employed in classrooms and workshops is an explicit attack on "central elements of self," a key marker for what psychologists have identified as second generation thought reform programs and which is designed to "neutralize a person's psychological defenses."[579] This method is grounded in the Maoist/ Freirean ideology of critical pedagogy.

Assessment

While there exists a valid field of "assessment" that leverages metrics of academic program success, as it is used in the student affairs literature, it means something dramatically different. This is an evaluative mechanism to determine how effectively thought reform techniques communicate the tenets of ideology to achieve "social justice outcomes." How far along is the student on the conveyer belt to "critical consciousness?"

Authentic

This is a rhetorical value-loaded trope used by antiracists to imply that whatever the issue or person or subject, the "antiracist" position is genuine while other positions are, by definition, "inauthentic." It exists in semantics as what we call an "essence statement." This is a common value-loaded adjective that, when used, supposes that the object of discussion or description is qualitatively genuine, unlike other versions of it. We see this in Antiracism with its employment

---

579 Richard Ofshe, Ph.D. and Margaret T. Singers, Ph.D., "Attacks on Peripheral versus Central Elements of Self and the Impact of Thought Reforming Techniques," *Cultic Studies Journal*, Vol. 3(1), 1986.

in having "authentic conversations" or in "bringing your authentic self" to work.

There is an abnormal element to the overuse of such terminology, a special pleading to be taken seriously and to be believed. Philosopher Soren Hallden analyzed this tendency toward psychological disturbances of a semantogenic type:

> The interest in essence definition has a background which is partly pathological. The man who engrosses himself in essence questions is a person who feels debarred .... He feels outside even linguistic and intellectual contact. [He voices] such definitions himself. If he does so he is at the same time claiming to be a member of the community, with respect to social contact even superior to his fellow members. Neurotic attitudes of this sort are not very uncommon.[580]

Behavior Modification

A program that utilizes psychological techniques to effect a change in behavior in a target person by manipulating beliefs, behavior, and environment. Today's rogue psychotherapists on campus use techniques developed in the 1940s by the American Kurt Lewin as well as severe techniques pioneered by the Maoist Chinese Communists and utilized in the Cultural Revolution of the 1960s and 1970s. Modern-day cults also utilize sophisticated behavior modification techniques.

---

580 Soren Hallden, *True Love, True Humour and True Religion: A Semantic Study* (Stockholm: CWK Gleerup, 1960), p. 107.

Bias Response Teams

These are campus squads mobilized by the campus DEI office to "investigate" reported instances of umbrage. Whereas these "teams" do not mount up retro vehicles as did the "firemen" in Bradbury's *Fahrenheit 451*, they do investigate or pass on the complaints to an investigative office. Folks who purport to take offense can report "incidents" to the campus DEI office anonymously, much like the situation in the medieval inquisition, when persons could report heretics or heretical activity anonymously. It also resembles the anonymous snitch system employed in the worst years of Stalin's Soviet regime in the 1930s and 1940s.

Entire political systems, such as that of the Soviet Union and Communist China, constructed societies that solicited reports of non-compliance and political deviation—persons were encouraged to report on friends, neighbors, and relatives. Deviationists were arrested, imprisoned, often executed, and routinely sent to concentration camps.[581]

Cargo Cult

A cargo cult is a crude copycat system that mimics the form or process of an original entity. It is designed to generate results from what is called "sympathetic magic," or the notion that a facsimile or model of something can generate the same results as an original. It emerged most prominently in the mid-20th century in some islands

---

581 Sheila Fitzpatrick, "A Little Swine," *London Review of Books*, Vol. 27, No. 21, November 3, 2005: https://www.lrb.co.uk/the-paper/v27/n21/sheila-fitzpatrick/a-little-swine

of the South Pacific as natives mimicked the high technology they had witnessed by building planes made of bamboo and by hacking out dirt runways in the jungle and lighting them with torches. All in a bid to "bring back the cargo" of the Westerner who had occupied the islands during World War II. Rather than empirical cause-and-effect, it relies upon fervent belief in magic and wishful thinking to explain the social world.

In higher education, examples of the cargo cult abound, most notably in the multitude of journals that have emerged to justify magic thinking and superstition, particularly in the realm of "social justice." Another example is the cargo cult of the co-curriculum and the full range of activities of "student affairs," which mimics the actual curriculum. DEI has its own cluster of supportive journals where, as conspiracy expert Jovan Byford notes, "pieces of information can be traded and exchanged, debated and contested."[582]

College Educator

This is the category descriptor that student affairs functionaries use to lift themselves up in professional esteem to the status of faculty. It is, in fact, a fraudulent act that uses a rhetorical sleight called the "ladder of abstraction." The LoA is used to make unlike things seem alike by putting disparate elements into the same abstract category. An example of this is how the media characterized the death of Michael Brown in 2014 in Ferguson, Missouri. They called the 6-4, 300-pound Michael Brown an "unarmed black teen," as if

582 Jovan Byford, *Conspiracy Theories: A Critical Introduction* (New York: Palgave Macmillan, 2015), p. 142.

the drugged-up criminal strutting in the middle of the street was no different than a 13-year-old on his way to violin practice—both are "unarmed black teens."

"College Educator" performs the same function on the college campuses. "Student affairs professionals" in ancillary bureaucrat support roles call both themselves and faculty "college educators" so as to achieve parity in the popular mind. This blurring of the distinction between the actual university faculty and the hirelings who comprise the bureaucracy is intentional.

Co-Curriculum

This is the cargo cult facsimile that parallels the actual curriculum taught by actual faculty in the university. It consists of fake college "faculty" who teach fake college courses in a fake curriculum that mimics the forms of academia. This is the method by which low-level administrative hirelings who manage dormitories and organize scavenger hunts to "finally get to use my master's degree" and pretend that they, too, are "college educators." This is a tangible manifestation of the "whole student" rationale that student affairs uses to gain access to students for "student development."

The co-curriculum began in the 1970s with the seminal article by Brown and Citrin, which articulated the ways and means.[583] It gained legitimacy with Kolb's 1984 book, followed by the work of George Kuh. The concept was hijacked by ideologues in the 2000s

---

583 Robert Brown and Richard Citrin, "Student Development Transcript: Assumption, Uses, Formats," *Journal of College Student Development,* Vol. 40, No. 5, (September/October, 1999)

as they realized that those who controlled the "co-curriculum" could control the milieu of the university and the "student learning" outside the purview of the faculty. Moreover, a lockstep ideology could be imposed on programs taught by non-faculty ideologues. "Institutes" run by ACPA train student affairs functionaries to employ the "curricular approach."[584]

Confidence Game, Con-game, Con, Hustle, "peanut hustle"

A confidence game is a type of swindle designed to extract resources from a *mark*, or *sucker*, by gaining the confidence of the mark and getting the person to turn over money or resources willingly. It constitutes a resource extraction strategy. It involves getting the mark to buy into a believable story that, of course, is untrue. A synonym for the Con is the *hustle*, which is "to make someone believe something false, usually so that that person will give you their money or possessions."[585] A hustle usually denotes a short-con, sometimes called a "peanut hustle" or "peanut grift."

The Big Con can utilize actors and stage settings. The more elaborate confidence games that launder ideas into respectability involve a scaffolding of subsidiary lies and fibs to increase the credibility of the central Con Story. For DEI, the scaffolding consists of a web of faux academic "peer-reviewed" journals—"cargo cult" journals—set up for the express purpose of laundering fringe ideas into academic respectability. The DEI Big Con is called *virtuous victimhood*.

---

584 Kathleen G. Kerr, Keith E. Edwards, James Tweedy, Hilary L. Lichterman, and Amanda R. Knerr, *The Curricular Approach to Student Affairs* (Sterling, VA: Stylus, 2020).
585 https://dictionary.cambridge.org/dictionary/english/con

Conspiracy Theory

An explanatory theory that is constructed from clues to make sense out of the world and is related to collective paranoia, a condition where facts are admitted or omitted depending on whether they confirm the theory. Codified confirmation bias, similar to the behaviors and beliefs of individual paranoiacs.

Courageous Conversations

This is a small-group behavior modification program, usually advertised as "talking about race" or "learning about race." It presents the extremist Manichean ideology of critical racialism and typically employs various behavior modification techniques employed by cults.[586]

"Critical Consciousness"

This is the phrase that describes a person who has accepted the evil/good, oppressor/oppressed ideology of critical theory in all of its variants, including critical race theory, intersectionality, and the rest of the grand panoply running under "social justice." A person who does not have critical consciousness is blinded by "false consciousness." This classic tautology is the sort that characterizes cults of all types. The phrase is linked to the Brazilian Maoist educationist Paulo Freire.

---

586 Glenn E. Singleton and Curtis Linton, *Courageous Conversations about Race: A Field Guide for Achieving Equity in Schools* (Thousand Oaks: Corwin Press, 2006).

Critical Race Theory

Critical Race Theory is a counter-Enlightenment project akin to its distant cousin Romanticism—it embraces "storytelling," "lived experience," "autoethnographies," *"testimonios,"* "fables," and out-right acknowledged fabrication in the form of "composite stories." Its major premises are all assumed and never substantiated. All subsequent assertions proceed from a handful of tenets that are a priori and unproven, much less ever discussed or questioned. All of what is important in life proceeds from the concept of race and the social fantasy that is constructed, with whites as de facto racist oppressors and everyone else a de facto victim.

Critical Race Theorists reject logic, reason, rationality, and the scientific method and offer instead "qualitative" methods to create unique "truths" and many "knowledges." At bottom, it's a cult grounded in Plato's Cave allegory, with critical racialists privy to hidden knowledge and dedicated to "unmasking" the veneer of power relations for the rest of us. It's Manichean in that it posits a stark world of good/evil, oppressed/oppressor, and it's pseudo-science in that it offers a comprehensive cosmology that purports to explain everything, even "predicting" the response of its critics (without answering its critics) and explaining anomalies and dis-confirmations as evidence for the theory. You know you're in the presence of high fraud when someone claims a theory explains everything that happens, to the point of claiming that disconfir-mations are actually *con*firmations of the theory.

Difficult Dialogue

This is a small-group behavior modification program, usually advertised as "talking about race" or "learning about race." In fact, like its sibling "courageous conversations," it employs critical racialism and typically inflicts various behavior modification techniques employed by cults. (See "courageous conversations").

Diversity

A synonym for "variety." This is a has been elevated into a shibboleth with almost unlimited positive valence even as it constitutes a code word for an underlying political agenda. It is not a "value."

"Do the Work"

This is an already clichéd term used by critical racialists to exhort folks to embrace the doctrine and "do the work" of antiracism, which means, first, accepting the primitive ideology associated with "antiracism" and, second, playing your role of contrition within that paranoid world. If you're a white person, it means confessing your racism and committing to "do the work" to become an "ally." If you are a "person of color," it means accepting that you have probably "internalized" your status as an "oppressed" victim and must "do the work" to overcome it.

Equity

This term is well-known as part of the triumvirate of "Diversity,

Equity, Inclusion," and it's likely the most problematic. In the racialist lexicon, this word supersedes "equality" and means something much more invidious—it expresses the Marxian notion of "From each according to his ability, to each according to his need" [*Critique of the Gotha Program*, 1875] and sanitizes its socialist/communist roots. Sovietologist Richard Pipes identified these roots many years ago before the neologism "equity" became popular.

No clear distinction can be drawn between "socialism" and "communism." Marx distinguished two phases of progress toward full communism: first, a transitional phase under which the old inequalities would survive even as their foundations were being destroyed, to be followed by a second, higher phase, in which the principle "From each according to his ability, to each according to his needs" would replace the principle "Equal work, equal pay." Lenin defined the first phase as socialism and the second as communism.[587]

Equity is not a "value."

"Exhausted"

This cliché refers to the fake psychological concept of "racial battle fatigue" contrived by non-academics and given currency by non-profit agencies and groups. The concept refers to a state of being fatigued with dealing with the daily emotional trials and tribulations that affect most all people, but which elevates these

---

587 Richard Pipes, *Communism: A History* (New York: The Modern Library, 2001), p. ix-x. The famous "needs" phrase is from Karl Marx's 1875 work *Critique of the Gotha Program*.

concerns to a special racial status, which in turn requires special dispensation for those suffering this "exhaustion."

Additionally, imagined slights and insults achieve the status of reality in the minds of racialists. Essential to the lexicon of Anti-racist paranoia, it unintentionally captures the state of dealing with the effects of hyper-vigilance and suspicion in the paranoiac. The paranoiac may well actually be "exhausted" from the debilitating effects of being always "on guard" against slights and insults directed against him from members of the paranoid pseudocommunity.[588]

Gaze

Essential to the edifice of paranoia constructed on the campuses is the development of paranoid behaviors and suspicions—these are codified in paranoid concepts, such as gaze, microaggressions, and surveillance. These terms/concepts constitute the repertoire of paranoid behaviors and rhetoric to forward the *Antiracist* agenda.

Grifter/Hustler

A grifter or hustler is someone who employs deception to extract resources from a *mark*. A fortune-teller is a small-time grifter. Corporate grifters or con-artists play Big Cons, like Bernie Madoff and Ken Lay of Enron. Most anyone who spins an exaggerated yarn to solicit contributions is a grifter. In some cases, persons who

---

[588] Mary-Frances Winters, *Black Fatigue* (Oakland: Berrett-Koehler Publishers, 2020).

tell their exaggerated tales may actually believe them. The ultimate grift is the extremist cult.[589]

Inclusion

A key term in the Antiracist paranoid lexicon, which is related only to how a particular person, usually a student, "feels" about his or her position at any particular time in any particular venue. Thus it is not and never has been a "value" (which is how racialism characterizes it) but rather an infantilized tool for emotionally deficient persons who constantly seek validation. Universities are not "inclusive" institutions; they are, in fact, *ex*clusive institutions to which one must apply and be accepted. Universities tell hundreds of thousands of persons each year that they do not "belong" and are not "included."

Informed Consent

A process that protects persons from unlawful human subject experimentation, a rigorous procedure that guarantees that subjects know the purpose of the research, understand the risks of the research, are not deceived by the researcher or the description of the research, and are informed of their rights under the research protocol (that they can terminate immediately for any reason).

---

589 Maria Konnikova, *The Confidence Game: Why We Fall for It . . . Every Time* (New York: Viking, 2016), p. 303-321.

Intergroup Dialogue

This is a small-group behavior modification program, usually advertised as "talking about race" or "learning about race." It applies the precepts of critical racialism and typically employs various behavior modification techniques employed by cults. (See "difficult dialogue" and "courageous conversations")

Kula Ring

A trading circle in Melanesia that utilizes magical items as currency in the generation of symbolic capital. Academia features its own Kula Ring of trade that involves the exchange of article citations to generate academic legitimacy without the confirmations and rigor required of genuine academia. Such mutual citation exchanges are a characteristic of conspiracy theory literature. "The most common manifestation of pedantry is a fondness for reciprocal citation, in which authors obligingly cite one another. The result is that the same sources are repeated over and over, which produces a kind of pseudoconfirmation."[590]

Mark

A *mark* is the target of a grifter, who wishes to extract resources from him or her by playing to the target's greed or vanity, which makes the mark tractable to illegal or quasi-legal get-rich-quick

---

[590] Michael Barkun, *A Culture of Conspiracy: Apocalyptic Visions in Contemporary America* (Berkeley: University of California Press, 2003), p. 28-29.

schemes. The mark is also uncharitably called a "sucker"—as in P.T. Barnum's famous quote: "There's a sucker born every minute."[591]

Milieu Management

Student Affairs staffers are acutely conscious of the need to make their ideology inescapable. They call this *milieu management*. This notion of milieu management was pioneered in the "student affairs" bailiwick by an influential thinker in the field, Burns B. Crookston. In a piece entitled "Milieu Management," Crookston advocated control of the milieu on the college campus with a single "student affairs" professional running the show—what he called the "principal student affairs officer (PSAO)."[592] The milieu, for Crookston, consisted of the "intellectual, social, esthetic, creative, cultural, philosophical, emotional, and moral environments as a totality; it includes the interactions among the individuals in all such groups." The goal of this "management" is to make the critical groupthink inescapable. Said Crookston:

Milieu management is a form of intervention that may be more complex than either instruction or consultation. This change strategy calls for marshalling all pertinent resources of the campus community to shape the institutional environment in ways which will facilitate desired change and maximize student development.[593]

---

591 Maria Konnikova, *The Confidence Game: Why We Fall for It . . . Every Time* (New York: Viking, 2016), p. 18.
592 Burns B. Crookston, "Milieu Management," *NASPA Journal*, Volume 13, Number 1, 1975, p. 46.
593 "A Student Development Model for Student Affairs in Tomorrow's Higher Education," *Journal of College Student Personnel*, 16(4), July 1975, p. 339.

NASPA

NASPA is the National Association of Student Personnel Administrators, but the name was "updated" to Student Affairs Administrators in Higher Education. It is a professional organization for student affairs personnel in colleges and universities, with approximately 15,000 members. Like ACPA, it serves as a repository for far-left ideology that is expressed in journals, books conferences, and various "institutes" sponsored by the group. Members believe themselves to be "college educators," like the faculty and that their mandate extends campus-wide in a process they call "milieu management."[594]

NADOHE

This is the National Association of Diversity Officers in Higher Education. It is a professional organization for diversity officers, with roughly 2,000 members. It is a highly ideological organization. Heavily steeped in far-left critical race theory, it does not reflect a diversity of educational approaches available. The NADOHE hosts conferences at which the DEI ideology is recapitulated and reinforced[595].

NACADA

This is the National Academic Advising Association, founded in 1979. While ostensibly an organization that supports the careers

---

594 https://myacpa.org/
595 https://www.nadohe.org/

of academic advisors, it sought "professional" status and as a result was captured by "social justice" ideology. Its brochures, articles, and conferences reflect this overreach. Members are urged to use their student-facing roles to inculcate social justice principles rather than simply "advise" students on their college careers.[596]

Paranoia

"Paranoia is a constitutional mental disorder that is limited in symptomatology to well-systematized and stable delusions of persecution and grandeur." Paranoids are constantly on guard, mobilized and ready for any emergency or threat. Whether faced with real dangers or not, they maintain a fixed level of preparedness, an alert vigilance against the possibility of attack and derogation. Unable to accept their own faults and weaknesses, paranoids maintain their self-esteem by attributing their shortcomings to others. They repudiate their own failures and project or ascribe them to someone else. Paranoiacs live in a hostile world, with enemies threatening them constantly.[597]

Privileged Identity Exploration Model (PIE)

A coercive psychological behavior modification program developed by Professor Sherry K. Watt and designed to undermine the target's sense of self to pave the way for the adoption of a new belief system. Her training confronts "privilege and the complexities of

---

596 https://nacada.ksu.edu/
597 James Page, *Abnormal Psychology* (New York: McGraw-Hill Book Company, Inc., 1947), p. 284 and Theodore Millon, *Modern Psychopathology* (Philadelphia: W. B. Saunders Company, 1969), p. 328.

intersecting identities in ways that bring about "intellectual vertigo" and "ontological dizziness." This sense of disequilibrium comes from having to *reconceive the self in relation to others in ways that are counter to one's understanding of one's social and political position in society.*[598]

Pseudocommunity

The pseudocommunity is the imaginary persecutory delusion constructed by a person suffering from paranoia. "The paranoid pseudocommunity . . . is an imaginary organization of real or imagined persons who are united in a plot against the patient."[599] Psychologist Norman Cameron originally developed the notion of the pseudocommunity in his contribution to the psychopathology of paranoia. Critical racialism constructs a pseudocommunity of "whites" on which to pin the blame for lack of success.

Moreover, the doctrine of *Antiracism* requires that whites act as if they are part of this social fantasy of persecutors. Without the pseudocommunity of guilty white people who acknowledge complicity in the invisible system of oppression, the conspiracy collapses; thus, whites are recruited vigorously into the pseudo-community by devices such as "conversations," "dialogues," "racial caucuses," and such like.

598 Sherry K. Watt, "Privileged Identity Exploration (PIE) Model Revisited," in Sherry K. Watt (ed.), *Designing Transformative Multicultural Initiatives* (Sterling, VA: Stylus, 2015), p. 41-42.
599 James D. Page, *Psychopathology: the Science of Understanding Deviance* (2e), (Chicago: Aldine Publishing, 1975), p. 296.

Racism

Racism is a type of prejudice grounded in racial or ethnic distinction, and this is all it is. Critical racialists have attempted to redefine the term so that it can be incorporated into the doctrine as an explicit expression of that doctrine, and nothing else. This "language loading" is characteristic of authoritarian ideologies, and it certainly is exemplified by Antiracism, critical pedagogy, and Critical Race Theory—for this family of doctrine, racism is described as "racism plus power," a formulation that goes back to 1972 and was coined by a teacher's assistant by the name of Patricia Bidol. This language loading attempts to coopt the word "racism" so that it exempts "persons of color" from culpability in acting racist.

Racial Microaggression

This is the most important concept in the lexicon of DEI's paranoid conspiracy. This constitutes the manufacture of "racism" where no racism exists and is measured only by the sensitivity of those who "experience" them. It has no objective reality outside the imagination of the trained potential paranoiac. Persons are trained to cultivate a hyper-sensitivity to the external environment and to maintain high alert for slights and insults and to automatically interpret ambiguous events as confirmations of the Antiracist ideology.

This "racial microaggression" is a malleable tool of transference whereby a person's insecurities, self-doubts, fearful imagination, personal prejudices, routine personal interactions, general woe, and outright failures can be transferred to an external enemy who is afflicting them in some way. As a scapegoat for externalization of blame, it is extraordinarily effective. The aggrieved can then report the "racial microaggression" to the appropriate office, anonymously if desired, which will investigate and act against the "guilty." The presumed guilty are not informed of the alleged transgression and the "investigation" is conducted clandestinely, sometimes without knowledge of the accused. The process is modeled not after American jurisprudence, but rather after the medieval religious inquisition. Or, more sinisterly, after the Soviet snitch system under Stalin in the 1930s.

Repetition

The act of repetition is a tactic of the racialists and of magic thinkers throughout history. Encouraging persons to repeat certain phrases and words as a kind of liturgy can build what sociologist Pierre Bourdieu called "symbolic capital." This is the generation of power from nothing.

The archetypical modern example appears in the works of bell hooks. Not in her fiction, but in her notional pedagogical work (which is equally fiction). The unwieldy phrase that she repeats in her works is "imperialist white-supremacist capitalist patriarchal biases."

The more repetition, the deeper cemented the fraud in the public psyche. People accept what is being repeated, not because of the quality of its argumentation but rather because of the quantity of its appearance. It is the written equivalence of group recitation of mock-holy pronouncements.

Resistance

Resistance is the label that paranoid racial conspiracy theorists give to any words, actions, arguments, normal skepticism, expressed doubts, or questions that arise as they impose their doctrine on students, faculty, and staff in the university. This term comes from the language of conspiratorial response.

Those who question the conspiracy, *themselves* become evidence of the conspiracy. Thus, the questioning of the conspiracy is proof that the conspiracy exists. This is a powerful marker that one is dealing with a conspiracy theorist. Any request for examples or evidence of the more problematic aspects of their conspiracy, *itself* becomes evidence for the conspiracy. The use of the term "resistance" or "resistant" (as in "diversity-resistant") is a distinct *tell* or *marker* for racialist conspiracy theorists. An entire faux-scholarly literature has emerged around this conspiracy term. Usage: "The students display 'diversity resistance.'"

Self-Disclosure

(see "vulnerability)

Student Affairs

An office in the university whose mission is to keep students fed, housed, healthy, and happy. It stands juxtaposed with "Academic Affairs," which administers the curriculum, what traditionally comes to mind with regard to higher education. Unfortunately, many bureaucrats in the student affairs office fancy themselves "college educators." Jealous of their faculty counterparts in Academic Affairs and inspired by Freirean "antiracist" ideology, they have steadily expanded their mandate on campus to haranguing students in what they call the "co-curriculum."

The two primary national non-profit organizations that comprise "student affairs professionals" nationwide are the ACPA and NASPA. These are centers of critical racialist ideology. Their extremist literature is largely non-academic and constitutes essays, narratives, poetry, "counternarratives," stories, "autoethnographies"—that is to say, *anecdotes*. In one sense the entire edifice of "student affairs" is constructed from the raw material of anecdotes.

Student Development

The euphemism that "student affairs" functionaries use when referencing their co-curricular programs outside the classroom. This vague trope empowers these functionaries to talk among themselves about their noxious subject matter without explicitly identifying it. Who, after all, could be against "student development"? Often used in tandem with or interchangeably with the equally vapid "student learning."

This is the body of psychological and quasi-psychological scholarship that speculates on how students develop psycho-socially, cognitively, and affectively. It has been co-opted by campus bureaucrats and now serves as the rubric for the university's coercive thought reform and behavior modification program. The program is designed to convert students to "critical consciousness." (see "student learning")

Student Learning

This is the euphemism used by "student affairs" that comprises the various tools and techniques to implement coercive campus thought reform programs, to include their co-curricular programs outside the classroom. Campus bureaucrats in "student affairs" adopted this term to up-sell themselves as "college educators" rather than as their actual role as ancillary support staff. It has enabled student affairs to extend its influence far beyond its mandate, and it does so under the cover of a benign and vague euphemism that masks the actual techniques, methods, and content of its thought reform program.

This trope empowers these functionaries to talk among themselves about their noxious subject matter without explicitly identifying it. Often used in tandem with or interchangeably with the trope "student development." Much of the "student learning" and "student development" literature draws upon psychological techniques to create the impression of academic legitimacy. (see "student development)

Social Justice

The overarching rubric for various strains of collectivist ideology designed to imbue the ideology with positive valence. The term is crafted to deflect criticism and even mild questioning of means and ends. The term removes the need for a person to think, and it confers virtue on the person using it in a kind of self-aggrandizement. Its lack of specificity, its general conferring of good feeling, its displacement of responsibility, and its widespread acceptance by institutions as rhetorical currency, renders "Social Justice" the narcissist's best friend. The urge to confiscate the property, wealth, position of some people and transfer it to others based on nothing more than a grasping, envious eye, is buried beneath the narcissist's self-conception.

The "social justice" dynamic constitutes confiscation and redistribution of wealth from those who produce it to those who do not, with a substantial portion of that wealth assigned to the planners who confiscate and redistribute wealth. This dynamic is presented this way:

> We believe that social justice is both a process and a goal. The goal of social justice is full and equal participation of all groups in a society that is mutually shaped to meet their needs. Social justice includes a vision of society in which the distribution of resources is equitable and all members are physically and psychologically safe and secure.[600]

---

600 Maurianne Adams, Lee Anne Bell, Pat Griffin, *Teaching for Diversity and Social Justice* (New York: Routledge, 1997), p. 3.

Hayek observed that the grasping calculation informed philosophers and social engineers for a millennium, in the form of "just price" and "just wage" theories, until the realization of experience finally penetrated the schemes of these planners.

The core meaning of this trope is Marx's dictum from his 1875 work *Critique of the Gotha Program*: "From each according to his ability, to each according to his need." Such egalitarian expressions have always appealed to utopians and social engineers. Every attempt to realize this dictum has resulted in economic and social failure at best and mass murder at worst. It continues its vitality today because of a studious aversion of actual history in favor of visionary social fantasy.

The notion of "social justice outcomes" reflects the age-old leveling impetus. If a fat man stands beside a thin man, "social justice" explains that the fat man got that way by taking advantage of the thin man.[601] "Social justice" constitutes the palatable public version of "socialism."

Surveillance

A key term in the lexicon of Antiracist paranoia. It is part of the social fantasy contrived by *paranoid personality disorder*.

Thought Reform

---

601 "We have so many people who can't see a fat man standing beside a thin one without coming to the conclusion the fat man got that way by taking advantage of the thin one," Ronald Reagan, "A Time for Choosing," Speech, 1964: https://www.youtube.com/watch?v=Ijhre9T_bv4

A coercive re-education program that employs psychological behavior modification techniques designed to change a person's belief system. Thought reform is grounded in the pioneering 1940s work of American psychologist Kurt Lewin and has been refined in subsequent decades to take advantage of techniques developed by the Communist Chinese under Mao and by modern cults. It is commonly called "brainwashing."

Thought reform is a repertoire of psychological and physical techniques designed to modify the behavior of a target person or persons. It is most often associated with authoritarian regimes, group therapy, and cults. Robert J. Lifton's eight-condition model of the thought reform program remains the chief tool whereby thought reform programs are identified. In the United States, the only widespread use of thought reform occurs in cults and on the college campus.

The program called "social justice education" universally applies this 8-point thought reform framework on the college campus, in credit-bearing courses and in "co-curriculum" workshops. Social justice educators, self-described as "scholar-practitioners," utilize the thought reform method.[602]

Trust

Trust is absolutely necessary for the process of thought reform and the destruction of a person's sense of self and that person's belief

---

602 Robert Jay Lifton, *Thought Reform and the Psychology of Totalism* (W. W. Norton & Company, Inc., 1961), p. 420-437.

system. It is impossible to overstate this factor. Without a person ceding "trust" to those who mean him psychological ill, the campus brainwash is interdicted before it begins.

We have spectacular examples of those who abuse trust. Dr. Lisa Spanierman is a psychologist at Arizona State University, who uses deception as a tool in her classroom as she manipulates certain students—white males—to feel guilty about issues or events that have nothing to do with them. She finds that these feelings of false guilt render them more likely to work for "social justice" causes, so she can then more easily mobilize them to do so in service to "social activism."[603]

Unsafe

A key term in the lexicon of Antiracist paranoia is this trope, which is reflexively applied to any situation in which the litany of *Antiracism* is not accepted and celebrated. Thus, if a student declares himself "unsafe" (usually psychologically) in a classroom in terms established by the *Antiracist* ideology, then this constitutes de facto evidence of a "microaggression" at best and outright racial or other type of discrimination at worst. The opposite of "unsafe" is "inclusion," which is again related only to how a particular person, usually a student, "feels" about his or her position at any particular time in any particular venue. The term "unsafe" relates to what psychologists call "safety behaviors" that are designed to preempt the perceived threat. "We might try to placate the people we think

---

603 Lisa Spanierman, "White Guilt in the Summer of Black Lives Matter," in Katharina Von Kellenbach and Matthias Buschmeier (eds), Guilt: A Force of Cultural Transformation (New York: Oxford University Press, 2022), p. 41-58.

are out to get us, or we might try to protect ourselves by keeping constantly on our guard. Safety behaviours are a typical feature of paranoia."[604]

Vulnerability

Essential to any thought reform program is to challenge the student's idea of self. This is designed to instill self-doubt and create vulnerability. A common name for this is "gaslighting," or convincing a person to doubt his own perception and understanding of the world. This attack permits the student self to be reconstructed along lines dictated by the ideology proffered. The fundamental precepts of the ideology are more easily transmitted via "student learning" if the student's natural skepticism is shut off. Thus, the student development thought reform program puts great emphasis on gaining the student's trust and getting the student to "make himself vulnerable." This is a constant trope in "social justice education," this desire to get students to open themselves to psychological attack.

The staffers who run these programs are encouraged in their literature to "model vulnerability" to get students to open up with "self-disclosure." Students should be wary of these persons, who practice a type of uncredentialed hip-pocket psychology.

---

[604] Daniel Freeman and Jason Freeman, *Paranoia: The 21ˢᵗ-Century Fear* (Oxford: Oxford University Press, 2008), p. 77.

White

Used as an adjective, it constructs neologisms as needed to expand the paranoid conspiracy theory's reach and scope. Examples: White Fragility, White Innocence, White Silence, White Adjacent, and such like. This is part of the externalization of the paranoiac's failure. It can also serve as a preemptive rhetorical move to provide cover for future failure.

White Adjacent

Rescue hypothesis used to explain anomalies in "Antiracism" that otherwise would disconfirm the paranoid conspiracy. When the Antiracist doctrine fails to explain instances of disconfirmation, rescue constructs are spun out that "explain" reality by virtue of proximity to "white" or "whiteness." As in "Asians are successful because they are 'white adjacent.'"

White Supremacy

This term has become so reflexive and ubiquitous that its magical origins have become obvious to even the casual observer. In primitive societies, shamans and witch doctors would craft a term to explain everything that was mysterious—this term was *mana*. Everything that was inexplicable in the realm of the known would be attributed to *mana*. This was used reflexively. The magic incantation was considered a valid and accepted concept, and it perpetuated the mystification of the actual world and legitimized it. If a fisherman returned with a full catch, it meant that his *mana* was strong. If the catch was miniscule, it meant that his *mana* was weak.[605]

"White Supremacy" is the modern *mana* of academic posers on the college campus and certainly in the realm of public discourse.

Whiteness

Whiteness is one of Antiracism's devil-terms. This vague term is useful because it's abstract. It's an empty bottle into which anything can be poured. In creating and defining the paranoid pseudocommunity, persons working in the Antiracist critical paranoia project have developed concepts and a lexicon of terms to provide a patina of legitimacy to the program.

An entire body of hoax literature has emerged from the paradigm of paranoia. This faux scholarship mimics science and includes outright fiction and fakery—in other words, it is a project of pseudoscience. "Whiteness" is one of the concepts that fleshes out this body of prejudiced propaganda. See also "White Fragility," "White Supremacy," "White Innocence."

---

605 H. Philsooph, "Primitive Magic and Mana," *Man, New Series*, Vol. 6, No. 2 (Jun., 1971).

INDEX

ACKNOWLEDGMENTS

I could not have accomplished this seemingly Sisyphean task without the support of my wife Lory—my confidant, idea maven, front-line editor, and in many ways co-author. She also put up with the multiple stacks of literally thousands of hard-copy articles and books scattered throughout our abode under the cover of "research." I also thank Shari and Loyd for their unwavering patience in providing months of material support and input for the creation of this volume.

My agent and editor Maryann Karinch of The Rudy Agency believed in me and the project from the start and found a superb home for the manuscript. I offer thanks and respect to many manuscript reviewers whom I would name, except that this might appear that I am spreading culpability rather than gratitude. And of course, I acknowledge the many students who have shared their stories from the campuses.

ABOUT THE AUTHOR

Stanley K. Ridgley, PhD is one of the Great Courses Professors the *Wall Street Journal* and *Washington Post* have dubbed a "rock star professor." He is the author of *BRUTAL MINDS*, the 2023 expose on higher education that reached #1 on Amazon's Democracy Bestseller list. Ridgley is also the author/presenter of *Strategic Thinking*, the million-dollar best-seller video course published by The Great Courses.

Dr. Ridgley is Clinical Full Professor of Management at Drexel University's LeBow College of Business. At Drexel, he serves on the faculty senate. He holds a Doctorate and Master's in International Relations from Duke University and an International MBA from Temple University. He has also studied at Moscow State University and the *Institut de Gestion Sociale* in Paris.

Dr. Ridgley is a former Military Intelligence Officer and served five years in West Berlin and near the Czech-German border, where he received the George S. Patton Award for Leadership in Bad Toelz, West Germany. Dr. Ridgley's intelligence activities *versus* the Soviet Union included signals and electronic intelligence as well as Russian translation and analysis. He served as a tactical intelligence officer on the German frontier with a combat arms unit and as a liaison officer during Soviet military inspections.

Dr. Ridgley teaches courses on Strategy and Competitive Advantage, Technology Innovation, International Business, and Competitive Intelligence. He has lectured and presented widely in the United States, Russia, China, India, France, Singapore, Spain, and Colombia. Dr. Ridgley is a staunch defender of Individualism and Enlightenment values in the university as the best defense against the seduction of authoritarians, charlatans, political *poseurs*, and noxious ideologues of every sort.

www.ingramcontent.com/pod-product-compliance
Lightning Source LLC
Chambersburg PA
CBHW020814270326
41928CB00006B/367